Arms and Politics
1958 – 1978
Arms Control in a
Changing Political Context

Robin Ranger

To the memory of
my father Robert
and my uncle Bill.
And to my mother Dickse
and my aunt Shirley.

Canadian Cataloguing in Publication Data

Ranger, Robin, 1945-
  Arms and politics, 1958-1978

Bibliography: p.
Includes index.
ISBN 0–7705–1627–0

1. Arms control. I. Title

JX1974.R35   327'174   C79–094163–5

This book has been published with the help of a grant from the Social
Science Federation of Canada, using funds provided by the Social
Sciences and Humanities Research Council of Canada.

Printed in Canada for
The Macmillan Company of Canada Limited
70 Bond Street
Toronto, Ontario
M5B 1X3

KZ
5624
.R345
1979

Contents

Acknowledgments

This book originated with my doctoral dissertation at the London School of Economics and Political Science. To the Department of International Relations there — the faculty and research associates, especially Professors Geoffrey L. Goodwin and Frederick S. Northedge — I owe an intellectual debt, both as an undergraduate and a postgraduate. This work is an attempt to repay that debt. My supervisor, Mr. Philip Windsor, inspired the questions this work attempts to answer whilst displaying his own inimitable intellectual flair. To Dr. Robert E. Hunter, then of the LSE, and now of the National Security Council, also my thanks. I am indebted to the International Institute for Strategic Studies and the Royal Institute of International Affairs for the use of their libraries and facilities, and for the intellectual stimulus and advice provided by their staffs and visiting speakers.

Professor Tom Millar of the Australian National University and Professor William T. R. Fox of the Columbia Institute for War and Peace Studies made it possible for me to spend the summer of 1969 at the Institute and to conduct essential research in the United States. This work was greatly assisted by Professor Marshall D. Shulman of the Columbia Institute for Russian Studies and by other scholars and officials too numerous to mention who, both then and subsequently, gave generously of their time and advice. Jerome H. Spingarn, Academic Liaison Officer of the U.S. Arms Control and Disarmament Agency, deserves particular thanks for his continued assistance. I am also indebted to the Harvard Center for International Affairs for permission to examine the records and attend the meetings of the Harvard – MIT Arms Control Seminar.

My thanks also go to the Canadian scholars and officials who assisted my research in Canada, notably John Holmes of the Canadian Institute of International Affairs (CIIA), and Lt.-General E. L. M. Burns, former Canadian Disarmament Representative to the Ten Nation Disarmament Conference (TNDC) and Eighteen Nation Disarmament Conference (ENDC). To Dr. George R. Lindsey, Director of the Operational Research Analysis Establishment (ORAE) of the Defence Research Board, now of the Department of National Defence, goes my special gratitude for enabling me to spend a stimulating year, from 1971 to

1972, as a consultant on arms control to ORAE. Both Dr. Lindsey and the Arms Control and Disarmament Division of the Department of External Affairs provided an invaluable insight into the practical problems of arms control, without being in any way responsible for the conclusions reached here. Subsequent work for ORAE into the problems of Mutual and Balanced Force Reductions provided further stimulus in the application to the real world of arms control of the theories advanced here. Dr. Colin S. Gray, successively of the CIIA, The University of British Columbia, (Assistant Director of) the International Institute for Strategic Studies, and now the Hudson Institute, has provided constant and accurate criticism of my work, together with a detailed critique of the manuscript of this book. The faults that remain are my own.

My academic colleagues at the Departments of Political Science or Studies at the University of Aberdeen, Queen's University, Carleton University, the University of British Columbia, the Royal Military College of Canada, and St. Francis Xavier University are all deserving of my thanks for their assistance, with particular thanks to Charles Pentland of Queen's University and his wife, Carol. My typists, Mrs. Claire MacDonald, Mrs. Shirley Delarge, Mrs. Stephonie Paterson, and Miss Anne Grady have all managed to make the illegible legible. A research grant from the University Council on Research of St. Francis Xavier University assisted in the final preparation of this work. Thanks are also owing to the Business Office, St. Francis Xavier University, for their helpful administration of the funding for this book, and to my research assistants, Gordon Carroll and Hugh Mellon, whose contributions were invaluable. Virgil Duff, executive editor of Macmillan of Canada's College Division, and my editor, Margaret Woollard, patiently persuaded me to make my ideas intelligible to the audience for which they were intended. Above all, my thanks to my wife Evelyn, whose perceptive criticism has been coupled with her unique encouragement to complete this work, without loss of her sense of humour. This is as much her book as mine, at least the good parts are.

R. R.
St. Francis Xavier University

Introduction

Despite the voluminous literature on arms control there have been few studies that stand back from current issues and inquire into the nature of the enterprise upon which arms controllers think they are engaged. This book attempts to do so. By appraising the whole of the intellectual, historical, and public-policy records on the subject of arms control from the mid-1950s up to SALT II and MBFR, it sets out to prove that the term "arms control" has been used, or rather misused, to cover two completely different policies, namely technical *and* political arms control. The distinction between these two concepts is crucial to a correct understanding of what has and has not been achieved in arms-control negotiations. The Western, especially the American, view by officials and academics has stressed the idea of arms control as a means of securing apolitical, technical solutions to the threats to strategic stability posed by technological innovations; and this view can therefore be characterized as the technical-arms-control approach. In contrast, the Soviets have sought to provide political counters to threats to strategic stability — threats seen in primarily political terms — and to further Soviet foreign-policy objectives; their approach can thus be described as political arms control.

The difference between these two approaches to arms control can be shown by tracing their origins in theory and practice from 1958 to 1962. By applying this distinction to the arms-control agreements reached from the 1959 Antarctica Treaty to the current negotiations for a SALT II agreement, one on MBFR, and a series of agreements to limit nuclear proliferation, it can be shown that the intellectual gulf between the Western and Soviet approaches to arms control has remained unbridgable. Western theories of technical arms control have failed to be translated into policy, whereas the Soviet Union has secured measures of political arms control. The so-called "arms-control" agreements we have had have been nominal, in that they have not significantly restrained the development and deployment of new weapons systems, and political, in that they have favoured both specific Soviet and, to a very much lesser extent, American foreign-policy goals. Additionally, these agreements have served the common superpower interest in visible improvements in their bilateral relations, through measures that both symbolize and advance superpower detente. The conclusion is that only measures of *political* arms control have proved and are likely to prove negotiable. In practice, U.S. policy has been, despite official claims to the contrary, to reject measures of technical arms control because these have proved non-negotiable and to accept instead measures of political arms control tolerable to the Soviets. President Carter is trying to reverse this trend, but, given past experience, his chances of doing so seem slim.

PART I The Evolution of the Technical and Political Approaches to Arms Control

1 Two Contrasting Concepts of Strategic Stability: Technical and Political Arms Control

The central thesis of this book is that American attempts from 1958 to 1978 to treat the *technical* symptoms of strategic instability through technical arms control have failed to impose any significant restraints on the strategic-arms competition between the two superpowers; and that, in contrast, the Soviets' countervailing policy (characterized as political arms control) of dealing with the *political* causes of instability has succeeded. A comparison of the evolution of Western and Soviet approaches to arms control shows their differences clearly, and indicates that there are valid grounds for questioning whether technical arms control has produced, or can ever produce, the results claimed for it by its proponents. At the risk of some oversimplification, the following brief survey of the differing conceptual frameworks of technical and political arms control highlights the fundamental opposition between the two approaches. These are subsequently considered in detail.

Technical Arms Control: Origins and Agreements, 1958-78

Recent official U.S. and academic questioning of the strategic theories underlying U.S. deterrence policy has sparked a continuing debate in which the defenders of the status quo have shown a remarkable attachment to the strategic theories of the early 1960s, including Mutual Assured Destruction (MAD),[1] and the arms race as an action-reaction phenomenon.[2] The majority view among strategists and arms controllers remained that the arms-control theory which evolved between 1958 and 1962 was the *summum bonum* of Western thinking on the subject, a dogma which it was heresy to question. Accordingly, as late as 1970 it could be said that there was a lack of new ideas and concepts in strategic studies, because "the [strategic] theorists did their job almost too well. They provided an intellectual apparatus which seems to be standing up to the test of time and is perfectly adequate for analyzing present strategic policies and most of the technological and political problems likely to occur in the future."[3] The conventional wisdom has remained that the theories that evolved between 1958 and 1962 have proven their adequacy by their transformation into practical agreements from 1963 to 1978. These were taken by the Western arms controllers as evidence that the Soviets were gradually being persuaded to accept both the correctness of arms-control theory and the resulting proposals for stabilizing the strategic balance.

Political Arms Control: the Soviet Approach

Essentially, the Soviet policy of political arms control evolved both as a reaction to the combination of Western arms-control proposals and because of Soviet political objectives, in so far as they were affected by these proposals. The Soviet Union's initial, central objectives were: to contain the threat of West Germany being armed with tactical nuclear weapons under what the Soviets considered inadequate controls by the United States; and to prevent the United States from exploiting its superiority in strategic nuclear delivery vehicles (which would have upset the tacit recognition of the Soviet Union's sphere of control in Eastern Europe reached at the 1955 Geneva Summit). The Soviet Union's defensive position as a superpower whose status the United States would not acknowledge resulted in its use of the 1958-61 test-ban negotiations to secure an unpoliced moratorium on testing. This left the Soviet Union, after its unilateral violation of the test ban in 1961 and the resultant U.S.–U.S.S.R. test series, much nearer parity with the United States in nuclear-warhead technology, and in possession of a politically effective deterrent to Western action against the Berlin Wall, which was erected just before the Soviet tests started. The same preoccupation with the interrelated questions of Germany's present and future status (divided or unified, neutralized or rearmed) and of West Berlin's undermining of the East German regime by permitting migration from East to West Germany was evident at the 1958 Surprise Attack Conference. While the West sought to discuss the prevention of a nuclear Pearl Harbor through arms control on strategic bombers and Intercontinental Ballistic Missiles (ICBM), the Soviet Union wanted to discuss a recognition of boundaries in Europe comparable to that finally achieved from 1969 to 1972. Multilateral recognition of boundaries was achieved at the Conference on Security and Co-operation in Europe (CSCE) from 1973 to 1975, and was formalized in its Final Act of August 1, 1975.

The technical bias of arms-control thinking was based on the arms controllers' belief that the stability of superpower deterrence depended heavily on military technology. This view was supported both by the strategists' preoccupation with the vulnerability of the U.S. Strategic Air Command (SAC) to a Soviet surprise attack and by the scientists' belief that self-contained technical solutions could be found to what were seen as the primarily technical problems of the arms race. These concepts were first expressed in U.S. policy at the 1958 Surprise Attack Conference and the 1958-61 negotiations for a nuclear test ban. Both failed to produce any agreements, but these failures were partially offset by the 1959 Antarctica Treaty, the first formal agreement not to militarize a specific area. More importantly, after the 1962 Cuban missile crisis, the Soviets agreed in 1963 to a hotline for rapid communications in a crisis and to the Partial Test Ban (PTB) Treaty. The latter treaty amounted to only a nominal curb on the development of nuclear weapons, since the extent to which underground testing could be developed was underestimated. A further agreement, embodied in a U.N. Resolution not to orbit nuclear weapons in outer space, removed one potential fear of surprise attack and paved the way for a series of declaratory steps that ran into 1964. These, in turn, set a precedent for further partial measures: in 1967, the Outer Space Treaty, and the Treaty for the Prohibition of Nuclear Weapons in Latin America (the Tlatelolco Treaty); in 1971, the treaty prohibiting the emplacement of weapons of mass destruction on the seabed (the Seabed Treaty), the revised hotline agreement, and the Agreement to Reduce the Risk of Nuclear War Outbreak; in 1972, the Biological Warfare (Weapons) Convention; in 1973, the Agreement on the Prevention of Nuclear War; and in 1975, the U.S. ratification of the 1925 Geneva Protocol on Chemical Warfare (Weapons).[4]

More importantly, from the arms-control viewpoint, the two main threats to international stability in the 1970s — the proliferation of nuclear weapons and the destabilization of the strategic balance — seemed to have been dealt with by the Non-Proliferation Treaty (NPT) of 1968, and by the 1972 SALT I and 1974 Vladivostok Accord. Although the NPT had been dealt a severe blow by India's explosion of a nuclear weapon in May 1974 (disguised as a Peaceful Nuclear Explosion), it was argued at the 1975 NPT Review Conference that the NPT regime still offered the best hope of containing the spread of nuclear weapons. Again, although the SALT I agreements of May 26, 1972, had imposed a freeze on offensive strategic missiles at the level of planned deployments only for the period of the Interim Agreement on the Limitation of Strategic Offensive Arms (1972–77), a ceiling was placed on strategic weapons and Anti-Ballistic-Missile (ABM) deployment was restricted to only two sites each for the United States and the Soviet Union. Subsequently, the agreements of June 1974 limited the superpowers to the single ABM site each had deployed, and introduced a Threshold Test Ban Treaty (TTBT) which prohibited superpower testing underground of nuclear weapons above 150 kilotons after May 26, 1976. This required the negotiation of a Peaceful Nuclear Explosions Treaty (PNET), not completed until 1976. Later in 1974, the November 24 Vladivostok Accord committed the United States and the Soviet Union to translate quantitative ceilings on their total strategic delivery vehicles and on the number of these that could be fitted with Multiple Independently Targetable Re-entry Vehicles (MIRV) into a SALT II agreement.

In addition to these developments, the idea of conventional troop reductions in Europe, which had been prevalent in arms-control writings of the late 1950s, was revived with the negotiations on Mutual and Balanced Force Reductions (MBFR) that began in 1973 and were still underway in 1978. A thinning-out of Forward-Based Systems (FBS) for delivery of tactical nuclear weapons in Europe also seemed possible, either via negotiations or via unilateral U.S. action. Thus, the technical arms controllers could point to an impressive record of success. Or could they?

None of these measures imposed more than the most marginal inhibitions on the military activities of the adherents, or on countries like France, China, and India, which rejected some or all of these agreements. The arms controllers' contention that strategic competition between the superpowers would have progressed even faster in the absence of such agreements was not only disingenuous but hardly in accord with their claims of offering self-contained solutions that would minimize the danger of changes in military technology, especially to the superpowers. Indeed, the claim of technical arms control that it offered apolitical solutions to technical problems without affecting the political relations of the parties created the paradox that, in fact, apolitical arms control became the chief modality of superpower detente. What happened was that the United States eliminated the controls that were required for technically effective agreements because these were unacceptable to the Soviet Union, with which the United States sought improved political relations. This represented a triumph of the Soviet view of arms control as a political process which could be used to limit, or enable the Soviets to exploit, the political impact of changes in military technology, rather than to restrain its development. The Soviet approach, therefore, has been described in this work as "political arms control"; and its implications can be juxtaposed with those of technical arms control to assess the real value of the arms-control agreements of 1963-78.

Ironically, the basis for this European settlement and for the precondition of superpower recognition of the mutuality of their interests proved to be the 1962 Cuban missile crisis. Neither the Soviets nor the Americans reacted by accepting, as the arms controllers had assumed, the need for arms-control measures, except for the hotline. Instead, both Mr. Khrushchev and President Kennedy recognized the need for a superpower detente which would recognize that their mutual interest in survival overrode their individual interests in altering the status quo in the two halves of Europe. Yet the inevitably tentative nature of a superpower detente, the implications of which were uncertain, meant that the new Soviet–American understanding had to be embodied in an agreement that would be both significant in itself, and perceived by the two sides as even greater in its symbolic importance. Since a nuclear test-ban treaty had acquired a great, even undue, importance as a Western objective, it could become the modality for superpower detente if the controls necessary for a Comprehensive Test Ban (CTB) were dropped. Such controls were unacceptable to the Soviets because they rejected the principle of inspection on Soviet territory. This attitude explains the emergence of the 1963 PTB and the discovery by the Soviet Union that nominal arms-control measures could embody the political understandings that it sought. Similarly, the Eighteen Nation Disarmament Conference (ENDC),[5] set up in 1962, could serve not only as a forum for discussing these understandings, but as one in which the Soviet Union's status was recognized by way of its position as co-chairman with the United States, a position of equality it had sought since 1957. Thus, by 1963, the Soviet Union's adaptation of the concepts of arms control to meet its political objectives had produced an implicit theory of political arms control. Soviet actions and statements, shorn of their propaganda, were consistent with the view that the political causes, not the technical symptoms, of strategic instability had to be dealt with through nominal arms-control measures; with the control provisions removed, they might make suitable modalities for reaching political understandings with the Americans and thereby nullify both threats to strategic stability and Russia's politico-military strength.

From 1963 to 1965, the greatest political threat seemed to the Soviet Union to be the U.S. proposal for a Multilateral Nuclear Force (MLF), which offered West Germany greater access to nuclear weapons. This reversed the trend towards detente which had been established from 1963 to 1964, and forced the Soviets to adopt offensive tactics to defeat what they perceived as a threat to their interests. From 1957 to 1959, the emerging concept of political arms control had led them to advocate the denuclearization of Europe, a nominal arms-control measure, in an effort to nullify West Germany's acquisition of two-key nuclear weapons (that is, U.S. nuclear weapons in West German delivery vehicles, which required U.S. and West German approval before their use — really a double-veto system). In 1964, the Soviets started to advocate an

NPT as a counter to the MLF. This tactic, combined with U.S. arms controllers' support for a global (rather than an anti-West German) NPT, and the MLF's inherent defects, acted to secure the MLF's demise in 1965. Instead, the NATO Nuclear Planning Group (NPG) was established in 1966. While trying, unsuccessfully, to oppose the NPG, the new collective leadership under Brezhnev and Kosygin apparently began to perceive the positive aspects of political arms control and to explore the possibilities of an extended political understanding with the United States via what the Soviets regarded as an NPT that was designed to secure inspection of West Germany's nuclear activities. The political and technical arms-control version of the NPT could be included in the same treaty, which the Soviet Union and the United States would implement in accordance with these two approaches. President Johnson's agreement in October 1966 to such a treaty ensured the re-establishment of detente, which was by then broadened into an acceptance of the mutuality of superpower interests and given expression through nominal arms control. The emergence of this new policy — of promoting superpower detente through political arms control while eschewing any technical restraints, however minor — was confirmed in 1967 by the Outer Space Treaty, whereby the superpowers agreed to forego a military option (orbiting nuclear weapons) that neither was then interested in — although they may now both be interested in such weapons for use against their opponent's satellites. Again, although the 1967 Tlatelolco Treaty only prohibited nuclear weapons from an area where no states possessed them, the United States refused to surrender its existing base and transit rights for nuclear-weapons carriers, as did the Soviet Union. Neither superpower would tolerate even the slightest technical arms control restricting its military capabilities.

The codification of the superpower understanding, embodied in the 1968 NPT, was both interrupted and confirmed by the absence of any effective U.S. objections to Soviet Russia's invasion of Czechoslovakia. SALT I was delayed until 1970, but once under way it proved a further success for the Soviet policy of political arms control. The 1971 arms-control agreements, like those of 1967, continued the trend towards a political understanding, this time being made more explicit at the 1972 Moscow Summit. The political context of SALT I indicated that the June 1974 accords and the Vladivostok Accord could be seen as following the Moscow model of making final the details of superpower co-operation in protecting their interests while confirming the spheres of American influence and Soviet control in Europe. In its most extreme form, the case for the success of political arms control would be that it had provided a modality for the Soviet Union to achieve its objectives of strategic and political parity leading to superiority, and recognition of the status quo in Eastern Europe. The arms controllers had gained no significant restraints on the development and deployment of new weapons, except those dictated by prudence and implemented by unilateral action.

Some Methodological Questions

Given this argument, the evolution and application of arms-control theory can be examined to compare its role in American diplomacy (and its success) with that of Soviet political-arms-control policy. In dealing with arms-control theory the problem has been one of too much rather than too little literature, so only the most influential or representative works have been cited here. The relative importance of these works has been assessed by interviewing the leading exponents of arms control in Great Britain and the United States. Service with the Canadian government as an arms-control consultant provided invaluable but unattributable insights into the governmental approaches to arms control.[6] The intellectual history of arms control and the perceptions of its theorists and practitioners are reasonably reliable, since extensive cross-checking, which confirmed the initial hypotheses outlined above, was possible. Indeed, one of the most interesting conclusions is that despite its failure to obtain its objectives, arms control was, in mid-1978, still a valid, albeit increasingly criticized, concept — according to its exponents in the Western alliance.

Assessing the Soviet approach was necessarily a matter of deduction, of asking what hypotheses could have explained Soviet policies in arms-control negotiations since 1958, and then of putting the relevant questions to the leading scholars in this area, since the study of Soviet policy in detail is beyond the scope of this work. Since most statements about Soviet policies and motives must be tentative, the conclusions suggested here seem as valid as any could be in a work that surveys so broad a period and field. Similarly, analysing the past two decades of arms control has involved generalizations about schools of thought and trends in policy which cannot take fully into account the judgments of every scholar[7] in the field or the entire complex of motives behind American arms-control policies.

Structurally, this book has been divided into five Parts (and an Epilogue). Part I deals with the evolution of American arms-control thinking from 1958 to 1963. It attempts to show how a technical emphasis was inevitable given its intellectual origins in U.S. strategic thinking and how it was reinforced by the influence of scientists working in the area of arms control. Part II shows how the Soviets reacted to the emergence of technical arms control as part of U.S.

foreign policy by developing their concept of political arms control. Part III demonstrates that, as applied in the nominal arms-control agreements of 1963-78, the dichotomy between technical and political arms control increased. The partial measures confirmed that both superpowers could agree to abstain from military activities from which they would both have abstained in any case. Part IV examines the NPT in detail to demonstrate that, contrary to the claims of the arms controllers, it could not do more than marginally inhibit the spread of nuclear weapons, the extent, speed, and destabilizing effects of which had been greatly exaggerated by arms-control theorists. Instead, the NPT extended the superpower detente embodied in the 1963 NPT into a broader understanding of the mutuality of their interests. Part V clarifies this approach as it was applied to strategic arms control through SALT I, the June 1974 measures, the Vladivostok Accord, and SALT II. It also covers the negotiations on MBFR. Its final chapter demonstrates that technical arms control has proved inapplicable because it has taken insufficient account of the political environment. Political arms control, on the other hand, which concentrated on political objectives, although using nominal arms-control agreements as the chief modality of superpower detente, has succeeded. The Epilogue shows how recent experience, especially that of the past two years (1976-78), has proved these propositions.

Ultimately, the conclusion that the central factor in the role of arms-control agreements has been the relatively neglected one of their changing political context must rest on the analysis presented here. But, taking this qualification into account, the value of arms-control agreements has been over-estimated in terms of the actual controls imposed, while the political implications of such agreements have been neglected. If at times the dichotomy of technical arms control and political arms control has been over-stressed, it has been because this necessary distinction has not been drawn before.

2 Scientists and the Refinement of Arms-Control Thinking: 1958-63

The previous chapter suggested that the American and Soviet approaches to the problems of securing strategic stability between 1958 and 1978 could be characterized by their respective emphases on technical and political considerations. This distinction (and the influence of arms-control thinking on American diplomacy) becomes clearer with an examination of the role American scientists played in negotiations for a nuclear test ban between 1958 and 1961. During these discussions American scientists refined the underlying assumptions of arms-control thinking. Chief among these refinements was that limited, technical solutions to specific problems could, and should, be divorced from the over-all political context of superpower relations.

Although the Geneva Test Ban Conference of 1958-61 failed to progress much beyond the findings of the 1958 Conference of Experts on the Detection of Nuclear Testing, it should have produced a reevaluation of arms-control theory. In fact, however, the reverse occurred. Since the arms controllers and strategists had invested their time, resources, and prestige in the technical approach to solving the problems with which they were confronted, they had no wish to question their own theories. Moreover, they were reinforced in this regard by the scientists' view of scientific methodology[1] and of their own role in government. Both were exemplified by the President's Science Advisory Committee (PSAC), established in 1957 to provide improved technical advice.[2] On nuclear testing, the PSAC consistently engaged in nominally technical studies which inevitably had major political consequences that its members refused to recognize. Thus, by 1963, American scientists had helped to make the initial assumptions of arms-contol thinking into unchallengeable propositions. The difference between the arms controllers' assumptions and those of political arms control was emphasized by the opposed American and Soviet interests in a nuclear test ban between 1955 and 1958. These help explain why the American scientists' input to policy making was so influential, while that of the State Department was so negligible. Consequently, in the Conference of Experts, the United States was left with a highly developed technical approach which lacked an appropriate political

framework. The continuation of this trend through the Geneva conference provided a link with the post-Cuban-missile-crisis negotiations
for a test ban that would symbolize superpower detente. The 1963
Moscow Partial Test Ban (PTB) Treaty, a measure of political arms
control, was initially approached by the Americans in technical arms-
control terms. This reflected their interpretation of the 1958-61 negotiations.

Both the existing literature and the arms controllers interviewed
tended to see the negotiations which led to the 1963 PTB as a search for
agreement on the modalities of inspection. This view was curiously
oblivious to the broader objectives of American policy. Only Robert
Gilpin, sceptical of Soviet intentions in the 1958 Conference of
Experts,[3] and Izzy Stone, suspicious of President Kennedy's motives in
1963,[4] stressed the role of a test ban as a symbol of detente in the
broader context of Soviet–American relations. The negotiations themselves, and the scientists' role in American policy making, can be
analysed here, rather than merely described, since they are covered by
the main works already available. Of these, Jacobsen and Stein[5] represents the most authoritative single source. Lincoln Bloomfield[6] has
provided an excellent account of the conventional American arms-
control view, this time of Soviet intentions. Spanier and Nogee's[7]
concept of "gamesmanship" in disarmament negotiations — that is,
the constant search for propaganda advantages in these negotiations —
recognized their political element, but from an oversimplified view of
the Cold War as a contest that the United States must win. Former
Ambassadors Dean (U.S.),[8] Wright (U.K.),[9] and Burns (Canada)[10] have
provided first-hand accounts which reflect the basic Western acceptance of what was, in retrospect, clearly a technical-arms-control view
of the negotiations. How far this differed from the Soviet political
approach to arms control becomes evident when it is related to their
political campaigns against nuclear weapons.

Soviet Policy on a Nuclear Test Ban: 1954-57

From Stalin's 1950 Stockholm Peace Appeal onwards, the Soviet
Union had tried to manipulate public opinion within the Western
democracies in an effort to inhibit both U.S. development of nuclear
weapons and its willingness to use them, especially in defence of
Western Europe.[11] This Soviet exploitation of a favourable political
asymmetry in order to offset its inferiority in strategic nuclear-weapons
delivery vehicles typified its stress on the political aspects of deterrence and nuclear testing. This political arms-control approach became
both more important and more feasible as an instrument of Soviet

policy at the time of Secretary of State Dulles's enunciation in 1954 of the massive-retaliation doctrine.

The newly emerged awareness of the danger of radioactive fallout from nuclear testing served to lend even further credibility to the Soviet stance. On March 1, 1954, for example, the U.S. fifteen-megaton Bravo nuclear test showered the Japanese trawler *Lucky Dragon* with radio-activity, and contaminated fish from the test area were reported to be reaching the Japanese market. Given the understandable Japanese sensitivity to any issue involving nuclear weapons or radioactivity, it was not surprising that "Hysteria swept Japan; American–Japanese relations became strained and the whole world resounded with criticism of the United States."[12] Subsequent Japanese research indicated that the Bravo shot had been a "dirty" — that is, a highly radioactive — bomb, using the fission-fusion-fission process to increase the production of long- and short-term fallout. This revelation increased the criticism of American atmospheric testing, and the U.S. Atomic Energy Commission's inept attempts to counter the growing anxiety served only to exacerbate the problem. These fears were reinforced by advances in the science of genetics and by studies on the pathological effects of radioactivity. Moreover:

A second source of concern . . . was the discovery that certain of the radioactive isotopes contained in the long-range fallout were extremely long-lived and had a particular affinity for human tissue. . . . [notably] strontium 90 with its half-life of 28 years.[13]

Therefore, the Soviets' disarmament proposals of March 19, 1955, may be seen as the first attempt to exploit the new U.S. vulnerability in disarmament diplomacy. They reversed the Soviet Union's years of failure to overcome the unfavourable effects of negotiating within the Baruch plan framework.[14] Their presentation also prepared the ground for the spirit of detente at Geneva in 1955.

Significantly, the Soviets decided that two of their three preconditions for implementation of the 1955 proposals would be a cessation of nuclear-weapons tests and an outlawing of these weapons.[15] By separating out a nuclear test ban for negotiations, they were clearly preparing to capitalize on the internal U.S. developments that had

. . . brought the finite containment school into tacit alliance with the control school and into open conflict with the containment scientists who remained committed to the desirability of maximizing America's nuclear capabilities.[16]

Adlai Stevenson's advocacy of a nuclear test ban in the 1956 presidential elections ensured its becoming a major political, as well as technical, issue in the United States, and undoubtedly confirmed the Soviet decision to use proposals for a test ban in its Sputnik diplomacy of 1957. This sought to exploit Soviet launching of the first artificial satellite, Sputnik I, to create an impression of strategic superiority over the United States. In reality, Mr. Khrushchev was negotiating from a position of gross strategic inferiority in terms of his ability to strike at the United States, and he knew it. But it was this very knowledge that made it even more important to create an impression of negotiating from strength and to reinforce the Soviets' political exploitation of their strategic deterrent versus Western Europe that had formed the basis for the 1955 Geneva detente, with its implicit U.S. acceptance of Soviet control over Eastern Europe. The spirit of Geneva might have disappeared with the Polish and Hungarian revolutions of 1956, but the American failure to interfere in either suggested to the Soviets that respect for their own sphere of control remained intact. Because Mr. Khrushchev was still securing his internal power, he sought to consolidate the Soviet position in Europe by resolving the Berlin and German questions in his favour. Thus, the political *lacunae* in the developing American concepts of arms control left the United States with a vulnerability that the Soviets hastened to exploit.

The Absence of a Political Framework in Arms-Control Thinking and the Conference of Experts: 1958

This background to the test-ban negotiations is essential to an understanding of the difference between the technical and political approaches to arms control. From 1957 to 1961 the Soviet Union undoubtedly took and held the initiative in this area. During those years, however, the Soviets did little more than temporarily halt American testing and cause considerable internal political difficulties for the British and West German governments in their deployment of, respectively, an independent deterrent, and tactical nuclear weapons under the two-key system. Mr. Khrushchev may not have hoped for much more, depending on how much his perennial optimism was tempered by realism. In any case, the relatively limited effect of their endeavours in test-ban negotiations serves to put the Soviets' success in its proper perspective. Paradoxically, it also helps to explain their flexibility. Because the Soviets' main interest lay in inhibiting both Western testing and reliance on nuclear weapons, they were untroubled by the need for accuracy required by arms-control proposals. Moreover, they could resume testing whenever they chose to do so.

Consequently, on April 30, 1957, the Soviet Union proposed to isolate the issue of nuclear testing for discussion.[17] This issue was accepted by the United States on August 29, 1957,[18] as the first for negotiation, but on the condition that it was coupled with a one-year suspension of tests while an international control system was established to cut off all future production of nuclear materials for weapons purposes. Although the U.S. administration was still strongly committed to the continued development and testing of nuclear weapons unless the Soviet Union made major concessions, Sputnik's launching on October 4, 1957, caused a reversal of this policy which resulted in an agreement to hold separate negotiations on the question of testing without any other conditions. Under internal political pressure from the Senate Sub-committee on disarmament (chaired by the late Senator Hubert Humphrey), and facing increasing diplomatic criticism for the refusal even to negotiate on a test ban, President Eisenhower accepted the suggestion of James Killian, the first presidential Special Assistant for Science and Technology and Chairman of the PSAC, that a committee be appointed to re-examine the issue. The resulting panel, under the chairmanship of Hans Bethe, reflected the emphasis on technicalities which we have seen to be so characteristic of arms control. The panel reported in April 1958 that a comprehensive nuclear test ban would not be detrimental to American security. It could be monitored by an inspection system that guaranteed sufficient probability of detection, and thus deterrence, of underground tests down to the one- to two-kiloton range.[19]

As the panel's membership suggested, it would report in favour of isolating the test-ban negotiations.[20] Secretary Dulles was reluctantly persuaded by the four officers in the State Department responsible for disarmament affairs that the diplomatic costs of rejecting separate negotiations were too high. On March 31, 1958, the Soviets announced that they would discontinue their nuclear tests, provided that other states did so as well. By doing this, they underlined the U.S. diplomatic weakness and showed the Soviet ability to utilize internal political factors in the United States to the Soviet Union's advantage. Similarly, timing their nuclear tests to end just before the announced U.S. series, which was scheduled to run into autumn, represented the integration of both technical and political factors that was typical of their policy. Secretary Dulles's suggestion that President Eisenhower propose technical talks on an inspection system and means of preventing surprise attack was adopted in Eisenhower's April 28 letter. The Soviets thereby secured their first objective, that of separate negotiations on the issue of testing. American insistence that the technical talks did not commit them to negotiate on a Comprehensive Test Ban (CTB) — which would in any case be dependent on a workable inspection system — ignored the intense political pressures for a test ban and, consequently, failed.[21] These attempts also neglected to take into account the Soviet fear of West Germany's catalytic potential if the December 1957 NATO Council decision to introduce two-key nuclear weapons was implemented.

The Soviets outmanoeuvred the diplomatically unsupported American scientists at the Conference of Experts from July 1 to August 21. The essential distinction between the ease of detecting suspicious events and the need for on-site inspections to prove they were not clandestine tests was obscured, and attention was concentrated on an inspection system using 180 seismic observation stations. Although this system was presented by the Soviets as able to detect all tests, it actually had a fairly high probability of detecting only above-ground tests down to one kiloton. To do so for underground tests below five kilotons would, according to the Western position, have required one hundred on-site inspections per annum. The Soviets, on the other hand, claimed that twenty would suffice.[22] The Soviet Union's political requirements were for a single detection system. A detection threshold close enough to that discussed by the Bethe panel on nuclear testing would make it virtually impossible for the West to reject negotiations, during which the inspection issue could be obscured by establishing unacceptable conditions for its settlement. In the interim, the West could be forced by internal public opinion and diplomatic pressure to implement its 1957 proposal for a moratorium on testing during talks. The final report of the Conference of Experts foreshadowed the main Soviet approach; by not making the right of inspection part of the Geneva system, the Soviets were able to claim that they would exercise the veto on any inspection by a control commission.

The Geneva Test Ban Conference: October 31, 1958, to August 30, 1961

The political arms-control approach secured the Soviet goal of an unpoliced moratorium, and also provided inhibitions to Western testing and deployment of nuclear weapons. The inspection issue, on which the Soviets were diplomatically vulnerable and which the arms controllers regarded as crucial, was suitably obscured. The three-year moratorium on tests, like the 1963 PTB, was significant precisely because neither resulted from negotiations in the arms-control sense of a process whereby the two sides resolve their differences over control in order to produce a mutually acceptable system. The Geneva Test Ban Conference and, later, the Eighteen Nation Disarmament Conference (ENDC) and its successor, the Conference of the Committee on Disarmament (CCD), did provide an on-going forum for discussion which helped to define the technical limitations of various control systems.

These gains alone, however, could never bridge the political gap between the Western principle of effective control and the Soviet rejection of inspection on its territory. Underlying the diplomatic manoeuvrings was a philosophical incompatibility. Technical-arms-control theory assumed that any effective limitation on developing military technology would create such strong incentives to cheat on the agreements necessary for stable deterrence that appropriate verification and sanctions against non-compliance would be necessary.[23] Yet such verification against non-compliance would be, from the political-arms-control viewpoint, inimical to the political understanding that such agreements should create. Equally, technical discussions which arms controllers hoped could bridge the gap between the United States and the Soviet Union on the number of inspections needed for a test ban were, to the Soviets, able only to reduce, not resolve, the problems in what was a politico-military question. By 1974, the inspection issue could — admittedly in a very different strategic and political context — be seen as secondary to the political interests of the superpowers in a Threshold Test Ban Treaty as evidence of continuing superpower detente. So also, in the negotiations on a U.S.–U.K.–U.S.S.R. CTB from 1977 onwards, inspection details were seen as less important to the Carter administration than the need for technical arms control and improved political relations with the Soviets.

In 1958, the Soviets regarded the temporary moratorium on American testing as a considerable gain, which the Geneva Test Ban Conference might enable them to prolong until such time as they wished or felt compelled to resume testing. President Eisenhower's extension of the moratorium into a commitment not to resume testing without warning attained his objective of lessening the political costs incurred by atmospheric testing. Paradoxically, however, it gave the Soviets less, not more, incentive to reach a formal agreement. Such an agreement would make a Soviet resumption of testing even more destructive of political understanding with the United States than under an informal understanding, since the tentative Soviet–American detente was still too weak to be symbolized by a CTB, or even a PTB. Moreover, the lack of integration of the technical and political aspects of a test ban in American diplomacy invited exploitation by the Soviets. Therefore, when the Soviet Union was beginning preparations for testing in mid-1960, President Eisenhower felt that the United States should discontinue the moratorium, but he also wished to avoid committing his Democratic successor.[24] President Kennedy and his arms-control advisors understandably wished to continue the test-ban negotiations, since the Fisk report and the National Security Council (NSC) recommendations of February–March 1961 both recommended that a further draft of a CTB would have considerable political impact, internally and externally, and would be more likely to restrain proliferation.[25] The change in the Soviet attitude on a test ban from one of distinct hardening in the second half of 1960 to complete non-co-operation in 1961 reflected the growing confrontation with the United States, especially the emergence of the West Berlin crisis. This development enabled the United States and Britain to offer greater concessions linked to effective controls. The U.S.–U.K. package of August 27, 1962,[26] which offered a CTB or a three-environment PTB, formed the basis for serious talks after the Cuban crisis; and it needed, therefore, to be seen both as an attempt to elucidate the alternatives for limited nuclear testing, without much hope of a response, and as one part of a more sophisticated use of disarmament diplomacy, including competition in General and Complete Disarmament (GCD) plans.

By 1962, the Kennedy administration and its arms-control advisors had reluctantly concluded that the Soviet Union would reject any on-site inspection. This accounts for the overly optimistic American reaction to Mr. Khrushchev's post-Cuban-crisis offer to reinstate the 1960 quota of three inspections per annum. Also significant was that, as part of the same offer, the Soviets accepted the distinction in the draft of August 27, 1962, between a technically effective arms-control CTB, with inspection, and a political-arms-control PTB which would institutionalize the probable superpower policy of refraining from testing in the atmosphere, outer space, or under water. The Soviets' considerable informal interest in an unconditional three-environment ban followed from its potentialities for furthering detente at no cost to the Soviet Union. Continued underground testing, which would not be prohibited by a PTB, would enable them to catch up with the U.S. lead in smaller warheads. Mr. Khrushchev's attempts to use the CTB proposal as the basis for his political arms-control policy after the Cuban crisis were explicable as the result of misunderstandings which arose out of the difference between political and technical arms control, and which were compounded by the importance that the CTB had acquired. This new importance made it difficult not to explore the CTB possibility first.

The Scientists' Effect on Arms-Control Thinking

Intellectually, the scientists' participation in the test-ban talks served to refine the underlying assumptions of the arms controllers. Rather than stressing the limitations of scientific methodology and dependence on the political environment as the necessary parameters for their calculations, the scientists exaggerated both the role of technically calculable factors and their own importance in test-ban negotiations. While such action was understandable in an internal U.S. political environment that was hostile to the very idea of agreements with the Soviet Union, the long-term effects ran counter to the scientists' wish for arms control. By over-stressing the possibility of securing a test ban independent of the superpowers' political relations through highly technical control measures, the scientists made physical controls an integral part of a nuclear test ban and, by implication, of any other arms-control agreement. Moreover, this stress on the technical aspects of one arms-control problem, nuclear testing, occurred during the formative period of arms-control theory. By 1963, when the PTB had demonstrated the need to modify arms-control thinking so as to give much greater weight to the politically desirable, as opposed to the technically possible, it was too late to alter this technical bias in the theory of arms control.

This last point is particularly important. As has been noted before, arms-control theory emerged out of a body of strategic thinking that stressed the dominance of technical factors in determining political actions, especially in a crisis. Arms-control thinking therefore had an inherently technical bias (see below, Chapter 3). But, and it is an important "but", arms-control thinking only emerged in U.S. government policy with the Surprise Attack Conference of 1958 (described below in Chapter 4). Although this reinforced the emphasis on technical factors as the key to arms-control agreements, it still left open the possibility that arms-control thinking could include a proper emphasis on the political factors in, and the political role of, arms-control agreements. That it did not was due in no small measure to the influence of those scientists involved in the nuclear test-ban negotiations, who were also, by and large, the scientists who were interested in arms control. Their emphasis on the technical aspects of arms control meant that, by 1963, when nominal arms control came to symbolize superpower detente, arms-control doctrine was too rigid to deal with political factors. That doctrine, and its exponents, retained certain fixed assumptions unchallenged until 1973-75, assumptions which still dominate current arms-control thinking. In order to understand why technical arms control became so dominant, some consideration must be given to its relationship to the main body of American strategic thinking, and especially to those aspects which made the theory so susceptible to refinement by the scientists and so different from the Soviet political approach. In the next chapter this essential factor is explored in detail.

3 The Origins and Development of Arms-Control Thinking: 1958-62

Arms-control theory has usually been treated by its Western exponents as a relatively unchanging and self-contained doctrine that deals with the effects of military technology on the stability of deterrence. Developments in this technology have been discussed in terms of a doctrine largely unchanged since the early 1960s; technological advances have not generated a questioning of this doctrine, because arms-control theory, like any dogma, has been able to answer these questions within its own logic. These theories, generated in the late 1950s, were in reality very much more a reaction to the then current preoccupations of American strategists than has usually been admitted by their proponents. But, once the central propositions of arms control became accepted and were institutionalized in the Arms Control and Disarmament Agency (ACDA), established in 1961, it became increasingly difficult to question the idea of regulating military technology and competition so as to maximize strategic stability without seeming to attack the most significant arms-control supporters of detente. The latter viewed the lessening of political tension between the superpowers as a product of arms control. However, as the Moscow Summit of 1972 demonstrated, superpower detente could, in fact, limit the influence of military competition on their political relations, so long as both the United States and the Soviet Union so desired.

In order to see how the corpus of arms-control thinking took a form which facilitated its refinement by American scientists, and why such control was acceptable to American policy makers, the development of this theory must be related to the concurrent evolution of American strategic theory, since both held the same underlying assumptions, which were, until recently, unquestioningly accepted as correct. Any intellectual history of arms-control theory, however brief, must survey the evolution of American thinking on deterrence, strategic war, limited war, and arms control, so as to emphasize that all four sets of analyses really consisted of logical deductions from a single set of hypotheses about military technology and stability. These hypotheses were, in turn, shaped by American assumptions about the desirability of stabilizing its deterrence of the Soviet Union, thereby creating a status quo which would facilitate the exercise of America's superior military technology for political ends. The writings cited in this discussion have been chosen because they are most representative of the mainstream of strategic theory from which arms-control theory developed.

The Role of Arms Control in Stabilizing Deterrence

In its original formulation by American policy makers after 1945, a state of deterrence was seen as existing where either side possessed forces able to inflict such damage as would be unacceptable to an aggressor when considered in relation to its possible gains. When both sides had such forces, deterrence would become mutual and produce a strategic stalemate.[1]

A more sophisticated theory of deterrence, developed between about 1955 and 1960, held this crude analysis to be imprecise in two respects: both the notion of "unacceptable" damage and the nature of the delivery systems for nuclear weapons were seen as requiring more rigorous definition. While there clearly existed an upper limit beyond which damage would become intolerable, there was much dispute as to where this limit lay; below this point there could conceivably be gains worth more in the perception of one superpower than the damage received. The concept of deterrence applied to a whole range of situations of which general war was only one. Therefore, instability could arise if one of the superpowers came to doubt another's ability to inflict such unacceptable damage, or if the threat of mutual destruction became so disproportionate to the threat posed by the attacker that, in either case, the deterrent threat lost credibility.

Analysis showed that the bomber was an extremely unreliable instrument of deterrence because, in view of its vulnerability to a preemptive attack, it was more suitable for a first strike.[2] This realization created an inherently unstable balance of deterrence (if both sides relied on bombers as their main strategic delivery vehicles), since, in a crisis, both sides might calculate that they would lose less by striking first. Limited conflicts would be deterred in this situation not through proportionate use of the main deterrent, but, it was hoped, through the mutual fear of the two protagonists that any clash might escalate into general warfare. Conversely, a stable strategic balance, by removing this fear, would make limited war more likely. Stability required that both sides possess second-strike forces, that is, forces able not only to retaliate after surviving the maximum possible damage the enemy could inflict in a first strike, but also to cause unacceptable damage to the attacker. (Secretary of Defense Robert S. McNamara later described this posture as one of mutual assured destruction [MAD].)[3] Additionally, both sides needed conventional forces sufficient to minimize an opponent's gains from limited war. All forces would have to be under tight political control to facilitate their use as counters in political bargaining during crisis management. Such control would also prevent unintended or undesired escalation of a conflict.

By these criteria, the balance of deterrence was unstable in 1958 because both the Soviet Union and the United States relied on deterrent forces that were comprised primarily of strategic bombers; and, whilst liquid-fuelled Intermediate Range and Intercontinental Ballistic Missiles (IRBM/ICBM) were being introduced, these had a slow reaction time (the time taken to prepare them for firing). These forces were neither protected nor capable of protection against attack. To add to the instability, American policy depended on the ability to threaten a first strike against the Soviet Union if it invaded Western Europe. When combined with the advantage of pre-emptive strike — that is, a strike made to anticipate an opponent's first strike — this dependency could easily make suspicion of surprise attack a cause of war.

In consequence of this unstable situation, the 1958 Surprise Attack Conference was held. Its intellectual origins in the United States were later summarized by Schelling and Halperin.[4] They saw the stabilization of the strategic balance as the most urgent measure of arms control. With the existing forces, little could be done beyond improving control over one's own forces and developing understandings with the other side to the effect that a pre-emptive strike was not intended. Similarly, if both sides could establish their own guidelines for regarding a war as limited, and if they could communicate these to each other, the danger of accidental escalation might be reduced. The introduction of second-strike delivery systems would stabilize the strategic balance, if these met the criteria fixed by arms-control requirements: that is, invulnerability to a first strike, siting of delivery systems to minimize collateral (incidental) damage to the population if attacked, and the ability to delay firing until the pattern of attack became clear.

Submarines carrying Polaris missiles, the first two of which went on patrol in 1960, were ideal from this viewpoint and had the additional advantage of being useless as counterforce weapons, since their warheads and accuracy were insufficient for the purpose. The Minuteman missile, originally conceived as a mobile weapon, was seen as being more suitable for limited strategic exchanges, provided it was emplaced in hardened silos. Once the balance of deterrence was stabilized, agreements might be reached to maintain it at minimal cost: for example; by limiting missile production, which would make a counterforce strategy impossible; by limiting the development and deployment of Ballistic Missile Defense (BMD) systems; and by making explicit the existing practice of not contributing to nuclear proliferation. Schelling and Halperin recognized that:

> Just as agreements that stabilize the strategic balance may make local war more likely, so agreements which serve to facilitate keeping local wars more limited make the outbreak of local wars more likely. If one of the things that prevents local wars is the fear of both sides that it will spiral to total war, then agreements which make it less likely that this will happen may end up by making local war more likely. On the other hand, this could be a reasonable price for greater assurance that local war would not go to total war.[5]

Consequently, America would, in co-operation with her allies, have to expand her conventional forces until they were able to fight limited conflicts and sustain a conventional defence of Europe for some time (up to ninety days) without being compelled to use tactical nuclear weapons. The latter were seen as making uncontrollable escalation probable for two reasons: first, each side had a spectrum of these weapons, making meaningful limitations between permitted and non-permitted weapons difficult; second, the distinction between nuclear and non-nuclear weapons had come to be accepted by both sides.[6]

Besides suggesting potential areas of agreement on the control of arms, Schelling and Halperin also gave some criteria for evaluating arms-control proposals. These could operate as planned, enable one side to cheat successfully, or break down, but the significance of failure would depend on the importance of the agreement. Since any understanding would be an innovation, it was important to get smaller agreements which had a chance of success rather than large agreements which might fail and prejudice the success of future steps. Similarly, the advantages, and therefore the likelihood, of cheating would be minimized in smaller accords.

Schelling and Halperin also argued against the balanced reduction of forces which the United States advocated at disarmament conferences. They felt it ignored the instability that would arise if unacceptable damage could no longer be guaranteed after a first strike because the number of delivery systems had been reduced below those needed for a second-strike capability. Inspection was no longer seen as merely negative, providing evidence of violations, but was expected to provide positive confirmation that one side was indeed doing what it said it was; that is, not planning a surprise attack in a crisis. The concept of positive verification was reflected in Schelling's proposal for an exchange of inspection teams at strategic air and missile bases, and other strategic points, in a crisis.[7] The most stabilizing arms-control agreements were those in which a violation could not give one country a decisive lead, but, because it acted as a mutual warning system, was readily detectable. The assumption behind any agreement must be that of mutual suspicion; each side had to be continually assured that the other was complying. It was the responsibility of each to demonstrate its compliance in any way it could; the only sanctions against violation were those the other side could impose.

In view of these circumstances, Schelling and Halperin's theme was that, ". . . a main deterrent of the likelihood of war is the nature of the present military technology and present military expectations", and that, "There is a feedback between our military forces and the conflicts they simultaneously reflect and influence."[8] These forces needed to be subject to limitation through arms-control agreements and unilateral action which, if reciprocated, ". . . can be of mutual benefit if they reduce the danger of a war that neither side wants, or contain its violence or otherwise serve the security of the nation."[9]

Theories of Arms Control and Strategy

The main developments in the formulation of American strategic doctrine help explain this concentration in arms-control thinking on the need to stabilize deterrence by technical control. Although the theorists did not start formulating the basic principles of American strategic thinking until the mid-1950s, their views showed a reasonable continuity with the handful of writings on the implications of nuclear weapons during 1945-46.[10] Secretary of State Dulles's enunciation of massive retaliation[11] had represented the first attempt to create a definite strategic doctrine for the United States. The academic reaction was typified by Bernard Brodie and Henry Kissinger,[12] both of whom criticized the application of strategic retaliation to the defence of those areas not vital to U.S. interests as a measure disproportionate to the threats involved. William Kaufmann showed that the doctrine was for this reason not likely to be credible to the enemy.[13] The question "if deterrence fails, is there any alternative to general war?" was answered by Henry Kissinger's summary of the discussion by a group representing the views of the U.S. foreign-policy establishment and its new adjunct, the strategic establishment.[14] He assumed that allied forces equipped with tactical nuclear weapons could hold off superior Soviet conventional forces because these would have to mass to attack, and would thereby present the ideal target for small nuclear weapons. If the Soviet Union attempted escalation to avoid defeat, the superior Western strategic forces would deter it by threatening a first strike. Robert E. Osgood[15] also came to the conclusion that a limited-war strategy was feasible and necessary for the United States. These views shaped and reflected the prevalent beliefs embodied in Dulles's article of October

1957, which announced that strategic forces would be backed up by local defences armed with "clean" nuclear weapons, that is, those with limited radioactive fallout.[16]

In the evolution of arms control, these views were significant because, like Halperin's later work on limited war[17] and Kahn's elaboration of the types of nuclear war,[18] they focused for the first time on the problems of reaching agreements with the Soviets on the establishment of limits in war before and after fighting started. The assumption was that if both sides possessed stable deterrent forces, the resulting strategic balance would make limited war more possible, but unless conscious efforts were made to keep it limited, escalation might result. The Korean War was studied as the only example of limited war in the nuclear age; it made possible examination of the different limits of geography and targets, the types of forces used, and the provision of sanctuaries not subject to attack. Great stress was laid on the fact that some limitations grew up out of circumstances and only later became observed as a matter of policy, while others — for example, maintenance of the fiction that Chinese communist troops fighting in Korea from 1950-53 were volunteers — stemmed from conscious policy. Without formal negotiations, the United States and China had come to perceive that certain sorts of immediate military advantages might be worth foregoing in return for establishing political or military limits to a war that neither wished to expand because only limited objectives were involved. Knorr and Read[19] extended these principles of limitation, communication, and common perceptions to strategic war: they argued that even in the case of a conflict which ceased to be limited to a particular theatre of operations, both superpowers would in fact be reluctant to destroy one another if they thought a more limited attack might break the other's will or force it to negotiate. Limited attacks could range from the symbolic explosion of small nuclear weapons over deserts to the destruction of evacuated cities. Communication would be largely through the unilateral decisions of each side, and each party would specify its demands and targets and try to establish certain of its own areas as sanctuaries, the violation of which would mean the escalation of the conflict. Their assumption of a strategic man, that is, an individual who would always respond rationally in terms of U.S. strategic thinking, was central to much of the American thinking on limited war.[20]

The strategic world view of those who wrote about deterrence, strategic war, and limited war was reinforced by the thinking of the games theorists who contributed to the debate, notably Thomas Schelling. The world which formed the basis for arms control was dominated by the two superpowers who could communicate and co-operate through a spectrum of means ranging from unilateral acts to formal negotiations and agreements. Although anxious to exploit the opportunities for political gains afforded by a strategic deadlock, neither power would wish to do so at the risk of causing a serious conflict that could escalate. If, by accident or by a misreading of intentions, such a clash occurred, both sides would exercise restraint based on this self-interest in avoiding nuclear war.

The idea of arms control was largely an extension of this analysis to include measures designed to keep the nuclear balance stable and to limit the scope of small wars. What gave these ideas their importance in the context of limited war was the realization in the late 1950s that the strategic balance was in fact even more unstable than had been thought. Clearly it was imperative to devise short-term measures to lessen the dangers of escalation through a mutual fear of surprise attack.

The Gaither Committee study of 1957 had shown that the proportion of aircraft that were able to retaliate after a surprise attack using Intercontinental Ballistic Missiles (ICBMs) was so low that, after allowing for Strategic Air Command losses to an alerted Soviet air-defence system, the United States might be unable to inflict on the Soviet Union the level of damage thought necessary to deter it.[21] The committee concluded that any retaliatory forces based on manned aircraft (or liquid-fuelled missiles not in hardened silos) would always be more suitable for a first strike because they were vulnerable to surprise attack. Since the *fear* of war could become the *cause* of war in an era of strategic and political uncertainties in superpower relations, arms-control measures were necessary to enable the superpowers to show that they were not in fact planning such surprise attacks on one another during times of crisis or confrontation.

This U.S. arms-control insistence on the need for superpower agreement(s) to lessen the possibility of either side initiating a strategic nuclear exchange out of fear of surprise attack led the United States to propose what became the Surprise Attack Conference of 1958. This conference was significant for three reasons. First, it provided the earliest juxtaposition of the U.S. approach to arms control as a primarily technical process with the Soviet view of arms control as a political process — a juxtaposition that left both sides convinced that their approach was valid and their opponent's was not. Second, the failure to reach any agreement with the Soviet Union should have led the U.S. arms controllers to re-examine the underlying concepts of technical arms control, but did not. Third, the balance of deterrence remained relatively stable in political terms throughout the period 1958-61 when it was supposed to be technically unstable. It was eventually stabilized technically through the introduction of Polaris-carrying submarines and Minuteman ICBMs that were able to ride out an enemy attack before retaliating and so provide a second-strike capability. However, the development of this capability was only marginally influenced by arms-control thinking, although the accelerated deployment by President Kennedy of these weapons owed much to the strategic arguments for second-strike forces. Whether or not his acquisition of a counter-force capability (that is, the ability to knock out the Soviet strategic forces at an acceptable cost to the United States) was an arms-control measure seems a moot point. Its proponents claimed that it was; if so, it was an odd sort of arms control.

PART II Initial American Arms-Control Initiatives and Soviet Responses: 1958-62

4 The 1958 Surprise Attack Conference

The emerging corpus of arms-control theory described in the previous chapter was refined in the nuclear test-ban negotiations, primarily because this was a context in which scientists were bound to be influential in determining American policy. The brief Surprise Attack Conference of November 10 to December 7, 1958, provided another opportunity for arms controllers to exert their influence. At this conference, the American delegation tried to implement the various arms-control proposals for mutual assurance against the self-reinforcing fear of surprise attack. In contrast, the Soviets sought to remove what they perceived to be the most likely cause of war in Europe — conflict arising out of their renewed pressure on West Berlin. Under these circumstances the level of tension between East and West could be escalated through West German action up to and including a catalytic strike — that is, a West German use of two-key nuclear weapons (which the Soviets believed the West Germans could seize and use in a crisis) to provoke a conflict with the Soviet Union in which the United States would be forced into supporting West Germany. The Soviets were also concerned about the continuing U.S. commitment to German reunification, with the concomitant refusal by the West to recognize East Germany or its borders.

It was in this context that the Surprise Attack Conference provided the first juxtaposition of political and technical arms control. The result was a strengthening of each side's view that its own approach was the only effective means of maintaining equilibrium between U.S. concern over the strategic balance and Soviet concern over the politico-military confrontation in Europe. Because neither superpower could grasp what the other was talking about, each went away feeling that it was even more important to press on with its own measures, a fact that was particularly important in shaping the development of U.S. arms-control theory. In 1958 this was a newly developed doctrine stressing the need for technical controls on strategic weapons to prevent the fear of surprise attack becoming, in fact, the cause of such an attack in a crisis. Its *technical* emphasis was, perhaps, inevitable in that particular context. However, an effective dialogue at the Surprise Attack Conference might have enabled the U.S. arms controllers to understand the Soviets' concept of the danger of surprise attack in Europe as a primarily *political* problem. Such a realization might have modified U.S. emphasis on technical controls to accommodate proper consideration of the political context in which they would have to be applied. Since arms-control theory was still in its formative stage, such an adjustment could perhaps have been made, though at the cost of upsetting some pretty strongly held notions on the dominance of technical considerations in arms control. Instead, the Surprise Attack Conference reinforced arms-control theory's emphasis on the technicalities of control and ensured that political factors would be shaped to fit a Procrustean bed of theory that stressed control over military technology independent of a political context. These developments left arms-control theory particularly vulnerable to the scientists' emphasis on technical considerations described above (see Chapter 3), and partly explained the importance of the Surprise Attack Conference in the evolution of thinking on technical arms control.

The extent to which the conference revealed emerging American and Soviet attitudes to technical and political arms control has been strangely neglected, except by Johan Holst.[1] Therefore, this chapter will concentrate on placing the conference in its appropriate political context — establishing the differing motives for participation, the positions adopted, and their effect on arms-control and arms-limitation thinking.

The Background of the Conference

From the Geneva Summit of 1955 onwards, the overriding political issue in Europe was the extent to which the temporary U.S. acquiescence in the Soviet sphere of control in Eastern Europe would become permanent and whether, as eventually happened in 1970-75, the Soviet Union would accept the status of West Berlin and Allied rights of access thereto in exchange for explicit American agreement not to threaten Soviet control over Eastern Europe. The argument could be made that it would require time for the superpowers to accept a status quo that neither would find wholly satisfactory or wholly stable, and to realize that they had to live with the less-than-perfect settlement acquired at the end of the Second World War. The increasingly stable balance of nuclear deterrence made it impossible to alter this arrangement through the use of force. Like most retrospective generalizations, this analysis of the underlying causes of instability, in Europe and between the superpowers, can only make the particular manifestations of instability intelligible by adding that at the time the relevant decision makers' perceptions of the strategic balance were much less sanguine than they are now. In part, this pessimism went with a tendency to view the problem in terms of generalized rather than precise threats.

Thus, the Soviets clearly saw West Germany — willing to risk war, or the threat of war, in an effort to obtain reunification — as a destabilizing force. In the Soviet view, West Germany was supported in its desires by the U.S. government, whose policy zig-zagged between President Eisenhower's often obscure pronouncements in favour of detente and Secretary of State Dulles's more bellicose statements. Since America's European allies were often uncertain of its real policy, the Soviets can be forgiven for their own uncertainty, and for their tendency to assume the worst. A particular focus of their concern was West Germany's access to nuclear weapons — through the early two-key system used from 1958 to about 1962; the Multilateral Nuclear Force (MLF), which seemed likely to be created between 1963 and 1965; or the MLF's substitute, the NATO Nuclear Planning Group (NPG). The very vagueness of the term "access" emphasized the uncertainty which characterized the Soviet Union's attitude towards the West German–U.S. nuclear relationship. Suspecting the worst, the Soviets took until 1966 to be convinced that West Germany was unable and unwilling to threaten a nuclear war for the recovery of East Germany.

West Berlin symbolized the problem of getting either the United States or the Soviet Union to accept the division of Germany, since the continued existence of West Berlin as a route through which East Germans could escape to the West threatened the survival of the Ulbricht regime in East Germany, which the West had no cause to support. Consequently, Mr. Khrushchev viewed West Berlin as a permanent threat to East Germany and so attempted to solve the refugee problem by threatening to limit access to, and egress from, West Berlin, either in the context of a resolution of the German problem or as an isolated measure. The resultant crisis exacerbated the Soviets' greatest fear, that West Germany might drag the United States into intervention on West Germany's Chancellor Adenauer's side by strengthening the Washington–Bonn axis. West Berlin therefore represented an independent cause of instability in Western Europe. The Berlin Wall of 1961 solved the Berlin problem by giving the Soviets all that they could reasonably expect: namely, an end to the outflow of East Germans. By this measure, the Soviets also made certain that they could gain no further concessions. Mr. Khrushchev's personal volatility always exaggerated each crisis and demonstrated the drawbacks as well as the advantages of Schelling's rationality of the irrational.[2]

The net result was an increased Soviet wish for some over-all solution to the political problems which in its view were the cause of instability. Simultaneously, the Soviets sought measures to limit military activity which might increase this instability. In this way, their thinking apparently parallelled that of the technical arms controllers who also sought to control destabilizing technological innovations. In the American view, the crucial balance was between the superpowers' strategic forces and the risk of unintentional war through surprise attack. These fears were increased by the Gaither Committee's report of November 7, 1957, which embodied the concepts of strategic instability and countervailing arms-control measures, both of which dominated U.S. arms-control thinking and policy until the post-Cuban-crisis detente of 1963. The report concluded that:

> . . . the Soviet Union could have a small operational force of, say, 100 ICBMs by the 1960s and thus could destroy American retaliatory forces. This report reflected the view of the arms controllers participating, notably William Foster, the effective chairman (director of the Arms Control and Disarmament Agency, 1961-69), Jerome Wiesner (President Kennedy's science adviser), and Paul H. Nitze (currently a member of the United States delegation to SALT). All these men saw the first-generation ICBM as an inherently destabilizing weapon, with its short flight time being considerably less than its reaction time, or [than] that of the great proportion of SAC; this complete vulnerability of retaliatory weapons made the ICBM essentially a first-strike weapon, creating a world of hair-trigger reactions in crises. This analysis made the report a polarizing document, leaving little choice between acceptance or rejection of its recommendations for short-term measures to lessen SAC's vulnerability, including negotiation with the Russians for mutual warning (unilateral and bilateral arms control) and a crash programme to create and deploy a hardened and dispersed second-strike ICBM force.

President Eisenhower discounted the report's major recommendations but endorsed the idea of a surprise attack conference.[3]

The difference between the technical-arms-control view and that of the Soviets with regard to what such a conference should discuss was apparent from the Rapacki plan, presented by Poland, with Soviet approval and probably at Soviet urging, in October 1957. The Rapacki plan represented the first coherent Soviet-bloc attempt to discuss security problems within the European framework that had emerged (however tentatively) in 1955. Previous Soviet efforts had treated these problems as the product of a framework that would be created by a political settlement. While it established a context for discussions on security, the plan also linked such discussions to the question of West Germany's position in NATO. This was intentional, since NATO's shift to reliance on tactical nuclear weapons and the concomitant introduction of two-key nuclear delivery systems would, in the Soviet view, increase West Germany's catalytic potential for war. In terms of analogies with the outbreak of the First World War used by arms controllers to argue for measures they saw as necessary to avoid a Third World War, the arms controllers were discussing the dangers of inflexible mobilization timetables and the provision of mutual reassurance of non-mobilization. To the Soviets, these were symptoms of the underlying political problem: in 1914, spheres of influence in the Balkans; in 1957, spheres of control in Europe. Senior Soviet academics have indeed used this analogy in private conversations with the author. Admittedly, these were conducted on a more rational basis than in the anti-German diatribes of Soviet propaganda. The Rapacki plan linked a political solution, the recognition of two German states, to the strategic problem of West German acquisition of two-key nuclear weapons. The former would be achieved and the latter prevented by creating an Atom-Free Zone in Central Europe, which would cover East and West Germany, Poland, and Hungary, with the four great powers guaranteeing implementation via ground and aerial inspection.

Differing Approaches to the Conference

By 1958 the United States and the Soviet Union were both anxious to discuss what each regarded as long-standing security problems made worse by certain military developments which made a bilateral solution desirable. For the arms controllers, the ICBM necessitated mutual reassurance against a surprise attack or a first strike which could be effective enough to be an acceptable option in a crisis. For the Soviets, West Germany's participation in the two-key system and NATO's lowering of the nuclear threshold increased the chances of escalation in a crisis. Soviet attempts to solve the West Berlin problem in the following year could precipitate such a crisis, necessitating measures of political arms control. These would try to insulate the political environment from the effects of military technology, whereas technical arms control sought to isolate strategic problems from their political environment and devise apolitical technical solutions to the problems of instability.

Accordingly, President Eisenhower's January 12 letter[4] stressed the idea of a conference of experts on surprise attack (as on nuclear testing) based on the idea of implementing controls against surprise attack that had been the theme of U.S. disarmament proposals since the President adopted the Rockefeller Committee's open-skies proposal[5] at the 1955 Summit Conference. The President's rejection of negotiations on the Rapacki plan accentuated the Soviets' dilemma: they wanted negotiations on the problem of surprise attack but defined it quite differently from the Americans. Since a conference of experts was the only possible negotiating forum, Soviet acceptance of such a conference was probably inspired by the hope that the agenda would cover what each side defined as the problem of surprise attack. Mr. Khrushchev's July 2 letter of acceptance[6] emphasized their view of the dangers of U.S. flights with nuclear-armed aircraft over Western Europe, flights which ignored the need for both sides to refrain from actions leading to an increase in the danger of war. Countermeasures should include, in the Soviet view, cessation of these flights, control posts at railway junctions, major ports, and highways, as well as other definite, though unspecified, disarmament steps. Another measure favoured by the Soviets was aerial surveys in key areas of vulnerability to surprise attack, notably eight hundred kilometres on either side of the boundary between Eastern and Western Europe. This linking of control proposals to specific disarmament measures reflected the Soviet belief that theoretical discussion of control was useless. Taken with the omission of airfields or missile bases in the Soviet Union as sites for observation posts, these suggestions emphasized Soviet preoccupation with the European strategic balance.

At the end of the month, on July 31, the United States suggested an October meeting of experts at Geneva to conduct a technical study of safeguards against surprise attack. Such a gathering would facilitate later agreement at a political level on the definition of regions in which safeguards would apply.[7] Already it was obvious that the two sides were approaching the talks with different agendas in mind. Indications were that the West rejected the European Aerial Inspection Zone as freezing the partition of Germany, and feared Soviet exploitation of U.S. eagerness to prevent surprise attacks as a means of securing a nuclear test-ban treaty. There was a complete Western failure to grasp what the Soviets were talking about. By assuming a Soviet conversion to the U.S. view of the experts' role in technical arms control, the Americans helped turn the negotiations into two parallel monologues. Moreover, that assumption ignored Secretary Dulles's known willingness to override experts' views for political reasons.[8] The Soviets may have been influenced by these unfavourable omens to delay their acceptance, since their campaign to end the four-power status of Berlin would be facilitated by a forum for discussing the dangers in the existing Berlin situation. If the conference started too soon and became deadlocked, it could break up before it was really needed. Therefore they waited until September 15 to propose November 10 as the starting date, and reiterated that the conference would be useful only "if its work aimed at practical recommendation on measures to prevent surprise attack [and] definite steps in disarmament".[9]

The composition of the delegations to the conference reflected the difference between the two approaches. As Holst observed, "The 'eastern' delegation amounted to forty-two experts and advisers . . . and consisted entirely of diplomatic personnel and military officers"[10] headed by Vasili V. Kuznetzov, a Deputy Foreign Minister experienced in disarmament negotiations. In contrast, the West had one hundred and eight members, including fifty from the United States. The chief of their delegation was William C. Foster, formerly Deputy Secretary of Defense and co-director (effectively director) of the Gaither Committee, later Director of the U.S. Arms Control and Disarmament Agency (1961-69), and, after his retirement, Chairman of the Arms Control Association (a lobby for technical arms control) from its foundation in 1972 onwards. Other prominent members of his delegation were George B. Kistiakowsky (later President Eisenhower's science advisor); Jerome B. Wiesner (also a member of the Gaither Committee, later President John F. Kennedy's science advisor, and a tireless advocate of technical arms control); and Albert Wohlstetter, plus several colleagues from the Rand Corporation.[11] Foster and the Western delegations operated under instructions forbidding any discussion of political issues, especially the politically very sensitive German question, and limiting them to discussion along pure arms-control lines — identifying the objects of control, defining techniques, revealing preparations for surprise attacks, and assessing their likely results. Such studies were to be hypothetical, although specific areas might be considered for purely illustrative purposes. Their general idea was for inspection posts with unrestricted communications which would monitor known points where surprise-attack preparation could take place. These would be supplemented by mobile inspection teams to examine suspicious activities revealed by aerial inspection, especially missile-launching platforms (fixed or mobile) and airfields. Surprise attack in the Western sense of a disarming counterforce strike would become more difficult and therefore less likely, although it would not be prevented.

In view of the fact that the Western side was forbidden to discuss West Germany's position in the Western alliance, which the Soviets saw as the main potential area of surprise attack, it is not surprising that the conference never got beyond discussing the agenda. It started on November 10 and ended with the adjournment for Christmas on December 7, despite Soviet efforts to arrange, presumably for political effect, its subsequent recall. The reiteration of irreconcilable concepts of technical and political arms control cannot be described as negotiation. It is therefore more appropriate to examine the major proposals made by each side, because these indicate their separate understanding of the dangers and possible solutions involved therein.

The Soviet Union used discussion of possible control systems to raise the political issues with which it was concerned. European arms limitation and related inspection (mainly aerial inspection and static ground observation posts) were to be complemented by measures to improve the political climate. The Soviet objective was not the reunification of the two Germanies, but their neutralization, to deprive them of nuclear weapons or delivery bases and to limit their conventional forces. Reduced offensive capability and detection of any build-up of forces would remove the major danger of surprise attack by separating West Germany's desire to challenge the Eastern European status quo from its requisite military capability. Automatically, the danger in maintaining West Berlin's anomalous status and thereby possibly precipitating a major confrontation would be reduced. The Soviet force-limitation proposals included: a ban on nuclear weapons, at least within the two Germanies; a one-third reduction in conventional forces in the two pact areas; an unspecified reduction in foreign bases in the same areas; and a ban on flights of aircraft with nuclear weapons over the high seas and over states (unspecified). The corresponding inspection system comprised an Aerial Inspection Zone (AIZ) of eight hundred kilometres (about five hundred miles) on either side of the Iron Curtain, and over Greece, Turkey, and Iran. Initially, the Soviets had included a zone covering both sides of the Bering Strait (the area east of 108°E and west of 46°W) and Japan. Later, however, they referred to aerial photography in areas of outstanding significance to avert surprise attack and these were defined as within the eight-hundred-kilometre AIZ. Ground observation posts at railways, ports, and highways were also proposed. These numbered twenty-eight in the Warsaw Pact and forty-eight in NATO, and six each in the Soviet Union and the United States, for a total of thirty-four in the East and fifty-four in the West. There were to be no more than four officers at each post, under the command of a national of the observed state.

The inspection provisions supported the earlier contention that the Soviet Union did not see the main danger to European stability as surprise air or missile attack. Its demands for an Arctic inspection zone were dropped, as were its 1955 proposals for observers at airfields.

Soviet political-arms-control policy could not be interpreted solely as a bid for propaganda advantages via apparently straightforward arms-control schemes that actually exploited its advantages in the current strategic balance. As gamesmanship, Soviet policy at the Surprise Attack Conference was inadequate; it failed to use the Western eagerness to discuss warning against surprise attack as the means to force discussion of the issues the Soviets were really concerned with, or to score diplomatic points. Their policy was consistent with the view of surprise attack attributed to them earlier in this chapter. This view dictated a link between any discussion of arms-control systems, which would be only nominal, and the more important underlying issues of the political context in which the system would operate and the political problems making it necessary. In contrast, the West held a belief in control as a subject for discussion on its own. Indeed, to the Soviets, technical arms control seemed to increase the dangers that it was supposed to limit, because it provided intelligence of strategic and tactical forces, and thereby made a surprise attack more likely to succeed. Moreover, as far as the Soviets were concerned, such measures did not tackle the political problems that had created the original danger. If warning were received of a surprise attack, the consequences would be the same as if the agreement had never existed. Accordingly, the Soviets stressed instead a Non-Aggression Pact between the NATO and Warsaw Pact members, which would, in conjunction with other measures of limitation and control, have signified a change in Western political attitudes. Most significantly, it would have marked an acceptance of the Soviet sphere of control in Europe and of the division of Germany, and have secured Western recognition of East Germany.

By the end of 1958 the United States was attempting to translate into policy the technical-arms-control concepts of stabilizing the strategic balance. The countervailing Soviet approach has been described as political arms control because it sought by political means to limit the political effects of changes in military technology and in the strategic balance, which were inimical to Soviet interests. In contrast, technical arms control emphasized physical controls on specific weapons systems. The differences between technical and political arms control evident in the 1958 conferences on a nuclear test ban and surprise attack became clearer with the Soviets' continued political campaign to secure acceptance both of their sphere of control in Eastern Europe and of their solutions for the instability created by the interlocking issues of the position of West Berlin and the division of Germany.

5 Political Arms Control in Soviet Diplomacy: 1958-62

The divergence between political and technical arms control became even greater with the failure of the Surprise Attack Conference. On the one hand, arms controllers continued to be preoccupied with consolidating their theories and getting these accepted by the U.S. government. On the other hand, the Soviets remained convinced that the absence of a coherent political framework in the West within which to negotiate both disarmament and arms-control issues afforded them the chance to gain political compensation for any of their deficiencies in the strategic balance. In practice, then, the distinction between political and technical arms control had become clear. This was demonstrated by the Soviet Union's pressure for Atom-Free Zones in 1959, by its use of General and Complete Disarmament (GCD) propaganda from 1959 to 1962, and by its persistent pressure for equal status with the United States in a continuing negotiating forum within which to discuss arms control and disarmament. Both the United States and the Soviet Union sought to stabilize a potentially unstable superpower confrontation in Europe, but only the Soviet Union used technical issues as modalities for achieving its political goals. In so far as the United States related political measures to arms control, it was only in an effort to provide a climate in which technical issues could be discussed without political considerations.

The Political Context of the Soviet Approach to Stability

On November 4, 1958, six days before the Surprise Attack Conference opened, Poland offered a revised Rapacki plan[1] which indicated the Soviet view of the causes and cures for tensions in Europe. Now included among the remedies was their suggestion that the denuclearization of East Germany, West Germany, Poland, and Czechoslovakia should be accompanied by a reduction of conventional forces that could be verified by unspecified control measures. NATO and the Warsaw Treaty/Warsaw Pact Organization (WPO) would continue. On the day the conference opened, Mr. Khrushchev demanded an end to the occupation of Germany and the conversion of Berlin to a free city, thereby emphasizing his view that West Berlin was an aspect of the German problem rather than a separate issue. He also demanded the withdrawal of NATO troops from West Germany in order to prevent a surprise attack, the demilitarization and neutralization of West Berlin under a U.N. guarantee, and an end to Soviet occupation rights in East Germany in an effort to force Western recognition of the German Democratic Republic (GDR). All of these demands demonstrated that Khrushchev viewed West Berlin only as part of the larger German problem. Included in a draft German peace treaty in a Soviet ultimatum of January 10, 1959, these proposals remained the objective of Soviet arms-limitation policy until, and possibly during, the West Berlin crisis of 1960-61.[2]

The idea of surprise attack remained intelligible to the Soviets only within Europe because this was the one area where they could envisage the existing confrontation as serious enough to generate a conflict likely to escalate into general war. In the Soviet view, insecurity, in the sense of a fear of attack, resulted from the absence of a European political settlement that recognized the status quo of their sphere of control in Eastern Europe. Provided that this was the subject for discussion, the Soviets were little concerned whether the forum was labelled political or technical. Their choice of the latter in 1958 was dictated by the Western arms-control framework in which technical discussions were seen as self-contained prerequisites to any decisions, including that of broadening the scope of negotiations. This Western adherence to a distinction that the Soviets could not accept ensured an impasse on the technical route to negotiations and led Khrushchev to seek a direct road to, and through, the Summit. Khrushchev had to decide whether the road to West Berlin led through arms-control negotiations at Geneva or political talks in Washington. One means of forcing the West to agree to his proposals was to increase the propaganda and diplomatic pressure on them via the nuclear-test-ban talks and Soviet GCD proposals. Such a campaign could also be advanced by reconstituting the U.N. Disarmament Commission in such a manner as to give the Soviet Union equality with the West and also bring in "Third World" representatives, whose anti-Western neutrality made them more susceptible to the techniques of Soviet diplomacy. These changes would also create an appropriate avenue for exploring any Western willingness to discuss the Soviet requirements for stabilizing the balance of deterrence.

Unquestionably, the Soviets recognized the possibilities for agreements with the West to minimize the shared, though not identical, risks that were created by their inability to resolve certain political and military problems which resulted from their conflicting interests. They used such agreements to secure both implicit Western acceptance of the political status quo and Western recognition of the fact that bilateral superpower understandings were the only practicable means of resolving conflicts. The Soviet emphasis on the political origins of military confrontation in Europe reflected their essentially Clausewitzian view of the relationship between force and politics, that "War is not a mere act of policy but a true political instrument, a continuation of political activity by other means."[3] Their approach stressed the need to balance the Western emphasis on strategic theory with a more realistic assessment of the political and psychological aspects of stability. The central difficulty with the German problem was that, although both sides recognized the dangers inherent in the possibility of surprise attack, their separate perceptions of those dangers prevented them from reaching agreement on mutually acceptable measures for its reduction. This was finally achieved through the Western acceptance of the Berlin Wall in August 1961 and the 1963 detente, with its tacit recognition by the Soviet Union that American strategic superiority was no longer likely to be used to upset the post-war settlement in Eastern and Western Europe.

The Soviet Union's 1959 Campaign for Atom-Free Zones in Europe

Nevertheless, American acceptance of the status quo in Eastern Europe seemed far away in 1959, when Mr. Khrushchev moved to head off what seemed to him to be the destabilizing U.S. distribution of two-key nuclear weapons authorized by the December 1957 NATO ministerial meeting in response to the Eisenhower administration's increased reliance on tactical nuclear weapons (described in Chapter 2 above). To do so he exploited the European and German internal political forces that were opposed to the placing of nuclear weapons in West Germany. Those same forces favoured instead neutralization as a prelude to reunification. Therefore, Soviet proposals for Atom-Free Zones (AFZ) rose from three in 1956 to twelve in 1957, dropped to ten in 1958, peaked at sixteen in 1959, dropped to one in 1960, rose to five in 1961, and dropped again to one in 1962.[4] Even more significant than the numerical increase was the Soviet concentration on AFZ proposals in the early half of 1959. Seven of the fourteen AFZ proposals made between January 10 and July 22 were, for the first time, made by Mr. Khrushchev himself. In the Soviet view, denuclearization was the only means of halting the dissemination of nuclear weapons. This position foreshadowed their opposition to the alleged proliferation represented by the Multilateral Nuclear Force (MLF) from 1963 to 1965. The inability of either Western diplomats or arms controllers to share the Soviet fears was evidenced by their lack of interest in denuclearization. British

Prime Minister Harold Macmillan, for example, had suggested a general freeze and reduction of troops and weapons in Central Europe.

The Herter plan[5] advanced at the Foreign Ministers' Conference of May 14, 1959, went even further in proposing that there would be no production of nuclear or biological weapons within mutually determined areas of comparable importance on either side of the line dividing Western Europe. In this way, the plan avoided the issue of storing nuclear weapons, but it did provide that non-production would be subject to verification by inspection. During the second stage, while the reunification of Germany and Berlin was being negotiated, there would be ceilings on foreign and national forces. The impossibility of achieving these objectives and the irrelevance of both the Macmillan and Herter plans to Western strategic or political objectives only emphasized the dichotomy between technical and political arms control. As technical-arms-control measures these proposals were inadequate; as political-arms-control measures they failed to counter the impression created by the Soviets that it was they who were advocating a detente in Europe and NATO that was blocking it.

In part, Secretary Dulles's distrust of arms control prevented the State Department from building up the necessary organization and understanding of this new aspect of diplomacy and curtailed any political input into arms-control thinking. Dulles's agreement with Chancellor Adenauer on maintaining a rigid status quo in Western Europe by placing Western unity ahead of superpower negotiations did, however, limit the Soviet ability to exploit the diplomatic advantage gained by political arms control. Therefore, the Secretary's death in April 1959 left the American and Allied governments much more vulnerable to the cumulative effects of Soviet policy.

The advantages the Soviet Union gained from having a clearly formulated policy of arms control were considerable. They combined clear-cut long-run objectives with great tactical cleverness in switching their proposals to suit the diplomatic needs of the moment. They seem to have been able to anticipate the relatively slow and ill-co-ordinated Western reductions with considerable accuracy, and to adjust their policy accordingly in order to gain their main objectives.

Agreement to a summit conference was easily achieved and Mr. Khrushchev's August–September 1959 visit to the United States helped him create the impression that the German situation, especially the status of Berlin, represented an aberration that threatened peace, and that satisfactory resolution of this problem would remove a dangerous anomaly. At Khrushchev's September Camp David Summit meeting with Eisenhower, the President's statements suggested that he was accepting the Soviet view of the Berlin problem. The September 27

Camp David communiqué promised a reopening of negotiations on Berlin, while the next day, at a news conference, Eisenhower said that he could not guarantee Allied rights in Berlin because "The situation is abnormal".[6]

Presumably, Soviet expectations from 1958 to 1960 ranged from substantive concessions by the Western powers to a change in their approach to the German question which recognized the Soviet fear of West Germany's catalytic potential for war. In the Soviet view, such a shift would make the West more ready to accept any limited unilateral actions the Soviet Union might feel forced to take in order to preserve its position in East Germany. In this sense, the real effects of the 1959 AFZ campaign and the political-arms-control policy on surprise attack (of which AFZ proposals were a part) became apparent in the separate West Berlin crisis after the Summit collapsed in 1960. As late as July 1962, the United States offered the Soviet Union a substantial concession by proposing an International Access Authority for West Berlin.[7] Since the crucial element in the Soviet theory of surprise attack was the potential U.S. support for West German attempts to upset the political status quo, and because the Ulbricht regime's security had been assured by the August 13, 1961, erection of the Berlin Wall, political arms control had succeeded, in so far as it changed Western perceptions of what constituted an acceptable settlement in Europe.

The Switch to General and Complete Disarmament (GCD): 1959-62

In his 1959 speech to the U.N. General Assembly, Mr. Khrushchev clearly required a new disarmament proposal that would appeal to the wider audience he was addressing. His objective was, of course, still to put the West sufficiently on the defensive that it would accept Soviet ideas on a German settlement. Accordingly, Mr. Khrushchev's speech on September 18 to the General Assembly, and the accompanying declaration, introduced the concept of abolishing war through GCD. The Soviet leader further proposed that this could be achieved in four years and that the resources released from arms production should be diverted to the Third World.[8] His declaration that nuclear war would be equally disastrous for all parties foreshadowed his later statement on January 14, 1960 reiterating this view, summarized in his oft-repeated aphorism that "There would be no victors in a nuclear war."[9] This marked the Soviets' explicit acceptance of deterrence. As an alternative to GCD, Khrushchev offered negotiations on limited measures. Rather than signalling Moscow's unreadiness for serious negotiations, this emphasis on GCD indicated that the respective Soviet and American views of acceptable partial measures were so far apart that agreement was unlikely.

Both sides agreed that they had problems which could be more suitably solved in collaboration, but they could not agree on either a definition of those problems or appropriate remedial measures. Mr. Khrushchev's partial measures included the main arms-limitation proposals, the propaganda accompaniments that had been advanced by the Soviets to date, and the proposals of March 10, 1955, as a third alternative for negotiation. The partial steps proposed were:

1. The establishment of a control and inspection zone and the reduction of foreign troops in the territories of the Western European countries concerned;
2. The establishment of an "atom free" zone in Central Europe;
3. The withdrawal of all foreign troops from the territories of European States and the abolition of military bases on the territories of foreign States;
4. The conclusion of a non-aggression pact between the member States of NATO and the member States of the Warsaw Treaty;
5. The conclusion of an agreement on the prevention of surprise attack by one State upon another.[10]

These proposals, especially (4) and (5), showed that Mr. Khrushchev remained prepared to engage in negotiations whenever it might be fruitful, but they also revealed his recognition that in the pre-Summit atmosphere propaganda could be more rewarding. The West had apparently reached the same conclusion. On the day before the Soviet GCD proposal was introduced, British Foreign Minister Selwyn Lloyd (the late Lord Lloyd) had attempted to recreate "the ideal of a relatively disarmed world that had been the basis for all Western disarmament proposals prior to 1955".[11] The Soviets were also able to exploit the popularity of GCD in the General Assembly by securing the unanimous adoption of a resolution that urged the discussion of GCD by the Ten Nation Disarmament Conference (TNDC),[12] which they had secured through negotiations arising out of the 1959 Foreign Ministers Conference.

At the TNDC's first and only session, which opened on March 15, 1960, the Western powers rapidly tabled their own three-stage GCD plan,[13] despite its technical imperfections, and thus signified their acceptance of GCD as the basis for propaganda exchanges. Like the Baruch plan of 1946 (or, more accurately, the Acheson–Lilienthal version thereof), GCD was excellent propaganda, since the Third World was more impressed by the possibility of diverting resources from the arms race to economic development than by the problems of maintaining the balance of deterrence in disarmament. The arms controllers' insistence on the need for adequate verification, together with the U.S.

reliance on overseas bases, forced them to raise what seemed to the Third World to be irrelevant obstacles to GCD. The effectiveness of the switch to GCD was evident in the extraordinarily mild Third World reaction to the Soviet resumption of nuclear testing on September 1, 1961; the statement made by the Belgrade Conference of Non-Aligned Countries merely requested that the moratorium on nuclear testing be resumed and asked President Kennedy, in a separate message, to resume negotiations with the Soviet Union.[14]

Both the propaganda utility of GCD and the need to have a continuing forum for the discussion of mutual security problems led the Soviets to seek a new disarmament conference. The need for such a forum had become more pressing because of Soviet withdrawal both from the TNDC in 1960 and from the Geneva test-ban talks in 1961. Therefore, in the McCloy–Zorin talks which led to the Agreed Statement of Principles of September 20, 1961,[15] the Soviets sought and obtained a troika-based conference (that is, one representing the Eastern, Western, and Neutral — pro-Eastern — blocs) that was committed to discussing GCD and to rejecting the U.S. principle of effective control in any agreement. The conference also established an important channel of communication with the new American administration. For the Soviets, this restored their position (lost when they unilaterally resumed testing) as the leading advocates of disarmament; it also facilitated substantive discussions with the United States. The successful U.S. counter-attack on the GCD front in the first half of 1962 reflects its increased integration of arms control and diplomacy with the Arms Control and Disarmament Agency's (ACDA's) establishment. That agency institutionalized, albeit within the framework of technical-arms-control thinking, the linkage between politics and technology that had previously been missing from American diplomacy. The Soviet Union's propaganda lead therefore decreased sharply, prompting Mr. Khrushchev to switch his emphasis from pressing the United States to acquiesce in his policies to engaging in direct negotiations which symbolized the superpowers' achievement of a *modus vivendi*.

At the first sessions of the Eighteen Nation Disarmament Conference (ENDC), from March 14 to September 7, 1962, GCD remained the dominant topic. But President Kennedy's American University speech on June 10, 1963, signalled the start of the post-Cuban-missile-crisis (October 1962) superpower detente, and the subsequent U.S.–U.S.S.R. negotiation of the Moscow Test Ban Treaty marked the end of GCD as a diplomatically useful instrument. It had helped press the West into discussing what the Soviet Union saw as outstanding security problems and, to a lesser extent, into accepting Soviet solutions, notably the Berlin Wall, to those problems. But once the superpowers could engage in an effective dialogue, from 1963 onwards, GCD became irrelevant to the central aim of political arms control, the securing of political solutions to strategic problems. With the U.N. Disarmament Commission's "omnibus" resolution of June 15, 1965,[16] which gave priority to a Comprehensive Test Ban (CTB) and a Non-Proliferation Treaty (NPT), the replacement of GCD by collateral measures as the main means of political arms control was complete. So also was the Soviet search for equality with the United States in negotiations, nominally achieved with the ENDC's establishment in 1962. Implicitly, this equality was achieved in the 1963 test-ban talks and the latter stages of the NPT negotiations, from 1966 to 1968; but it was not formalized until 1969, when the superpowers enlarged the ENDC into the Conference of the Committee on Disarmament (CCD) and separated out the Strategic Arms Limitation Talks (SALT) between the two superpowers. The Moscow Summit of 1972, which marked American acceptance of the Soviet Union as a political and strategic equal, also symbolized the fulfilment of yet another political arms-control objective that had emerged between 1958 and 1962.

Arms Limitation and the Changes in Negotiating Forums: 1954-72

From May 1945 onwards, the post-Stalinist Soviet leadership sought participation in an institutionalized framework for negotiations on disarmament and arms limitation that would accurately reflect their increasing political influence and military strength.[17] The 1955 Summit signified Western acceptance of the Soviet Union as a major European power and, tentatively, of its sphere of control in Europe as well. This led the Soviets to press for equality of the two blocs in disarmament talks at a suitable opportunity. That occasion came with the Western use of its voting majority in the General Assembly to endorse its proposals of August 29, 1957, to the Sub-committee of the U.N. Disarmament Commission. The Soviet Union withdrew from the existing negotiating bodies, and thereby forced the West to accept its conditions for the resumption of talks in 1958 by using the Conference of Experts to introduce the principle of equal bloc representation. This principle had been effectively embodied in the 1958 Surprise Attack Conference, despite Western attempts to deny that this was the case. The Geneva test-ban talks of necessity included only the nuclear-weapons powers of the time — the United States, Great Britain, and the Soviet Union — but they also marked the beginning of the institutional distinction between the two superpowers and others in arms-control talks. The short-lived TNDC (March – June 1960) institutionalized equal representation of five states each from East and West. Its replacement had to meet two new Soviet requirements: first, that it serve as a superpower negotiating body, since Soviet unilateral violation of the testing moratorium in September had ended the Geneva talks, with their potential for bilateral U.S.–U.S.S.R. discussions; and, second, that the new body be based on the new Soviet theory of three blocs — East, West, and Third World. Accordingly, the ENDC, established in the 1961 General Assembly, had the United States and the Soviet Union as co-chairmen of a body composed of the TNDC's members plus eight nominally non-aligned states.

Thus, from the institutional inferiority of 1954, the Soviets had secured East-West bloc-to-bloc equality and American acceptance as a (lesser) superpower by 1962. This victory was achieved through balancing the possibilities for effective discussion of Soviet security problems with the West against the opportunities for securing a better forum for substantive talks or for propaganda, depending on which best served the Soviet Union's purpose.[18] After the Cuban crisis, partial agreements — notably the Partial Test Ban (PTB) Treaty of 1963 — that confirmed bilateral superpower respect for each other's interests were sought and obtained by the Soviet Union. Subsequent smaller measures served to confirm this relationship. During negotiations on the NPT from 1964 to 1971, it became increasingly clear that the ENDC really comprised two separate conferences, one between the superpowers on essentially political agreements furthering their bilateral relationship, and a second on the other members' terms for acceptance of these agreements. This new and highly important relationship, which involved the acceptance of the Soviet Union as an equal superpower by the United States, was formalized in 1969 with the co-chairmen's agreement on ENDC's enlargement. Japan and Mongolia were added to the conference on July 3 and were followed on August 7, 1969, by Argentina, Hungary, Morocco, the Netherlands, Pakistan, and Yugoslavia. This raised the membership to twenty-six (effectively twenty-five, since France continued her 1962 refusal to participate in disarmament discussions) and the name was changed to "The Conference of the Committee on Disarmament" (CCD)[19] to allow for any further additions. With the opening of the preliminary discussions on the Strategic Arms Limitation Talks (SALT) on November 17, 1969 (agreed to in principle by the superpowers when they signed the NPT on July 1, 1968), the superpowers confirmed that their unique relationship made it easier for them first to negotiate on a bilateral basis and then to persuade the affected members of the international community to accept the results.

Thus, from 1954 to 1972, the orientation of political arms control led the Soviet Union to place extreme importance on the negotiating forum. This same issue was regarded by the technical arms controllers as primarily functional in nature because they placed less emphasis on the political relationships between the superpowers and the consequent need, in the Soviet view, to make appropriate institutional arrangements.

Political and Technical Arms Control

The three examples of political arms control discussed above show how the Soviets consistently stressed the political rather than the technical elements of strategic stability in their attempts to discuss the issues raised by arms-control theory. Allowing for propaganda and the absence of any theoretical discussion of arms limitation comparable to the intensive Western development of arms-control theory, it could be argued that by 1962 the Soviets had developed a distinctive approach to the problems of strategic stability. The assumptions of political arms control differed sharply from those of technical arms control, but each represented the basis from which the Soviet and American governments were to approach a nuclear test ban and other measures to stabilize the superpowers' strategic and political relations after the Cuban missile crisis.

PART III   Detente Through Arms Limitation: 1962-63

6 The Changing Roles of Technical and Political Arms Control

Detente, in the correct sense of a relaxation of tension, was achieved between the superpowers in 1963. The prevalent arms-control view had been that this breakthrough was made possible by the change in Soviet policy towards strategic stability. Essentially, that change involved Soviet acceptance of certain technical-arms-control measures which included the hotline, the Partial Test Ban (PTB) Treaty, and the agreement not to station weapons of mass destruction in outer space. However, this view underestimated the complexity of the political changes involved, and overestimated both their rapidity and extent. Furthermore, it exaggerated Soviet acceptance of technical-arms-control's underlying assumptions and ignored the compatibility of the nominal arms-control agreements with political arms control. As Thomas Wolfe has pointed out, Mr. Khrushchev had always alternated between seeking unilateral and bilateral solutions to outstanding problems with the West.[1] Political (like technical) arms control suggested bilateral as well as unilateral measures.

The main effects of the Cuban missile crisis on strategic stability were, paradoxically, to confirm that the balance of deterrence was much more stable than the theoretical calculations of arms controllers had suggested. Moreover, the crisis also served to point out to Soviet leaders that, contrary to their expectations, the United States was likely to seek only minimal political advantages from her strategic superiority. Contrary to the impression created by Secretary of Defense McNamara's Ann Arbor speech of June 16, 1962, the United States was not prepared to fight and win a strategic nuclear war as it had done with conventional wars in the past. Although the Soviets apparently feared that political restraint would not be exercised on U.S. strategic superiority, the Cuban crisis demonstrated that such political restraint was there. Therefore, while technical arms control became even more irrelevant in Soviet eyes, their own policy of political arms control acquired a new importance.

The actual political restraint on America's technical strategic superiority shown during the Cuban crisis needed to be institutionalized through an agreement that both superpowers could recognize as symbolic of detente. However, such agreement could not be made explicit, for fear both of a domestic reaction from hard-liners and of increased uncertainty about the nature and extent of this detente. Since a test-ban treaty was already under discussion in the Eighteen Nation Disarmament Conference (ENDC), and had acquired considerable symbolic importance, a PTB would provide a symbol of detente without involving any significant restraint on military research. (The precedent for such a measure was the Antarctica Treaty of 1959.) The ability of the superpowers to agree on a hotline (a direct communications link between Washington and Moscow), mutually perceived as necessary, would indicate whether their detente was strong enough to warrant proceeding with a PTB in 1963.

The interaction among the changes in Soviet perceptions brought about by the Cuban crisis, the role of the Antarctica Treaty as an instrument of arms limitation, and the progress on the hotline agreement had to be viewed in the changed political context of the post-Cuba detente if the PTB's significance as a political instrument of arms control was to be understood.

Soviet Perceptions of the Cuban Crisis

Although all discussion of the Soviet leadership's *weltanschauung* must be necessarily speculative, Mr. Khrushchev's behaviour during and after the Cuban crisis suggested that he emerged convinced that no conceivable political gain was worth the risk of nuclear war. He also felt that President Kennedy, too, was prepared to consider the possibility of nuclear war only if America's vital interests, as he saw them, were threatened.[2] So the West Berlin crisis created by Mr. Khrushchev from August 1961 to October 1962 disappeared. Clearly, by threatening nuclear war, the Soviet Union could gain nothing, and would, in fact, risk the confrontation it wished to avoid, in which West Germany would involve the United States. On the other hand, the Americans had dropped their apparent willingness to use their strategic superiority to win a nuclear war. It was the Soviet belief that the Americans could, and might, use this superiority, as Soviet strategic thinking implicitly (and later in the 1970s explicitly) said such force should be used — for political gains — that had made political arms control so important an instrument of restraint in the first place.

In retrospect, the use of nuclear weapons in the Cuban crisis seemed unlikely, although both President Kennedy and Mr. Khrushchev appear to have regarded this as a serious possibility. Consequently, both leaders were determined to avoid the smallest possibility of a nuclear exchange, either then or subsequently. The extent of the change in

American policy was evident in public addresses by American states-men before and after the Cuban crisis. On June 16, 1962, in a speech at Ann Arbor, McNamara publicly adopted the declaratory policy that he had advocated at the NATO meeting at Athens in May of that year:

> . . . to the extent feasible, basic military strategy in a possible general nuclear war should be approached in much the same way that more conventional military operations have been regarded in the past. . . . [the] principal objectives should be the destruction of the enemy's military forces, not of his civilian population.[3]

But, on October 2, 1962, in his first public statement on the Cuban crisis, President Kennedy stressed war prevention through deterrence:

> Third: It shall be the policy of this nation to regard any nuclear missile launched from Cuba against any nation in the Western Hemisphere as an attack by the Soviet Union on the United States, requiring a full retaliatory response upon the Soviet Union.[4]

Politically, the crisis emphasized the Soviet Union's need to con-solidate its position and to secure recognition of its right as a global superpower to compete with the United States beyond their most immediate areas of interest. This necessitated a re-examination of the existing understandings about the nature of superpower rivalry and the means for controlling it. Such control would have to be political, and therefore would involve political, not technical, arms control. Presi-dent Kennedy's American University speech of June 16, 1963, sum-marized the change in American attitudes which made such political agreements possible. He rejected a *pax Americana* as the basis of peace and emphasized that both superpowers and their allies had:

> . . . a mutually deep interest in a just and genuine peace and in halting the arms race. Agreements to this end are in the interests of the Soviet Union as well as ours, and even the most hostile nation can be relied upon to accept and keep those treaty obligations . . . which are in their own interest.
>
> So let us not be blind to our differences, but let us also direct attention to our common interests and to the means by which these differences can be resolved . . . nuclear powers must avert those confrontations which bring an adversary to a choice of either a humiliating retreat or a nuclear war.[5]

Thanks to Mr. Khrushchev's prior intimation of agreement on a PTB, the President was able to look to agreement on a nuclear test ban. However, his implication was that this would be comprehensive. In fact, he knew a treaty would have to be similar to the U.S.–U.K. draft PTB treaty of August 27, 1962, which, as Sorenson admitted, formed the basis for the Western negotiations in Moscow.[6] The Moscow talks, which took only ten days, resulted in the initialling of the PTB Treaty on July 25, 1963, only six weeks after the American University speech.

Together with the other agreements reached in 1963-64, the PTB has usually been described as an arms-control measure. Did their acceptance by the Soviet Union mean that the Soviet leaders had altered the approach hitherto described as political arms control? The issue was especially important for policy because of the intellectual dominance of technical-arms-control ideas within the Kennedy administration. It was also crucial because Kennedy's advisors, who were responsible for negotiations on the agreements, interpreted Soviet co-operation in negotiating the Non-Proliferation Treaty (NPT) from 1966-68 as confirmation of the Soviet Union's acceptance of technical arms control. Alternatively, it can be argued that what the Soviets really accepted were specific, limited agreements which represented only nominal, political, arms control. The Soviet Union valued the 1963-64 measures because the United States chose to see them as important when the Soviets were trying to re-establish the principle of superpower negotiations in the security sphere. What mattered to the Soviets was the fact of agreement wherever it could be reached, rather than its substance, provided that this achieved its political ends without jeopardizing Soviet interests.

Since the 1959 Antarctica Treaty originated in similar political circumstances, it needed to be considered as an earlier example of an arms-limitation agreement of the 1963 type. The hotline, the PTB Treaty, and the U.N. Resolution on the Peaceful Uses of Outer Space, together with the Soviet entry into the International Atomic Energy Agency (IAEA), were all parts of a continuous political process that effectively ceased with President Kennedy's assassination in November. The remaining partial measures, notably the cutback in military budgets and in the production of fissile materials in 1964, were both a continuation of those of 1963 and an attempt to continue detente in decreasingly favourable circumstances. Thereafter, political arms control became important for the Soviets as a means of halting the Multilateral Nuclear Force (MLF) from 1964 until October 1966, at which time political arms control again became a means of furthering superpower detente.

The Antarctica Treaty as an Example of Arms Limitation

The 1959 Antarctica Treaty has been sparsely covered in the arms-control literature, presumably because it did not constitute arms control in the sense of establishing significant limits on military capabilities. It "demilitarized" an area which had never been militarized and for which no meaningful military uses could be found. Its inspection provisions allowed for unlimited inspection of non-military activities. So the Antarctica Treaty epitomized political arms control, that is, the use of nominal arms-control measures to achieve detente between the superpowers. But the same was true of the 1963 arms-control measures, with the partial exception of the hotline agreement, and of all subsequent partial measures. Accordingly, my argument was reinforced for redefining the objectives and origins of arms control primarily in the political, rather than in the technical, milieu.

The treaty's genesis lay in the 1957-58 International Geophysical Year (IGY) agreement that scientific work should be carried out in the Antarctic without prejudice to the existing and often conflicting territorial claims by nine of the twelve eventual signatories: Argentina, Australia, Chile, France, New Zealand, Norway, South Africa, Great Britain, and the United States.[7] The other three — Belgium, Japan, and the Soviet Union — established scientific bases there during the IGY. It is possible that Soviet motives for joining were purely scientific and without any diplomatic overtones, but Australian apprehensions seemed to focus on the prospects of either a military presence or espionage. These fears were expressed to the U.K. and U.S. governments, and on April 28, 1958, President Eisenhower took the initiative and invited the Soviet Union to participate in the Conference of Experts and the Surprise Attack Conference. He linked his invitation to a request that the other eleven participants in the IGY experiments join in discussions to continue their activities under a treaty that would both allow this research and, at the same time, freeze the legal status quo in Antarctica for the IGY's duration.[8]

The Western views of the need for such a treaty can be summarized as follows:

While this situation [of bipolarity] persists, any solution which completely froze one of the world's major political contenders out of the Antarctic while aggrandizing the other would not be an agreed solution. The Soviet Union must either be included in an Antarctic settlement or such a settlement must be imposed. Only an agreed settlement could produce a final, unmodified division of the Antarctic between the present sector claimants plus the United States. This situation may incline the West to favor some sort of international approach which would neutralize and make tolerable Soviet participation.[9]

After the treaty was signed on December 1, 1959, it was argued, on arms-control grounds, that:

The Treaty was by no means such an insignificant event as is sometimes supposed. The failure to agree on demilitarization would not only have made possible the use of the area for the testing of atomic weapons, for which suitable areas become increasingly scarce. It could also have conceivably brought about a race for the establishment of missile and other military installations in the Antarctic, which would certainly not have been without military value, a race that conflicting territorial claims would have made particularly intense. Next, the Treaty represented perhaps the first effective acceptance by the Soviet Union of the principle of inspection. Finally it represented a practical experiment in inspection and control — in effect, creating one of those zones of limited armaments so frequently discussed at this period — which might provide important lessons for later agreements in other areas.[10]

However, using political-arms-control criteria, the picture appeared rather different. The Soviet Union's political status as an equal had again been recognized by the United States, and this created a favourable precedent for the Summit of May 1960 that was intended to crown Khrushchev's policy of bilateral accord with Eisenhower. The treaty supported the concept of Atom-Free Zones (AFZ) so vigorously advocated by Mr. Khrushchev earlier in 1959 as the one contemporary example of formally agreed demilitarization. It also enabled the Soviets to evade the valid Western accusation that they had always rejected inspections by pointing to the inspection provisions of Article VII, especially paragraphs 3 and 4.[11] The inspection actually involved only Soviet installations, not its territory, which was almost always excluded in its schemes for Central European disengagement. Significantly, the Soviet Union abstained from exercising its right of inspection from 1959 to 1978, whereas the United States made four inspections. In any case, the reports of May 1964, July 1967, and July 1971 and 1975 confirmed that the treaty was being observed.[12] The precedent had thereby been set for an Arctic inspection zone that would inhibit Strategic Air Command (SAC) operations, as was proposed by the Soviets on November 17, 1956, April 30, 1957, and November 28, 1958.[13] This was revived as late as November 1964 in the first publication of a specific disarmament proposal that was jointly authored by an American and a Soviet scientist.[14] Some American scientists had still not learned the lessons of the 1958 Conference of Experts.

The difference between these two assessments of the treaty from the viewpoint of, respectively, technical and political arms control emphasized how different the objectives of these two approaches were. From the Soviet viewpoint the Antarctica Treaty and the effective continuation of the nuclear-testing moratorium in December 1959[15] should have established an atmosphere of superpower detente conducive to Western acceptance of the sphere of control in Eastern Europe and a solution of the West Berlin problem. A parallel would be with the 1955 Geneva Summit, where the Soviet sphere of control was tacitly accepted by the West. The necessary atmosphere of detente had been created by the Soviet disarmament proposals of March 10, 1955, and by Soviet agreement to withdraw from its zone of occupation in Austria, enabling an Austrian Peace Treaty to be signed.

Neither the preliminaries nor the Summits could have had other than primarily atmospheric effects, including U.S. acceptance of the Soviet Union as a superpower that enjoyed strategic equality with the United States and a legitimate sphere of control in Eastern Europe. The repercussions of the Soviet shooting down of a U.S. U-2 reconnaissance plane were used by Mr. Khrushchev to break up the 1960 Summit; this was soon followed by the separate West Berlin crisis in late 1960. Because of these incidents, the Antarctica Treaty did not create the hoped-for detente, so that, when the detente of June 1963 emerged, the new agreements overshadowed the Antarctica Treaty. Nevertheless, the latter survived — with the durability that is characteristic of political-arms-control treaties (which are built on political realities), rather than of arms-control attempts to have self-interested observance of treaty obligations replaced by intensive inspection to detect treaty violation.

The Hotline Agreement

To understand the similarities between the political climates of 1963 and 1959, it is helpful to consider the negotiation of the hotline, which confirmed for the Soviets that their detente with the United States was sufficiently strong to be embodied in the PTB. Additionally, the hotline has remained the only measure of arms control whose implementation in any way resembled its theoretical form and performed the functions claimed for it by arms controllers.

The establishment of communications between opponents in order to facilitate crisis management had been a major theme of arms-control thinking from the first, especially in Schelling's works.[16] Therefore, the hotline seemed to represent Soviet acceptance of one of the basic ideas of arms control and its underlying assumptions. But the difference between this simple technical arrangement, with its far-reaching political implications, and the variety of complex arms-control proposals for mutual reassurance during crises[17] made it arguable that the hotline was really a common-sense arrangement that arose out of practical difficulties experienced in the Cuban crisis. Hedley Bull, here as elsewhere, more accurately assessed the relevant political realities in predicting that:

In times of international crisis, whether produced by political tensions or technical accidents . . . there may be no more important safeguard than the ability of persons at the centre of power in the countries concerned to establish contact with each other directly and at once.[18]

The strategists' belief in a delicate balance of terror that created a reciprocal fear of surprise attack had produced inspection schemes that could be characterized as impossible where relevant, irrelevant where possible, and counter-productive in both cases. These included: reciprocal inspection of strategic bases; observation posts in key road, rail, and air junctions; and tacit understandings on the avoidance of activities likely either to create suspicion of attack or to prevent verification that an attack was not being executed.[19] But if superpower relations were characterized by this degree of antagonism, the thinking behind such arrangements should have stressed (but did not) that they could hardly be negotiated. Where superpower relations might permit effective arms-control negotiations, the fear of surprise attack, in Western terms, would have decreased so far as to make the additional reassurances superfluous. There remained, of course, the difficulties in resolving technical obstacles to an effective warning system. The incentive for agreement on such systems rested on two American assumptions: that strategic war might be risked on the basis of probabilistic calculations, and that this could be modified by the information provided by these technical verification measures. In practice, U.S. and Soviet preoccupations with differing versions of surprise attack (a problem the Soviet Union was well aware of, since these differences were underlined at the 1958 Surprise Attack Conference) meant that they would approach the evidence of such an attack differently.

Soviet policy on the hotline fell into two phases. Before Cuba it appeared as part of a whole set of Western proposals which were irrelevant to the real problem of surprise attack. After Cuba, the hotline, as a practical necessity, was separated out for negotiation. With the failure of the Comprehensive Test Ban (CTB) talks in the spring of 1963, it became the last chance of resurrecting the policy of detente through political arms control. Because of this urgency, the April 5 agreement-in-principle was an important political event, although the formal understanding was not signed until June 30,[20] after both President Kennedy's American University speech on June 10 and Mr. Khrushchev's immediate acceptance of what both leaders tacitly recognized would be a conference to conclude, very quickly, a PTB, to be held in Moscow in July.

The Soviet refusal to consider the hotline concept until after Cuba was significant, because it fitted in theoretically with their other proposals for ground observation posts in Europe that were intended to lessen the dangers of surprise attack.[21] Since these proposals were also made by the West, the Soviet failure to conduct even exploratory talks meant either that they were not interested in these proposals or that they viewed their proposals, apparently similar to those of the West, in a very different way. The latter seemed more probable, if the Soviet view of the role of ground observation posts was considered in the light of their drawing of analogies between the surprise-attack problem and the 1914 situation.[22] In the absence of a political agreement on their respective spheres of influence, either in August 1914, or in the post-Second-World-War era, the competing powers could hardly trust assurances of non-mobilization or of the absence of preparations for a surprise attack, whether through diplomatic channels or simple inspection systems. Ultimately, crisis limitation depended on sacrificing potential or actual advantages for the sake of preventing escalation or expansion of a conflict. Accordingly, Soviet support for ground observation posts, inadequate by Western technical standards, was explicable if their interests lay in establishing not a foolproof inspection system but a symbol of agreement on preserving the Soviet position in Eastern Europe.

The Soviet Union was, in fact, working for a recognition of the mutuality of superpower interests, in which each would recognize the importance of the other's interests and of protecting those interests by reducing the risks of confrontation that would endanger them. It was precisely because a PTB would embody an American recognition of Soviet interests that the PTB became the major instrument of political arms control in 1963. The arms-control effects of that instrument were both militarily negligible and politically irrelevant. The first symbol of detente, and the one which made the PTB possible, had been a hotline that was something of a last hope, offered by the United States and accepted by the Soviet Union partly because its obvious technical utility could be used to minimize its political significance if negotiations failed. Conversely, success would signal political progress that would lead to the PTB. It was an appropriate irony that the only technically effective arms-control measure, the hotline, should have inaugurated political arms control as the chief modality for superpower detente.

7 The 1963 Partial Test Ban Treaty as an Instrument of Superpower Detente

The Moscow Partial Test Ban (PTB) Treaty of 1963 was almost exclusively an instrument of political rather than technical arms control. This was evident from the failure of negotiations for a Comprehensive Test Ban (CTB), which confirmed that Mr. Khrushchev and President Kennedy were interested in a PTB to formalize, and therefore advance, the emerging superpower detente. At every stage of the negotiations President Kennedy sacrificed the arms-control requirement of an adequately verified CTB for a PTB that could be unilaterally verified and which represented only the most marginal inhibition to the development — already in progress — of warheads for the Anti-Ballistic Missiles (ABM) and Multiple Independently Targetable Re-Entry Vehicles (MIRV). The PTB achieved its political goals. Subsequently, advances in underground testing techniques allowed tests of ABM warheads of about five megatons by both superpowers in 1971-72, while both continued to reject a CTB under which they could unilaterally verify compliance with the PTB. The eventual Threshold Test Ban Treaty (TTBT) of 1974 still permitted testing up to 150 kilotons, enabling MIRV to be perfected and, therefore, failing to act as a qualitative corollary to the quantitative limitations imposed by the 1972 SALT I agreements. Although, by 1978, the new U.S. President, Jimmy Carter, had persuaded the Soviet Union (and Britain) to negotiate on the CTB he favoured, the Soviets seemed unlikely to accept, at least for long, an effective CTB, a measure of technical arms control they had always rejected.[1]

In late 1962, the Soviets had resurrected the on-going negotiations at the Eighteen Nation Disarmament Conference (ENDC) for a CTB, in order to explore the possibilities of a primarily political test-ban treaty. This showed how Soviet moves within the framework of what Western analysts regarded as arms-control negotiations could be misinterpreted as indicating acceptance of the necessity for arms control. As the tactical objectives of political and technical arms control were often similar, especially in negotiations, the underlying differences between these two approaches only became evident as negotiations progressed in the PTB talks and in the Non-Proliferation Treaty (NPT) negotiations from 1963 to 1968. In so far as the Soviet Union had stressed the need for a CTB, this stemmed from the political significance of the implied restrictions on the use of nuclear weapons.[2] It was also a product of the lesser (because of their less-developed nuclear-weapons technology) Soviet dependence on miniaturization techniques for nuclear warheads which could be tested underground under a PTB. Moreover, their 1961-62 test series had provided the Soviet Union (and the United States) with virtually all the information they needed on explosions in the atmosphere; therefore, a CTB would benefit the Soviet Union strategically by limiting U.S. development of MIRV, ultra-small tactical weapons, and ABM warheads, in the unlikely event that a CTB could be negotiated.

With the U.S. development of seismic detection methods, there arose the problem of bridging what was rapidly becoming a political difference over the number of on-site inspections in a CTB. The difficulty had apparently emerged in late October and early November of 1962 in conversations between Ambassadors Dean and Kuznetzov, in which the American suggested eight to ten such inspections instead of the previous minimum of twelve. The problem was also brought to light in discussions between Jerome B. Wiesner, presidential Special Assistant for Science and Technology, and the Soviet scientist, Yevgeni K. Federov.[3] Given the President's anxiety to renew negotiations, his representatives may have implied that the United States might accept something very near to the Soviet offer on July 26, 1960, of three on-site inspections per annum. The final American offer of seven certainly was closer to the Soviet position.[4] On December 19, Mr. Khrushchev offered President Kennedy " . . . 2–3 inspections a year . . . in seismic regions where any suspicious earth tremors occurred".[5] This expanded the Soviets' earlier offer of December 10 to accept two or three automatic seismic-recording stations on their territory. The President felt that with apparent agreement in principle to on-site inspections, which was the key to the Western CTB position, the remaining differences could be settled by negotiations. These began in Washington on January 14, 1963. However, both the Soviet refusal to discuss how on-site inspections were to be conducted and the Western insistence on the need for seventy-six nationally owned and operated control stations in the Soviet Union[6] cast doubts on whether either side wished to progress with a CTB. On January 31, 1963, the Soviets requested that the negotiations be transferred to the ENDC, suggesting that the attempt at a quick agreement on a CTB had failed. This course of events made it more difficult to switch to the obvious alternative of a PTB.

The major difference between the U.S. dual offer on August 27, 1962, of either a CTB or PTB and the Soviet position was the latter's insistence that a PTB must include a moratorium on all underground testing, even if the treaty forbade only those tests with a seismic threshold of 4.75 or more on the Richter scale. From 1958 to 1961 this would have ensured a continuation of the unpoliced moratorium that the Soviets already enjoyed. Therefore, their 1963 proposals could be more accurately described as requiring a limited CTB and a moratorium, whereas the U.S. proposals of August 27, 1962, were described specifically as a three-environment PTB. The implications for political and technical arms control were clear. Given the inability of the U.S. government to secure acceptance of a CTB agreement with the Soviet Union, the United States would have to indicate to the Soviets that a PTB could be used to effect a change towards less antagonistic superpower relations. In that case, however, the development of nuclear weapons would be left largely unchecked. A PTB would be as undesirable from the viewpoint of technical arms control as it was desirable for Soviet political-arms-control policy. It would permit continued testing; more important, it would offer a change in the political atmosphere that would be more favourable to joint superpower agreement on more immediate problems. The three most important of these for the Soviet Union were: implicit U.S. acceptance of the status quo in Eastern Europe; the prevention of further West German access to nuclear weapons through the newly emergent Multilateral Nuclear Force (MLF); and U.S. agreement to regard superpower competition for local influence outside Europe in localized terms. President Kennedy's American University speech and the preceding informal talks broke the log-jam. On July 2, Mr. Khrushchev ruled out a CTB on the inspection issue but agreed to accept a three-environment PTB, without the unpoliced moratorium on underground testing on which the Soviets had always previously insisted. He also attempted to link a PTB to a NATO–Warsaw Treaty Organization Non-Aggression Pact.[7] The linkage was not pressed, however, and remarkably speedy negotiations, which started on July 15, 1963, produced a treaty that was initialled on July 25, signed on August 5, and which entered into effect on October 11.[8]

The Partial Test Ban Treaty as an Instrument of Arms Limitation

Clearly, the Moscow Treaty met those objectives of political arms control that were shared by American diplomacy in 1963, but bypassed any possibilities for arms control. In large measure, the superpowers' motives for signing the PTB Treaty were political in nature: the treaty capitalized on the symbolism that had come to be attached to nuclear testing as representing a barometer of their strategic balance and political relations. It did not contain any significant contribution to limiting subsequent advances in strategic arms competition.

The Role of Negotiations

The treaty banned only tests in three environments which were of marginal military utility, although the ban on atmospheric testing certainly handicapped the development of effective ABM systems. National inspection systems offered sufficient probability of detection to deter violation. In 1958 the Conference of Experts had concluded that a one-kiloton test up to an altitude of fifty kilometres could be detected at a distance downwind of two to three thousand kilometres, or five hundred kilometres upwind under favourable circumstances, and 1,300 kilometres in any direction under unfavourable conditions. Underwater explosions, even if small, could be detected at distances of about ten thousand kilometres.[9] Western refinement of verification techniques — notably in the areas of large-aperture seismic arrays and the Vela detection satellites that were able to detect testing in the air or outer space[10] — gave a virtual certainty of detection. Accordingly, the incentives for violation had largely disappeared.

Presumably, the Soviet Union had rejected a three-environment treaty ban from 1958 to 1961 because it preferred an unpoliced moratorium that would minimize the cost of its resumption of atmospheric testing. The PTB could hardly have resulted from the 1958-61 negotiations because the earlier studies on detection and inspection systems for underground tests were largely irrelevant to the 1963 treaty and to the Soviet Union. Soviet disinterest in the technicalities of inspection that were regarded as crucial by the arms controllers was summarized thus:

In August 1958 Soviet expert representatives signed a report saying that every unidentified underground seismic event could be inspected by an international control organization. Three months later the Soviet political representatives asked for a veto by the Soviet Union of any inspection of Soviet territory. Between December 1958 and the end of 1960 the Soviet Union had agreed to the text of seventeen treaty articles and two annexes which provided for permanent control posts in the Soviet Union largely manned by foreigners, and for a small number of on-site inspections in the Soviet Union every year. But in November 1961 they repudiated the whole of the experts' report of 1958 and all the agreed treaty articles and annexes.[11]

The Soviets had also rejected both a single-environment ban, as proposed by the West on September 3, 1961, and the original PTB that was offered on August 27, 1962, because neither were in their political or strategic interests at that time. However, the Cuban crisis changed Soviet perceptions of both by November 1962. Henceforth, they moved rapidly to secure a test ban. Even though they assumed that capabilities for verification of violations were irrelevant to an agreement, they agreed to three on-site inspections in order to meet the Western demands for these as a matter of principle.

The only over-all contribution of the test-ban talks from 1958 to 1961 or from their resumption at the ENDC in March 1962, was to provide, via the discussion of technicalities, a means for continuing negotiations in an area in which each superpower desired agreement. Although their separate reasons for wanting agreement were sufficiently different to make this apparently impossible, these same technicalities could have a moderating effect: they might lessen the adverse political effects of rejecting particular proposals while, conversely, minimizing the importance of any unsuccessful initial moves towards an agreement. This dual usefulness of technical discussions explains the use of the CTB framework for discussion in late 1962 and early 1963 and the Soviet acceptance of the hotline proposal on April 5, only four days after the West's final offer of seven on-site inspections per annum. The acceptance of the hotline enabled the United States to move out of the CTB position and to use the existing PTB position to reciprocate Mr. Khrushchev's indicated desire for political accord. Without Soviet acceptance of the hotline proposal, President Kennedy would have been unable to break free from the domestic constraints that resulted from the previous negotiations. Although the advantages of the ENDC as a continuing negotiating forum were again evident in the MLF–NPT discussions from 1964-68, the role of negotiations was quite different from that envisaged by arms-control theory; that is, of arriving at mutually acceptable means for securing common interests.

The Lack of Arms-Control Effects

By permitting underground nuclear testing the PTB did nothing to halt vertical proliferation (the quantitative and qualitative expansion of the existing nuclear arsenals of the United States, the Soviet Union, and Britain), and little, or nothing, to inhibit horizontal proliferation (the spread of nuclear weapons to new powers). The distinction between vertical and horizontal proliferation was stressed by the Indian government, partly to justify its refusal to sign the Non-Proliferation Treaty (NPT) and development of its nuclear option. France continued atmospheric testing until 1975 and was joined by China in 1964. Any Nth power could either follow suit by using the withdrawal provisions or by testing underground, as India did in May 1974. Additionally, states could effectively test their nuclear weapons in laboratories, *without* exploding them. Israel seemed to have done this by 1975, and South Africa might have done so by 1978. The 1962-63 negotiations showed how narrow the gap between on-site inspections had become in technical terms. The final gap between the U.S. offer of seven and the Soviet offer of three inspections per annum could only be political — that is, bridgeable, if the internal groups in the United States and the Soviet Union who favoured continued testing could be persuaded to reverse their positions. This seemed unlikely as long as testing was thought to stabilize the strategic balance. In these circumstances, underground testing provided the ideal balance between the political requirements of detente and military needs. There was also the added security of insurance against a technological breakthrough by the other side, assuming that the general principle of the parallel nature of scientific advances continued to hold true in the nuclear-weapons field.

Confirmation that the PTB represented a largely political agreement between the superpowers came from their tolerant attitude towards each other's breaches of Article 1 (B) whereby the parties promised not to carry out any nuclear explosions:

(B) in any other environment if such explosion causes radioactive debris to be present outside the territorial limits of the State under whose jurisdiction or control such explosion is conducted.

The first violation by the Soviet Union, on January 15, 1965, produced a remarkably amiable diplomatic exchange[12] and testified to the qualitative change in superpower relations to which the PTB had contributed so greatly. In response to the Soviet oral reply that the amount of radioactive debris released was too insignificant to constitute a violation, the United States indicated on January 26 that, although the Soviet Union's action constituted a technical violation, it was accidental. This view was confirmed by the State Department's request on November 19, which merely asked the Soviet Union "to take precautionary measures so that the limited test-ban treaty would be observed."[13] No further technical violations were the subject of published correspondence, although some may have occurred. For example, between 1969 and July 1970 ten tests were reported as venting radioactive material[14] bringing the total of such incidents to eleven.[15]

Clearly, then, the PTB was regarded by the superpowers as no more than an attempt to impose marginal restraints on the development of nuclear weapons. The fundamental irrelevance of the test-ban negotiations from 1958 to 1962 followed by their short and uncomplicated transition into treaty form in the PTB, emphasized how far the PTB departed from the theories of arms control. Those theories held that negotiations were a process of defining terms for an agreement that would impose some limitation on the present and future deployment, use, or development of weapons. In actuality, the PTB served as a modality for codifying a revised understanding of the superpowers' mutually dependent political relationship.

The political intent of the superpowers became clearer with their resistance to subsequent attempts by other powers to extend the PTB to at least some underground testing, because such action would have converted it from a purely political instrument of arms limitation to one of partial arms control.[16]

Political Implications of the Moscow Treaty

The political implications of the Moscow Treaty were as significant as its arms-control effects were negligible. The PTB made possible the evolution of the two detentes, so aptly described by Philip Windsor as a process of sharply distinguishing dealings between the United States and the Soviet Union and those between the Eastern and Western alliances as a whole.[17] In October 1966, President Johnson made his "peaceful engagement" speech in which he informed Mr. Gromyko that the NPT would be regarded as the touchstone of Soviet-American understanding:

... the U.S. was working towards a separate form of detente with the Soviet Union [and] appeared disposed to permit her European allies to do the same.[18]

Although, as Robert Hunter has observed, the superpower detente was a relatively fragile understanding about a few central issues, notably the political stability of Europe, mutual deterrence, and the prevention of nuclear confrontations,[19] these were precisely the areas of most concern to the Soviet Union. Its political-arms-control policy had contributed greatly to securing its objectives. The extension of detente through arms limitation via the NPT helped the Soviets to invade Czechoslovakia without a significant cost in terms of their relationship with the United States, and to halt what they regarded as undesirable trends in intra-European detente. At this point, the Soviets knew that their action would cause no more than a temporary interruption in the superpower detente.

From 1969 onwards, the Nixon and Ford administrations, and their foreign-policy architect, Dr. Henry A. Kissinger, attempted to mitigate the inherent conflict between these two detentes, and thereby emphasized arms control's tendency to recommend measures like the NPT which stressed the bilateral superpower detente. That this was an inherent product of technical-arms-control thinking was suggested by the main arms-control measures introduced by President Nixon: SALT I, MBFR, and the possibility of unilateral U.S. force reductions in Western Europe. The PTB initiated the process of using relatively ineffective technical-arms-control measures as instruments of political arms control; that is, the political containment of technical imbalances or instability. The 1963 Moscow PTB Treaty gave the Soviet Union parity of esteem with the United States, and the Soviets were careful to reinforce that status with a series of partial measures of arms control which ranged from agreements on the peaceful uses of outer space (made in the fall of 1963), to the Threshold Test Ban Treaty (TTBT) signed in 1974. These measures indicated the continuing trend towards superpower detente (a trend since sharply reversed) and provided a bridge to the institutionalization of strategic (as well as political) equality in SALT. The latter came to symbolize the uniqueness of superpower relations in the nuclear age.

8 The Contrast Between Arms-Control Theory and Political Practice Reinforced: Partial Measures, 1963-72

The development of the distinction between technical and political arms control took place after the Partial Test Ban (PTB) at two distinct but related levels. The negotiations for the Non-Proliferation Treaty (NPT) and the Strategic Arms Limitation Talks (SALT) involved the major political interests of the superpowers; inevitably, therefore, they introduced political considerations into what American writers persisted in regarding as essentially arms-control discussions — although the fact that these talks were about political arms control should have been evident from the concurrent negotiations on lesser measures of restraint. These will be considered here as a group, in order to emphasize how a series of measures recommended by arms controllers were adapted to political arms control by the removal of any element of effective control. With consistent regularity, the result of these partial measures was simply a declaratory agreement to refrain from certain military activities that neither side was likely to engage in anyway. These agreements were used by the superpowers to signify their continuing, if often uncertain, political accord. In this way, progress on peripheral issues helped to ease the passage of difficult sections in the NPT and SALT negotiations. Paradoxically, the theoretically apolitical nature of these partial arms-control measures disguised their full political implications, and so confirmed their suitability for formalizing the evolving superpower relationship. Their apparently limited technical nature also served to limit criticism within the United States and from her allies.

Throughout these negotiations, an extremely subtle series of moves was perceived by the American participants as a relatively straightforward attempt to implement arms control because, theoretically, these were relatively apolitical measures. The Soviets were almost certainly more aware of the long-term political effects of reinforcing the superpower detente. Both the United States and the Soviet Union were anxious to keep the Eighteen Nation Disarmament Conference (ENDC) and its successor the Conference of the Committee on Disarmament (CCD) as continuing forums in which to explore possible areas of bilateral negotiation. Once they themselves were discussing these areas, the superpowers could keep the Geneva conference occupied with more marginal matters and thereby limit the other members' ability to criticize the arrangements they had made.

Continuing the 1963 Detente: The Peaceful Uses of Outer Space and Declaratory Measures to April 1964

The partial measures from 1963 to 1972 fell into three groups. Each of these had a different relation to the emergence of the superpower detente, but together they provided a political and chronological continuity. After the August 1963 PTB and the December 13 U.N. Resolution on the Peaceful Uses of Outer Space,[1] Mr. Khrushchev suggested in Moscow, the same day, a possible reduction of Soviet forces and a reduction in military spending for 1964.[2] He later proposed, on December 31, a formula for the peaceful settlement of disputes, including an undertaking "not to resort to force to alter existing state frontiers",[3] that was to form a key element in the 1970 West German treaties with the Soviet Union and Poland. It was also to form a key element, from the Soviet viewpoint, of the August 1, 1975, Final Act of the Conference on Security and Co-operation in Europe (CSCE), although the value of such promises by the Soviets was negligible. Given the lack of verification of compliance, all four measures were, appropriately for the Christmas season, important for their thoughts of peace on earth and goodwill among the superpowers, rather than for their contents. In their efforts to carry over this spirit of detente into 1964, the United States, the Soviet Union, and Great Britain agreed on April 21 to cut back on the production of fissionable materials for weapons purposes.[4] As the Soviet pledge could not be verified, and no evidence was ever produced of their compliance, the agreement was purely symbolic, especially as both the Western powers had been planning such cutbacks in production anyway.

The April 1964 agreement also marked a temporary halt in the process of creating detente through arms limitation, which, since its commencement in November 1962, had lasted for eighteen months. However, the political and diplomatic momentum that had been built up during those months sufficed to carry superpower discussions at the ENDC through their initial unproductive phase in 1964 and on to the definition of proliferation as a negotiable issue in mid-1965.

Clearly these declaratory measures were not arms control, but neither was the 1963 U.N. Resolution banning the stationing of nuclear weapons in orbit, subsequently embodied (with minor modifications) in the October 1967 Outer Space Treaty.[5] The genesis of these measures lay in the arms controllers' view of the need for limitations on the military use of Intercontinental Ballistic Missiles (ICBM) and orbital weapons because of the threat they posed to the stability of deterrence. These views had been expressed throughout 1957,[6] and were summarized at the 1958 conference, notably in the Western proposal for the observation and inspection of ballistic missiles, made on December 3, 1958.[7] This system would have included resident-observer teams who would watch for indicators of capability, preparation, and launching of a surprise attack. Intrusive inspection was an integral feature of this, as of many other arms-control proposals:

Effective direct observation of missile forces is the key to reducing the threat of surprise by ballistic missiles. This suggests that all launch sites be brought under direct observation. Flight test facilities should be included in this category since they can be — and sometimes are — used as operational launching sites, although modified inspection procedures might be acceptable for such sites. Integral parts of an inspection and observation system, which we consider, are aerial search and assessment activities.[8]

This indicates that the arms controllers viewed control over ICBMs as necessary to stabilize the balance of deterrence, prevent unrestrained military competition in outer space, and limit potential future instability that might result from the new technology involved. The views of Brennan[9] and Bull[10] were representative of the arms controllers' position and its limitations. Typically, Bull envisaged the main objectives of arms control in outer space as being Soviet tolerance of U.S. reconnaissance satellites and an understanding that both sides benefited from greater certainty about each other's military activities. Brennan stressed the dangers of a Fractional Orbital Bombardment System (FOBS) or of the (then not very probable) introduction of esoteric space weapons.[11]

Bull's point was well taken, but basically did little more than apply common sense to the problem of strategic stability. Indeed, this was what a great many arms-control ideas did, so that neither these concepts, nor their acceptance by the Soviets, were perhaps quite the intellectual or technical breakthroughs they were claimed to be by the more ardent Western proponents of arms control. Once the basic concept inherent in the notion of the balance of deterrence was accepted, namely that both superpowers shared a common interest in stabilizing this balance in political and technical terms, a whole series of arms-control measures suggested themselves. Thus, the idea of the hotline, accepted in 1963 and upgraded in 1971, reflected the obvious superpower interest in crisis management to avoid unintended escalation or expansion of a conflict. The Basic Principles of Relations of May 26, 1972, and the 1973 Agreement on the Prevention of Nuclear War similarly recognized the inevitability of superpower interdependence in the nuclear age. Indeed the partial measures considered in this chapter could be seen simply as reaffirmations of this interdependence. Nor could a superpower agreement to refrain from disseminating nuclear weapons be seen as a particularly original notion whose acceptance marked a breakthrough in superpower relations. Neither the United States nor the Soviet Union was contemplating dissemination between 1963 and 1968. Soviet fears that the United States was contemplating dissemination to West Germany arose out of misunderstandings of the role of the Multilateral Nuclear Force (MLF) and it was clearly in the interests of those who had nuclear weapons to limit the nuclear club to its extant members. It was equally obvious, except to the arms controllers, that potential proliferators could be expected to disagree with this view, as India did before joining the nuclear club. Similarly, with the 1972 SALT I and the Vladivostok Accord of 1974, which were expected at the time to lead rapidly to a SALT II, the U.S. arms controllers and Secretary of State Kissinger argued that the notion of some quantitative freeze on strategic nuclear delivery vehicles at levels well above those needed for mutual deterrence was relatively obvious and not so difficult to negotiate as might be expected. The Anti-Ballistic Missile (ABM) freeze at two and then one site each for the superpowers in 1972 and 1974 was also a simple, perhaps too simple, solution to the problems of avoiding the costs of ABM deployment. This was not to deny the importance of the more complex technical-arms-control arguments whose implications were not self-evident, such as the threat to strategic stability posed by Multiple Independently Targetable Re-entry Vehicles (MIRV). But this was to say that the basic principles underlying the arms-control agreements we have got were perhaps less revolutionary and more commonsensical than they seemed to their Western proponents.

By September 1963, the U.S. government was prepared to surrender all arms-control requirements for effective control on the placement of nuclear weapons in outer space, using ICBMs, in favour of an agreement with the Soviets that was aimed at consolidating the superpower detente.[12] The Soviets had sought the agreement as one of a series of such measures. With regard to the resulting resolution, an impartial source has commented that:

. . . it merely called upon Governments to refrain from extending the arms race into space and did not require the cessation of any activities known to be already under way. It recalled and reaffirmed United States previous statements of intention in this regard.[13]

The changing U.S. position on the control of ICBMs demonstrated both the incompatibility of technical and political arms control, and the American willingness to give priority to political considerations in order to promote superpower detente.

Bilateral Detente Reaffirmed: 1967-72

The absence of any such agreements until late 1966 suggests that both superpowers were engaged in the complex process of redefining their relationship. That redefinition was expressed primarily through the NPT and SALT, but it was also supported by the 1967 Outer Space Treaty, the 1971 Seabed Treaty, and the 1972 Biological Warfare Convention.

The Outer Space Treaty was agreed to in the U.N. General Assembly on December 19, 1966, signed by the superpowers on January 27, 1967, and entered into force on October 10, 1967, embodying and furthering the process of superpower detente.[14] The new U.S. President, Lyndon B. Johnson, and the new Soviet government (where General Secretary Leonid Brezhnev was already establishing his dominance) had both come to effective power in 1964, but, by 1966, had reached agreement on the two arms-control issues acting as the barometer of detente. The United States had agreed to drop a Multilateral Nuclear Force (MLF) and accept an NPT that they saw, in technical-arms-control terms, as containing global nuclear-weapons proliferation. The Soviets saw it, much more realistically, in politico-military terms, as preventing West German access to nuclear weapons. Soviet Foreign Minister Andrei Gromyko's statement of October 10, after a meeting with President Johnson and Secretary of State Dean Rusk in Washington, that "It looks like . . . the United States and the Soviet Union are striving to reach agreement"[15] on an NPT really meant that they had agreed on *their* terms for an NPT. This underlined the strength of the bilateral superpower detente at a time when America's allies were strongly objecting to the agreed Soviet–U.S. draft-NPT because, in their view, it embodied too great a degree of superpower understanding.

Indeed, from 1966 onwards, the strengthening of the bilateral Soviet–U.S. relationship found expression in the opposition attempts by the other members of the ENDC/CCD and by the U.N. General Assembly to impose arms control on the superpowers. In these circumstances, the Seabed Treaty adopted the precedent that had first been set by the Antarctica Treaty and then by the Outer Space Treaty — namely, an area of negligible military utility was reserved for peaceful purposes, but any military activity that was desired by the superpowers could continue uninterrupted. For example, the United States had allowed the Soviet tests of a fractional orbital bombardment system (FOBS) as consistent with the Outer Space Treaty because the FOBS was not an *orbital* nuclear weapon. It was an ICBM fired into a very low ballistic trajectory, 100 miles above the earth, instead of the usual 800 miles, giving it a ten minute shorter flight time and a marginal advantage in a surprise attack, especially against U.S. bomber bases.[16] Although McNamara played down FOBS' utility, he missed the important arms-control lesson: the Soviets developed weapons that met *their* strategic needs. In 1967, FOBS made sense for them, given the sites of the U.S. Strategic Air Command (SAC) and the Soviet lack of sufficient long-range Submarine Launched Ballistic Missiles (SLBM) to strike SAC. The United States, in turn, insisted that her seabed sonar systems could be retained under the terms of the Seabed Treaty. The latter could effectively ban the emplacement of weapons of mass destruction on the ocean floor, since both superpowers had established that there were no military advantages in doing so.[17] After demanding the complete de-militarization of the seabed in their March 19, 1969, draft treaty, submitted at the ENDC, the Soviets reversed their stand in late August and accepted a ban on weapons of mass destruction on the seabed outside a twelve-mile coastal zone.[18] An appropriately harmonious relationship had been re-established for the start of both the SALT talks in November and the U.S. campaign to secure West German ratification of the NPT. The latter was also a major Soviet objective that had been delayed by their 1968 invasion of Czechoslovakia. Initially, both the Soviet Union and the United States had resisted any outside attempts to broaden the Seabed Treaty. Canada, for example, had demanded that the signatories' right to assistance in verifying compliance should include a right to apply to another state party to the treaty or to the U.N. Secretary General.[19] At a later date, Sweden suggested an article that would commit the signatories to continued negotiations on a more comprehensive prohibition on the military use of the seabed.[20] The Canadian and Swedish demands were deprived of their effectiveness in the revised draft treaty of September 1, 1970.[21] This was signed by the superpowers on February 11, 1971, and entered into force on May 18, 1972.

It could be argued that the Seabed Treaty took the principle of political arms control too far by emphasizing the Soviet desire to reaffirm its political understanding with the Americans through agreements that would "control" either those arms that neither side wished to develop anyway, or those that other parties owned or might possess in the future. The euphoria and relief which had enabled the 1963 agreements to be seen as the precursors of substantive measures of arms control were replaced for the remainder of the decade by the scepticism born of the massive increase in strategic arms. When the strategic-arms race appeared to have been removed from the context of superpower relations, the former continued to escalate without, initially, adversely affecting the latter; in no way was the arms race subject to greater control. Increasingly, it became evident that SALT was becoming a means of dealing with the politically undesirable effects of the strategic-arms race on superpower detente, rather than with the arms race itself. This realization reinforced the general scepticism with regard to the superpowers' declared interest in arms control.

The Tlatelolco Treaty: 1967

Doubts mounted concerning the superpowers' interest in arms control when each made separate attempts to reject the Tlatelolco Treaty, a Latin American effort to "denuclearize" that continent. The treaty embodied for the first time the concept of verification by challenge, but the unlikelihood of this being invoked, combined with the treaty's limited acceptance, emphasized the political improbability of operationalizing any arms-control ideas.

Initiated by Mexico in 1963,[22] the treaty sought to prevent any introduction of nuclear weapons into Latin America by external powers. It also sought to provide a regional NPT that would commit its signatories to the non-acquisition of nuclear weapons, while allowing them the right to develop peaceful nuclear technology and explosives. For the first time a group of countries allied to the United States had produced their own measure of political arms control. It paralleled the superpower practice of furthering their political objectives through codifying existing restraints on particular forms of military activity. These restraints were eventually embodied in Articles 13–18 of the treaty. They added to the existing safeguards against the diversion of fissionable materials for weapons purposes (to be negotiated with the International Atomic Energy Agency [IAEA]) and provided for special inspections that were to be arranged by the Council of the Agency for the Prohibition of Nuclear Weapons (OPANAL) — an agency established by Articles 7 and 8. Such inspection could be requested: ". . . by any Party which suspects that some activity prohibited by this Treaty has been carried out, either in the territory of any other party *or in any other place on such latter Party's behalf.*"[23]

That these articles embodied the principles of political rather than technical arms control was evident from the political difficulties of invoking their provisions. Arms-control studies of inspection systems had failed to emphasize sufficiently the importance of the frequency with which such verification provisions could be invoked without destroying the underlying political conditions for the continuation of inhibitory mechanisms.

For the superpowers, the question was whether American requirements for the retention of their military facilities in Latin America could be reconciled with Soviet and Cuban demands for their removal. The United States was reluctant to sign Protocol I of the treaty because, although they had secured an interpretation that the transit of nuclear weapons through the Panama Canal was permitted, they wished to retain the option of deploying nuclear weapons in Puerto Rico and the Virgin Islands. Those in their Guantanamo base in Cuba were unaffected, since Cuba refused to sign.[24]

Officially, Soviet rejection of both the treaty and Protocols stemmed from their failure to inhibit U.S. use of transit and base facilities in Latin America. The real motives, however, were twofold. The Soviet Union's failure to adhere would not impair Soviet-American relations, since the United States had never been enthusiastic about the treaty; but the Soviet Union did need an excuse for not signing, in view of the Cuban opposition to the treaty and the possibility, realized in 1970, of establishing facilities at Cienfuegos, Cuba, to service and increase the effectiveness of Soviet missile-carrying submarines.[25] The Americans' muted reaction suggested that both superpowers would tacitly accept the utility of their Latin American bases while excluding from superpower arms limitation attempts to denuclearize the area.

Understandably, the Chinese and the French ignored the treaty, and the relative disinterest of the nuclear-weapons states in the treaty as a political instrument seemed to be shared by many of the more important Latin American states. At the end of 1972, only sixteen states had deposited their instruments of ratification, together with a declaration which waived the requirements of Article 28 (1) of the treaty, and brought the treaty into force for themselves.

Despite the Tlatelolco Treaty's attempts to combine the advantages of political arms control with a technical-arms-control verification system, it left Latin America with only slightly greater diplomatic restraints than before on the introduction of nuclear weapons from within or without. The obvious difficulties, both domestic and international, of invoking the verification-by-challenge procedure, especially outside nuclear installations, made challenge unlikely. The ambiguous position of the three possible Nth powers (Argentina, Brazil, and Chile) was that denuclearization did not preclude the development of nuclear-weapons options, dramatized by the 1975 Brazilian agreement to purchase a complete nuclear power plant and fuel cycle (crucial to weapons production) from West Germany. This agreement, although experiencing technical problems, was still in force in 1978, despite intense U.S. opposition for three years. Thus, the treaty emphasized the dichotomy between political and technical arms control.

Like the other partial measures, the effectiveness of the Tlatelolco Treaty depended upon a political commitment that was represented only by the signatories' pledge to refrain from developing or deploying weapons where they were either unlikely or unable to do so in the first instance. A declaration by Latin American states which lacked the means to manufacture nuclear weapons and which were unlikely either to accept them from or be offered them by the United States or the Soviet Union could hardly be described as a major advance in arms control. Moreover, the treaty imposed no constraints on the existing deployment of nuclear weapons by states that already owned them; the United States retained its transit and base rights, while the Soviet Union maintained its bases in Cuba. It is worth noting, however, that the technical emphasis on the control aspects of arms-control agreements remained intellectually influential enough to produce verification procedures so complex as to preclude their effective operation. This was especially true given the absence of meaningful sanctions against violation. The Tlatelolco Treaty was one example of such thinking. Another was the 1970 U.S. offer, in SALT I, of a ban on MIRV flight testing and of on-site inspection to verify the non-deployment of MIRV, as distinct from the original proposal (from within the U.S. bureaucracy) for a unilaterally verified ban on flight testing.[26] A third example would be proposals for restraints on anti-submarine warfare (ASW) (or "sanctuaries" from ASW) for submarines carrying SLBMs. It should also be noted that this emphasis on control found no place in political-arms-control thinking. Since arms-control agreements were important for their political effect, the question was what kind of agreement could be secured by control measures acceptable to the parties (for the two superpowers, unilateral verification), rather than what kind of controls were necessary to verify a technically significant agreement.

The Biological Warfare Convention: April 1972

The trend towards largely declaratory statements of arms limitation was continued with the Biological Warfare Convention (the origins and implications of which I have traced elsewhere).[27] The most important features of this convention, in terms of the central dichotomy between technical and political arms control suggested in this book, was that neither the United States nor the Soviet Union agreed to controls on a militarily significant activity, such as would have been represented by a verified convention banning chemical warfare. Instead, both superpowers agreed to a declaratory commitment to destroy their stocks of biological-warfare agents, but insisted that any complaints of violation be channelled through the Security Council, where they could exercise their veto. This was not to say that the Biological Warfare Convention did not represent a significant step in arms limitation. What it does say is that the reaffirmation of the superpowers' political agreement against the use of biological warfare, or, by implication, chemical warfare, was implicit rather than explicit, and was supported only by political verifications and sanctions that fell far short of the requirements of arms control.

Partial Measures as Political Arms Control: 1963-72

In summary, this chapter has argued that of all the partial measures considered, from the 1963 U.N. Resolution on the Peaceful Uses of Outer Space to the 1972 Biological Warfare Convention, each fulfilled the criteria of arms limitation rather than arms control. Each agreement was essentially related to the ongoing political context, and was intended to reinforce the superpowers' mutual interest in, and commitment to, bilateral detente through limitations on military activities of little use to them, or, indeed, to other parties. The attempts, described in this chapter, to restrict the superpowers' military freedom of action were resisted, as were any attempts by third powers to assert their rights. Therefore, the theory that arms-control measures were as much in the interests of third parties as of the superpowers seemed more than ever open to question. On the other hand, the political-arms-control view, implicitly espoused by the Soviet Union, that measures of arms restraint had become a mutually acceptable modality for embodying superpower agreement on their political as well as strategic interests seemed justified. Significantly, after the SALT I agreement of 1972, the superpowers apparently felt that there was relatively little further need for multilateral partial measures, as none were introduced to the CCD between 1972 and 1975. The only other significant measure was the U.S. 1975 ratification of the 1925 Geneva Protocol on the use of chemical weapons. This committed the United States to refrain from the first use of such weapons in time of war, except as riot-control agents and defoliants.[28]

Part IV of this volume attempts to show how this process of reinforcing political understandings through the nominal arms-control measures of the NPT and SALT was accomplished from 1963 to 1970. Thereafter, the NPT diminished in importance, while the Moscow agreements of May 1972 and the concurrent negotiations on Mutual and Balanced Force Reductions (MBFR) became increasingly significant because they meant that the initial objectives of political arms control — strategic and political parity with the U.S. — had been achieved. During that process, any contributions to arms control were minimal and incidental.

9 The Changing Focus from Surprise Attack to Non-Proliferation: 1964

With the Partial Test Ban (PTB) of 1963 and the subsequent partial measures of arms control outlined in the previous chapter, the role of political arms control became one of symbolizing the superpower detente. Because of these developments, 1964 may be regarded as a crucial year in the development of political and technical arms control. Although there appeared to be a complete impasse between the United States and the Soviet Union on arms-control measures during 1964 and 1965, the divergence between technical and political arms control had actually been greater from 1958 to 1962. Thereafter, the United States moved closer, albeit often unconsciously, towards accepting the political-arms-control notion of using nominal arms-control steps to embody and further superpower detente. In the technical-arms-control view the Soviets moved to accept this thinking with the Non-Proliferation Treaty (NPT) and, in the 1972 Strategic Arms Limitation Talks (SALT I) agreement, to accept the idea that quantitative restraints on strategic weapons were desirable once both sides had achieved a Mutual Assured Destruction (MAD) capability. In reality, there was little evidence to support this view. The Soviets had stuck to their concept of furthering superpower detente by nominal arms-control measures, and had accepted a purely formal recognition of their planned strategic force build-ups in SALT I and the 1974 Vladivostok Accord. So, rather than the United States and the Soviet Union's converging on a common understanding of arms control as a technical and political process (as was commonly argued), the United States had, actually, moved to accept the Soviet approach.

Since 1964 was a year in which these changes were inherent rather than actual, it serves as a suitable point from which to survey the developments which made these changes possible. Midway through the narrative, some indication is given of the complexity of factors whose interaction formed the broader context for negotiations on the NPT.

Technical and Political Arms Control: The Dominance of Politics

From 1958 onwards, when the United States implemented a policy based on the emerging theories of arms control, the Soviet Union responded with a policy that evolved into political arms control. That concept had always been part of Soviet policy, although often inchoate, but it was made increasingly coherent by the necessity of responding to American initiatives. Between 1958 and 1962, the two concepts of technical and political arms control were developed to the point of maximum divergence. The Conference of Experts, the Geneva test-ban talks, and the Surprise Attack Conference had refined arms-control theory into an explicit body of doctrine of how to control the undesirable technical effects of weapons, irrespective of the political relations between the superpowers. Simultaneously, political arms control had developed into a set of implicit assumptions — notably that arms control was dangerously irrelevant to the central problems of strategic stability because it downplayed their political context, especially in Europe. Therefore, by 1962 the two concepts of technical and political arms control were so clearly developed and divergent that there was no possibility of negotiations based on these two approaches. The 1963 hotline and PTB broke this impasse, because the United States moved to accept the idea of political arms control. Thereafter, this came to be the preferred modality for signifying political accord between the superpowers. However, it imposed no restraint on U.S. military technology, so that what the United States claimed to be arms-control measures were really disguised steps towards political arms control.

The process of adapting technical-arms-control measures to political arms control began with the 1963 PTB. This symbolized the bilateral reassurance of strategic stability that was needed by both superpowers after the Cuban crisis. The partial measures that were adopted until April 1964 served a similar purpose. After a hiatus that lasted until October 1966, the political leadership of both superpowers shifted away from this limited view of political arms control as providing for a relaxation of tensions after a major crisis and on to the broader concept of political arms control as the chief modality for a major superpower detente stressing their unique bilateral interdependence in the nuclear age. This did not, of course, prevent the Soviets from engaging in a massive build-up of their strategic and tactical nuclear forces, from creating a navy equal to that of the United States, and from quantitatively and qualitatively increasing their conventional air and ground forces. They could do this whilst trying to maintain their version of detente precisely because of this concept of superpower interdependence, which was espoused by technical arms controllers and policy makers in the Democratic and Republican administrations from 1963 to 1978, especially by Dr. Kissinger and, from 1977, President Jimmy Carter. Because both sides, from increasingly divergent motives, wished to use political arms control to create an image of detente, the United States and the Soviet Union both resisted any attempts to restrict their respective freedom of military action that would have resulted from effective partial measures. To have done otherwise would have assigned a negative role to the concept of political arms control, the positive aspects of which found expression in the NPT.

The Evolving Political Setting: 1963-68

Essentially, the new role of arms limitation resulted from the changed international political context that had been created by the post-1963 superpower detente. This enabled the United States and the Soviet Union to distinguish between their own bilateral relationship, the intra-European detente, and their more active but limited competition for influence outside Europe, with its attendant risks of limited conflict and the need to prevent such conflict between their allies from affecting their superpower supporters. Such competition did increase sharply with the Soviet and Cuban intervention in Africa from 1975 onwards. However, the far-reaching change in the 1960s in Soviet-American political understandings demanded a series of interim reassurances that would formalize the evolution of what Marshall D. Shulman has characterized as their "limited adversary relationship"[1] into something that would involve greater co-operation. Such reassurances were provided by tacit co-operation on partial measures of arms control and, more significantly, by the NPT. Paradoxically, both sides came to attach great importance to an NPT, but for totally different reasons. The Kennedy and Johnson administrations saw the treaty from the perspective of the arms controllers, who had urged the necessity of preventing proliferation, which they saw as rapid and destabilizing. The Soviet Union seemed to view the only destabilizing proliferation as U.S. dissemination of nuclear weapons under the two-key system, of knowledge about their use and manufacture, and of delivery systems to U.S. NATO partners, especially West Germany. The theoretical divergence between the Western and Soviet definitions of the dangers of proliferation and the means for their resolution was thus at its height from mid-1963 until mid-1965. During this period the Multilateral Nuclear Force (MLF) proposal was an increasingly important instrument of U.S. foreign policy, but by mid-1965 it had been decisively defeated by its inherent defects and by the fact that the U.S. government, under the influence of the arms controllers, rated a global NPT higher than the MLF. Given that the Soviet precondition for an NPT was the dropping of the MLF, it was clear that the MLF would have to go. So by mid-1965, the Soviet Union, which had been advocating an anti-dissemination NPT, found that the main threat to strategic stability (as they defined it), the MLF proposal, had been removed.

The NPT thus became the ideal vehicle for emphasizing the bilateral, superpower aspects of detente. Removal of the MLF meant that the main political-arms-control problem had been dealt with. An NPT would be symbolic of superpower accord but otherwise of little relevance to technical arms control, since its control provisions could not prevent proliferation. This view was shared by President Johnson, who failed to see its implications for his European allies. Hence, the NPT emerged as the chief modality for superpower detente from October 1966 to the beginning of the SALT negotiations in November 1969.

Inevitably, the process which produced this arrangement was more complex than my chronological overview has implied. From the last of the 1964 partial measures to mid-1966, two sets of developments created uncertainty as to how far the tentative relaxation of tension embodied in the PTB could be extended. Initially, it was unclear whether the PTB's use of an apparent arms-control measure to implement political arms control could be continued, given the absence of suitably adaptable measures. The uncertainty disappeared when the NPT became a negotiable proposition in 1965. Additionally, the changes of leadership in the United States and the Soviet Union raised new uncertainties about the objectives and the means that each country would adopt. President Kennedy's assassination in November 1963 removed a unique personal element from Mr. Khrushchev's relations with the United States. The shared experience of the Cuban crisis apparently had given both leaders considerable incentive to secure detente as a prelude to a more fundamental reconstruction of the superpower relationship. Mr. Khrushchev indicated this to the new Johnson administration by continuing with the various partial measures into 1964. The removal of the Soviet leader from power in October of that year signalled a tougher line in Soviet foreign policy under Mr. Brezhnev. The combination of the Soviet Union's campaigns against the MLF, against the succeeding 1965 NATO Nuclear Planning Group (NPG), and against West Germany's Ostpolitik clashed sharply with President Johnson's concept of bridge-building between East and West, especially between the two halves of Europe.[2] Soviet acceptance of the fact that the MLF was finished and that it could not fundamentally change West Germany's political status in Western Europe combined to make the NPT a symbol of superpower relations, implicitly from mid-1965 to mid-1966, and explicitly thereafter. Both new governments had found it necessary to extend rather than to contract their areas of mutual understanding; accordingly, they agreed to separate out the superpower detente by means of the NPT.

These changes were reflected in the negotiation positions that the superpowers took at the Eighteen Nation Disarmament Conference (ENDC). These indicated the shifting American and Soviet perceptions of their political relations, the implications thereof for strategic stability, and the consequent roles of political and technical arms control. Additionally, the Soviet rejection of theoretically impeccable arms-control proposals for a bomber bonfire emphasized the importance of relating these to the political balance between the United States and the Soviet Union, between the superpowers and their local allies, and within the regions where the proposed arms-control measures were to operate.

Redefining the Bases for Negotiation:
The January 1964 Superpower Proposals to the ENDC

The U.S. five-point plan that was tabled on January 21[3] and the Soviet nine-point reply of January 28[4] represented a reappraisal of the possibilities for agreement on partial measures in the light of their new relationship. Although they continued to use their respective approaches of technical and political arms control, the declining propaganda content in their proposals suggested a greater, if still limited, interest in seeking joint solutions to the problem of strategic stability. Those problems were still defined by the Soviets in terms of West Germany's catalytic potential, now represented by the MLF proposal. Both sides' approaches were characterized by uncertainty as to whether any significant agreement was possible. For both, achieving detente in relation to past hostilities (as with the 1963 PTB) was now less important than gaining some proof of superpower ability to co-operate in measures of political arms control. For the Americans, proof of such ability was an NPT with the nominal technical goal of stopping all proliferation; for the Soviets, it was an NPT stopping West German access to nuclear weapons through the MLF. Understandably, the transition to the political-arms-control NPT was gradual, making these distinctions relative rather than absolute. But the post-PTB declaratory treaties (see above, Chapter 8) did represent a continuation of the earlier aspect of political arms control, in that they sought a relaxation in superpower relations after a major crisis, which was quite distinct from the hesitant emergence in 1964 of the NPT as a negotiable issue. On the other hand, if the U.S. plan of January 21, 1964, is indicative of arms-control thinking modified by diplomatic considerations and is at the same time seen in contrast to Soviet replies based on political-arms-control principles, the continuing difference between the two intellectual approaches is apparent.

Propaganda

Although the Soviets continually and bitterly attacked the MLF, compared with past disarmament discussions, use of propaganda was relatively restrained, suggesting a greater mutual interest in substantive negotiation. Mr. Khrushchev's appeal on December 31, 1963, for an agreement on a peaceful settlement of disputes was answered by the Americans' point 1. The Soviets repeated their call for a NATO–Warsaw Treaty Organization Non-Aggression Pact (Point IV), thus emphasizing their continuing interest in U.S. recognition of East Germany.

The Strategic Balance and the Bomber Bonfire

The United States offered a verified freeze on the number and characteristics of strategic nuclear offensive forces (point 2). Although this was unacceptable to the Soviets because it would have institutionalized U.S. superiority, it was intended to indicate to the Soviets a fundamental change in the American position. That change had come with U.S. recognition of the limited political utility of strategic nuclear weapons and its rejection of any attempt to maintain the disarming counter-force capability that McNamara had discussed in his 1962 Ann Arbor speech. The accompanying point 3 called for a halt in the production of fissionable material for weapons use. This was largely propaganda that was designed to reinforce the idea of a ceiling on strategic forces. The Soviets repeated the common practice of exploiting strategic asymmetries to the proposer's advantage by suggesting the evacuation of all foreign troops from European overseas bases (Point I) and the elimination of bomber aircraft (Point VIII). The Soviet-proposed prohibition of underground tests (Point IX), like the U.S. strategic-freeze proposal, combined superficial propaganda appeal with a serious message. The Soviets knew that the United States regarded the PTB as an anti-proliferation measure, so a CTB could act against proliferation if the inspection problem could be resolved. Soviet suggestions for a decrease in over-all force levels (Point II) and a cut in military budgets (Point III) similarly repeated traditional proposals but in a context which suggested that some agreed moderation in strategic competition might be desirable and possible.

The tension between attempts to extend the scope of political arms control and the traditional disarmament diplomacy practised by both sides was exemplified by the "bomber bonfire" proposal. The U.S. replied to the Soviets' Point VIII on March 19, 1964, with the suggestion that both powers should agree to the verified destruction of an equal number of B-47 and TU-16 (Badger) bombers at the rate of twenty per month for two years, or more if those stored for emergency mobilization were included. This would provide a tangible reduction in strategic delivery vehicles, ensure that these were not transferred to other states, and thereby restrain the proliferation of sophisticated weapons systems.[5] In arms-control terms, this would prevent the destabilization of local deterrent balances that could complicate both superpowers' control over their respective allies and over bilateral crisis management.[6]

The technological factors that created a predisposition to a disarming counter-force first strike, where both forces were equipped with aircraft, represented only the technical aspect of the problem of surprise attack. Since the 1955 Czechoslovakian arms deal with Egypt, the Soviets had used the supply of arms to the Third World as a major means of extending their political influence; and they could expect to use TU-16 Badgers for this purpose when these were no longer required by the Soviet Union. In 1964, however, the Soviets had about one thousand Badgers in service which, together with the 800 Intermediate- and Medium-Range Ballistic Missiles (I/MRBM) in Eastern Europe, represented most of the Soviet medium-range system for delivering nuclear weapons against European and U.S. carrier forces. In contrast, the U.S. B-47 was three years older than the Badger and the last 500 were being phased out of the Strategic Air Command (SAC).[7] Therefore, the Soviets adhered to their proposal of destroying all bombers and after further exchanges the issue effectively lapsed in December 1965.[8]

The whole exchange epitomized the stagnation of negotiations, but the substantive questions concerning the choice between the MLF proposal and an NPT were provisionally resolved in favour of the latter. In this instance, the American use of arms control reinforced the Soviet perception of arms control as an extension of the Western technique for disguising political differences within a technical framework. Because the bomber bonfire proposal complemented the U.S. suggestion for a strategic freeze that would have institutionalized the Soviet strategic inferiority, it could only have accentuated their distrust of arms control's claims to political impartiality and their scepticism of U.S. allegations regarding the global dangers of proliferation, while simultaneously advocating the dissemination of U.S. nuclear weapons to Western Europe.

Europe and Surprise Attack

Europe's central importance in the Soviet concept of the strategic balance was evident in the Soviets' reintroduction of ground observation posts (Point VII), linked to the reduction of forces and denuclearization in Central Europe (Points I and IV). The Americans' point 4 referred to observation posts alone. Apparently, each side would maintain its

1958 position, although neither assigned such a high priority to the problem of surprise attack in this context. Previous negotiations had shown that, while both agreed that there existed a chance of surprise attack in Europe, the problem was perceived so differently by the superpowers as to prevent any negotiated reduction of the risks involved. Moreover, these had been diminished by political and technical changes which reduced the danger that either side would engage in pre-emption during a European crisis. Furthermore, such a crisis was in itself more difficult to envisage. The post-Cuba detente had altered the political relationship with the United States that had dominated Soviet thinking, and American fears of a nuclear Pearl Harbor had been assuaged by their acquisition of what they regarded as an assured destruction capability. In the Soviets' eyes, West Germany's catalytic potential could only re-emerge with the MLF and they considered this a major threat to stability from 1963 onwards. Halting the MLF involved discussing non-proliferation as well as non-dissemination; therefore, proliferation assumed the dominant role in their political-arms-control policy. Previously, that policy had been concerned with the problem of surprise attack for the four years between 1958-62 and, concurrently, with partial measures in 1963. Their 1964 introduction of proliferation as an issue needed to be related to developments in the field of nuclear sharing in 1963 and earlier.

Non-Proliferation and Non-Dissemination

Diplomatically, the 1964 proposals were more than usually ambiguous. They reflected the rapid evolution of contradictory positions between the superpowers and within the Johnson administration. The U.S. point 5 comprised: first, a promise not to transfer nuclear weapons "into the national control of states which do not now control them, and that all transfers of nuclear materials for peaceful purposes take place under effective international safeguards";[9] second, acceptance of similar safeguards on peaceful nuclear activities by nuclear-weapons powers; and third, a verified CTB. Because the last two points were obviously unacceptable to the Soviet Union, this actually marked a regression in the American position to one of even stronger support for the MLF. The U.S. draft General and Complete Disarmament (GCD) Treaty outline of April 18, 1962, had included a non-dissemination and non-acquisition agreement, whereby non-nuclear-weapons states promised not to acquire control over nuclear weapons or to manufacture them.[10] These changes clearly reflected the dominance of the MLF supporters within the new administration, in that they removed any American positions that could be construed as an obstacle to the MLF. The Soviets' Point VI reflected their awareness of this by demanding that both direct and indirect access to nuclear weapons should be excluded by an agreement that would prohibit the transfer of nuclear weapons, or indirect access to them through military blocks, for example, through NATO's MLF.[11]

These two proposals (point 5 and Point VI) reflected the major source of confusion in the discussion of proliferation, that is, its different definition by the superpowers. This obscured the question of whether the NPT that was signed four and a half years later represented political or technical arms control, because, once the NPT had contributed to the MLF's demise, it imposed greater controls on the commercial nuclear activities of America's allies but left the Soviets free of even the token International Atomic Energy Agency (IAEA) inspection that was accepted by the United States and Great Britian. The arms-control concept of proliferation was that a rapid spread of nuclear weapons to all those states that were technically capable of their manufacture would create an inherently unstable international system, with a vastly increased danger to the superpowers of accidental involvement in nuclear war. That process could become irreversible unless the United States and the Soviet Union negotiated an enforceable NPT by no later than the end of the decade.[12] This definition of proliferation reflected a global view of American security interests, whereas the Soviets' understanding of and opposition to proliferation derived from their preoccupation with the security of their control over Eastern Europe and the political defence of these interests against West Germany. Although the details of American dissemination policy, the MLF, the NPT, and the Soviet reactions are described in the succeeding chapters, the interaction among these four cannot be understood without the background discussion of the major political and strategic issues which brought both superpowers to include them in the January 1964 proposals for an agreement to halt the spread of nuclear weapons. Viewed in retrospect, perhaps this assumed more importance than it deserved, since 1964 was a turning point for American foreign policy. At that time, the attempt both to negotiate detente with the Soviet Union and to strengthen relations with Western Europe via the MLF was challenged by both European and Soviet opposition to the force. This led to the substitution of a bilateral superpower detente which gained expression in the NPT. An appreciation of how much 1964 was a year of transition and how uncertain the prospects for relations with the United States and Western Europe must have seemed to Mr. Khrushchev and his successors involves placing their proposals on proliferation in the context of past Soviet experiences with American policy towards dissemination within NATO.

PART IV   The Non-Proliferation Treaty: A Case Study in the Failure of Arms Control

10 Dissemination, the MLF, and Proliferation

In 1964, the Soviet Union faced three distinct problems — in addition to that of its continuing strategic inferiority — in the field of nuclear weapons. The first of these concerned U.S. willingness to disseminate to its European allies both the knowledge of nuclear weapons and the weapons themselves under safeguards that the Soviets regarded as inadequate. The second was the expansion of this policy to include the Multilateral Nuclear Force (MLF). And the third was China's development of nuclear weapons. However, the fear of West Germany dominated Soviet thinking. Moreover, Soviet opposition to the acquisition of nuclear weapons, or bases for them, by any of America's allies created a misleading resemblance to American theories regarding the need to halt proliferation. The basic Soviet view of the German problem warrants emphasis here, because therein lie the origins of the Soviet Union's concern over the conflict in American policy between opposition to proliferation and the use of controlled dissemination to resolve NATO's political problems. The latter provided the basis for the emergence of the general idea of an MLF in the late 1950s, and seemed at the time to represent simply the extension of a long-standing U.S. policy towards its NATO allies.

The United States' controlled dissemination policy originated in the years 1955-58 with the belief that once Great Britain's national nuclear forces had been created (however undesirable that might be), it was better to accept them as part of an alliance than to embark on an unsuccessful attempt to secure their renunciation. The Nassau Agreement[1] of December 1962 was influenced by the strategic rationale that if an ally had an independent deterrent, it should be as invulnerable to surprise attack as possible. The special rules that applied to Great Britain were extended to France through the agreement's offer of Polaris-carrying submarines to President de Gaulle as replacements for the vulnerable aircraft of the *force de frappe*. Although it was rejected, the offer could be seen by the Soviets as implying that a sufficient desire for nuclear weapons by a major European ally would meet with reluctant acquiescence by the United States. The Soviets, like the

European desk of the American State Department, assumed that the West German government wanted nuclear weapons. That assumption led them to believe that the United States was willing to provide NATO members with the knowledge of, and the weapons for, a two-key nuclear system. By combining both these aspects of controlled dissemination, by the end of 1962, the MLF had become in principle, if not in practice, the main American instrument for ensuring that proliferation and dissemination within NATO would be controlled without being militarily or politically destabilizing. Ideally, the MLF could absorb the French and British deterrents, and thereby reduce the appearance, and perhaps later the substance, of their independence. This would justify U.S. assistance in their modernization. Potential nuclear powers, notably West Germany, could be persuaded that benefits from partnership with the United States exceeded those of independence in the nuclear-weapons field. The European questioning of American willingness to guarantee them against Soviet attack had increased with McNamara's determination to provide for a conventional war in Europe. This questioning was met with the response that such attack would be countered by the nuclear backstop provided by the MLF.

This ill-defined theoretical framework of the MLF abruptly became the basis of U.S. diplomacy with Western Europe in February 1963 because of General de Gaulle's January veto on British entry into the European Economic Community (EEC). To a dominant coalition of interests in the Kennedy administration, an MLF became the only means for containing the centripetal tendencies within NATO. Despite grave doubts among its prospective European members, it was expected by October 1964 that a treaty to establish the MLF would be signed in December, for ratification early in 1965.

The MLF and West Germany

Soviet political-arms-control policy towards the MLF or towards any other form of West German access to nuclear weapons was dominated by the paranoia that had been evident since the 1958 Surprise Attack Conference. Throughout the negotiations on the MLF and the NPT this paranoia was a self-reinforcing hypothesis strengthened by the fact that the MLF and the NPT were defined in terms of quite different theoretical frameworks. The substantive interests of the superpowers became intelligible only when defined in the context of negotiations on the NPT, which frequently degenerated into an unresolvable debate about strategic theology. The Soviet theory of the MLF produced the demand that every hypothetical avenue to such a force be blocked as a precondition for an NPT. The Americans, on the other hand, wished to leave open at least a theoretical option for a European deterrent because of the repercussions of not doing so in West Germany and among the MLF advocates in the State Department.

The Soviet picture of the MLF combined logical deductions with false premises that were based on traditional assumptions of German Machiavellism. If the MLF functioned under a veto of all members, including the United States, it would give each state no greater access to nuclear weapons than it already had. Although true of at least the first stage of the MLF, this made it hard for the Soviet Union to understand how the force could play the role that the United States seemed to be claiming for it in alliance politics. Because of these American claims, the Soviets assumed that the MLF did, in fact, represent some increase in Allied control over the ability to fire nuclear weapons. In their view, once the force was established, the United States could surrender its veto to the NATO Council, which was dominated by West Germany. The more the MLF became a bilateral U.S.–West German project, from October 1964 to late 1965, the greater became the Soviets' fear that the re-establishment of their special relationship would tie Washington to Bonn once again. In any case, the MLF could become an integrated European force (without the United States as a member) that would be under ultimate European control. "European" in this context was thought to refer to West Germany, which, through the MLF, might acquire control over strategic nuclear weapons as well as its existing access to tactical weapons. Therefore, in the NPT negotiations the European clause created a stumbling block because it would allow a future European federation to include the British and French nuclear deterrents in a European force. This must have seemed intentionally disingenuous to the Soviets. In the Soviet view, if the Americans wanted an NPT, they were unlikely to hold up an agreement for the sake of maintaining a hypothetical and improbable option for their European allies. But under West German pressure, a nominal federation could be created with control over the British and French deterrents. By invoking the European clause, the United States could then supply nuclear weapons to such a federation without breaking the NPT. Such Soviet arguments were no more theoretical than those frequently employed by arms controllers.

The crucial element in the Soviet assessment of the MLF was the nature and extent of West German influence within the Atlantic alliance. This had declined in 1963 despite a large army and increased economic strength. The Berlin Wall and the Cuban crisis had removed the most likely causes of war and had made America's relations with the Soviet Union less dependent on the military strength and diplomatic cohesion of NATO. Chancellor Adenauer had alienated President Kennedy with his insistence on the rigid policies of the Dulles era, but the gradual introduction of the more flexible *Ostpolitik* had offered West Germany a new chance to exploit detente for her own aims. As expanded by Foreign Minister Schroeder in 1964, the *Ostpolitik* would use West German economic power to exploit the greater freedom that was allowed the Eastern European states by the Soviet policy of polycentrism, which decreased its political control over them. Had this control been less primitive, such a limited threat could have been contained without undue difficulty.[2] As it was, and as the Soviet government was well aware, West German success might lessen its economic dependence on the Soviet Union and cause the introduction of political changes that could necessitate such action as the 1968 invasion of Czechoslovakia. This could possibly undermine detente both in Europe and between the superpowers. On the other hand, the MLF could have provided West Germany with strategic and political support for the *Ostpolitik*.

Ironically, the 1968 Soviet invasion of Czechoslovakia actually emphasized its political weakness while demonstrating the strength of superpower detente.[3] In 1963, however, this detente was just beginning; the MLF constituted American policy towards Europe, and West Germany was moving towards a more active policy in Eastern Europe. Under these circumstances, the Soviets had to oppose the MLF because it could give West Germany the power to reverse any trend towards superpower detente. Their fear was the obverse of the West German one that the U.S.–U.S.S.R. understanding could lead to the abandonment of reunification as the (declared) goal of the United States and NATO.

Illusion and Substance in Soviet Policy Towards the MLF

Defining the political reality of the MLF for the Soviet Union was more than usually difficult because its propaganda obscured the basic elements that have been outlined above and reflected the underlying perception that had shaped its understanding. The Soviet picture of West Germany could be likened to that held by the Cold War warriors in the United States with regard to the Soviet Union. The cycle of political paranoia was completed for the Soviet Union by the Western failure to take account of how the MLF could look from Moscow. The American contention that no government could produce a rational theory of the MLF — if it was based on such irrational assumptions as the Soviet Union's — ignored the ability of governments to entertain contradictory ideas. The MLF that the Soviets saw was no more removed from political reality in some ways than the MLF of its more ardent supporters. Both tended to sound like bad strategic theologians, since governments are ill-suited to conduct theoretical debates either internally or with each other. For example, U.S. attempts to persuade the

Soviets that the MLF was an anti-proliferation device that had, in fact, been designed to divert West German desires for nuclear weapons into safe channels served only to confirm Soviet fears. They already believed that West Germany wanted greater access to nuclear weapons, and could see that if the MLF did not provide this directly it would certainly increase West German incentives and opportunities to do so.

China and Proliferation

China's role in Soviet foreign policy tends to be assessed according to whether this is seen as European- or China-oriented.[4] The European-centred approach that is favoured here has not prevented China from being considered important in relation to three aspects of proliferation. The Soviet emphasis on the dangers of disseminating nuclear technology to allies was accentuated by their one experience of doing so, by providing aid to the Chinese program between 1957 and 1960. This assistance was decisive in enabling China to manufacture nuclear and thermonuclear weapons quickly.[5] The common interest and ideology that the aid was intended to serve had disappeared with startling rapidity and must have had an effect on almost every aspect of Soviet policy, especially its perception of similar assistance to other states. Even in 1964 the possibility must have been apparent that the Soviet Union could become involved in constructing an Asian balance of power to contain the Chinese influence. The collective Soviet leadership in power after October 1964 clearly favoured this idea, and it was later elaborated by Mr. Brezhnev into a doctrine which was not unlike that of John Foster Dulles. It must have been obvious by 1965 that Soviet interests were unlikely to suffer greatly from the development of an Asian nuclear balance. India was the obvious counterpart to China, even if an Indian bomb might lead to Japan following suit, with or without U.S. assistance. A Non-Proliferation Treaty (NPT) might inhibit China's use of its bomb for political aims while an appropriate politico-military balance was evolved. Therefore, its first nuclear explosion in October 1964 might have strengthened a secondary Soviet argument for pressing on with an NPT the main object of which was to contain West Germany. With this background the negotiations can be considered in more detail.

11 Differing Soviet and American Objectives in the NPT Negotiations

Up to this point it has been argued that, by 1963, technical-arms-control theory had become a highly developed conceptual framework, but that its implementation by the United States had proved virtually impossible. Thus, what the Americans were calling arms-control policy was in practice much nearer political arms control. Instead of imposing controls on the technical aspects of the superpowers' strategic-arms competition in order to secure strategic stability, the United States and the Soviet Union came, with the 1963 Partial Test Ban (PTB) and subsequent partial measures, to use nominal arms-control measures to further their political understandings of their respective spheres of influence and the modalities of competition outside these spheres. This distinction between technical and political arms control became crucial during the negotiations for and the conclusion of the 1968 Non-Proliferation Treaty (NPT).

Preventing the proliferation of nuclear weapons had become a major preoccupation of the arms controllers during that period. These theorists had created a detailed theoretical framework of the dangers involved and the means for their prevention, such that the implementation of an NPT became a test case for the real applicability of their theory.[1] For their part, the Soviets had developed an equally coherent, although less explicit, theory of the dangers that would result from greater West German access to nuclear weapons. They made the prevention of this a major objective of political arms control, but only when it was compatible with the overriding need to advance their detente with the United States. From 1963 to 1970, the two policies of technical and political arms control were in conflict over the nature and extent of the NPT. That conflict was finally resolved in favour of political arms control and a precedent was thereby set for the outcome of the Strategic Arms Limitation Talks (SALT), which started just before the NPT was ratified in 1970.

Heretofore, the Western world had accepted the arms-control viewpoint of the NPT as the only valid interpretation of the problem of proliferation. In order to understand how the Soviets perceived the related problems of proliferation and the dissemination of nuclear weapons by the American government, Soviet perspectives on American dissemination policy must be considered from 1958 — when this became a major problem to the Soviets — until 1965, when the NPT emerged as the best available means by which to check what they saw as an American policy that threatened strategic stability.

Not surprisingly, the Soviets saw proliferation as a political issue and, accordingly, American policy on the dissemination of nuclear weapons always seemed ambiguous to them. This latter fact serves to refute the arms-control idea that successive American administrations refrained from any measures which could be interpreted as proliferation.[2] This same failure to distinguish sufficiently, in either arms-control theory or U.S. policy, between the technical justifications for actions and their political consequences accounted for the confusion at the beginning and end of the NPT negotiations. From 1958 to 1965, the U.S. government appeared to the Soviets to be considering a politically dangerous form of dissemination within NATO. On the other hand, from 1966 to 1967 (and from 1977 on, on politico-economic grounds), NATO's European members found themselves opposed to U.S. proposals for safeguarding nuclear-fuel supplies because these safeguards threatened Western Europe's political ability to influence the superpower bargain that the NPT had by then become. In contrast, arms-control literature and American policy statements treated the NPT as an arms-control measure that was aimed at halting the otherwise rapid and destabilizing spread of nuclear weapons. This process was seen both as inimical to U.S. political and strategic interests and, in so far as the Soviet Union was becoming a status quo power, against Soviet interests as well.[3] Since Soviet objectives — that is, the prevention of West German access to nuclear weapons and the strengthening of the superpower detente — were political in nature, the whole negotiating process was asymmetrical. As usual, the United States based its position on arms-control theory and the Soviet Union based its on the principles of political arms control. This made agreement possible only where the two differing views of proliferation and dissemination suggested compatible modalities that were intended to serve fundamentally different objectives.

Soviet Perspectives on American Dissemination Policy: 1958-61

The dominant trend in American dissemination policy was not opposition to proliferation but to the use of controlled dissemination of nuclear weapons and of information on their use to meet NATO's politi-

cal demands for a greater share in U.S. strategic planning for the
defence of Western Europe. Understandably, the Soviet Union feared
that such dissemination could increase West German influence in
NATO, or even create the possibility that West Germany might obtain an
independent nuclear capability. In the context of East-West relations
prior to Chancellor Brandt's *Ostpolitik* of 1969 and onwards, the realization of the latter would be an extremely destablizing factor. Soviet
opposition to West German acquisition of cruise-missile technology
and to the United States' deployment of the neutron bomb in Western
Europe from 1977 onwards emphasizes the consistency of these Soviet
views.

Dissemination became an issue for the Soviet Union in December
1957. At that time, the NATO Council decided to assuage the Western
European fears that had been generated as a result of Sputnik by
supplying nuclear weapons under the two-key system and planning for
an Intermediate Range Ballistic Missile (IRBM) force under Supreme
Allied Command Europe (SACEUR). This was the genesis of the Multilateral Nuclear Force (MLF).[4] Until 1963, this concept of an MLF was
essentially a policy that the United States would adopt only if its
Western European allies supported the idea, which they did not. The
1960 U.S. proposals to NATO for an MLF, President Kennedy's speech in
Ottawa, in May 1961, and the references to nuclear sharing in the 1962
Nassau Agreement should, therefore, be seen as the tentative explora-
tions of an MLF concept whose precise nature and purpose were both
unclear. To the Soviets, the MLF would have seemed a much greater
threat than it actually was, given the previous U.S. policy of extremely
limited and carefully controlled dissemination. The U.S. amendments
made to the MacMahon Act (1946) on July 2, 1958, which had forbidden the U.S. government to disclose information on nuclear weapons

> . . . authorized under certain specific conditions the transfer to our allies
> of: (1) the non-nuclear parts of atomic weapons, (2) fissionable nuclear
> materials suitable for the development of, or use in, nuclear weapons,
> (3) sensitive information concerning nuclear weapons, and (4) nuclear
> equipment such as military reactors.[5]

In the Soviet view, this represented a developing trend in U.S. policy
that had begun with President Eisenhower's desire to assist U.K. development of its independent nuclear weapons. The need to train the
newly formed West German army had already caused the MacMahon
Act to be modified in 1955, in order to allow "the transfer to NATO
countries of information on nuclear defense plans, on the external
characteristics of nuclear weapons, and on the training of NATO personnel in the employment of U.S. atomic weapons."[6]

As I suggested in Chapter 4, the catalytic potential created by the

American dissemination policy may have been a factor in the circumstances that caused the Soviet Union to attend the 1958 Surprise Attack Conference,[7] at which began the asymmetrical process whereby the United States had to adapt its generalized arms-control requirements for an NPT to limit West German access to nuclear weapons. During the NPT negotiations from 1965 to 1968, the Soviets added to their central objective of stopping further German access to nuclear weapons through the United States and NATO. An additional goal, at least in declaratory Soviet policy, was halting proliferation in the two regions where the Soviet Union was becoming increasingly involved, the Middle East and Asia. The potential Nth powers involved were Israel, Japan, India, plus, in the longer run (the late 1970s onwards), South Korea and Taiwan, South Africa, and, in the 1980s, Brazil and Iran.[8]

The first juxtaposition of the narrower arms-control concept of nonproliferation and the broader arms-limitation emphasis on nondissemination came in 1961. In that year, the U.N. General Assembly approved the Irish Resolution[9] that advocated a simple NPT and the more complex Swedish Resolution[10] that aimed at preventing dissemination. The United States and the Soviet Union reacted in accordance with their established perceptions. The United States distinguished between two categories of dissemination, "(1) the manufacture or acquisition of ownership of nuclear weapons", which it opposed on arms-control grounds, and "(2) the deployment of nuclear weapons",[11] which it upheld as necessary to Allied defence. The Soviet Union opposed both types of dissemination and urged the immediate conclusion of an agreement with the other three nuclear powers (the United States, Britain, and France) to enter into an undertaking "not to deliver nuclear weapons or information concerning their manufacture to other countries". It should also stop the spread of nuclear weapons, whether through acquisition by new states or through a decision to make available nuclear weapons "to one or another military bloc as a whole".[12] Admittedly, these 1961 proposals expressed support for the Rapacki plan and other proposals for nuclear-free zones. Nevertheless, they may be taken as the point where Soviet ideas on how to limit or eliminate West Germany's nuclear role in the alliance began to switch from the unsuccessful denuclearization framework to one of nonproliferation. This new line of thought was more compatible with, although dissimilar to, that of the U.S. arms controllers. What Alastair Buchan has so aptly characterized as President Kennedy's "private nightmare about nuclear proliferation which can have borne very little relation to the kind of scientific advice . . . available to him,"[13] made the President and the newly created Arms Control and Disarmament Agency (ACDA) more receptive to the idea of an NPT.

Exchanges during 1962 served only to emphasize that the United

States saw both the problem of and the solution to proliferation in arms-control terms; it supported the Irish Resolution but gave no major political commitment to an NPT.[14] With equal consistency, the Soviets continued to see the problem of U.S. dissemination to West Germany in terms of the potential for an independent nuclear capability. The reappearance of the dialogue of the deaf, so evident at the 1958 Surprise Attack Conference, manifested itself at the Eighteen Nation Disarmament Conference (ENDC) on the issue of non-proliferation, despite the use, after the 1962 Cuban crisis, of political arms control to establish better political relations. The conflicting priorities between the MLF and the NPT, from 1963 to 1965, meant that despite intense political activity on these issues, the sense of diplomatic stagnation remained. In order to place the tentative American moves towards an NPT in 1965 in the correct context, the Canadian representative to the ENDC made clear, in retrospect, the arms-control interpretation that the United States had always pushed for an NPT:

During the 1963 and 1964 sessions of the Disarmament Committee there were many more discussions of the problem of preventing further dissemination of nuclear weapons, but the positions of the two parties remained precisely as they had been in July 1962. The United States in private diplomatic conversations and in public statements in the Disarmament Committee has tried, but with no success, to persuade the Soviet Union that a multilateral NATO force would be so constituted that it would not permit any participant to become an independent power. There has been no real shift in these deadlocked positions in the last three years. Nikolai Fedorenko, representing the Soviet Union, at the meeting of the United Nations Disarmament Commission on April 26, 1965, covered almost precisely the same ground as did Mr. Zorin in the 1962 statement quoted above.* Again the United States representative, the late Adlai Stevenson, had to rebut the allegations of West Germany's revanchist aims and lust for nuclear weapons. He said that: "a non-dissemination agreement in accordance with the resolution proposed by the delegation of Ireland would be the best way to meet this concern, and we urge the Soviet Union to join in seeking such agreement. If we argue endlessly about future fears and let pass our chance to conclude a non-proliferation agreement while there is yet time, we will all lose.†

*See Mr. Fedorenko's statement in U.N. Document DC/PV, 72, pp. 36-41.
† U.N. Document DC/PV, 73, pp. 10-11.[15]

The MLF and the NPT, 1963-65

Soviet fears of West German access to nuclear weapons were greatly accentuated by the emergence of the MLF as the chief means for securing President Kennedy's grand design of Atlantic interdependence in February 1963, after de Gaulle's veto on British entry into the Common Market. This American use of a technical modality for achieving its political objectives forced the Soviets to counter with a similar move. Initially, they used the NPT as the means by which to defeat the MLF, until late 1966, and then as an instrument of superpower detente. The interaction between the technical and political aspects of the MLF may be summarized as follows.

The Soviet Union's extreme hostility to the MLF was based on its general effect, namely that it would increase West German political influence. It also resulted from the possibility that the MLF might eventually enjoy the same ultimate autonomy as the U.K. Polaris force if the MLF was either an integrated force, where the United States had surrendered its veto, or a largely European force, under European control with no U.S. veto. Theoretically, mixed manning would prevent any one state from gaining control, but this would clearly be dependent on who the participants eventually were.[16] Soviet attacks on the MLF caused NATO's Western European members to lend greater verbal support than they might otherwise have given to a project about which they had the gravest doubts. These were articulated only when the technical MLF studies resulted in the October 1964 decision by the United States that the MLF would consist of twenty-five surface ships, each carrying eight A-3 Polaris missiles, with the United States and West Germany each paying 40 per cent of the costs and the remaining European powers 20 per cent. An MLF treaty was to be signed by the end of 1964.[17]

Great Britain and France made it clear that they would go to extreme lengths to oppose the project. This led President Johnson to toy with the idea of a bilateral American–German MLF, and to appoint, on November 1, 1964, a committee under the chairmanship of former Deputy Secretary of Defense, Rosswell Gilpatrick, to examine the relative priorities of the MLF as against an NPT. The Gilpatrick Committee reported in favour of an NPT on January 21, 1965. The publicity with which President Johnson received this report and his subsequent statement on the dangers of proliferation suggested that he had adopted the arms-control view of the need for an NPT and already saw it as a possible means of achieving a better understanding with the Soviet Union.[18]

The committee's curious assumption, apparently shared by the President, that opposition to the MLF had to be equated with support for an NPT can only be explained by the pervasiveness of arms-control thinking and ACDA's support for an NPT as a means by which to increase its bureaucratic influence. Because American policy was cast in terms of a dichotomy between the MLF and the NPT, the Gilpatrick Committee was bound to suggest provisional backing for an NPT, given the MLF's manifest defects. Western European and Soviet opposition to the MLF were also equated with support for an NPT.

In fact, the issue of nuclear sharing in NATO had always been quite separate from that of sharing within the framework of U.S. planning for the defence of Western Europe. In June 1965, discussions on NATO nuclear planning led to the creation of the McNamara Committee, which was formally constituted as the Nuclear Planning Group (NPG) in December 1966. This indicated that by early 1965 President Johnson had withdrawn even his internal support for the MLF.[19] He and the Gilpatrick Committee had been influenced by the Deutsch study, commissioned by ACDA, in which it was confirmed that the West German government had no desire to manufacture nuclear weapons, but would go along with any U.S. proposals which, like the MLF, would lessen West Germany's perceived insecurity.[20] This study also reinforced the arms-control view that the United States had to choose between the MLF and the NPT. But although the United States seriously explored the possibilities for an NPT for the first time in 1965, its government was less committed to the NPT than the arms controllers wished and later suggested. The subsequent over-commitment of the United States to securing an arms-control NPT partly resulted from the energetic and skilful campaign by ACDA Director William C. Foster and his deputy, Adrian Fisher, to translate the Gilpatrick Committee's provisional encouragement of the NPT into a presidential endorsement. This was finally achieved in mid-1966.

The Arms-Limitation Reaction to the Arms-Control NPT

The Soviet Union parallelled these shifts in U.S. policy by adopting the NPT in order to prevent greater West German access to nuclear weapons. This purely negative objective was achieved by mid-1965, with the MLF's destruction. The influence of Soviet policy was important, however, only in so far as its apparent support for an NPT reinforced the arms controllers who were opposed to the MLF. From mid-1965 to mid-1966, Soviet attempts to remove the NPG as a condition for its acceptance of the NPT failed. However, the political leadership in both the United States and the Soviet Union came increasingly to see the NPT as a suitable instrument for extending the policy of detente through nominal arms control. Therefore, from October 1966 onwards the NPT became a dual-purpose instrument, serving quite different purposes for each of the two superpowers. For the Soviets, its primary purpose was the establishment of an explicitly bilateral detente with the United States. The securing of controls over West German nuclear activities was an incidental benefit that became less important after Chancellor Brandt's election in 1969. Controlling West Germany's catalytic potential and improving relations with the United States had been the central aims of political arms control since 1958; there was, consequently, an essential continuity in Soviet policy, from its opposition to, successively, two-key nuclear weapons, the MLF, and the NPG, to its support for an NPT as a political instrument. For the United States, on the other hand, the NPT was an instrument of technical arms control and a means of furthering detente. The political defects in technical-arms-control thinking were shown by the Johnson administration's inability to resolve the contradictions between the arms-control and detente objectives of the NPT. If it was an arms-control measure, it would require active Soviet co-operation in its enforcement and involve heavy diplomatic costs in terms of U.S. relations with its allies. A political-arms-control NPT symbolizing superpower detente needed only to meet the Soviet Union's minimum requirements for restraints on West Germany and to provide a system of controls over fissionable materials that would marginally inhibit proliferation. This was what the 1968 NPT did in practice. However, American attempts to make it work as an instrument of arms control served only to alienate the Western Europeans, who saw in the nominally technical issue of safeguards a political indicator of how far the United States was prepared to sacrifice European political interests in order to enforce an arms-control measure that was aimed at furthering a bilateral superpower detente. Similarly, American influence in India was still further reduced by U.S. attempts to secure Indian signature to the NPT, because India was determined to assert its political independence and improve its strategic position, making it impossible for it to sign the NPT.

Because the NPT provides the most detailed evidence for the effectiveness of political arms control (in contrast to the failure of arms control proper), the succeeding chapters will show how, during the NPT's negotiation, the central dichotomy between political and technical arms control enabled the Soviets to obtain their objectives. The United States failed to obtain an effective NPT, but this was probably an impossibility under any circumstances. The Americans were also relatively unsuccessful in implementing even the NPT's limited restraints on proliferation. This technical failure was in sharp contrast with the treaty's political success in extending the superpower detente, which in turn made possible the 1972 SALT I agreements.

12   The NPT:
The Basic Superpower Bargain

It was clear to all, except its technical-arms-control advocates, that the Non-Proliferation Treaty (NPT) represented the Americans' unconscious adoption of political arms control. During the period from April 1965 to October 1966, the basis of the superpower bargain was laid. The United States would drop the Multilateral Nuclear Force (MLF) in exchange for the Soviet Union's nominal adherence to a global NPT that would be couched in arms-control terms. In return, the Soviet Union accepted, albeit reluctantly, West German participation in NATO's two-key (double-veto) nuclear delivery system and in the new Nuclear Planning Group (NPG). Once the Gilpatrick Committee had suggested that an NPT might be given priority over the MLF, an arms-control modality (the NPT) became the best available vehicle for the political-arms-control objective of preventing greater West German access to nuclear weapons. The Soviet Union pursued this aim to the point of threatening the NPT, but never beyond, until President Johnson recognized, in October 1966, that the treaty's real importance was in the promotion of superpower detente, not arms control, although these two strands in American policy continued to conflict.

The universalist American arms-control approach to preventing proliferation meant that, in the Soviet and eventually also the U.S. view, securing an NPT involved the sacrifice of particularist objectives in Western Europe. The Soviet Union had to accept the NPG, while the United States sacrificed the MLF, and both experienced a sharp deterioration in their relations with their respective allies in Eastern and Western Europe. Ironically, these political costs were unnecessary in the case of the United States and West Germany because their underlying security interests remained effectively identical. But the modalities through which these interests were expressed and implemented were bound to create conflict, as with Mutual and Balanced Force Reductions (MBFR). Arms controllers tended to concentrate on the technical details of possible arrangements for an inspection system for the NPT, or, for example, reductions, unilaterally by the United States, or through the SALT and/or MBFR negotiations, in their Forward-Based

Systems (FBS) — for delivering tactical nuclear weapons in Europe — without fully realizing their political implications. In the West German view, this seemed to reduce the importance that the United States placed on preserving West German interests in U.S.–U.S.S.R. negotiations. This distinction between substantive interests and the modalities of their expression was the main cause of strained relations between the United States and its allies during the NPT negotiations. It explained many of the difficulties that were encountered by the United States and the Soviet Union in transforming their relatively straightforward political interests in bilateral detente into an NPT.

The pattern of negotiations was characteristic of those which led to nominal arms-control agreements and, as usual, their real significance was political. The United States and the Soviet Union argued their respective cases from quite different premises, put forward irreconcilable drafts, engaged in acrimonious restatements of their positions, but finally agreed to a compromise which gave each side its overriding objective of political accord within the framework of an agreement that was capable of interpretation as arms control.The Soviet request of March 31, 1965, that the U.N. Disarmament Commission (comprising all members of the U.N. General Assembly) be convened, therefore indicated an interest in exploring the new possibilities for an NPT opened up by the Gilpatrick Committee's report. Because the commission was usually used for general discussions, the Soviet signal that they wanted it for serious negotiations (for political arms control) with the United States was clear and clearly understood. The United States quickly proposed a draft NPT to the commission's successor, the ENDC, on August 17, 1965.[1] The Soviets, however, foreshadowing their tactics in SALT of making unreasonable demands, rejected this draft in an attempt to bar even West German participation in the emerging Nuclear Planning Group (NPG), creating an impasse in negotiations until March 1966.

The negotiations on the NPT involved two parallel exchanges. The first and simplest dealt with transforming into treaty form an agreement similar to that of the Irish Resolution, whereby nuclear-weapons states would promise not to disseminate, and non-nuclear-weapons states not to acquire, nuclear weapons. The second exchange involved defining control over, or access to, nuclear weapons in such a way as to reassure the Soviet Union that the United States would not surrender its veto over the use of any nuclear weapons that it supplied to its allies, and to convince the Western Europeans that such an agreement would not interfere with consultation on the deployment and use of these weapons within NATO. Accordingly, the NPT that was signed on July 1, 1968, embodied a series of interrelated bargains; it improved the superpowers' political relations, and implemented both the technical-arms-control objective of limiting proliferation and the political-arms-control aim of non-dissemination to West Germany, even allowing for any "dissemination" connected with its role in NATO's nuclear planning. This was, of course, the dissemination of information on nuclear-weapons technology, strategy, and delivery systems.

The Question of West German Access to Nuclear Weapons

West Germany's role had been made an issue by the Soviets in an attempt both to reverse the trend in U.S. dissemination policy of giving West Germany access to two-key nuclear weapons and to undercut Bonn's influence in Washington. The latter was already weakened by the collapse of the MLF proposal that West Germany had supported largely out of loyalty to the United States. Such a reduction in the influence of America's staunchest ally and also the greatest military power in NATO, whose political influence was being felt increasingly in Eastern Europe, would have greatly benefited the Soviets by emphasizing just how bilateral the detente embodied in the NPT was. They failed to secure their objectives because these were probably unobtainable without threatening the basis of the U.S.–F.G.R. alliance, and were irrelevant to the arms-control concerns which motivated U.S. policy on the NPT.

With its amendments of March 25, 1966,[2] to its original draft NPT, the United States had gone as far to meet Soviet fears of proliferation, especially of dissemination to West Germany within NATO, as was compatible with its arrangements for the supply of nuclear weapons under American veto, training, and planning for their use. The nature and technical adequacy of the U.S. veto was clearly spelt out,[3] as was its declaratory policy on the non-dissemination of nuclear weapons to states without the substantial independent nuclear-weapons capability that was required for American assistance under the 1958 amendments to the MacMahon Act. Previous criticisms of the American failure to appreciate Soviet concerns over West German access to nuclear weapons notwithstanding, March 1966 marked a turning point. The Soviet Union could no longer claim that West Germany was a military threat, as was privately admitted by its diplomats. With the MLF removed, the role of tactical nuclear weapons in deterring a Soviet attack on Europe would assume an increasingly important psychological, as well as strategic, role in reassuring the Europeans of their security. Any request that these arrangements be modified would have the same detrimental political effect in the West as the Soviet schemes for denuclearization in the late 1950s. Moreover, the West German government, after the election of the Grand Coalition that was formed on December

1, 1966, was very different from the Adenauer–Strauss regime that ruled at the height of the confrontation over West Berlin. Under Chancellor Kiesinger (who had succeeded Erhard a year earlier) and Foreign Minister Willy Brandt, West Germany moved towards an acceptance of the status quo in Eastern Europe that came with the 1972 ratification of the 1970 treaties with Soviet Russia and Poland and the November agreement with East Germany. The *Ostpolitik* might pose new political difficulties for the Soviet government but these lay in the ideological, economic, and political rather than the strategic spheres. Therefore, far from being interested in controlling proliferation through the NPT, the Soviets remained largely indifferent to this issue. Rather, they used the treaty to attack NATO, and thereby foreshadowed their campaign for a European Security Conference. The arms controllers' commitment to an NPT forced them to persist with it, despite its divisive effects, unless the Soviets pressed so hard as to threaten the NPT's withdrawal.

From April to August 1966, Ambassador Roschin attacked the amended draft for leaving open the possibility that a nuclear-weapons state (the United States) could transfer such weapons to a non-nuclear-weapons state (West Germany), provided that the transferer (the United States) retained its veto. By the end of July, Roschin was insisting on the need to embody a non-transfer commitment in the NPT. This was largely a semantic issue, disguising a political attack, since the U.S. draft covered this issue. In fact, the final joint draft of August 24, 1967, applied the non-transfer commitment only "to any recipient whatsoever"[4] instead of the more explicit "transfer into the national control of any non-nuclear State, either directly or indirectly, through a military organization" (Article I (1) of the U.S. 1965 draft).[5] The marginal growth in the restrictions against the increasingly hypothetical possibilities contained in the European option so vigorously attacked by Roschin could hardly have been the real justification for his prolonged delaying tactics.

The real causes were those outlined above and, with the most favourable interpretation, a genuine Soviet difficulty in grasping the implications of the NPG. The Soviet leaders' reluctance to commit themselves to an NPT followed from the treaty's inability to give them more than they had already secured. Its negative aspects, in dividing Western Europe and the United States, in attacking West Germany, and in halting the MLF were clear. The positive aspects involved accepting the deposed Khrushchev's concept of political arms control as the preferred instrument for strengthening superpower relations. It was also increasingly evident that, whatever the Johnson administration's interest in arms control, it could not tolerate further Soviet anti-German and anti-NATO propaganda without any sign of progress on an NPT.[6]

The first indication of changing Soviet attitudes came at the International Atomic Energy Agency's (IAEA) Tenth General Conference, from September 22 to September 28, 1966. When the Polish and Czechoslovakian delegates offered to put their nuclear installations under agency safeguards if West Germany followed suit on the opening day of the conference, East Germany had made a similar offer, and all of these were endorsed by the Soviet Union.[7] On October 10, Foreign Minister Gromyko visited Washington for the customary discussions with the Secretary of State prior to the U.N. General Assembly. They laid out their respective positions on the NPT, and apparently Mr. Gromyko had been authorized to indicate Soviet acceptance of NATO's nuclear arrangements if that was necessary to effect agreement, since both then had a long discussion with the President. From his subsequent comments, President Johnson seems to have viewed the NPT as a keystone in the new policy of bridge building that he had announced three days earlier.[8] This explains Mr. Gromyko's optimistic statement after the meeting that indicated an NPT was in sight.

The Soviets had secured final abandonment of the MLF concept of nuclear sharing, in return for reluctant acquiescence in West Germany's continuing to receive U.S. nuclear weapons (with a presidential veto on their use), while still participating in the NPG. The European clause that was inserted in the first U.S. draft NPT in order to placate the West German government was likewise dropped in the final version, although the Soviet Union did not object to a unilateral U.S. interpretation that the NPT would:

... not bar succession by a new federated European state to the nuclear status of one of its former components. ... While not dealing with succession by such a federated state, the treaty (NPT) would bar transfer of nuclear weapons (including ownership) or control over them to any recipient, including a multilateral entity.[9]

Safeguards on commercial nuclear activities were seen by the Soviet Union as a necessary part of an anti-West German non-dissemination agreement. They became symbolic of the divergence between the United States and its Western European allies because of Soviet pressure to impose more stringent restraints on what it described as self-inspection of West German nuclear installations by the European Atomic Energy Community (EURATOM), of which West Germany was a member. Technically, there were no insurmountable obstacles to EURATOM's inspection being supervised by the IAEA; although negotiation of the necessary ageements inevitably took a long time, they were finally concluded in 1974. Here again, ACDA arms controllers' blindness to the political implications of pressing for rapid agreement in

1966-67 on how safeguards were to be negotiated, and their insistence on rapid progress in the negotiations after the NPT was signed in 1968 served only to emphasize to the Western Europeans the extent to which the NPT had come to symbolize superpower detente at the expense of lesser powers. The changing importance that came to be attached to the issues of West German access to nuclear weapons, safeguards, and non-proliferation was reflected in the negotiations on the NPT from 1965 to 1968.

13 Initial Negotiations over West German Participation in Nuclear Planning: 1965-66

During the first stage of the Non-Proliferation Treaty (NPT) negotiations, from February 1965 to October 1966, the arms-control requirement for an NPT which did not rule out a revival of the Multilateral Nuclear Force (MLF) diverged completely from the political-arms-control aim of limiting West German access to nuclear weapons. Paradoxically, the major source of confusion was the question, raised by the MLF, of the distinction between the control of nuclear weapons, in the English sense of physical possession of the weapons and the independent ability to fire them, and contrôle, the French term, meaning access to, and participation in, planning and policy making. In this case it meant contrôle of NATO strategy, especially nuclear strategy,[1] where the United States was still keeping its NATO allies very much in the dark. The Soviet Union thought West Germany was seeking, and could obtain, control through the MLF, whereas in fact it sought only contrôle. The Soviet Union lumped the two together under the term "access" to nuclear weapons, which it never defined. This explained the confusion between the two separate, albeit interrelated, questions of U.S. dissemination policy vis-à-vis West Germany, and the attempts to secure superpower agreement on resolving this issue through the modality of an NPT, a measure that was only nominally aimed at preventing proliferation. The Soviet objective of limiting the undesirable political effects of specific weapons deployment was reconciled with requirements of arms control once the United States had defined its concept of control as precluding an independent West German ability to fire American nuclear weapons.

The 1965 NPT Drafts: Political versus Technical Arms Control

In 1965 Soviet support for an NPT represented an extension of its 1964 attempts to use an NPT to stop the MLF, but this time in the changed climate that had been created by the Western European opposition to the MLF and the resultant Gilpatrick Committee's report. At the U.N.

Disarmament Commission meeting (April 26 – June 15), the Soviets sought an NPT that would ban West German participation in an MLF or in the NATO nuclear-planning committee that had been established on May 31. They emphasized that an NPT must be comprehensive, banning access both directly, through the acquisition of national control over nuclear weapons, and indirectly, by way of participation in their control through military alliances.[2]

The United States was moving in a quite different direction, towards an arms-control agreement similar to that of the 1961 Irish Resolution. This involved promises by the nuclear-weapons powers not to give, and the non-nuclear-weapons powers not to acquire, nuclear-weapons technology, as well as IAEA controls on commercial nuclear activities.[3] Although the Soviet and American viewpoints were still irreconcilable, the Arms Control and Disarmament Agency (ACDA) used the Soviet support for an NPT to commit the United States to giving a limited NPT priority over Allied cohesion via ACDA Director Foster's article in the July edition of *Foreign Affairs*.[4] Although he argued that such an NPT was not incompatible with an MLF or an Atlantic Nuclear Force (ANF) and would indeed depend on Soviet willingness to accept these in exchange for an NPT aimed against China, the Soviets were aware that this meant that they could secure the demise of the MLF if they made its removal a precondition for an NPT. Accordingly, they suddenly requested a quick Eighteen Nation Disarmament Conference (ENDC) meeting that lasted from July 27 to September 6. With Great Britain and Canada preparing to table drafts for an NPT, the United States had to commit itself, and embodied their drafts in its draft of August 17,[5] which amounted to a limited NPT that was modelled on the Irish Resolution. Thus Soviet diplomacy had substantially strengthened the arms controllers in ACDA against the MLF's protagonists in the State Department and left the question of U.S. support for an NPT open.

The three issues that the U.S. draft left open were the European clause, safeguards, and indirect access to nuclear weapons. The Soviets regarded the first as removable given the demise of the MLF, and the second as solvable once agreement could be reached on the third. The contradictory Soviet positions on the Nuclear Planning Group (NPG) reflected their commitment to the NPT as an anti-West German measure, rather than as an anti-proliferation device. Although the NPG was clearly the substitute for the MLF, and one which enabled the United States to give precedence to the NPT, the Soviets appeared prepared to accept the NPG as compatible with the NPT only as long as the alternative was a lowering of the treaty's priority in U.S. policy, and a resurgence of the MLF. Once the NPT had helped defeat the MLF, the Soviets tried to use the treaty to exclude West German access to nuclear weapons under the two-key system and any dissemination of information on nuclear weapons via the NPG. Their attacks continued until they threatened the NPT itself, at which time they were temporarily modified. This explains why the Soviets denounced the NPG in 1965, accepted it privately after the U.S. draft NPT was tabled, but then for the next year insisted that it was, after all, unacceptable. This issue was not resolved until October 1966 when the United States indicated that its terms for the NPT as they stood were final.

The Soviet draft NPT that was tabled on September 24, 1965[6] reflected both their objective of preventing nuclear sharing in NATO and their lack of concern with the broader U.S. concept of proliferation.[7] But this draft did mark a definite shift from the denuclearization and Atom-Free Zone (AFZ) approaches that had been used from 1957 onwards, to one of non-proliferation as a means for containing West German access to nuclear weapons, its political influence in the Western alliance, and the alliance's political cohesion and military effectiveness.

The Politics of Arms Control in Washington

These negotiations need to be related to the internal bureaucratic debate in Washington, where ACDA was attempting to convert the Gilpatrick Committee's provisional endorsement of an NPT into a case for an arms-control NPT as a major objective of U.S. foreign policy. The nuclear-sharing problem was first dealt with through the McNamara Committee, and later the NPG. This involved convincing the President and the European governments that an MLF could not further Allied cohesion, whereas an NPG would, in return for which the Europeans would support, or accept, an NPT and associated safeguards, at least in the interests of their security, if not for arms-control reasons. Persuading the Soviets to enter into substantive negotiations could also demonstrate the treaty's potential for reversing the deterioration in superpower relations. This depended on whether or not the Soviet Union could be convinced that the MLF would be dropped if, and only if, it accepted the NPG and NATO's existing nuclear-sharing arrangements, as well as a nominal commitment to non-proliferation. Ultimately, the arms-control features of an NPT were, in large measure, surrendered in order to secure the political accord that had become the objective of political arms control. Both superpowers subsumed their original aims as these became demonstrably unrealizable. Reluctantly, the Soviet Union came to accept that it could no more stop all West German access to nuclear weapons than the United States could halt India's development of a nuclear option. Both the Soviet Union and the United States realized that these limits to their influence gave increased value to any framework that would inhibit the form of proliferation to which they objected. This realization served to strengthen their agreement not to let this adversely affect their political relations. Until mid-1966, the Soviet Union persisted in her attempts to secure West Germany's exclusion from nuclear planning while support for the treaty was built up in Washington to assuage fears of the MLF's resurrection. Soviet moves towards accepting an NPT for these purposes were evident in September 1966, and this made possible the furtherance of bilateral detente with Mr. Gromyko's meeting with President Johnson and Secretary Rusk in October.

The Soviets also had before them a negotiable NPT in the form of the U.S. amendments of March 25, 1966,[8] which defined the concept of non-dissemination in a manner that was acceptable to the Soviet Union. The resultant revised draft NPT was still couched in arms-control terms, since the spring Senate hearings on the Pastore Resolution[9] in support of the NPT had enabled ACDA to expound the arms-control case for an NPT to the point where it became accepted American policy. Paradoxically, the NPT had in fact become an instrument of detente rather than one of arms control, as was evident from the succeeding negotiations from 1966 until its entry into force in 1970.

14 The Re-emergence of Superpower Detente through Political Arms Control and the Resultant Political Problems: 1966-70

President Johnson's acceptance of the Non-Proliferation Treaty (NPT) as an instrument both of arms control and of detente created some problems. It accentuated the U.S. difficulties in dealing with the consequent political opposition from its NATO allies to the proposed safeguards system and caused a resurgence in Soviet fears of West Germany, but in the context of safeguards rather than in that of access to nuclear weapons. The resolution of these difficulties took from November 1966 to November 1967, which delayed the final negotiations on the NPT and its signature until July 1, 1968. The Soviets' subsequent August 21 invasion of Czechoslovakia, although probably inevitable, was facilitated both by the political understanding that was embodied in the NPT and by Soviet acceptance of preliminary meetings to the Strategic Arms Limitation Talks (SALT), which were to be inaugurated by a September 30 Summit meeting between President Johnson and Messrs. Brezhnev and Kosygin. After August 21, 1968 the absence of a coherent political framework in arms-control thinking was demonstrated by the Johnson administration's unsuccessful efforts to reconcile reassurance of their NATO allies with attempting to persuade them to sign the NPT. Essentially, President Johnson seemed to believe, or to accept his advisors' belief, that the substantive corpus of arms-control literature was a body of knowledge from which measures of detente could be drawn and implemented without undue difficulty.

In 1966, the issue of safeguards over supplies of fissionable material was regarded by arms controllers as purely technical. They were, thus, unable to cope with European opposition in the October NPT negotiations to the over-emphasis on superpower detente at the expense of inter-Allied and intra-European relations. The arms controllers exacerbated the confusion between technical modalities and their political

objectives by trying to answer what were essentially political objections couched by the Europeans in technical terms as if they were
simply technical queries. This exasperated the Europeans, as well as
the Japanese and Indians, and confused the Soviets, who had always
viewed the NPT from the political-arms-control viewpoint and therefore
assumed the Americans realized that the basic issues were political.
This political view of the NPT and SALT was shared by the United States
from 1969 onwards, since President Nixon and his Special Advisor on
National Security (and later Secretary of State), Dr. Henry A. Kissinger,
recognized the need to balance the political and technical factors in
arms control in order to position it nearer to the political-arms-control
approach. The Nixon administration distinguished between the political and technical aspects of the NPT by trying to secure West German
signature and Soviet agreement to start SALT, which would ensure that
both countries' anxieties were dealt with in a suitable manner.

After October 1966, progress on the NPT fell into four main phases.
For a year, until November 1967, the members of the European Atomic
Energy Community (EURATOM) — that is, Belgium, Luxembourg,
France, Italy, the Netherlands, and West Germany — successfully
fought for a safeguards agreement that would preserve EURATOM as a
symbol of their political interests and protect the same against those of
the superpowers. From then until July 1, 1968, the United States and
the Soviet Union were preoccupied with transforming the resultant
agreement into treaty language in preparation for signature, and with
the Summit that would launch SALT to secure their bilateral detente.
Soviet Russia's invasion of Czechoslovakia on August 20, 1968, confirmed the fundamentals of this detente, but made it inadvisable for
these to be made too explicit. At the same time, U.S. arms controllers
were pressing for the NPT's signature, regardless of political consequences, from September to December 1968. During the next fifteen
months, the Nixon administration differentiated between the technical
and political aspects of the NPT, but recognized their interrelationship
and thereby secured reluctant Western European acquiescence in a
superpower detente. Additionally, the election of Willy Brandt's
SPD–FDP coalition government in West Germany in September 1969
changed the political context of Soviet–West German relations, in that
it lessened the Soviet concern to secure an NPT that would control West
Germany.

The Political Implications of Nuclear Safeguards, October 1966 – November 1967

After the October 1966 meeting between President Johnson, Secretary
Rusk, and Soviet Foreign Minister Gromyko, the superpowers were

basically agreed on the need for, and the nature of, an NPT; therefore, the subsequent success of the bilateral negotiations on the NPT was hardly surprising. The by then familiar situation of both powers working for what was nominally an arms-control agreement but really a largely symbolic instrument of political accord produced relatively rapid progress, considering the much greater complexity of the NPT compared to earlier agreements. This parallelled the growing complexity of the superpower relationship, just as the treaty's mixed reception exemplified the problems of implementing bi-polar co-operation in a multi-polar world. Discussions between Ambassadors Roschin and Fisher at the U.N. in the Fall led to the settlement of the remaining differences of detail and the preparation of new draft-treaty language. The superpower co-operation was evident in the absence of Soviet attacks on the Multilateral Nuclear Force (MLF), Atlantic Nuclear Force (ANF), or Nuclear Planning Group (NPG) in the 1967 Eighteen Nation Disarmament Conference (ENDC) sessions which led to the U.S.–U.S.S.R. draft NPT of August 24.[1]

But once the NPT had become primarily a political instrument, the safeguards issue became symbolic of the political differences between EURATOM's members and the United States. This was not to deny the commercial importance of safeguards, but rather to emphasize that economic considerations were secondary to, although used as a cloak for, a political dispute. The European Economic Community members were determined to preserve EURATOM, not for its negligible contribution to nuclear research, but because it, and its inspection system, represented part of the community structure and therefore the rights of medium and small powers to state the conditions under which their nuclear activities would be inspected for the convenience of the superpowers. The U.S. arms controllers, thinking in terms of mutual reassurance against proliferation wherever it was technically possible, had difficulty in grasping this political argument. The Soviet Union understandably concentrated on inspecting West Germany, but refused to follow the example of the United States and Great Britain in offering on December 2 and December 4, 1967, to place their non-military nuclear activities under International Atomic Energy Agency (IAEA) inspection.[2] The Soviets were not concerned that the removal of EURATOM inspection would leave France's peaceful nuclear installations uninspected, since France, both under and after de Gaulle, could be expected to share their opposition to West German nuclear weapons. European opposition to Soviet bullying and U.S. pressure was such that it was not until November 2, 1967, that the North Atlantic Council reluctantly agreed to a revised compromise draft as the basis for negotiations, over a year after the Gromyko–Johnson agreement-in-principle on an NPT.

The Soviets delayed acceptance of this draft until the ENDC reconvened on January 18, 1968. They required two months to be convinced that, in order to obtain their essential aim of inspection by the IAEA, they must accept EURATOM as its agent.[3] The resultant Article III on safeguards was incorporated unaltered in the final treaty,[4] and its convoluted language reflects the uneasy compromise that it embodied. The EURATOM problem was dealt with by American insistence that it would interpret Article III in such a way as to permit EURATOM's continued operation under an agreement whereby the IAEA would double-check EURATOM's auditing of fissionable materials.[5]

Thus, Article III met the needs of the Soviet Union and of EURATOM. Its members' first round of negotiations with the IAEA proceeded satisfactorily in the summer of 1970, after the Soviet Union, as part of its more conciliatory German policy, assured the U.S. government that the NPT would in no way be interpreted as inhibiting West German development of peaceful nuclear technology.[6] This Soviet concession also resulted from EURATOM's insistence on withholding ratification of the NPT until satisfactory safeguards were negotiated, Japan's insistence on equally favourable terms before it ratified the treaty, and the Nixon administration's unwillingness to oppose this stand. The establishment of a U.K.–F.G.R.–Netherlands consortium on March 21, 1969, for the purpose of manufacturing uranium 235 (the crucial element in triggering a thermonuclear explosion) via the gas-centrifuge method reminded the Soviets of the problems that are created by technical changes that favour proliferation, at a time when a resumption of their aggressive tactics towards Germany would have been counter-productive.

The subsequent slow pace of the EURATOM–IAEA negotiations which began in November 1971 resulted from a combination of obstruction by France for political reasons and the complexity of the issues involved.[7] The technical difficulties of effective but non-intrusive inspection had been underestimated by the arms controllers. The essentially political nature of the NPT was underlined by the Soviet Union's failure to react to the U.S. announcement on March 5, 1972, that it proposed to continue supplying fissionable materials for peaceful purposes after the expiry of the NPT deadline for the conclusion of the EURATOM–IAEA negotiations.[8] The U.S. argued that agreement might reasonably be expected in 1973, so that halting fuel supplies, the only sanction for non-compliance with the NPT, would militate against securing safeguards. Putting too much pressure on EURATOM's members would make them less rather than more willing to conclude a safeguards agreement with the IAEA.

Arms Control as a Political Instrument, 1968-70

The NPT's role as a barometer of superpower relations was indicated by Mr. Gromyko's acceptance of the long-standing U.S. invitation to SALT on June 27, only a few days before signature of a treaty that was intended, in the Soviet view, to recognize its strategic and political parity with the United States. The impending Summit conference between President Johnson and Premier Kosygin, which was to be announced on August 21, demonstrated the NPT's success in creating a deceptive climate of detente, despite the Soviets' cautious insistence that the NPT must be signed before SALT started. Their attitude typified their cautious, conservative approach to both sets of negotiations, a caution contrasting sharply with the sense of urgency felt by the U.S. technical arms controllers. They wanted to halt potentially destabilizing proliferation and new strategic weapons that were emerging, notably Multiple Independently Targetable Re-Entry Vehicles (MIRV) and Anti-Ballistic Missile (ABM) systems, whilst there was still time to do so. The Russians did not wish this, and so could use the NPT and SALT for political arms control.[9]

The Soviet Union's invasion of Czechoslovakia on August 20, and the consequent collapse of the Summit conference, together with the reassessment of Soviet intentions by the United States and Western Europeans, created a new set of uncertainties in American arms-control policy. Soviet suspicions of West Germany also revived, although expressions of these could be largely discounted as attempts to shift attention away from the real cause of the invasion, namely the Soviet Union's fear of political change in Eastern Europe. Progress towards Western European signature and ratification of the NPT came to be seen by the Soviet Union as evidence of the priority that the United States assigned to arms control, and therefore of the extent to which this could be manipulated to serve Soviet political interests. This also gave the Soviet Union some base from which to measure the relative importance that it should attach to relations between the United States and its allies and to those between the United States and the Soviet Union. The Johnson administration had placed its major emphasis on arms control at the expense of relations with Western Europe during the NPT negotiations because these were thought to strengthen detente. This in turn suggested that the United States might be prepared to accept Soviet arguments in SALT for cutting back on Forward-Based Systems (FBS) that could reach the Soviet Union. Other Soviet motives for agreeing to SALT in 1968 probably included: attempting to restrict U.S. development and deployment of new strategic-weapons systems (notably MIRV and ABM, plus the Underwater Long-Range Missile System — ULMS, later renamed, confusingly, the Trident missile and the Trident submarine — and the B-1 bomber); exploiting the increasing internal criticism of the U.S. military; and further dividing the United States from its allies by increasing the difference between detente for the superpowers and detente in Europe. Once the United States and the Soviet Union had signed the NPT, the crucial issue for the Soviets became the way in which the United States tried to secure the signatures and concessions that they were prepared to demand from West Germany in return for Soviet ratification. While their view of SALT was influenced by the NPT, the Soviets also attempted to use their acceptance of a definite date for talks as a means of persuading the United States to implement the political-arms-control NPT, that is, one that would control West Germany's nuclear activities and strengthen superpower relations while affecting proliferation only incidentally.

Arms Control After Czechoslovakia, August–December 1968

The inherent contradictions between the technical emphasis and the political implications of arms control were at their height during this period. On September 26, 1968, the Senate Committee on Foreign Relations' report on the NPT[10] recommended — by a vote of only seventeen to thirteen, with three abstentions — that the Senate give its advice and consent to ratification. The reservations emphasized the political implications of the way in which the modalities of the NPT's signature were handled. The report noted that:

. . . several members took the position that, while they supported the treaty, they believed the Committee should defer final consideration until January because of the Soviet behavior. Weighted against this . . . was the prevailing view that . . . the treaty . . . is of such significance as a potential barrier to proliferation that any delay in taking final Committee action was inadvisable.[11]

The minority view stressed that their objections "concern both the substance of the treaty and its relationship to the tragic events in Czechoslovakia."[12] Furthermore, "other countries have indicated their belief that this is not an opportune time even to sign the treaty. It seems to the undersigned that this is an even less opportune time for us to take an even more final step and consent to the treaty's ratification."[13]

These reservations accurately reflected the fears of the United States' allies, especially in Europe, and showed a greater grasp of political reality than the administration, whose policy clearly demonstrated the influence of the assumption in arms-control theory that such measures could be divorced from the political environment. On October 6, Secretary of State Rusk recognized that the general atmosphere must be satisfactory if SALT were to succeed, but his Undersecretary, Katzenbach, was telling the Assembly of the Western European Union (WEU) only ten days later that the dialogue with the Soviet Union must continue in spite of Czechoslovakia, presumably through SALT. However, in the same month, Mr. Katzenbach was also in Yugoslavia, apparently discussing possible co-ordination of defence against Soviet attack.[14] The ever-present divergence between the requirements of arms control and diplomacy reached its height in this context at the NATO ministerial meeting of November 15-16 (brought forward from December).[15] Apart from marginal military changes, its declaration stated that "any Soviet intervention directly affecting the situation in Europe or the Mediterranean would create an international crisis with grave consequences."[16] The language, reminiscent of that of the Cold War, reflected Dean Rusk's reported remarks to a private group on November 15 that a Soviet attack against Austria, Yugoslavia, or Rumania would be a direct threat to Western security.[17]

However, a few weeks earlier, Arms Control and Disarmament Agency (ACDA) Director Foster had stressed that Czechoslovakia must not halt progress on the NPT or SALT.[18] He thereby revealed how a commitment to what the Americans perceived as a needed arms-control measure could lead to a certain insensitiveness on their part to the psychological and political reactions of their allies. This sort of callousness had characterized the NPT negotiations. In former Secretary of Defense McNamara's discussions of November 11 with Premier Kosygin,[19] he repeated his views of the arms race as an action-reaction phenomenon, by emphasizing the importance of a quick freeze on Anti-Ballistic Missiles (ABM) to enable the United States to slow down development of its MIRV, the flight testing of which had begun that June.[20] The Soviet Union expressed agreement with the need for speedy progress on the NPT, but offered no substantive concessions because it preferred to attack West Germany at the U.N. While the Soviet Union sought to erase the memory of Czechoslovakia and its previous disinterest in SALT by pressing for these, the United States adopted an extremely defensive stance, apparently because it was unwilling to attack the Soviet Union too severely for fear of jeopardizing SALT. This U.S. reluctance to criticize the Soviet invasion of Czechoslovakia was all the more odd, because if, in fact, the Soviet Union wanted SALT to start as quickly as it said it did, then this would put the United States in an advantageous bargaining position from which to condemn the invasion without threatening SALT.[21] This suggested that they had misunderstood the Soviet approach and that the arms controllers were anxious, after President Nixon's election victory on November 21, not to offer any hostages to an administration that was likely to be less favourable to their views than Johnson's. For the arms controllers, Allied objections were less important than the NPT's entry into force and the start of SALT before the diplomatic momentum that had been so painfully acquired on arms control was lost. Therefore it was pointless to jeopardize the agreements — which in the arms-control view were essential to the long-run security of all states — for the sake of limited U.S. action that would not reverse the Soviet occupation of Czechoslovakia, abhorrent though it might be. This argument was valid only if preventing proliferation was the overriding objective of U.S. policy and generally accepted as desirable by other states. SALT certainly added to the problems within the Alliance by bringing out fears of a superpower condominium, the unresolved dilemma of arms-control policy.

After August 20, 1968, the basic dichotomy increased between arms control and arms limitation, even though it had apparently lessened with the NPT's signature and agreement on SALT. The Soviet Union did not see SALT as urgent because confirmation of the superpower detente had been embodied in the NPT. It could thus balance the start of SALT against other political objectives — notably securing West German adherence to the NPT and dividing the United States from its European allies by underlining the different implications of detente for the two. The Johnson administration's rejection of any linkage between arms control and politics had become excessive because of its fear of delaying the NPT. The administration urged its acceptance regardless of the deleterious effects upon the Alliance, and that ensured its failure.

The Nixon Administration's Attitude to Arms Control and the NPT's Ratification: January 1969–March 5, 1970

For the Soviets, the most important changes in American arms-control policies were those in priority and emphasis which brought them much nearer to political-arms-control policies in practice, even though they still derived from the differing assumptions of American strategic theory. But neither the new President nor Dr. Kissinger was inclined to favour arms-control agreements at the expense of Alliance cohesion. Where these agreements appeared desirable for the United States, as in SALT, they would endeavour to avoid as much friction as possible. This policy explains the extensive consultations with NATO on SALT, starting with the President's visit of March 1970, and the exclusion of FBS (for delivering tactical nuclear weapons) in Europe from the discussions, notwithstanding that SALT affected the substance as well as the atmosphere of superpower relations much more than the NPT. This awareness of the political implications of American strategic policy evident in Dr. Kissinger's writings was reflected in the more moderate assessment of the consequences of proliferation and the NPT's role in restraining it. Unfortunately, this awareness later disappeared, especially in Dr. Kissinger's handling of the SALT negotiations and agreements.

Proliferation continued to be officially regarded as, *a priori*, inimical to U.S. interests, as it might decrease U.S. ability to exercise influence over Allied powers with nuclear weapons in times of crisis. However, it was recognized that the process would be neither so rapid, so destabilizing, nor so widespread as the previous Democratic administrations had supposed. The NPT was, moreover, regarded as only a partial answer to the fundamental security problems which faced political Nth powers, the major concern of which would continue to be the evolution of the local power balances and the attitudes with which the superpowers received these. The fundamentals of American policy were laid out in President Nixon's Foreign Policy Report of February 1970[22] (in which Dr. Kissinger's influence and style were evident). These included a much greater willingness to allow most regions, with the exception of Western Europe, to reach their natural equilibrium with very limited U.S. involvement. The implication was that limited proliferation might be tolerated. With Western Europe emerging as the main focus of a foreign policy that was aimed at limiting American commitments, it was clear that the NPT's Article III safeguards would be regarded as providing a better framework for the major expansion of commercial nuclear power in the 1970s. EURATOM would be left relatively free to conduct its negotiations as it thought fit, provided that its conditions were technically reasonable. Similarly, West Germany would be encouraged, rather than pressed, to sign.[23]

This change from the frenetic urgency of the Johnson administration to a more diplomatically acceptable pace for the NPT's ratification partly reflected the departure from government office of almost all those arms controllers who had either remained from President Kennedy's era or entered subsequently. Additionally ACDA's influence was reduced through Dr. Kissinger's reorganization of the National Security Council (NSC) as the central body for determining and implementing U.S. foreign policy. Henceforth, ACDA's new director, Gerard C. Smith, had to make policy recommendations through the NSC Senior Review Group. Dr. Kissinger's insistence that papers contain packages of options, with the implications of each course of action spelt out, rather than single departmental recommendations, still further reduced ACDA's bureaucratic influence. Moreover, ACDA's institutionalization of arms-control thinking came to have much less influence. Although arms-control thinking remained part of U.S. policy, its zenith could be said to have been between 1963 and 1968, until President Jimmy Carter's 1977 administration re-installed technical arms control and arms controllers in all fields. Dr. Kissinger's approach, from 1969 to 1976, was to regard SALT as the only significant area of arms control. He argued for SALT on technical-arms-control and political grounds, while settling for political SALT agreements with no technical impact — except, adversely, on the United States. Proliferation was not regarded as an important problem in the Nixon–Kissinger administrations (1969-74), although it re-emerged as an issue in 1976, partly under the pressure of the presidential elections. The NPT was, therefore, implemented in a very different internal and external milieu from that in which it had been conceived.

It was typical of an arms-control agreement allegedly in the universal interests of all states that the U.S. government was left to obtain progress on the NPT on its own in 1969, and to incur both internal and external political costs, while the Soviet Union offered only two declaratory gestures. The Eastern European countries ratified the NPT at the rate of one per month from May to July (Hungary, May 27; Poland, June 12; Czechoslovakia, July 22). Bulgaria gave her ratification on September 5 and East Germany on October 31.[24] The Soviets also expressed a continued interest in SALT in Mr. Gromyko's address to the Supreme Soviet on July 10,[25] but otherwise displayed a studied indifference to its future as the July 31 opening deadline came and went. This was quite inconsistent with an interest in arms control[26] but accorded well with political arms control. In the summer of 1969, the United States was preparing for a Fall diplomatic campaign to secure signatures for the NPT in an uncertain climate. The first sign of political progress came in August, with the abrupt Soviet reversal of position on the Seabed Treaty to one of accepting the U.S. position that it ban only the emplacement of weapons of mass destruction and not passive detection systems, as the Soviets had previously insisted. Like the 1963 U.N. Resolution on the Peaceful Uses of Outer Space, this treaty essentially codified a superpower policy of detente and indicated that further and more substantive co-operation might be possible.

The major breakthrough on the NPT was the West German election in September and the subsequent emergence of an SPD–Free-Democrat government with Willy Brandt as Chancellor. Brandt was committed to signing the NPT as soon as the issue of peaceful nuclear development had been formally resolved, and to providing ratification following the conclusion of the EURATOM–IAEA safeguards negotiations. The Brandt government's *Ostpolitik* would also recognize the boundaries that had been established in Eastern Europe since 1945. As this had been a major objective of Soviet policy since 1945, the relative importance of the NPT in containing West Germany's political influence dropped sharply. The Soviet Union hastened to ease the new Chancellor's political difficulties with the Christian Democratic Union (CDU) opposition by providing assurances that no obstacles would be placed by the Soviet government in the way of Bonn's development of peaceful nuclear technology.[27] This had been the central political issue for West Germany in the safeguards dispute since 1966. Soviet assurance that their original aims vis-à-vis West Germany were being met led to their agreement on October 25 to participate in preliminary talks on SALT, beginning on November 17.[28] Thus the process of detente through political arms control was resumed little more than a year after the invasion of Czechoslovakia.

With joint superpower signature to their instruments of ratification of the NPT on November 24 and West Germany's signature on November 28,[29] the European aspects of the NPT could be regarded as settled. This left the problems of securing the adherence of the potential proliferators and the suppliers of uranium ore. The continued resistance to the NPT resulted from the contextual nature of the security problems that gave rise to proliferation. In other words, potential proliferators — especially India and Israel — were concerned about their own very specific security problems, and felt that the NPT's generalized structure took insufficient heed of these. Additionally, Czechoslovakia's invasion had confirmed that the NPT did not offer a joint superpower alternative means of guaranteeing the security interests of lesser powers, but that these would be disregarded where they conflicted with those of the United States and the Soviet Union. Therefore, India's (and therefore Pakistan's) refusal to sign was to be expected, as was Israel's. Only Japan's signature on February 3, 1970, could be regarded as a significant advance, although its value was reduced by the implicit reservations that were reflected in its November Defense White Paper and declared intention to follow West Germany's attitude in signing and setting conditions for ratification. Australia's signature on February 27, 1970, certainly resulted from American pressure but it too was accompanied by reservations which implied that the Australian government wished to retain the option of developing nuclear weapons in view of the unreliability of the U.S. alliance and the possibilities of utilizing a special nuclear relationship with France.[30] On the other hand, while Australia could eventually rely on indigenous fuel supplies, it would initially have to obtain both these and nuclear reactors from abroad. Therefore, its signature to (and January 23, 1973, ratification of) the NPT could be likened to Japan's, that is, as a means of legalizing the development of a technical option on nuclear weapons. South Africa and the A.B.C. Latin American group (Argentina, Brazil, and Chile) continued to refuse their signa-ture. The 1970 ratifications of Sweden (January 9), Rumania (February 4), and Yugoslavia (March 4) signified little.

When the superpowers deposited their instruments of ratification on March 5, 1970 to bring into force the NPT,[31] it seemed more than ever a symbol of superpower detente, the effects of which in inhibiting prolif-eration could not be more than marginal and would depend on de-velopments in technology and international politics over the next decade. This less sanguine view is in sharp contrast with the American optimism of July 1968, but it reflects the growing scepticism over the claims of classical arms control. The Soviet Union had by no means changed its position on these; rather the United States seemed at the time to be adopting the view of arms control as a modality for political agreement as embodied in the concept of political arms control.

15   The NPT's Success as an Instrument of Political Arms Control

The Non-Proliferation Treaty (NPT) was always an instrument of political arms control. This was evident from its inherent inability to limit proliferation more than marginally. In practice, after the American attempt to restrict proliferation via the NPT, neither the United States nor the Soviet Union seemed willing to expend its influence in order to limit proliferation. Hence, the NPT codified the existing policies of the nuclear-weapons powers, even though neither France nor China signed, and extended safeguards over fissionable materials that were to be used for commercial purposes. The latter was accomplished most notably by placing America's bilateral safeguards agreements with recipients of such materials under the supervision of the International Atomic Energy Agency (IAEA).

The superpowers' attitude towards potential Nth (nuclear) powers was exemplified by their lack of opposition to India's increasingly explicit development of a nuclear-weapons option that it clearly intended to exercise, probably during the 1970s.[1] After unsuccessfully trying to halt India's development of a weapons option by offering guarantees that lacked credibility, and then threatening the withdrawal of economic aid between about 1966 and 1968, the United States adopted a policy of reluctant acquiescence towards the Indian option. This was reflected in its 1972 acceptance of trilateral U.S.–IAEA–India safeguards against the diversion of U.S.-supplied commercial nuclear materials for military purposes. This arrangement left India free to divert other nuclear materials for such purposes and removed its only incentive to adhere to the NPT — that is, its need for nuclear fuel supplies. Additionally, the United States continued shipment of heavy water, essential for the functioning of India's nuclear reactors. The Soviet Union made no significant effort to exert its increased influence in India (symbolized by the August 1971 Soviet – Indian Treaty of Alliance) to restrain Indian development of its nuclear-weapons option. The United States, like the Soviet Union, found itself putting into operation, in a regional context, the political relationship of limited competition and co-operation that had been embodied in the NPT. The superpowers' attitude at its ratification was basically the same as that after India's 1974 nuclear test. Whilst not pleased, they recognized that they could do little to prevent the evolution of a distinctively Indian strategic posture, including its nuclear option.

Moreover, India's changing perception of the nuclear option that it had been developing since 1955 emphasized that behind nuclear proliferation lay political and strategic motivations. The generalized framework of the NPT made it inadequate for dealing with specific political and technical problems. The need to consider proliferation in specific political and technical terms was equally evident from the NPT's failure to affect the other two most probable proliferators, Israel and Japan. Both cases made evident the inherent flaws in the generalized arms-control theory of proliferation.[2] The respective positions of the nuclear-weapons powers and the potential proliferators with regard to the NPT emphasized that it was unlikely ever to have had the effects claimed for it by Western arms controllers and that it had always been an instrument of political arms control.

The Treaty's Failure to Increase Existing Political Restraints on Dissemination

Besides extending the boundaries of the superpowers' bilateral detente, the NPT codified existing American and Soviet policy on limiting dissemination and proliferation. The United States confirmed that NATO arrangements for the dissemination of nuclear weapons would include a retention of the U.S. veto and exclude the transfer to West Germany of any independent capability to fire these, either unilaterally or in conjunction with other European members of NATO. In exchange, the Soviet Union offered a declaratory commitment to inhibit proliferation outside NATO, but interpreted detente negatively, as legitimizing the Soviet ability to impose its will on states within its sphere of control (as in Czechoslovakia) and to assert its influence elsewhere as a global superpower (as in the Middle East). America and Great Britain remained nominally opposed to proliferation, but continued to distinguish between refusing aid that could increase the number of nuclear-weapons powers and the accepted American policy of dissemination assistance to those who had independently acquired nuclear weapons — including the provision of information and weapons with a U.S. veto under the two-key system to NATO allies without their own weapons. If, as seemed increasingly desirable, the United States wished to modernize the deterrent forces of Great Britain — an adherent to the NPT — and France — which had refused to sign but would behave as if it had[3] — this would be allowable under the treaty.[4] The Article III safeguards primarily affected the United States as an exporter of nuclear power plants and fuels but acted only to complete the on-going transfer of its thirty-three bilateral agreements for co-operation in the civil uses of atomic energy to trilateral agreements, with the application of IAEA safeguards.[5] Thus, the arms controllers secured the inspection system that they regarded as necessary to prevent the classic arms race caused by uncertainty over technical capabilities and accentuated by political distrust.

Theoretically, compliance with the treaty was ensured by the non-dissemination of supplies to non-signatories and the threat that violators would cease to receive fissionable materials. However, the difficulties of implementing these provisions and the problems that would be raised by a state's seizure of fissionable materials[6] illustrated the uncertainties of how far such a generalized commitment could be enforced in particular political circumstances.

The Soviet Union was virtually unaffected by the safeguards clauses. Although it had once aided China's acquisition of nuclear weapons, it seemed unlikely to consider a repetition of that action. Article III of the NPT legitimized Soviet control of nuclear activities in Eastern Europe and further confirmed its sphere of influence, especially in East Germany, but also permitted monitoring of West Germany's nuclear activities. The Soviet Union seemed unlikely to export nuclear reactors outside its bloc.

Thus, the treaty formalized both the existing tacit superpower understanding not to aid in proliferation and the more specific policies that had emerged from the talks. Those on intra-NATO dissemination policies were embodied in Articles I and III, which turned the U.S. safeguards system into a multilateral obligation with the hoped-for result of ensuring that other nuclear exporters would follow suit. The Security Council guarantees[7] added nothing to those given unilaterally by the United States and Great Britain, as the U.S. Secretary of State and the U.K. Secretary of State at the Foreign Office reassured their respective publics.[8] These reminders that any guarantee, especially a nuclear one, depended upon the context in which it had been given would have been less surprising had it not been so often ignored in technical-arms-control thinking. This is not to argue that from the superpower viewpoint the NPT was irrelevant. On the contrary, it was regarded in 1968 as of major political importance by both of them, if for very different reasons, but it could be regarded only incidentally as a technical-arms-control measure.

The best confirmation of this was the lack of significant effects on proliferation from the Chinese and French failure to sign the NPT or to cease their nuclear testing in the atmosphere (discontinued by France in 1977). Actually, the Chinese nuclear capability had changed less than the American perception of it as destabilizing because it was likely to be used. This view was prevalent from 1964 to 1968[9] but it was a complete reversal of that held at the time of President Nixon's March 1972 visit to Peking and Dr. Kissinger's proposal of a pentagonal power balance, comprised of the United States, the Soviet Union, Western Europe, China, and Japan. That the arms controllers had exaggerated the Chinese threat was evident in 1969 when their policy was summarized by me as:

... following the pattern of regarding proliferation as acceptable until nuclear weapons are acquired, whereupon further proliferation becomes undesirable. The Peking Government supported the spread of nuclear weapons among socialist states with the classic arguments; in the right hands they contribute to peace by increasing defensive potential, ensuring that superpower allies will honour their obligations and guaranteeing their owners against nuclear blackmail. Since their first test explosion in 1964 they have issued few statements on proliferation but these show a complete policy reversal, suggesting it is unnecessary now China, the guardian of socialism, is a nuclear power. Proposals for a no-first-use-of-nuclear-weapons agreement with the U.S. support this line of asserting China's nuclear status, besides attempting to maximize the benefits from her minimal force. China has expressed its anti-further-proliferation stand in its own way.[10]

Further evidence for the validity of the central distinction between technical arms control and political arms control was the accuracy of my 1969 predictions as to the treaty's lack of effect on the policies of the five nuclear-weapons powers, which were:

... unwilling to contribute to proliferation. They may differ in emphasis but agree that it would not benefit them, could reduce their influence (especially for the three smaller powers) and have such incalculable long-term results as to be undesirable. The sections of the NPT whereby the nuclear powers agree not to disseminate nuclear weapons and to make available the peaceful benefits of nuclear power therefore do no more than set out the existing policies of those who signed it (U.S.A., U.K. and Russia) and those who will not (France and China). They gain a new set of inhibitions against proliferation and an inspection system offering some protection from a nuclear version of the classic arms race through uncertainty.[11]

Even if considered as a technical-arms-control measure, the NPT introduced no new policies except in the sphere of superpower relations, where their condominium was institutionalized through the modality

of political arms control. This had an opposite effect on proliferation —
that of stimulation rather than that of constraint as intended by the
Western technically oriented arms controllers. They had naively im-
agined that such a condominium would be directed solely against
proliferation, that is, the policies of potential Nth powers. The reactions
of the latter to this superpower plan are considered in the next two
chapters.

16   The NPT's Failure to Inhibit Proliferation in India

The three states which, in 1968, were considered the most likely Nth powers, having both the technological capability to build nuclear weapons and the strategic incentives that were likely to lead them to exercise this option, were India, Israel, and Japan. Pakistan was considered a possible fourth. In each case, the central question in evaluating the Non-Proliferation Treaty (NPT) as an instrument of technical arms control was whether it could be expected to restrain the rate of proliferation during the next decade. Since the arms controllers could argue that the same anti-proliferation measure would have been more effective if it had been implemented when first suggested in 1960, the question of timing also had to be considered. Could the NPT or a similar instrument have worked, in the sense of inhibiting proliferation, once this was perceived as inimical to U.S. interests? Western arms controllers could defend the NPT's relative failure with the paradox that, once a country had developed even the basis for a weapons option, it might be too late to halt its development. Such an argument would involve acceptance of the proposition in this book that technical arms control was usually impossible when seen as necessary and was therefore inherently incapable of controlling the dangers that it often wrongly diagnosed. On the other hand, it must always be remembered that few Western arms controllers have argued that arms control in general, or even preventing proliferation in particular, should or could have been an overriding goal of U.S. or Western policy. Technical arms control could never be more than one among many policy objectives, although it was elevated to a major American goal from 1966 to 1968. Without repeating the available detailed analyses of the nuclear policies of India, Israel, Japan, and Pakistan, the real effectiveness of the NPT could be assessed by a brief survey of each of the three countries' development of a weapons option. This would reveal whether at any point the treaty could have seriously delayed their weapons programs without involving an unacceptable price for the countries supplying nuclear aid. The best recent summaries of both these particular four countries' positions and of the evolution of proliferation under the NPT system as administered by the Nixon–Ford administrations under Henry Kissinger's guidance are listed below.[1] As their publication dates indicate, there was a revival of interest in proliferation, coupled with increasing doubts among arms controllers that the NPT system would limit proliferation, and equal doubt that the United States or its allies would, or could, act to shore it up or provide effective substitutes. The Carter administration re-elevated halting proliferation to a major issue in 1977, and its non-proliferation policy is therefore treated separately in the Epilogue.

India: The Sixth Nuclear Power

India's explosion of a nuclear device underground at Rajasthan on May 14, 1974, dramatically illustrated the NPT's basic weakness. Whether it halted proliferation or not depended on the importance attached to this arms-control objective — in comparison with other foreign-policy goals — by the two superpowers and the suppliers of nuclear plants and fuel, in this instance Canada and the United States. Soviet efforts to constrain India's acquisition of a nuclear option had been conspicuous by their absence, although Soviet influence over India had increased between 1968 and 1974 as America's waned. Even so, U.S. efforts to persuade India to accept the NPT had been minimal because its acceptance had ceased to be a major foreign-policy goal with the advent of the Nixon administration. Canada's position was more illustrative of the dilemmas facing nuclear-plant suppliers.

The Canadian position was a difficult one. Canada was a strong supporter of the NPT and its safeguards system and had urged their widest possible acceptance, especially by potential proliferators. At the same time Canada had a history of co-operation with India on nuclear energy which had led it to provide India with a small NR (CIRIUS) reactor in 1956. The safeguards agreement of April 28, 1956 committed India to use the fissionable products from this reactor only for peaceful purposes and to accept International Atomic Energy Agency (IAEA) safeguards as soon as that organization came into existence. This India refused to do, although in 1960 it did accept joint inspections and audits of Canadian fuel. The success of this initial venture in nuclear co-operation led Canada to provide in 1964 technical and financial aid for the construction of the RAPP I and II nuclear reactors of the CANDU model. This policy was strongly supported by Atomic Energy of Canada Limited (AECL), the Crown corporation charged with the responsibility of developing Canadian nuclear-power plants and selling them abroad. The CANDU reactor was unusual in that it was fuelled by natural uranium. This opened up the prospect of nuclear self-sufficiency for India, which had reserves of uranium and thorium (while U.S. reactors depended on enriched uranium, obtainable only from the United States or Great Britain). The first Canadian doubts about supplying India with a nuclear option came after the October 1964 Chinese test of that country's first nuclear weapon and the ensuing debate in India on its possible acquisition of a counter-balancing nuclear deterrent. These doubts were reinforced by the Indian decision in the same year to build a chemical-separation plant to produce plutonium from nuclear fuel-rods. But it was difficult to see how Canada could insist on more stringent safeguards without questioning India's good faith and jeopardizing the generally good Canada–India diplomatic relations. Additionally, it was hoped that India would solve the problem by accepting the then emerging NPT and its safeguards system. India's rejection of the NPT when it was signed left Canada in a dilemma. If it wished to restrain the Indian development of a nuclear option, an option increasingly clear to Canadian diplomatic and scientific advisors, it would have to cut off all nuclear aid to India unless India accepted IAEA safeguards on its nuclear activities. But the arguments against such drastic action were strong. It was not clear whether such safeguards could prevent Indian development of its nuclear option, the pressure for which could be increased by an abrupt cessation of Canadian aid. This would also lessen any Canadian influence on India to remain a non-nuclear-weapons power and to accept IAEA safeguards. Such action would also be unpopular politically, since India was viewed by Canadian politicians and the electorate in terms of the image — created by Gandhi and Nehru — of a peace-loving leader of the Third World. This view, together with support for nuclear aid to India for economic development purposes, was shared by the dominant figure in Canadian foreign policy from 1945 to 1968, Lester B. Pearson. Pearson was, successively, Under Secretary of State for External Affairs — the senior civil-service post — (1946-48); Secretary of State for External Affairs (1948-57); and Prime Minister (1963-68). The only interruption to his (and the Liberal party's) dominance of the federal government was the prime ministership of Progressive Conservative John Diefenbaker (1957-63), during which no coherent direction was given to foreign policy, which was, therefore, continued by the Department of External Affairs on Pearsonian lines. Mr. Pearson's successor as Liberal Prime Minister, Pierre Elliott Trudeau, was also personally inclined to favour the Third World, as was his Special Assistant on foreign affairs, Dr. Ivan Head. Not surprisingly, then, the decision was taken to use the traditional Canadian policy of quiet diplomacy to urge acceptance of IAEA safeguards and non-nuclear-weapons status on India.[2] This policy scored an apparent victory when, in 1971, India accepted trilateral Canada–India–IAEA safeguards on the

RAPP I and II reactors, following the 1970 conclusion of a similar trilateral agreement covering the U.S.-assisted Taripur reactor which was then under construction. The ease with which the transition could be made from a peaceful nuclear technology under IAEA safeguards to the status of a nuclear power was illustrated by the Indian nuclear explosion of 1974. Canada reacted by suspending both shipments of nuclear equipment and material to India and all nuclear co-operation between the two countries. This was a classic example of locking the stable door after the horse had bolted. Canada had become "the first country to give away nuclear weapons without making any of its own".[3] Nevertheless, the effects of the Indian nuclear explosion needed to be seen in perspective: "India is not now a nuclear power but may choose to become one in the next year or so, at least if conventional aircraft are considered suitable as delivery systems. But India cannot hope to be a strategic nuclear power for a decade."[4] None the less, it seemed hard to disagree with the Indian argument for a nuclear option as a safeguard against uncertainties in relations with China.[5] These arguments and the evolution of the Indian position on the NPT need to be put in the broader context of changing Indian perceptions of their national and security interests.

Indian Perspectives on Security

The Indian situation thus typified the major problem in halting proliferation: namely, the near impossibility of preventing a state with the economic requirements for a significant peaceful nuclear-power industry from acquiring an involuntary nuclear option which could be exercised once the necessary technological base had been built up and fuel supplies ensured, either indigenously or through a political alliance. From 1955 to 1961, India built up a dual-purpose nuclear-power base, nominally for civilian purposes, but always intended to provide a weapons option if needed. This was perceived as necessary with the discovery of India's strategic interests in the period between the limited conflict with China in 1962 and the Indo-Pakistan war of 1965. The realization, in mid-1966, that the NPT would become a reality brought the question of India's nuclear option to the fore in New Delhi. The Cabinet finally decided that India could not renounce the political, economic, and military potential represented by a nuclear program outside the NPT framework, but that it would accept trilateral safeguards on the supply of fissionable materials from the United States as long as these were necessary to ensure continued American aid in financing and building nuclear-power plants. Parallel with these, facilities for the production of weapons-grade fissile material, notably plutonium-separation and gaseous-diffusion or -centrifuge plants, could be constructed, along with the necessary delivery vehicles. From 1955 to 1974, the problem in halting proliferation by India was that Western refusal of assistance with India's nuclear program could retard its economic growth and thus act against a major objective of Western foreign policy. Moreover, India could turn to the Soviet Union for assistance which would probably be forthcoming. As the late Leonard Beaton and John Maddox observed as early as 1962,

In the period between 1955 and 1960, she [India] began the steady creation of a self-sufficient nuclear base which, with extensive Canadian and British co-operation, is now fully established. The programme has been under the direct supervision of the Prime Minister, Mr. Nehru, who is Minister of Atomic Energy. The Department of Atomic Energy has as its Secretary Dr. Homi J. Bhabha, who is also Director of the Atomic Energy Establishment, Trombay, the Chairman of the Advisory Atomic Energy Commission and the Director of the Tata Institute for Fundamental Research.[6]

Beaton and Maddox concluded that:

The most reasonable inference is that Mr. Nehru, advised by Dr. Bhabha, has decided to give the country the option to produce a military device in 1963 in case this should be politically or militarily necessary.[7]

The authors properly distinguished between the decision to exercise an option and that of developing even a small stock of atomic bombs with the necessary delivery systems, which would take considerably longer to construct. Given the basis of Indian foreign policy under Prime Minister Nehru and a growing climate of diplomatic hostility to proliferation, which he seemed to share, it doubtless seemed wise to refrain from immediate action since that might interfere with nuclear supplies to India and produce an apparently unnecessary political conflict between the West and India.

The 1962 clash with China over the McMahon Line started the psychological reaction away from Prime Minister Nehru's foreign policy of non-alignment which, as his officials were well aware,[8] neglected defence issues. India's limited defeat in the 1965 clashes with Pakistan, and China's first nuclear-weapons explosion using U-235, in 1964, accelerated this trend towards a more realistic Indian foreign policy. Accordingly, India's nuclear option assumed major importance to Mrs. Gandhi's cabinet in 1966-67 because of India's basic security problems and the way these were perceived at the time. These questions did not appear to have been considered adequately by Western arms controllers, perhaps because by the time the Indians began to do so, the intellectual framework of the NPT, and indeed the basis of the treaty itself, were too firmly established to accommodate an analysis which challenged some of its major assumptions. At its simplest, India's dilemma was that it faced potential threats (from China, Pakistan, rebellious border areas, and internal factions) against which the conventional forces that it could afford might not be able to offer an effective guarantee. Therefore, there came a cross-over point at which the marginal utility of conventional forces dropped below that of nuclear weapons. Additionally, once China became a nuclear-weapons power, India, as the other regional great power in Asia, could hardly avoid following suit.

The Indian debate on the development of its weapons option, and the importance of not surrendering it, via the NPT, reflected the emergence of a community of Indian strategic analysts whose views came to be shared by the political, bureaucratic, and military decision makers. India's conventional weakness against China had become an accepted belief, much as NATO's inferiority against the Warsaw Pact's politically usable forces was an article of faith to NATO in the 1950s. In both cases, the actual strategic balance was a great deal more complex and less favourable to the weaker side when the military balance was placed in a political context. In both instances, too, the reaction was to regard nuclear weapons as a potential answer both to the problems of conventional defence in an unfavourable geographic setting (for India the two fronts against China and Pakistan; and for NATO the lack of depth and the unbalanced deployment of forces) and to the problem of nuclear blackmail. On the one hand the threat to NATO seemed to be that Soviet nuclear weapons could stalemate those of the United States, which would create an umbrella over conventional aggression. On the other hand, India faced a position where, as the first Director of the Institute for Defence Studies and Analyses put it:

Thus if China has strategic options which India does not have — or denies herself — then not only is China likely to win the psycho-political game, but she could precipitate a crisis over the border states or elsewhere in which India could be blackmailed into paralysis.[9]

The Chinese nuclear tests in October 1964 and on May 14, 1965, and the three in 1966 on May 9, October 27 (using a guided missile), and December 28 indicated China's likely possession of at least Intermediate Range Ballistic Missiles (IRBM) with thermonuclear warheads by the early 1970s. These would suffice to threaten India since, using Lhasa as the centre,

. . . a circle with a radius of 800 miles would cover the inner cities of Delhi, Calcutta, Jamshedpur and Kanpur. Range (therefore) presents little problem to China's aircraft (whereas almost all equivalent Chinese targets were 1,500 – 2,500 miles from bases in Northern India).[10]

The asymmetry between an India without a weapons option or some form of delivery system and a China which would clearly possess a guaranteed minimal strike capability by 1970 seemed so great as to raise the possibility to India of China's political use of its nuclear capability.

India and the NPT

India's diplomatic opposition to the NPT from 1965 onwards was based increasingly on her special security needs, meaning at least a requirement to preserve an Indian option against Chinese nuclear blackmail. Neither the NPT nor the superpower security guarantees provided an adequate answer to this threat.[11] While arms controllers saw India as the test of whether proliferation could be halted, the background to the Indian decision showed that its motives for acquiring nuclear weapons were only partly those that were recognized in arms-control theory; they also derived from the interaction of specific strategic, economic, and political factors. These made it questionable whether India's perceived security requirements could be met within the framework of a multilateral treaty. Moreover, the 1968 treaty did not seem likely to halt the acquisition of an option that had started over a decade before, despite India's existing dependence on external aid to bring its nuclear program, or at least the military aspects thereof, to self-sufficiency by the end of the decade. In this sense it could be asked whether the NPT had not come ten years too late seriously to inhibit the Indian acquisition of nuclear weapons, even though it had been designed to do so.

Because the arms controllers drew on their interpretation of the British and French cases in dealing with India, there existed, for them, certain similarities between the problems which faced these NATO members in relying on external guarantees for their security and those which faced India. Against the allegedly greater dangers of nuclear war if proliferation occurred, all three states had insisted that they were unlikely to be any more enthusiastic about a nuclear exchange if they had nuclear weapons, since their limited forces could be used only in a counter-city role. But were there any more credible answers to their perceptions of strategic threats which differed from those of the United States? While NATO in the late 1950s had been concerned over potential Soviet aggression which might arise out of a border clash or Berlin incident, India had experienced the three conventional uses of force that Chinese nuclear weapons could exacerbate if these ever-present threats were again translated into open hostilities. These were: limited war with China (1962); or Pakistan (1965); plus Chinese aid to guerrilla fighters amongst dissident border tribes (notably the Nagas and Mizos). India argued on both specific grounds and general considerations of prestige that it had an equal case with Britain and France for acquiring nuclear weapons and should not be singled out for discrimination because it was doing so later. Its subsequent December 1971 defeat of East Pakistan reinforced Indian arguments for nuclear weapons as a regional great power.

The development of the Indian nuclear option in relation to progress on the NPT supports the main arguments in this book. Technical arms control, both in theory and as applied in U.S. diplomacy, shared the tendency of modern strategic theory to make insufficient allowance for the necessarily specific political context in which it was to be applied. The Soviet Union never accepted the framework of technical arms control but used the NPT as the means by which to achieve its political goal of superpower detente. If the prevention of proliferation was even a moderately important objective of the superpowers, logically they should have offered a specific guarantee to retaliate against any state which either used or threatened to use nuclear weapons against India (there are indications that this was sought but rejected) in exchange for its ratification of the NPT. This could have been combined with threats to withhold military, and possibly economic, aid if India did not comply. As well, they could have threatened to impede its nuclear program by withholding technical and economic aid, and endeavouring to persuade Canada and South Africa to cut off fuel supplies. The United States and Canada secured safeguards on fuel supplies that met treaty standards but at a high diplomatic price. The increasing internal support for Indian nuclear weapons produced a conflict between non-proliferation and other Western foreign-policy objectives that were more important in the aggregate. Because the Soviet Union's objectives in the NPT were to prevent dissemination of nuclear weapons to West Germany and to strengthen the Soviet concept of superpower detente, they understandably ignored the question of proliferation by India. They concentrated on building India up as a counterweight to China, one that would be formally allied to, and dependent for military supplies on, the Soviet Union. The steady deterioration in Sino-Soviet relations, after an initial improvement following Mr. Khrushchev's fall, culminated in the border clashes that started on the Ussuri River on March 2, 1969. That these were not totally unexpected was suggested by the steady build-up of Soviet forces in the Far East since 1963, to about forty divisions.[12] Speculation that the Soviet Union was considering a pre-emptive strike against Chinese nuclear installations reached its height in the summer of 1969. The use of Indian weapons against China would not conflict with Soviet interests. A further complication, unforeseen by Western arms controllers, was the increasing domestic reaction in the United States against American involvement in Southeast Asia because of the Vietnam War, with its longer-term implications — clear to the governments in the area, if not in Washington — that the United States would largely withdraw from the Pacific. President Carter is currently attempting to implement this withdrawal, with mixed success. These developments suggested that America should leave India to its own devices, nuclear or otherwise, but retain what influence it could. In effect, both superpowers tacitly acknowledged the limits of their influence with a regional great power that they envisaged as an ally against a third party, China.

The central paradox which prevented non-proliferation remained that, once potential proliferators were faced with the NPT, they could plot a way around its restrictions, especially since research on Peaceful Nuclear Explosions (PNE) was allowed under Article IV. Ultimately, proliferation depended on a country's political perceptions, given a technical option, and an NPT that was cast in generalized terms which could never deal with the specific problems involved. Also a factor was the superpowers' lack of interest in halting proliferation once it became apparent, as it did from 1966 onwards, that the political costs of doing so far outweighed the probable gains. The real problem of proliferation bore as much relation to the technical-arms-control picture of it as did the grin the Cheshire Cat left to face Alice: it symbolized a significant image rather than a substantive problem which could be solved. Halting proliferation was not something the NPT could do on its own and neither the United States nor the Soviet Union was prepared to use the treaty for this end, because it had become evident by 1972 that proliferation would be slow, limited, and unlikely to be destabilizing for the next decade. This forecast was essentially correct. There is, indeed, a substantial body of analysts who argue that the same is likely to be true of the 1980s, although the technical-arms-control view is the reverse: proliferation will be rapid, widespread, and destabilizing. Hence the Carter administration's efforts to increase drastically the barriers to proliferation, so far with little success.

The answer to the question of whether India's acquisition of a weapons option could have been stopped by technical-arms-control action either before or under the 1968 NPT is both yes and no. The United States could have refused all further nuclear aid after President Kennedy's accession to power, in the same way as the Soviet Union had withdrawn its assistance from China's weapons program slightly earlier. The U.S. action would have been far more effective, because in 1961 the Indians, unlike the Chinese, lacked a gaseous-diffusion plant for producing U-235, or even a chemical-separation plant for weapons-grade plutonium. The Soviet Union might have stepped in to aid India, but this was and is unlikely in view of its experience with China. Politically, the United States would have alienated India at a time when the former saw India as a potential counterweight to China. A cut-off of nuclear aid was, therefore, unlikely in 1961. Yet by 1972 Indian-American relations were at their nadir and the United States had switched its diplomatic support to China. This made it appropriate for the United States both to withdraw all nuclear assistance before the reactors that were currently being built with American assistance became operational and gave India effective self-sufficiency, and to persuade Canada to do the same. The Nixon administration's failure to take this action could be attributed both to a lack of interest in arms control and to the influence of the nuclear-industry lobby. But would any U.S. administration have cut off one of its country's few remaining means of influencing India, for the sake of retarding its acquisition of a minimal deterrent that threatened no significant U.S. interests? Since the answer would always be negative, the arms controllers were right in assuming that Indian proliferation *could* have been halted by drastic American action, perhaps even as late as 1968, but wrong in supposing that any American government *would* pay the necessary price and in ignoring possible off-setting nuclear aid by the United States. The NPT's effectiveness was limited because even President Johnson was prepared to pay only a limited price to control proliferation. This was evident from the treaty's lack of effect on the other nuclear-weapons powers and potential proliferators.

17 Completing the Potential Proliferation Picture Under the NPT: Pakistan, Japan, and Israel

The Non-Proliferation Treaty (NPT) had only a minimal effect on the four states which comprised the emerging Asian nuclear balance in the early 1970s when the NPT was relevant to limiting proliferation (if, indeed, it was ever relevant). South Korea and Taiwan were both pursuing a nuclear option, but discreetly, much as India had done. Their significance was realized only in the reassessment of the proliferation problem from late 1976 onwards, discussed in the Epilogue. China continued its nuclear-weapons program and refused to sign the NPT, but refrained from dissemination. The other regional great power, India, accelerated the development (started over ten years before) of its weapons option, partly because this option seemed threatened by possible U.S. enforcement of the NPT by refusing fuel supplies. Pakistan was so far from developing a weapons option that unilateral U.S. policy on assisting development of its single reactor could have prevented it from acquiring nuclear weapons even without the NPT. However, the treaty did legitimize U.S. claims to prevent the unrestricted development of nuclear technology, here as elsewhere. America also tried to control Japan's nuclear program, but its efforts to compel Japan to adopt a military role that would be consistent with its status as the world's third superpower conflicted sharply with arms-control requirements. This contradiction in U.S. policy was exemplified by the repeated suggestions of Melvin Laird (U.S. Secretary of Defense, 1969-73) that Japan should consider acquiring nuclear weapons, and the U.S.–Japan agreement to co-operate in developing a gaseous-centrifuge plant for manufacturing the enriched uranium needed to fuel Japan's nuclear-energy reactors.

Pakistan

Pakistan's technological capability for manufacturing nuclear weapons was extremely limited, although its political incentive to do so was very high, once India, its major enemy, had detonated a nuclear device in 1974. This occurred only three years after India had inflicted a major conventional defeat on Pakistan by destroying its Eastern half, reconstituted as the nominally independent, Indian-dominated State of Bangladesh. The arms controllers were, therefore, correct in assuming, in the early 1960s, that Pakistan would seek a nuclear option if India did so, especially if it did so successfully. But they were wrong in assuming that a Pakistan option could be limited only by the NPT, especially since Pakistan could not be expected to adhere to the treaty so long as India refused to do so — which was likely to be indefinitely. But Pakistan's option could also be restrained by unilateral U.S. action, both direct, on nuclear materials it supplied, and indirect, on other nuclear suppliers (as with ultimately successful U.S. pressure from 1976 onwards on France) not to supply the nuclear reprocessing plant Pakistan needed to obtain weapons-grade nuclear material. Again, the key issue was whether the United States would incur the political costs involved. Indian nuclear weapons were intended to deter Chinese nuclear blackmail, either directly, or, for example, in support of Pakistan against India, as the arms controllers feared might occur in a situation like the Indo-Pakistan War of December 1971, although their fears were not realized. What was unclear was where the instability would lie in a bi-polar Indo-Pakistan, or tri-polar Sino-Indo-Pakistan balance of deterrence. Admittedly, all the parties' first-generation delivery systems would be technically vulnerable to a pre-emptive strike, but the chances of this happening seemed minimal, as the Soviet Union's decision in 1969 not to carry out such a strike against China suggested. Moreover, China, India, and Pakistan would be anxious to conserve their minimal nuclear forces for deterrence, rather than to use them in a politically useless attack that would expose them to reprisals against their governments and centres of nuclear production. The arms controllers' fears of an unstable Asian balance of deterrence seemed to derive from the 1957-58 theory that sufficient technical vulnerability to a disarming first strike could create sufficient incentives for such a strike in an extreme crisis. This concept had been open to question in its original superpower context, but seemed completely inapplicable when the arms controllers once again transposed their ideas of superpower stability out of their original context and into a quite different setting, this time in Asia.

Pakistan's refusal to adhere to the NPT was based less on its search for a weapons option than on the political impossibility of adhering to the NPT while India refused to sign. Diplomatic pressures for Pakistan's adherence were minimal. Although Pakistan seemed committed to an alliance with China, the Soviets undoubtedly hoped to weaken it. This objective would not be helped by pressing Pakistan to ratify the NPT, since India's development of its nuclear option had left Pakistan dependent on alliances with China and the United States. Soviet use of American interest in arms control in order to further Soviet political interests was particularly evident in its refusal to put pressure on Pakistan, whose embryonic nuclear option was vulnerable to such pressure. Unlike India, Pakistan represented a possible Nth power that could be inhibited from contributing to proliferation, but only by the United States or its allies. Pakistan's failure to adhere to the NPT was unlikely to do more than slightly modify the process of acquiring a nuclear option because it was placed within the context of whatever safeguards, outside the NPT system, had to be accepted, reluctantly, by Pakistan to maintain its option. It was clearly committed to do so, albeit discreetly, but the rate at which it would do so would depend on the availability of technology, and on the political and strategic complexities of the relevant balance of power. In this instance, it was the triangle of Pakistan–India–China relations and superpower attitudes and actions.

Japan

Japan was unusual in its involuntary acquisition of a sophisticated weapons option (to be complete by 1980). Ironically, its possible exercise of this option had become a legitimate subject for discussion from 1966 onwards, by reason of the questions of status in international politics that were raised by its terms for signing the NPT. While lacking the perception of a specific threat that had stimulated China's acquisition of weapons and the Indian pursuit of an option, Japan faced a generalized security problem as the emergent third superpower in an underdeveloped area. It was confronted with a nuclear-armed China and a sufficiently decreasing American presence in Japan and South Korea to make it want an eventual nuclear capability with which to secure the U.S. nuclear guarantee, as was the case with the British and French nuclear forces in Europe. Changing Japanese attitudes towards nuclear weapons were implicit in its criticisms of the NPT's provisions for safeguards, security guarantees, and the imbalance of rights and obligations. Japan refused to sign until West Germany had done so, and until it had made the 1970 Defense White Paper declaration that, "As for defensive nuclear weapons, it is considered that Japan may have them in theory, without contradicting the Constitution."[1]

Together with the U.S. agreement of November 21, 1969, to return administrative rights over Okinawa to Japan by 1972, the White Paper signified that Japan, like West Germany a decade earlier, was ceasing to be an object of other states' foreign policy and was slowly asserting its own rights. Further evidence of this came with Prime Minister Tanaka's visit to Peking in October 1972. How the NPT intended to prevent the acquisition of a nuclear option under these circumstances was never clear. The main factors behind the growing Japanese willingness to consider the development of a short lead-time option were the involuntary option represented by Japan's advanced nuclear-power program (dictated by a shortage of indigenous fuels), the availability of a medium-range delivery system (Phantoms and F-15s) and the technology to develop a long-range system (represented by the Japanese satellite program), and above all the changing political situation. President Nixon's Guam doctrine of July 1970, with its theme of the Asian states' reliance on their own forces for protection against any but obvious external aggression, clearly marked a reversal of the American containment of China, a policy into which the United States had drifted after 1949. It was, therefore, clear that it would be increasingly difficult for Japan, or indeed Taiwan and South Korea, to accept assurances that the United States was as committed to their defence as ever. That Japan was still spending a minimal amount (about 1 per cent of its GNP) on defence, was still only discussing exercising its option, and had finally ratified the NPT in 1977 was a tribute neither to the NPT, nor to U.S. security policies in Southeast Asia. Rather, this reflected Japan's realistic assessment of its ability to continue reliance on the U.S. conventional and nuclear umbrella whilst this was feasible. How long this would be became questionable with the Carter administration's Pacific withdrawal and its uncertain handling of withdrawing U.S. troops from South Korea. Meanwhile, Japan's nuclear industry had grown enormously, cutting the time it would take to exercise a credible and reliable nuclear option. Japan's admission of its need to reserve the possibility of an option represented a notable triumph of security over technical-arms-control interests and a virtual absence of Soviet pressure on Japan to adhere to the treaty.[2] The contradiction between nominal adherence by the superpowers to the NPT's objectives and their wish to manipulate the Asian balance of power to their political advantage explained why, in addition to its inherent limitations, the NPT would not be used by the Soviet Union to inhibit Indian development of nuclear weapons. In the Soviet view, these were a counter to China's deterrent. Once again, political interests had taken priority over technical-arms-control requirements.

Proliferation in the Middle East: Israel

Israel's security problem was unique in that it depended on the use of massive retaliation for its continued survival. Its attitude to the NPT, however, was consistent with that of all the major powers that were affected by it. Israel rejected technical arms control in favour of political and strategic interests. The inherent difficulties of maintaining deterrence via conventional means for the indefinite future were bound to suggest a nuclear option, especially for a country spending 25 to 35 per cent of its GNP on defence, and which had had to fight what it regarded as at least five defensive wars against its Arab neighbours. (This counts the 1947 War of Independence and its revival in 1948; the 1956 War and the 1967 Six Day War; the undeclared 1970 air war against Egypt; and the 1973 Yom Kippur War.) Additionally, there was the continuous war against Arab guerrillas and against terrorists, both Arab and international. This explains the development, with French assistance, of the Dimona reactor (made public only in 1960), which became operational in 1964 and gave Israel "a very developed option [that it was] capable of exercising ... within a short period".[3] This prediction was borne out by the increasing evidence, from 1975 onwards, that Israel had ten to twenty nuclear weapons, with a fifteen- to twenty-kiloton yield, "ready and available for use" and might, indeed, have been prepared to use them if facing conventional defeat in the 1973 war.[4]

There has been much discussion of the Israeli deterrent in American strategic and arms-control literature, much more so than in Israel itself, because once the question of security arose, such a debate within Israel was regarded as inimical to the national interest. But it was unlikely that any Israeli government would adhere to a treaty the inspection system of which would remove the psychological deterrent of an uncertain but not negligible option.[5] As Israeli representative Yosef Tekoah diplomatically expressed this on May 29, 1968, to the United Nations, in the debate on the final NPT draft: "For obvious reasons, my country has a special sensitivity to the security aspect. We are involved in an unresolved conflict in which our security is being threatened and which has thrice in two decades erupted into armed hostilities."[6] The real control over Israel's proliferation lay in its relationship with the one power which desired to halt proliferation, the United States. The latter had supplied military assistance and an implicit guarantee against genocide. As Henry Kissinger put it, the United States was committed to supporting the existence of the Israeli (Jewish) population, but not to supporting its existing (post-1967 and -1973 wars) boundaries. The understanding seemed to be that the American commitment to protect Israel would probably lapse should Israel announce its possession of nuclear weapons. All the NPT could do was to legitimize U.S. restraints as a substitute for Israeli adherence. The treaty was overtaken by the growing Soviet-American confrontation in the Middle East, exemplified by the Soviets' decision to re-supply the

Arabs with arms during the 1973 war, a clear violation of previous superpower understandings. The official cessation of French arms supplies after 1967, made Israel totally dependent on the United States for the arms required for existence. Minimizing the political use of its nuclear potential became a small price to pay as the incentives rose to develop it technically. The only Soviet interest in restraining proliferation in the Middle East was a guarantee that any crisis management would be exploited to the benefit of the superpowers first, and only secondly for the benefit of their allies, preferably to the advantage of Egypt until its break with the Soviets in 1972-73. The Soviet Union's dissemination of vast quantities of conventional hardware to the Arab world, especially to Egypt until 1973, and then to Syria, accorded not with the spirit of the NPT but with the traditional Soviet use of force for political purposes. This policy was extended, through political control, to include any declaratory or actual restrictions on hostile forces, such as Israel's nuclear option.

The NPT and the Nth Powers: The Triumph of Political Interests

Where the NPT should have restrained the spread of nuclear weapons, or the option to manufacture them, the treaty's technical-arms-control provisions were nullified by a combination of local political interests and those of the superpowers in Asia and in the Middle East. The Soviet Union and the United States were both exploiting the agreement that had been embodied in the NPT to compete locally for influence. The Soviet Union did so largely by ignoring the requirements for technical arms control; the United States was forced to subsume these requirements under broader considerations. The most probable proliferators, India, Japan, and Israel, all understood the dangers of proliferation but felt that these were exaggerated by the arms controllers and that the resultant lesser dangers were acceptable risks in a world of insecurity for medium powers. Pakistan shared these views. In this book, the central question has been whether the NPT would halt proliferation because the arms-control analysis of the process of proliferation was correct. That the analysis was fundamentally incorrect was suggested by the disinclination of the superpowers to use the NPT to inhibit proliferation more than marginally, as the United States tried to do, or by their tendency to ignore the issue except in the West German context, as the Soviets did.

Further evidence of U.S.–U.S.S.R. concern to consolidate their ever-broadening political relations through nominally technical arms-control measures was found in their 1972 Strategic Arms Limitation Talks (SALT I) agreement to place a purely quantitative freeze on strategic missiles. Together with discussions on Mutual and Balanced Force

Reductions (MBFR), this completed the cycle of political arms control. This had gone from unilateral Soviet political restraints on the United States from 1958 to 1961, to superpower detente with the 1963 Partial Test Ban (PTB), and extended into a superpower understanding of the mutuality of their interests in the 1968 NPT, the political consequences of which for Europe were spelt out in the Moscow Summit of May 1972 and in SALT I. The implications of these developments will be considered in the following chapters.

PART V   Bringing Arms Control and
Arms Limitation Full Circle:
Stabilizing the Strategic Balance
via SALT and MBFR

18 SALT I:
The Failure of
Strategic Arms Control

The Non-Proliferation Treaty (NPT) represented the greatest effort by the U.S. government to transform a measure of technical arms control into policy. From 1966 to 1968, President Johnson sought to enforce the arms-control aspects of the NPT and to combine these harmoniously with its political benefits to superpower detente. President Nixon recognized the contradictions between preventing proliferation and preserving the United States' political interests with powers other than Soviet Russia. Political expediency required that the United States adopt a more lenient attitude with regard to securing adherence to the treaty. Accordingly, the NPT could only marginally inhibit proliferation and provide a safeguards system for the commercial use of fissionable materials. The NPT confirmed suggestions, made earlier in this volume, that the technical requirements of arms control were almost always too complex for the political environment. This made arms-control theory inapplicable in political practice. The result was the emergence of political arms control as the Soviet counter to technical arms control, and, by the late 1960s, as an instrument for the positive pursuit of their political and strategic goals, which, by the late 1970s, seemingly included strategic superiority and the use of force for Soviet political ends. Since the idea of strategic arms limitation had been present in arms-control thinking since its formulation, it was inevitable that, once the Soviets had sufficient strategic forces to negotiate from a position of parity, SALT would start. The question was whether these talks would produce effective technical arms control, with the Soviets accepting the need for this, or whether, on the contrary, the Soviets would continue their policy of political arms control. This could not only preclude any strategic arms limitation, it could enable the Soviets to slow down the U.S. strategic build-up, whilst increasing their own, as critics of SALT were to argue happened. Henry Kissinger preferred to see SALT as the chief modality for securing their political interests and preserving strategic stability.

SALT I: The Failure of Arms Control

Superficially, the SALT I agreements[1] of May 26, 1972, seemed to con-
tradict the apparent subsuming of arms control's technical requirements for strategic stability under the political-arms-control concept —
developed between 1963 and 1968 — of preserving stability through
political accord between the superpowers. In SALT I, the Soviet Union
agreed for the first time to accept quantitative limitations on its
strategic forces. These apparently included a ceiling of 313 on the very
large SS-9 missiles; the Soviets also accepted reciprocal unilateral
verification via reconnaissance satellites. Nevertheless, when put in
the political context of the Moscow Summit's wide-ranging superpower accords on the mutuality of their interests, or compared with the
arms-control proposals for restraint or reductions in strategic-arms
development and deployment, SALT I represented arms control only
incidentally. The Soviet Union had accepted a limited quantitative
freeze that enabled it to achieve qualitative superiority and effective
qualitative parity in strategic weapons with the United States. In exchange, the United States recognized Soviet strategic and political
parity and, implicitly, the boundaries of its control in Eastern Europe.
SALT I was, as Dr. Kissinger emphasized,[2] primarily a political agreement that allegedly saved both sides from allocating more resources to
strategic weapons than they would have done without the agreement.

SALT I was pure political arms control. The superpowers seemed, in
1972, to have accepted, tacitly, political arms control as the best means
for recognizing their increasingly interdependent strategic and political interests.[3] At the Moscow Summit, the United States and the Soviet
Union had rejected any attempts to restrict those developments that
were regarded as most destabilizing by arms controllers. These included the threat to Mutual Assured Destruction (MAD) that was
represented by ABM and the introduction of Multiple Independently
Targetable Re-entry Vehicles (MIRV). In the arms-control view, both of
these developments appeared to resurrect the dangers of a reciprocal
fear of surprise attack that had been prevalent in the 1950s.

The Arms-Control View of SALT

Discussion of the arms-control problems that would be posed by ABM
systems had started as early as 1957, in the President's Science Advisory Committee (PSAC) and elsewhere. The first and simplest theory of
the need for an ABM moratorium held that if either side deployed even a
relatively ineffective ABM (the U.S. Nike–Zeus or the first-generation
U.S.S.R. Galosh), the other side would be forced to make worst-case
calculations, which would exaggerate the effectiveness of their

opponent's ABMs and necessitate countermeasures. These could include counter-deployment of an ABM system (the 1967 U.S. Sentinel system versus the 1964 U.S.S.R. Galosh), increased procurement of Intercontinental Ballistic Missiles (ICBM) beyond those needed for a MAD capability (1,000 U.S. Minutemen against the 800 or less argued for by Carl Kaysen and Jerome Wiesner in 1961), and, most importantly, penetration aids (penaids). By about 1962, the development of penaids (MRV and MIRV) and projected improvements in accuracy were responsible for producing the second, more complex, theory of the need for a SALT agreement. Although Secretary McNamara included both views in his action-reaction theory of the arms race,[4] the initial, simple theory, which stressed the arms-control need for an ABM moratorium, dominated discussion from 1957 to 1966 and was incorporated into U.S. arms-control proposals from 1966 onwards. From 1967 onwards, when knowledge of MIRVs became public, the arms controllers could emphasize that they had been urging MIRVs so as to discourage Soviet and U.S. ABM deployment. This would allow time to negotiate a moratorium on MIRV flight testing and, ideally, a Comprehensive Test Ban Treaty that would impose limitations on the development of ABM and MIRV warheads.[5] These measures would slow down or halt MIRV deployment and make it a low-confidence weapon that would be too unreliable for a first strike, instead of a high-confidence weapon that could make possible a successful attack against land-based ICBMs. This would necessitate the development of new delivery systems such as the Underwater Long-Range Missile System (ULMS), now named Trident.[6]

Once again the arms controllers had developed an explicit theory of a threat to the stability of deterrence, and of necessary countermeasures. Soviet deployment of a limited ABM was interpreted according to these arms-control theories, without taking sufficient account of the institutional factors (such as the influence of the Soviet Air Defense Command) or perceptions (notably the Soviet stress on defence and its strategic inferiority until 1967-68). The arms controllers reacted to the Soviet commencement in 1964 of a limited ABM system around Moscow by suggesting a mutual moratorium on ABM deployment.[7] The official Soviet reply, that the ABM was defensive and therefore *a priori* less destabilizing than offensive missiles,[8] was consistent both with the Soviet deployment of a much larger air-defence network than the United States had, together with an extensive civil-defence program, and with known Soviet perceptions of the ABM. In the West, however, it was regarded as evidence of intellectual backwardness because it was not in accord with the arms controllers' intellectual framework. Three years later, the same gap in perceptions of the ABM was evident in Premier Kosygin's statement on February 9, 1967, in which he rejected an ABM moratorium in isolation because "an antimissile system may cost more than an offensive one but it is intended not for killing people but for saving human lives."[9] Later in the year, Secretary McNamara repeated the arms-control arguments for an ABM moratorium to Premier Kosygin at the Glasboro Summit (June 23–25). Again the Soviets stuck to the propositions that ABMs were defensive, and that a moratorium on their deployment could not be discussed in isolation from restraint on offensive weapons.[10] Mr. Kosygin was not only being logical, from the Soviet viewpoint, he was also probably suffering from the sense of technical overkill experienced by all who received the famous McNamara anti-ABM briefing. The combination of innumerable statistics and their presentation by the intellectually formidable Secretary of Defense, arguing that they *proved* ABM was bad, was unforgettable (even experienced analysts took two days to recover). Unfortunately, it typified the technical-arms-control approach. The figures were selected to agree with the underlying assumptions, whereas the assumptions, and all too often the figures themselves, were open to question, if not wrong.

On March 2, 1967, President Johnson accepted the fact that talks on limitations must cover offensive and defensive missiles.[11] This reflected the arms controllers' growing preoccupation with the need for an ABM moratorium as a prelude to limiting destabilizing developments in offensive weapons, a view shared by Secretary McNamara. Both he and the arms controllers were prepared to accept Soviet strategic parity, as foreshadowed in his commitment in November 1964 to limit U.S. offensive forces to one thousand Minutemen, fifty-four Titan II ICBMs, and forty-one Polaris-carrying submarines.[12] This decision followed from the concept of Mutual Assured Destruction (MAD) as giving a fixed level of strategic forces as sufficient for the United States (given the invulnerability of the ICBM in the 1960s), with only very limited additional forces for damage limitation. These ideas had crystallized in the minds of American decision makers between 1961 and 1963. To put their views in perspective, it must be remembered that, as late as 1965, McNamara was insisting that the Soviets had given up, forever, any hope of catching up with the United States in strategic forces. By 1978, this statement had proved to be the complete reverse of the truth. But with McNamara's departure from office in 1967, and the delay in starting SALT because of the invasion of Czechoslovakia in 1968, the divergence between the arms controllers and the U.S. government increased. The start of SALT proper in 1970 meant that the Nixon administration was entering into an implicitly political dialogue with the Soviets, which necessitated, as with previous arms-control negotiations, an adjustment of the technical requirements of arms control to the political considerations of political arms control. As the arms-control requirements for SALT became increasingly complex, the possibilities for an agreement that would meet arms-control criteria decreased. Indeed, the changing U.S. diplomatic position on a SALT agreement had always shown that any limitation must be the product of the internal and external political environment.

SALT in American Government Policy

As with the NPT, the U.S. government had to adapt the arms-control requirements for agreement with the Soviet Union to the political relations between the superpowers and to Soviet perceptions of what any agreement need contain. Initially, the Johnson administration supported the arms controllers by offering a freeze on strategic missiles in their proposals of January 1964.[13] Although this freeze would have institutionalized Soviet arms inferiority at the time, it was intended to introduce the concept of a ceiling on offensive and defensive forces once mutual deterrence was perceived by both sides as being assured.

From November 10, 1966, when Secretary McNamara confirmed that there was "considerable evidence of Russian ABM deployment around Moscow",[14] the Johnson administration tried to start discussions on a mutual ABM freeze before internal political pressures, notably those from the Joint Chiefs of Staff, forced an American counter-deployment of ABMs. This explains President Johnson's pressure for SALT in 1967, and Secretary McNamara's emphasis on the undesirability of the anti-Chinese Sentinel ABM when he announced its deployment on September 18, 1967.[15] The Soviets' failure to accept President Johnson's invitation to SALT until June 27, 1968, emphasized that they were as interested in its political implications (expanding the understanding embodied in the NPT) as they were unable to understand the arms controllers' fears of strategic instability. This is why the Soviets were willing to wait until after the Nixon administration had weathered the full force of the internal U.S. opposition to the Safeguard ABM, in the August 1969 Senate debate,[16] before they would accept the preliminary talks on SALT, which started in November. During this hiatus, from June 1968 to November 1969, the only Soviet concern seemed to be that of preventing the resurrection of forces in the United States that were opposed to superpower detente, since no suggestions were made by the Soviet Union for an ABM or MIRV moratorium as an urgent measure.

Since the SALT negotiations proper lasted only two years (April 16, 1970–May 1972), the Americans had to persuade the Soviets of the second, more complex, case for an ABM and MIRV moratorium, or, failing this, accept the Soviet view that any agreement must embody the minimum limitations on strategic forces in order to be consistent with the broadening of the superpowers' political understanding. The Nixon administration's forced abandonment of the arms-control requirements for a SALT agreement, which Dr. Kissinger had probably never wholly endorsed, was evident from the progress of the SALT negotiations.[17] There were, in fact, two sets of negotiations. The formal ones, the so-called "front channel", were effectively bypassed by Henry Kissinger's "back channel", his personal negotiations, with presidential approval, with the Soviet Ambassador to the United States, Anatoly Dobrynin, and through him, or directly, with Leonid Brezhnev, the Politbureau, and their strategic and military advisors. Initially, in 1970, the Soviets rejected a verifiable ban on the deployment and testing of MIRV. They did so because the prevention of deployment would have involved continuous monitoring of ICBM and SLBM warheads. They offered no adequate reason for rejecting limitations on testing, but this rejection was necessary to enable them to catch up with the Americans on MIRV technology. President Nixon's personal intervention in early 1971 was necessary to convince the Soviets that his administration viewed a SALT agreement as essential to the political understanding that the Soviets desired. His action led to the understanding of May 20, 1971, that the initial offensive limitation would be temporary and would freeze only selected categories of missiles, and that a more permanent ABM solution would be required. The resulting U.S. package of July 1971 showed how far the Nixon administration had been forced away from the arms-control view of SALT by the Soviets. The United States proposed only an ABM limitation of two to three hundred ABMs to protect missile sites (as opposed to Soviet demands for a limit of one hundred ABMs around each capital), and a numerical equality in launch vehicles, except for limitations on the very large Soviet SS-9. The United States also suggested December 1971 as the cut-off date for all new construction.[18] The Soviet leaders waited until the end of April 1972 to reach an agreement in principle, and only then did so because they were obliged to by the President's impending visit, which resulted in the forced finalization of SALT I in May. This was only accomplished by Henry Kissinger's effectively accepting all Soviet demands and ignoring or overruling the advice of the technically far more qualified United States SALT negotiating team, led by Gerard C. Smith and including Paul Nitze. Kissinger's conduct made sense, given his assumptions that the technical details of SALT I were relatively unimportant because strategic superiority was unachievable and so politically useless, whereas detente with the Soviets was politically vital — for the forthcoming presidential elections and the future of mankind. These assumptions are, however, difficult to reconcile with Dr. Kissinger's concurrent and subsequent concern for the stability of the strategic balance, defined in technical terms. Notwithstanding the internal political difficulties that were involved in reaching SALT I, it seemed clear that the Soviets were interested in the agreement not on arms-control grounds, but because the President had insisted that such an agreement was a corollary to the political and economic accords that were sought by the Soviets.

The Dominance of Arms Limitation in SALT I

The separate "Treaty . . . on the Limitation of Anti-Ballistic Missile Systems" — the ABM Treaty — was "of unlimited duration", except that either party could withdraw at six months notice (Article XV) and it was to be reviewed every five years (Article XIV). It allowed each side two ABM systems limited to 100 ABM launchers and 100 ABM missiles, together with their associated radars. Effectively, this allowed the United States to complete its ABM site at Grand Forks, North Dakota, which protected a Minuteman ICBM field, and to deploy, if it wished, an ABM defence of Washington. The Soviet Union would retain its ABM defence of Moscow and could deploy an ABM defence of one of its ICBM fields. Qualitative improvements in ABM systems, except for radars, were allowed. Other Surface-to-Air Missiles (SAM), launchers, and radars were not to be tested "in an ABM mode" (Article VI [a]).

In assessing SALT I it is important to distinguish between what the agreement actually achieved, which was the codification of both sides' planned offensive force deployments from 1972 to 1977 (the duration of the Interim Agreement . . . on the Limitation of Strategic Offensive Arms), and what the technical arms controllers claimed that it achieved, which was the establishment of a climate of restraint in superpower strategic-weapons procurement. These force levels and the structure of the Interim Agreement — which was, from 1975 onwards, to be the subject of much dispute over whether the Soviets had violated it — are set out in Tables 18:1 and 18:2 below.

From 1964 to 1972, the Soviets had consistently opposed the arms controllers' views regarding the necessity for an agreement that could prevent the destabilization of the strategic environment. In their view this was growing more rather than less stable, by reason of the political relations with the United States that were embodied in the PTB and in the NPT, and which more than off-set any technical changes that might favour a resurrection of the theories on the dangers of a first strike through technical advantages that the Soviets had never accepted anyway. They were, however, prepared to accept that such fears could become self-fulfilling prophecies in the United States and therefore moved to head them off once SALT succeeded the NPT as an embodiment of superpower political understanding.

Table 18.1 *Interim Agreement and Protocol . . . on the Limitation of Strategic Offensive Arms . . . With Agreed Interpretations,* Common Understanding, and Unilateral Statements. (Signed at Moscow, May 26, 1972; entered into force for five years, October 3, 1972.)[19]

	ICBM Silos	SLBM	"Modern" SSBN*
U.S.	1,054	656 (or 710, if SLBM replace 54 older Titan ICBM). "Modern" SSBN allowance then	41 44
U.S.S.R.	1,618 (included sub-total of 313 "Modern Heavy Missiles")	740 (or 950, if SLBM replaced: (a) ICBM deployed before 1964 (210 SS-7 & 8); and/or (b) SLBM on "older" submarines; 10 H-class SSBN, each carrying 3 SS-N-5 SLBM). "Modern" SLBM allowance reminded at	62 62

*SSBN = Ballistic Missile Submarine, Nuclear.

Notes:
(i) U.S.S.R.: SLBM *excluded* 12 G-I- and 11 G-II-class diesel submarines, each carrying 3 SS-N-4 SLBM (G-I class) or 3 SS-N-5 (G-II class).
(ii) *U.S.S.R. Unilateral Statement, May 17, 1972.* Total Western forces (the United States, the United Kingdom, and France) could not exceed 50 SSBN, carrying 800 SLBM, without corresponding increases in Soviet forces. The United States did not agree to this.
(iii) The Protocol defined the levels of SLBM and SSBN for the two signatories and also defined the Soviets' "older" ICBM as those deployed prior to 1964 and allowed the Soviets to replace SLBM on "older submarines" up to the specified levels, without further defining "older submarines".

Table 18.2 *Agreed Interpretations, Common Understandings, and Unilateral Statements . . . Regarding the* ABM *Treaty Interim Agreement*

(1) *Agreed Interpretations*
　　(a) 12 Initialled Statements
　　　　(A) to (L):　　　　　　　　Initialled by the heads of the SALT delegations, May 26, 1972.

　　(b) 6 Common Understandings
　　　　(A) to (F):　　　　　　　　Understandings reached during the SALT negotiations, 1972

(2) *Unilateral Statements*
　　(a) 7 Statements by U.S. Delegation (A) to (G):　　Made during the SALT negotiations, May 1972

　　(b) 1 "Statement of the Soviet Side":　　　　　　May 17, 1972, with U.S. response, May 24, 1972

Notes: (i) Dr. Kissinger and the Nixon administration insisted, in 1972, when seeking Senate approval of the SALT I package, that these Agreed Interpretations, Common Understandings, and Unilateral Statements were an integral part of the Interim Agreement, since they defined its key terms. Especially important was the definition of a "heavy modern ICBM".

　　　In Initialled Statement J, "the dimensions of land-based ICBM silo launchers will not be significantly increased"; Common Understanding A defined "significantly increased" as not more than "10-15 per cent of the present dimensions of land-based ICBM Silo launchers". This limited "light" ICBM to a volume of seventy-five cubic metres, under half the size of the Soviets' then heaviest ICBM, the SS-9.

(ii) As an Executive Agreement by the U.S. President, the Interim Agreement would not legally require U.S. Senate consent to ratification, but Section 33 of the 1961 Act creating the U.S. Arms Control and Disarmament Agency (ACDA) bars action to reduce or limit U.S. arms except by treaty or "unless authorised by further affirmative legislation by Congress". The Interim Agreement was therefore submitted to the U.S. Senate and House of Representatives for approval by a Joint Resolution. Given as Public Law 92-448, 92nd Congress, H.J. Res. 1227, September 30, 1972, only *after* the inclusion of Senator Henry M. Jackson's (D – Washington) Amendment (the Jackson Amendment) which "requests the President to seek a future treaty that, *inter alia*, would not limit the United States to levels of international strategic forces inferior to the limits provided for the Soviet Union. . . . ".

Nevertheless, the majority of the U.S. technical-arms-control community welcomed SALT I, and regretted only that it had not tackled the qualitative aspects of the strategic arms race, notably MIRV. But this could be dealt with in SALT II. There was general agreement that the Soviets had accepted the principle of MAD as the basis for superpower deterrence and that neither superpower understood the other's deterrent philosophy. This development would greatly assist a SALT II agreement. The freeze on ABM deployment was regarded as evidence of Soviet acceptance of this principle of mutual vulnerability. Against the criticism that nothing had been done to restrain qualitative developments in strategic weapons, it was argued first that the strategic arms race would have gone on even faster in the absence of SALT I, and second that SALT I had produced a climate in which the United States could restrain its strategic force spending in the expectation that the Soviet Union would follow.[20]

Table 18.3 *Projected Strategic Force Deployments, mid 1977*[21]

	Without Moscow Agreement		Under Moscow Agreement	
	U.S.S.R.	United States	U.S.S.R.	United States
Land-based missiles	1,900	1,054	1,330	1,000
Sea-based missiles	1,200	656	950	710
Heavy bombers	140	500	140	500
Deployed strategic warheads	3,400	11,000	2,600	11,000
Equivalent megatonnage	5,500	4,550	4,000	4,450

Source: Weapons characteristics based on the International Institute for Strategic Studies, *The Military Balance*, 1971–72.

Dr. Kissinger's various briefings on SALT emphasized that "Never before have the world's two most powerful nations, divided by ideology, history and conflicting interests, placed their central armaments under formally agreed limitations and restraint", and that "there is at least reason to hope that these accords represent a major break in the pattern of suspicion, hostility and confrontation which has dominated U.S. – Soviet relations for a decade. The two great nuclear powers must not let this opportunity slip away by jockeying for marginal advantages."[22] Significantly, Dr. Kissinger separated himself from the pure technical school of arms control by also stressing that SALT I needed to be put into its proper political context as the symbol of superpower detente, which amounted to an implicit admission that SALT I might have more political than strategic significance.

The U.S. arms controllers expected SALT II to remedy the qualitative defects of SALT I by including some or all of the following: for MIRV, a ban on deployment that could be verified by on-site inspection, and/or limitations on the flight testing that was required to create a high-confidence counter-force weapon; for ABM, a freeze at one site each for the United States and the Soviet Union. In order to limit weapons testing, a Comprehensive Test Ban (CTB) treaty would be required. It might also be possible to envisage reductions in strategic force levels.[23] However, subsequent developments did not fulfil these expectations. The Interim Agreement expired on October 3, 1977, without being replaced or susperseded by a SALT II. Moreover, it seemed, by mid-1978, that no SALT II negotiable with the Russians would be acceptable to the U.S. Senate, or vice versa. Thus both in 1972, and even more so in 1978, it was evident that SALT I was in reality a triumph of political arms control, because it epitomized the policy of using nominal arms-control agreements as a modality for codifying political understanding by the two superpowers. The pace of strategic-arms acquisition by the two superpowers did not slow down, but accelerated to the point where, by 1975, it began to threaten the detente relationship, a threat realized by 1976-78.

SALT I could therefore be seen as a model for arms control in three senses. First, it reflected the arms-control community's insistence on the need for mutual restraint in the superpowers' strategic-arms race in order to avoid the destabilizing effects of ABM and MIRV. Second, SALT I rejected any technical restrictions on superpower development and deployment of new weapons systems (except for the restraint on ABM) in favour of an essentially political agreement that formalized strategic programs for 1972-77 at about their planned levels, and attempted to ensure that changes in strategic force levels that were in favour of the Soviet Union need not adversely affect Soviet-American relations. Thirdly, in eschewing technical restraints on weapons deployment in favour of an agreement that insulated this from the general context of improved superpower relations, SALT I confirmed a superpower policy of furthering detente through arms control.

SALT I both followed the pattern set by the arms-control agreements of the 1960s and confirmed that this would be the pattern for the 1970s. Of the 1974 agreements, the Threshold Test Ban Treaty (TTBT) avoided a true CTB, one that would have halted all underground testing and inhibited improvements in MIRV warheads, in favour of a TTBT that allowed tests up to a threshold of 150 kilotons, which was sufficient to perfect MIRV warheads. The ABM freeze simply formalized the status quo of one site for the United States to defend the Grand Forks ICBM field and one site for the Soviet Union with which to defend Moscow. The Vladivostok Accord appeared to impose far-reaching restraints on the superpowers' strategic-weapons deployment that would stretch into the 1980s, but proved on closer examination to do little more than legitimize their extensive programs for qualitative and, in the case of the Soviet Union, quantitative improvements in their strategic forces. Nothing was done to restrain qualitative force improvements (such as MIRV, or greater accuracy), which threatened the stability of the strategic balance.[24]

19 The 1973 Agreements and the 1974 Arms-Control Treaties: Vladivostok and Beyond

Superficially, the momentum of SALT I seemed to be carried forward in the next two years. In 1973 the two superpowers concluded an Agreement on the Prevention of Nuclear War and an Agreement on the Basic Principles of Negotiations on Strategic Arms Limitation which were to lead to the Vladivostok Accord of November 24, 1974. This limited the total U.S. and U.S.S.R. strategic forces to 2,400 strategic delivery vehicles, of which only 1,320 could be Multiple Independently Targetable Re-entry Vehicles (MIRV). The agreement was to be translated into a SALT II treaty in 1975, or at least in time for the 1976 presidential elections. But Dr. Kissinger's SALT II never did materialize, and President Carter is still searching for *his* SALT II. In the interim, June 1974 saw two superpower treaties, one establishing a ban on underground nuclear tests above a threshold of 150 kilotons and another freezing Anti-Ballistic Missile (ABM) deployment at the one existing ABM site the United States and the Soviet Union each had. On the other hand, a closer examination of these agreements suggested that like SALT I and its predecessors, the 1973-74 accords represented political rather than technical arms control. This proposition was reinforced by an examination of strategic-force deployments, since the SALT I agreement was expected to slow down the strategic-arms acquisition process. Here, as elsewhere, the trends in the Soviet force build-up that became evident in 1974 were much clearer by 1978, as was the extent to which they were at, or over, the SALT I ceilings, quantitatively as well as qualitatively, and so analysed in the Epilogue.

Strategic-Force Deployments After SALT I: 1972-75

In principle the offensive force limitations of SALT I allowed the Soviets a major quantitative advantage in their strategic forces, to be balanced by qualitative improvements in U.S. forces with the deployment of MIRV. But even this limited goal, falling far short of what arms controllers regarded as necessary, was threatened by the extraordinarily rapid

Soviet build-up of forces combined with its development of new missiles with MIRV, greatly increased throweight (payload), and accuracy. In 1974, it became clear that they would, by 1975, be deploying their fourth generation of strategic missiles, the SS-16, -17, -18, and -19 ICBM (for details, see Annex). A new medium-range bomber, the Backfire, started deployment in 1974 and could have a strategic capability against the United States, a hotly disputed capability, denied by Dr. Kissinger, but insisted on by his critics. Indeed, the Backfire issue helped to torpedo Kissinger's attempts to reach a SALT II. In Submarine-Launched Ballistic Missiles (SLBM) and "modern" Ballistic Missile Submarines, Nuclear (SSBN) the Soviets were completing the last of their thirty-four Y-class, with a building rate of six to eight SSBN per year, including the new D-II and D-III classes. These would replace the 210 "older" ICBM (SS-7 and -8), enabling the Soviets to reach their SALT I ceiling of 950 SLBM in 62 "modern" SSBN soon after the expiration of the Interim Agreement in 1977. Since these ICBM- and SLBM-deployment plans were clearly known to the Soviets when they negotiated the Interim Agreement, it was clear that they had built its quantitative ceilings around these plans, whilst, as became clear from 1975 onwards, leaving loopholes for the qualitative improvements — especially in throweight and heavier ICBM — which the United States had sought to restrain; and, indeed, claimed to have restrained. For the Soviets, then, SALT I had meant no effective, technical arms control.

The same was true of the U.S. strategic-force modernization programs, although these were on a much more modest scale. But MIRV deployment was proceeding as planned, the ULMS Trident SSBN/SLBM system was scheduled for deployment in 1978 (a deadline that was not met), whilst a new, larger ICBM to succeed the Minuteman (the M-X) was under development. Outside the Interim Agreement limits, the new strategic bomber, the B-1, was scheduled for production in 1976 (although President Carter cancelled it in 1977) and, less noticed in 1974, but more significant for SALT, the Long-Range Cruise Missile (LRCM) was under development in submarine, sea, air, and ground-launched versions. (For details see Annexes.) The issue of whether, and how, to limit the Soviets' Backfire bomber and the cruise missile, as the LRCM was known, was to prove a major obstacle to a SALT from 1975 to the present. There were real technical and strategic problems involved and, as the SALT/detente issue became politicized, these problems served as technical expressions of political views for or against SALT II and, via SALT II, of the whole nature of the superpowers' political relationship. Even halfway through the life of the Interim Agreement, however, technical arms controllers were doubting whether it imposed any restrictions on the strategic arms race and, accordingly, were demanding the rapid conclusion of an effective SALT II.

They were more optimistic about the 1972 ABM treaty. Their major objection to ABM systems had been that, according to the action-reaction model of the strategic arms race, a light, small-scale U.S. ABM system would trigger Soviet MIRV deployment, to be countered by a heavy U.S. ABM. But MIRV deployment by both sides was proceeding under SALT I despite a freeze on ABM related only indirectly to arms-control requirements. On the U.S. side, political pressure against ABM, based on an uncritical acceptance of oversimplified arms-control arguments, had made an ABM moratorium politically desirable for the Nixon administration. Additionally, the cost-effectiveness of the Spartan/Sprint point defence of the U.S. ICBM force remained questionable given Soviet progress in MIRV. Completing the Grand Forks ABM site in 1974 and developing new ABM systems were therefore politically attractive options whose strategic costs could be minimized. Ironically, the United States had had a good strategic bargaining counter, the full twelve-site Safeguard system, which had been politically difficult to use, and so was used badly. In contrast the Soviet Union had had a bad strategic position (the Galosh-based defence of Moscow) that was easy to exploit politically and so was used well. The Soviets never appeared to have accepted the arms-control case that ABM was destabilizing, except as a self-fulfilling U.S. prophecy. But they could see the advantages in halting a sophisticated and effective U.S. defence of hard sites (ICBM silos) at one site, with a politically unusable option for a second site defending a soft target (Washington). In exchange, the Soviets had limited a less sophisticated defence of a soft target (Moscow) and acquired a usable option to deploy an improved ABM in defence of an ICBM field. In fact, they traded this option for the politically useful 1974 one-ABM-each agreement and a major research and development effort in ABM.

SALT II Negotiations

Taken as a whole, the limitations imposed by SALT I on the strategic arms race were almost wholly ineffective in terms of the technical criteria specified by the arms-control community, although immensely successful politically in fostering the image of superpower detente. In defence of SALT I it was argued that it was a necessarily cautious first step in strategic arms control whose deficiencies, notably its failure to deal with the qualitative aspects of the strategic arms race, would be remedied in the SALT II negotiations and the resultant agreements. The three key issues were: first, whether MIRV testing and deployment could be limited; second, what forces were to be included; and third, whether some over-all limit on total strategic forces could be agreed upon. Throughout the SALT II negotiations, the United States approached these questions from the viewpoint of technical arms control while the Soviets stressed their political approach to arms control.

In accordance with the arms-control view that limitations on MIRV were vital, the United States had offered in SALT I a ban on research, development, testing, and production and deployment, to be verified by on-site inspection. Such inspection was unacceptable to the Soviet Union, which countered with a proposal for an unverified ban on MIRV deployment. An obvious compromise would have been a ban on MIRV flight testing and deployment, the ban on flight testing being monitorable by national means of verification.[1] Whether such monitoring could prevent all clandestine MIRV testing was doubtful, but it could inhibit the development of the high confidence needed in MIRV as a first-strike weapon. The Soviets showed no interest in such a compromise, apparently remaining, in SALT II as in SALT I, completely uninterested in significant limitations on MIRV development and deployment,[2] an area where they lagged behind the United States. Indeed, instead of responding seriously to these U.S. proposals for technical arms control, the Soviets concentrated on proposals designed to embarrass the United States and institutionalize their strategic superiority. The Soviets repeated the demand made in SALT I that U.S. Forward-Based Systems (FBS) for delivering tactical nuclear weapons in Western Europe and on aircraft carriers should be counted as strategic weapons because they could, theoretically, strike the Soviet Union on one-way missions.[3] There was no suggestion that the 750 Soviet Intermediate- and Medium-Range Ballistic Missiles (I/MRBM) targeted on Western Europe be reduced in return. This proposal to reduce FBS was clearly intended to create strains between the United States and her Western European allies, who rightly regarded FBS as symbolizing a U.S. nuclear guarantee. This deadlock in the SALT II negotiations, partly caused by the emerging Watergate scandal that produced increasing paralysis in Washington, meant that 1973 saw only two arms-control agreements between the United States and the Soviet Union. The significance of both was political rather than technical.

The first, the Agreement on the Prevention of Nuclear War of June 22, 1973, signed during Mr. Brezhnev's visit to Washington, confirmed the political-arms-control principle of using nominal arms-control measures to symbolize and advance superpower detente. This detente was by then remarkably far advanced when compared with the limited detente of a decade earlier, which had produced the 1963 Partial Test Ban (PTB). Under the 1973 agreement the superpowers seemed to move from detente to entente, agreeing "that they will act in such a manner as to prevent the development of situations capable of causing dangerous exacerbation of their relations, as to avoid military confrontations, and as to exclude the outbreak of nuclear war between them and between either of the parties and other countries" (Article I). If there was any risk of nuclear conflict from relations between the superpowers, or between

any other states, the United States and the Soviet Union "shall im-
mediately enter into urgent consultations with each other and make
every effort to avoid this risk" (Article IV).[4] The arms-control principles
underlying this agreement were impeccable, although it was not clear
that it bound the superpowers to do anything they would not already
do, but the agreement aroused considerable concern among America's
NATO allies. They still depended on the American nuclear guarantee for
their security and were concerned lest the agreement be interpreted by
the Soviet Union as meaning that in the event of a Soviet threat to use
nuclear or non-nuclear force against Western Europe, the United States
would place a premium on securing an understanding with the Soviet
Union to avoid the use of nuclear weapons, rather than invoke their
deterrent threat against the Soviets. These fears were symptomatic of a
general Western European anxiety that the Moscow Summit and SALT I
had generated an atmosphere of detente or entente far greater than was
warranted by the real state of superpower relations, where a rising
Soviet Union faced a declining America. This interpretation of superpower relations was apparently confirmed by the signing on June 21,
1973, of the Agreement on the Basic Principles of Negotiations on
Strategic Arms Limitation, which bound the United States and the
Soviet Union to "make serious efforts to work out the provisions of the
permanent agreement on more complete measures on the limitation of
strategic offensive arms with the objective of signing it in 1974".[5] Here
again, it seemed that U.S. anxiety to secure arms-control agreements
with the Soviet Union was leading the United States to make commitments the political wisdom of which was debatable. This was especially true in 1973, when the Soviets were pressing for discussion of the
FBS issue in SALT II and U.S. NATO allies could not be certain that the
United States would reject these pressures, although in fact it did in
1974.

Despite this commitment to secure an agreement in 1974, the SALT II
negotiations remained bogged down in the face of Soviet intransi-
gence. Dr. Kissinger sought to break this deadlock in his visit in May
1974 to Moscow by using a "conceptual breakthrough". He proposed
two formulae for a SALT II agreement. The first was to set a total figure
within which each side would have the "freedom to mix" the proportion of ICBMs, SLBMs, and strategic bombers, a principle that was, in
fact, to form the basis for the Vladivostok Accord. The second would
attempt to control land-based missiles by setting a limit on their total
throweight. The United States also offered to halt further deployments of MIRVed missiles if the Soviets agreed to limit their future
deployment of such missiles. A ban on MIRVs or their further flight
testing was not offered.[6] The Soviets rejected these proposals at this

stage but could see that from the political viewpoint it would be extremely desirable to have some nominal arms-control agreements to symbolize superpower detente at the forthcoming June Summit meeting between Mr. Brezhnev and President Nixon. They therefore agreed to Kissinger's fallback proposals for a Threshold Test Ban Treaty (TTBT) and a freeze on ABM deployment at one site each (both measures of political arms control), for the 1974 Moscow Summit.

The July 1974 Agreements

The failure to agree to limit MIRV flight testing in SALT II had left a Comprehensive Test Ban (CTB) as the chief means of restraining MIRV development. If neither the United States nor the Soviet Union could test their MIRV warheads, the perfection of the high-confidence weapons necessary for a first strike could be prevented. Additionally, if ABM warheads could not be tested, either on their own or in combination with MIRV to test MIRV shielding, the development of improved ABM systems could be slowed down. These arms-control arguments for a CTB were reinforced by improvements in the ability of the United States and the Soviet Union to detect each other's nuclear tests with their own seismic detection systems. Their unilateral verification capabilities could detect tests as low as 10 kilotons, although with considerable expense and difficulty tests of up to 50 kilotons might be muffled to produce seismic readings corresponding to an explosion of 10 to 20 kilotons.[7] Since these were arguments by proponents of a CTB, they may have been too favourable to such a treaty, as may have been their conclusion that such cheating would have been of little technical value to justify the considerable risks of being caught. U.S. demands for on-site inspection to verify a CTB, demands always rejected by the Soviet Union, were part of the charade which enabled both superpowers to continue nuclear testing while claiming to be in favour of a CTB. Because the United States would not drop its demands for on-site inspections, a CTB remained out of reach; hence the compromise of a TTBT prohibiting underground nuclear tests above levels within the unilateral detection capabilities of the superpowers. A TTBT with a threshold of, say, 10 to 20 kilotons would have been a technically effective arms-control measure significantly inhibiting MIRV development. But the threshold of 150 kilotons allowed in the June agreement was too high to restrict MIRV, while the delay in enforcement of the TTBT until March 31, 1976, would allow both sides to complete their current tests of larger-yield warheads. Admittedly, the TTBT would prohibit the testing of ABM warheads which were in the one- to six-megaton range, but both sides had completed extensive testing programs giving them the data needed to develop new

ABM systems. The TTBT of July 3, 1974, could not therefore be considered a technically effective arms-control measure as it did not inhibit the development of MIRV or of "mini-nukes", smaller, cleaner tactical nuclear weapons, including, we now know, the neutron bomb.

Superficially the U.S.–U.S.S.R. July 3 agreement to limit their ABM sites to the one they each have currently deployed seemed a more substantive measure of arms control. Yet it really did little more than make political capital out of formalizing the technical status quo. The United States was politically unable to use its SALT I option to deploy an ABM in defence of Washington. The Soviet decision to give up its technically attractive option to defend an ICBM field indicated that its defensive technology lagged behind U.S. offensive technology. If ABM systems were thus politically unavailable to the United States and technically unattractive to the Soviet Union, their mutual restraint from deploying ABMs could hardly be hailed as a triumph of arms control since it did not restrain the deployment of an effective weapons system that would otherwise have been deployed. Additionally, since the U.S. ABM system was superior to the Soviet one, the freeze was an asymmetrical bargain favouring them. How long these allegedly permanent restraints on ABM deployment would last also seemed open to question, given both sides' intensive development of improved ABM systems.[8] No arms-control agreement had yet prevented the deployment of effective weapons systems, which is what the ABM treaty would eventually be doing. The treaty did, on the other hand, provide a framework which, suitably modified, would enable the superpowers to formalize any higher level of ABM deployment which they might come to see as desirable in the future, while maximizing present restraint. The legitimization of unilateral verification of compliance via satellite observation also codified an existing superpower practice conducive to arms control.

The Vladivostok Accord

If, then, the July 1974 agreements did little to inhibit destabilizing innovations in strategic technology, what of the Vladivostok Accord of November 24, 1974? Superficially, it seemed to provide the first over-all limits on the superpowers' strategic forces and was claimed by Dr. Kissinger to "put a cap on the strategic arms race". It limited the United States and the Soviet Union to "a certain agreed aggregate number of strategic delivery vehicles" (SDV), the number subsequently being clarified as 2,400, while there would also be a "certain agreed aggregate number of ICBMs and SLBMs equipped with MIRV", a number later fixed at 1,320.[9] Significantly, Soviet demands that FBS be included were dropped in the face of Dr. Kissinger's determination not to allow this issue to affect adversely American-Western European relations. But the Soviets still got something from their creation of a non-issue. The United States agreed, in return for the dropping of FBS, not to regard the new Soviet Backfire bomber, which could reach the United States with in-flight refuelling, as an SDV under the limits of the Vladivostok Accord.[10] These limits seemed less restraints than generous ceilings when compared with existing and projected forces allowed under SALT I. At the time of the Vladivostok Accord, the United States had a total of 2,213 SDVs (composed of 1,054 ICBMs, 656 SLBMs, and 503 strategic bombers). The Soviet Union had a total of 2,488 (composed of 1,612 ICBMs, 736 SLBMs, and 140 strategic bombers).

The limitations on MIRV were more apparent than real, since what was limited was the number of MIRVed SDVs, not their throweight, that is, their ability to deliver a given payload over intercontinental distances. It also remained open to question whether the United States could effectively deter any Soviet violation of this provision. The Vladivostok Accord thus did not constitute technical arms control in that it did not substantially restrain the development and deployment of new strategic-weapons systems which might, like MIRV and Maneuverable Re-entry Vehicles (MARV), threaten the stability of the strategic balance. That these agreements failed to restrain the strategic-arms competition between the superpowers became even clearer if those limitations achieved at Vladivostok were compared with those considered necessary by arms controllers, which varied from the realistic to the Utopian. A representative realist was Paul Nitze, who was, until his resignation in June 1974, the U.S. Department of Defense representative to the SALT negotiations.[11] He argued that, to be effective, a further SALT agreement would have to include three elements: "The first, and perhaps the least likely of success, is to continue the effort to negotiate roughly equal ceilings on the throweight of MIRVed missiles at a low enough level to be meaningful; i.e., low enough to postpone significantly the day when a high percentage of the hardened silos of the other side would become vulnerable to a counterforce attack."[12] This concept of qualitative restraints on equal MIRV payloads at low enough levels to minimize mutual fears over a potential first strike was proposed by Dr. Kissinger in his visit to Moscow in March 1974 and rejected by the Soviet Union in favour of a quantitative ceiling on MIRVed SDVs at about 1,000 for each side.[13] Second, Nitze proposed "roughly equal ceilings on overall missile throweight, MIRVed and unMIRVed with realistic allowances for the bomber equivalent of missile throweight."[14] The Pentagon had argued for this position to counter the imbalance between the Soviet throweight of about seven million pounds (rising to ten to fifteen million pounds under their modernization programs) as against the U.S. missile throweight of two million pounds plus a bomber payload that varied, depending on the mission, from two to thirty million pounds. Third, Nitze argued the need to "negotiate a schedule of phased reductions in these ceilings to lower levels, even lower if possible, than planned U.S. deployment levels."[15] These were minimum conditions for a technically effective SALT II agreement which were not met in the Vladivostok Accord. Additionally, there were strong arguments for restraints on Anti-Submarine Warfare (ASW) to preserve the invulnerability of SLBMs. More Utopian proposals included an elimination of U.S. and U.S.S.R. land-based ICBMs as vulnerable to counterforce strikes and therefore destabilizing in a crisis, or for a substantial reduction in the alleged overkill capabilities of current strategic forces.

The extent to which the Vladivostok Accord failed to limit the potential strategic instability from MIRVs' counterforce capability could be seen from rough calculations for the vulnerability of land-based ICBMs. The Soviet force of 313 SS-9 could, when MIRVed, destroy 95 per cent of the U.S. Minuteman force, while a modernized Minuteman force of 1,000 MM IIIs could, with foreseeable improvements in accuracy, take out 70 to 85 per cent of Soviet silos.[16] Whether such mutual vulnerability to a counterforce first strike would, in fact, produce instability in the strategic balance in a broader, political sense was, of course, open to question; so was the issue of whether the Soviet Union would seek political gains from its strategic superiority. But the important point was that such crisis instability had been assumed to follow from a technical vulnerability to a first strike by the arms controllers since 1958 and remained, in their view, the greatest single threat to strategic stability in 1975.

Thus the limitations imposed by SALT I and the 1974 agreements on the strategic arms race were almost wholly ineffective in terms of the technical criteria specified by the arms-control community. Dr. Kissinger's claims that the Vladivostok cap on the arms race "is substantially below the capabilities of either side" and that it substantially reduced "the element of insecurity inherent in an arms race"[17] were deliberately disingenuous. He was accurate only in suggesting that the political instabilities resulting from the superpower arms race might have been mitigated. The rate of development and scale of deployment of MIRV had not been restrained, either at Vladivostok or by the TTBT. The ABM freeze at one site each simply legitimized a status quo that was unlikely to be as permanent as was implied. But the 1974 arms-control agreements had, like SALT I, been completely successful in a political sense, facilitating the improvement of Soviet-American relations as long as neither power attempted to make political gains from any theoretical strategic superiority. Both SALT I and the 1974 agreements showed that the Soviets continued to reject Western notions of arms control and strategic stability in favour of a belief that military superiority should be productive of political gains. This had created an asymmetrical bargaining process in which the United States and its allies were forced to pay a high political price in order to gain agreements whose arms-control effects were minimal. So long as these agreements also produced a genuine reduction in tension, this process of detente through arms control was constructive. But now that the United States had accepted the Soviet Union as a superpower with whom it enjoyed a relationship of adversary-partnership, arms-control agreements also needed to reflect Soviet acceptance of Washington's parity with Moscow. Parity had to be a two-way relationship if it was to produce co-operation.

The Questioning of SALT:
Soviet "Violations" of SALT I and Political Changes

Paradoxically, then, the Vladivostok Accord, rather than paving the way for a SALT II, prevented it. By provoking widespread and effective criticism from both the liberal and conservative technical arms controllers, the Accord re-focused attention on the crucial political issues that had been subsumed in the technical minutiae accompanying much of the assessment of SALT I's success or failure, and of the consequent shape SALT II should take. The three key questions posed by the Soviets' continuing build-up of their strategic forces were: their political motives for doing so; why even the very limited SALT I agreements had failed to stop this where the United States administration had claimed they would do so; and, above all, what the future of the Soviet-American relationship would be — entente, detente, or a new Cold War? Because SALT I and II had been made, like previous superpower arms-control agreements, the barometer of their political relations, the new SALT debate, from 1975 onwards, had increasingly broad political implications not only for relations between Washington and Moscow, but also for events within Washington and for domestic U.S. politics. Nor were Washington's allies, within and outside NATO, without interest in this debate: the major Western European powers had been especially concerned about the apparent move towards a superpower condominium signified by SALT I, and were increasingly apprehensive about Soviet long-term designs on them, and about the reliability and credibility of the American nuclear guarantee. It was, therefore, an increasingly sensitive political arena in which charges of Soviet exploitation of the ambiguities of SALT I were made from early 1975 onwards.[18] These charges are still being debated; but the fundamental issues — if not the answers — were always relatively clear, clearer than much of the resulting debate would suggest. They reaffirmed the basic argument that arms control cannot be treated as an apolitical, technical process. Arms-control measures always have political effects, although their importance can vary, as can the complexity of their technical content and the political relevance of these technicalities.

In the case of the Soviet conduct in SALT I, the legal rather than the strategic technicalities caused confusion because of the unique treaty structure involved in the Interim Agreement. As explained above in Chapter 18, it fell into two parts: the Interim Agreement (Table 18.1, p.158) and the ABM treaty which could be called the Treaty proper, or SALT I, Part I, since it was equally binding on both parties; and the attached web of interlocking Agreed Statements, Common Understandings, and Unilateral Statements (Table 18.2, p.159); these also interpreted the ABM treaty. This could be called the United States interpretation of SALT I, or SALT I, Part II. This is not an exaggeration: the Soviet government never formally, legally, accepted any of these American interpretations, although agreeing with, or taking note of them. Nor did they allow into either SALT I, Part I, or the ABM treaty any precise definition of the key terms. Given the Soviet history, since 1917, of observing the precise letter of any treaty it accepted, this suggests that, knowing their planned deployment of offensive strategic forces from 1972-77, and their development program for ABM systems, they framed SALT I, Parts I and II, to allow these deployments and developments to proceed without legally violating SALT. Politically, they used SALT to further the image of detente, as, indeed, they are still trying to do, albeit with less success each year since 1975. Since they never accepted the technical-arms-control case for restraint on strategic forces, the Soviets never believed SALT I had any spirit of arms control, except insofar as this spirit was perceived in the West, a political perception they encouraged. In contrast, the Nixon – Kissinger administration stressed the importance of the spirit of SALT I, as did President Ford under Dr. Kissinger's guidance. In this instance, Dr. Kissinger's conduct could be defended by the argument that SALT and detente were the prerequisites for the survival of civilization. It is less easy to justify his conduct, except in terms of political expediency, in telling the Senate, Congress, and the American people that SALT I, Part II, was as binding on the Soviets as SALT I, Part I. It would have been more accurate to say that, since the Soviets refused to commit themselves to legally binding definitions of the key terms in SALT I, Part I, the United States had set out its definition of these, which it would insist the Soviets comply with, or, if they did not, the U.S. would abrogate the Treaty — the normal penalty for non-compliance. Similarly, Dr. Kissinger should have stressed that the Standing Consultative Commission (SCC) established on December 21, 1972, as required by SALT I, to monitor compliance with SALT (Parts I and II), had no real power to do so. The SCC could only act as a forum for diplomatic charges of violation and their rebuttal, as with possible Soviet violation or exploitation of SALT. This basic analysis makes it clear that the Soviets faced a spectrum of choice: they could observe their version of SALT I (Part I only: the meaningless quantitative ceiling); they could observe the U.S. version of SALT I (Parts I and II: imposing the first qualitative restraints on the strategic arms race); or they could mix competition and restraint. They appear to have chosen unrestrained competition, knowing that the Nixon – Kissinger commitment to SALT as a symbol of detente would make it politically so costly to charge the Soviets with violating SALT I (Part I), or ignoring SALT I (Part II), that no such charges would be made.

Indeed, rather than make such charges, the U.S. government would be the first to defend the Soviets against them. The answer to Fred C. Iklé's classic question on arms-control agreements, "After violation — What?",[19] was, for the Soviets: "Nothing". Kissinger, especially after Watergate, could not even afford to hold out on a SALT II. President Ford needed it politically, for the 1976 presidential elections, and he needed it to head off strategic instability (which it would not have stabilized) and political instability (which a SALT II could have stabilized, had the Soviets been co-operative rather than competitive).

Once the two-part nature of SALT I is understood, the pattern of Soviet adherence to Part I — which was legally binding on the Soviets and too politically expensive to violate too often — and of Soviet indifference to Part II is intelligible. The question remaining is, then, the effect of their actions on SALT I: was the strategic environment less stable at the end than at the beginning of the Interim Agreement? The answer was that it was clearly less stable by technical-arms-control criteria. Given that SALT I had failed to restrain the deployment of MIRV, the most important qualitative improvement in Soviet forces that SALT I could stop was their increase in throwweight, the importance of which was discussed above, and in Circular Error Probability (CEP) (linked to throwweight). SALT I (Part II) tried to do this, but a comparison (Table 19.1) of the new Soviet ICBM with the ones they replaced shows the effect of not enforcing its provisions.

Table 19.1 Soviet ICBM: Increases in Throweight, Volume, and CEP under SALT I* 1972-77

Type	First Deployed	Volume (cubic metres)	Throweight (**) (thousand lbs.)	Warhead Yield (†)	CEP (††)	Number Deployed [July] 1972	1977
"Light" ICBM (†††)							
SS-11 Sego	1966	69	1.5–2	1–2 MT or 3x KT MRV	0.5–0.3	970	840
SS-13 Savage	1968	30	1		0.7	60	60
Replacements							
SS-17	1975	118	6		0.3	—	40
SS-19	1975	96	7	6x KT	0.3–0.2	—	50
"Heavy" ICBM							
SS-9 Scarp	1965	c. 247	12–15	18–25 MT	0.5	290	238
Replacement							
SS-18	1975	247	15–18	15–25 MT	0.3–0.2	—	50

Notes:

(*) SOURCE: Colin S. Gray, *The Future of Land Based Missile Forces*, Adelphi Paper No. 140 (London: IISS, Winter 1977), pp. 32–35. Volume estimates are mine.

(**) Throweight is payload

(†) KT (kiloton) range = 1,000 tons TNT equivalent
MT (megaton) range = 1 million tons TNT equivalent

(††) Circular Error Probability: measure of accuracy, circle radius within which half of missiles fired will fall

(†††) Under SALT I (Part II) a "light" ICBM was defined by the United States as one with a volume of under seventy cubic metres. In January 1976, Dr. Kissinger accepted the Soviet redefinition of a "light" ICBM as one with a volume not exceeding ninety-six cubic metres.

Arms controllers had also stressed the importance of stopping ABM deployment and development, yet even here the ABM treaty, apparently part of SALT I (Part I), failed to achieve its objective. The Soviet SA-2 and SA-5 SAM and associated radars were tested "in an ABM mode" against high-altitude targets (over 100,000 feet) for eighteen months, ceasing only after the test series was complete. The problem was that the definition of "in an ABM mode" was a unilateral American one. This poses the "SAM-upgrade" problem, that is, the possibility of giving the Soviets' large SAM network (over 10,000 launchers) some ABM capability. Additional testing of ABM radars, and deployment of a major new radar had also taken place.

SALT II: The Stalled Search, 1975-76

This debate on Soviet violations of SALT created a right-wing backlash in the United States, especially in the Republican party, that forced President Ford, by March 1976 — out of fear that Ronald Reagan might wrest the Republican nomination from the President — to put a hold on Dr. Kissinger's quest for a SALT II. But Dr. Kissinger's quest probably never had much chance of success. The Vladivostok Accord (the accompanying *aide mémoire* defining the key terms is still secret) failed to cover two important issues: the Soviet Backfire bomber and the U.S. cruise missiles. Dr. Kissinger's briefing on the Accord put him on record as saying that he did not think the Backfire would be counted as a strategic delivery vehicle (SDV). But increasing technical evidence, which Dr. Kissinger tried to suppress, emerged that it had some strategic capability against the United States, making it a political issue. Whatever the strategic value of the Backfire, once it was seen to have a strategic capability, not counting it as an SDV seemed an excessive concession to the Soviets, even by the lax standards of SALT. The cruise missile created an even greater problem for SALT II; even if this was only held to cover air-launched cruise missiles (ALCM) — a view subsequently rejected by the Soviets in 1977-78—how was the ALCM to be counted? The eventual interim solution, to count ALCMs carrying strategic bombers against the Vladivostok sub-ceiling of 1,320 MIRVed SDV came late to produce a SALT II for 1976. The Soviets clearly assumed that Dr. Kissinger and President Ford would eventually offer extremely favourable terms. They were right. At his January 20, 1976, Moscow meeting with the Soviet leaders, Kissinger reportedly offered SALT II concessions allowing the Soviets to build up to 275 Backfire bombers over the next five years, with no limits thereafter. In contrast, the United States would refrain from deploying cruise missiles on submarines and limit them to twenty-five ships for ten years.[20] Ironically, here, as with President Carter, the Soviets underestimated two increasingly important factors in superpower arms control. The first was the growing doubt within the United States about the value of arms-control agreements with the Soviets that allowed or appeared to allow them to build up their forces while those of the United States were restrained. The second was the questioning of detente, sparked by the failure of SALT I to meet even its most modest objectives, or to lead to a SALT II, coupled with the Soviet Union's increasingly harder line, internally and externally, culminating in its intervention (using Cuban troops) in Africa, starting in late 1975 in Angola. The resultant swing in the American electorate away from the euphoria of the detente, or even entente, atmosphere of the 1972 Moscow Summit was symbolized by President Ford's deletion of the word "detente" from his campaign vocabulary.

At the strategic level, the high hopes technical arms controllers had had for SALT — both as a process of mutual strategic education (actually of the backward Soviets by the advanced Americans, to "raise their learning curve") and as a series of agreements limiting the strategic arms race — had been dashed. The new Carter administration might reverse this adverse trend, the technical arms controllers argued, if it adopted their theories, which it did, and translated these into practice, which it could try to do. But it seemed all too likely to approach arms control with the lack of awareness of its political dimensions that had all too often characterized U.S. arms-control policy. The lessons of the SALT I negotiations and terms, of the Vladivostok Accord, of the failure to enforce the U.S. interpretation of SALT I, and of the search for a SALT II were that U.S. acceptance of anything less than actual and perceived strategic parity with the Soviets would produce adverse results. Moscow had not demonstrated reciprocal restraint in weapons acquisition, but had been encouraged to capitalize on, and increase, its strategic advantages versus Washington. The same trend had been evident in the Vienna Talks on Mutual and Balanced Force Reductions (MBFR — a NATO acronym rejected by the Soviets).

These had sought to translate into practice some of the long-standing proposals for arms control and reductions in Europe, the most heavily armed area in the world. Starting in 1973, in the afterglow of the 1972 Moscow Summit, MBFR had also seemed to offer a means of halting the Warsaw Pact Organization (WPO) increase in conventional forces targeted against NATO. But, as the lack of progress in these talks until 1976 (and, in fact, to 1978) showed, arms-control negotiations were primarily concerned, from the Soviet viewpoint, with the relevant political relationships, either between the superpowers, or between them and their European allies and adversaries. Stability, for the Soviets, remained defined in their politico-military terms, not in terms of the technical requirements of Western arms controllers. The survey of arms control in Europe that follows serves to underline its essentially political nature.

20 Arms Control in Europe: Origins, 1955-65*

*This and the next two chapters draw on my *Mutual and Balanced Force Reductions: Underlying Issues and Potential Developments*, ORAE Memo, no. M74, January 1976.

Two decades after the first major arms-control conference — the Surprise Attack Conference of 1958 — discussions were once again under way with the objective of stabilizing the balance of deterrence in Europe. The three main sets of negotiations were: those between NATO and the WPO on Mutual and Balanced Force Reductions (MBFR), that started in 1973; the Conference on Security and Co-operation in Europe (CSCE) that started in 1972 and finished in 1975; and the talks on Forward-Based Systems (FBS) for delivering tactical nuclear weapons that had been touched on in SALT I and SALT II. Additionally, these negotiations were the subject of a growing debate on their role, together with that of tactical nuclear weapons, in NATO strategy. In each instance the Western countries retained their emphasis on technical, and the Soviets their emphasis on political, arms control. This became clearer if their current positions were placed in their appropriate historical and intellectual contexts, since both superpowers had in fact attempted to apply their different concepts of arms control to the European theatre since these emerged in the late 1950s. From 1958 to 1964, Western arms-control analysts attempted to apply their new theories to produce schemes of technical arms control for Europe, while the Soviet Union concentrated on the essentially political concepts of Atom-Free Zones (see Chapter 5, above), and the various Rapacki plans for denuclearization. Additionally, the Soviet Union regularly proposed ground observation posts (GOP) and measures for preventing surprise attack that looked at first glance like measures of technical arms control but which were technically inadequate, and political in intent. With the emergence of the Non-Proliferation Treaty (NPT) as the chief focus of superpower interest in arms control in 1965, attention shifted away from arms control in Europe until 1968 when the concept of Mutual and Balanced Force Reductions (MBFR) emerged in Western policy as a counter to U.S. domestic pressures for reductions in its forces in Western Europe. NATO pressures for negotiations with the WPO on MBFR interacted with the Soviet campaign for a European Security Conference (ESC), that started in 1964, to produce, with Brezhnev's acceptance of MBFR talks in his 1971 Tiflis speech, two sets of discussions on security in Europe. The political one, in which the Soviet Union had more to gain, was the CSCE, while the technical one, in which the West had more to gain, was the MBFR talks. The FBS issue was particularly interesting as an example both of the differences between the technical and political approaches to arms control and of the way in which their different modalities could lead to the same objective. Similarly, the Western debate on the role of tactical nuclear weapons in the defence of Western Europe, started by U.S. plans (in 1973) to modernize their nuclear stockpile in Western Europe, showed the continuing dominance of the technical approach to arms control in U.S. thinking. To see how this had influenced Western thinking as a whole it was necessary to turn back to the 1958 Surprise Attack Conference to see how the then emergent concepts of technical arms control had shaped U.S. proposals for reassurance against surprise attack in Europe, and how these ideas had subsequently developed.

The Technical Approach to Arms Control in Europe: 1958-64

As has been shown in Chapter 4, the main focus of the Western delegations to the 1958 Surprise Attack Conference was on preventing strategic surprise attack, but surprise attack in Europe was also considered. The lengthy "Explanatory Document of the . . . Proposed Plan of Work Submitted by the Western Experts"[1] concentrated on strategic delivery vehicles but also mentioned armoured fighting vehicles and mobile artillery. Some of the types of evidence which might be used for indicating the imminence of surprise attack might include:

Concentrations of ground forces or their logistic support; increase of transport capabilities; the movement of missiles or other warhead delivery devices to units; change in scale and scope of maneuvers; increase of personnel.[2]

The document went on to suggest that ground observers were,

. . . the most effective means of ground inspection aimed at reducing the danger of surprise attack. However, their effectiveness is a function of their freedom of movement within or over the area under observation, of the adequacy of their means of transportation and communication, and of their rights and privileges. The use of technological aids can extend the sensory capabilities of observers and thus increase their effectiveness.[3]

These proposals were examined in more detail in the "Third Explanatory Document" of December 5, 1958,[4] which suggested a highly complex system of observation to monitor virtually all significant military movements within a given area (presumably Eastern and

Western Europe, although the document managed to avoid saying this). These proposals included the "Exchange and Verification of Blue prints of Force Data" (3.2); "Observation of Ground Forces" (3.3); and of "Transportation Centres" (3.4); and the establishment of "Communications Facilities" (3.5). The conclusion was that "significant results might be obtained even with a modest force of resident and mobile observers. . . . so long as the rights of observers . . . are not unduly curtailed."[5] Such measures went far beyond anything that could be acceptable to the Soviets and emphasized the Western or, more properly, the technical-arms-control view that:

We [the West] did not envisage this as a political negotiation but a meeting of experts to discuss technical/military problems in respect of systems of observation and inspection designed to reduce the danger of surprise attack.[6]

This theme was reiterated in the statement of December 18, 1958, by U.S. Representative William C. Foster that: "We have sought to promote technical discussion and understanding. You [the Soviet Union] have sought discussion of a selection of political proposals, for the most part not susceptible of technical assessment."[7] The problem of stabilizing the NATO–WPO balance of deterrence was thus dealt with in the technical, nominally apolitical framework characteristic of the U.S. and Western approach to arms control. This was evident from a brief examination of subsequent arms-control proposals for stabilizing the East-West European military balance which formed the intellectual framework within which the idea of MBFR was to be developed from 1967 onwards.

Technical Arms Control and European Stability

While the Soviets were concentrating on proposals for political arms control in Europe, Western technical-arms-control thinking remained preoccupied with the strategic balance. Indeed, the most striking feature of the intellectual refinement of arms control (outlined in Chapter 3) was how little attention was paid to the problem of stability in Europe. The four central works summarizing arms-control thinking as it had evolved by 1961-62[8] contained virtually no discussion of arms control in Western Europe, except for Bull's reference[9] to the Western stress on mutual inspection against surprise attack at the 1958 Surprise Attack Conference and the reiteration of these measures in the Western plan for General and Complete Disarmament (GCD) of March 16, 1960.[10]

The only substantial new academic work on arms control in Europe was by Alastair Buchan and Philip Windsor.[11] This showed how far Western thinking had become dominated by U.S. concepts of technical arms control. It stressed that disengagement, that is, a political settlement involving the neutralization of Germany as a preliminary to military withdrawal, was no longer considered feasible since political negotiations could only follow from a reduction of tension and the achievement of basic military stability, the objective of technical arms control. Once this military stability was achieved without sacrificing political stability, it might be possible to reduce forces in Eastern and Western Europe.[12]

The danger of accidents as long as both sides relied on nuclear weapons for their forward defence in Europe was stressed, as was the danger that if they relied primarily on conventional forces the possibilities of surprise attack might be higher.[13] The central arms-control problem was that "the prevention of 'accidental war' depends both on the prevention of technical accident and on the establishment of adequate means of verification and control to prevent any such accident from triggering a nuclear exchange."[14] The problem of surprise attack was discussed largely in the context of Schelling's work on the reciprocal fear of surprise attack, where the fear of war becomes a cause of war, and reflected the technical concept of arms control.[15] Possible measures to lessen this fear in Europe could include inspection and control procedures, using air surveillance and mobile ground teams, as in NATO plans for a zone of inspection including the two Germanies, Poland, Czechoslovakia, and parts of France and the Low Countries; but this level of inspection would lead to demilitarization. A more practical measure would be the advance notification of major military manoeuvres.[16] This idea has re-emerged at the CSCE, as a Confidence Building Measure (CBM). To deal with the problem of a general ground attack, static inspection teams were proposed at major airfields, main roads, railways, and, possibly, ports. "Because it was limited and static, an inspection system designed to check build-up would be more likely to command early agreement, it would not work to the disadvantage of either side, and it would serve its purpose effectively."[17] The United States had, on December 12, 1962, proposed at the Eighteen Nation Disarmament Conference (ENDC), an exchange of military missions between the headquarters of NATO and the WPO.[18] Arms reduction could contribute to stability if it brought about parity between NATO and the WPO, especially on the Central Front and particularly if the Soviet superiority in tanks (then 14,000 to NATO's 6,000) could be reduced.[19] Here again, the arms-control concepts of the early 1960s have re-emerged in NATO proposals for MBFR.

With the post-Cuban-missile-crisis detente of 1963, arms-control attention shifted from the problem of surprise attack towards the nonproliferation of nuclear weapons. Typical works of the mid-1960s contained few references to arms control in Europe, reiterating the old ideas of observation posts as protection against surprise attack and discussing the idea of inspected or demilitarized zones in Europe.[20] Only in the late 1960s did the problems begin to arise of U.S. domestic and economic pressures for a reduction in its forces in Europe (the result also of the Vietnam War), though even then arms-control thinking was still dominated by the issues of non-proliferation and the desirability of U.S. deployment of an ABM system, a question linked to the possibility of SALT.[21]

Diplomatic Developments

A similar lack of movement away from the ideas of the 1958-61 period was evident in the few Western diplomatic proposals for arms control in Europe. The 1960 U.S. position was based on the hastily prepared Coolidge Commission report and stressed the need for safeguards against surprise attack, including zones for aerial and ground inspection, and for stopping the spread of nuclear weapons.[22] The U.S. Working Paper on "Reduction of the Risk of War Through Accident, Miscalculation, or Failure of Communication"[23] of December 12, 1962, also included suggestions for the advanced notification of major military manoeuvres and the conduct of confirmatory and supplementary observations, especially "Movements and maneuvers by ground forces of considerable strength . . . conducted in the proximity of frontiers."[24] Additionally, observation posts at principal ports, major railroad junctions, intersections of key highways, and significant airfields were proposed, together with additional observation arrangements, the exchange of military missions, and communications in military emergencies.[25]

These proposals summarized the then existing thinking on technical arms control in Europe which progressed little further until MBFR emerged as an issue. In 1964 the United States re-introduced the idea of observation posts to the ENDC to reduce the risk of war through misunderstanding, though these were tied to the strategic superpower balance by the suggestion that they be placed in the United States and the Soviet Union, as well as in Eastern and Western Europe.[26] Great Britain followed up with a Working Paper on Observation Posts restating the technical-arms-control case for them.[27] Neither proposal met with any response from the Soviet Union. These suggestions for observation posts, this time in the context of a NATO–WPO Non-Aggression Pact, re-emerged in 1965 along with the idea of "parallel troop reductions in West and East Germany by the United States and the Soviet Union" which would not change the military balance, but would "preserve the balance at less cost".[28]

Therefore, by 1965, two important factors in shaping the concept of MBFR were already clear. The first, the emergence of U.S. domestic pressures for U.S. troop reductions in Western Europe, was obvious. The second, the intellectual stagnation of thinking and policy on arms control in Europe, was not. But it was impossible to understand how much MBFR was a product of technical-arms-control thinking without realizing that the new ideas of this thinking, formulated from 1958 to 1961, had become generally accepted within U.S. and Western policy-making circles. This is not to say that all Western policy makers accepted the ideas of technical arms control, only that those concerned with arms control had come to accept the ideas of 1958-61 as the conventional wisdom of their field. One of the most important of these ideas was that of the dangers of allowing either the East or the West to acquire sufficient advantage in a first-strike attack to make fear of surprise attack a cause of escalation. Pressures from the United States for reductions in its forces in Western Europe were therefore bound to interact with the classic arms-control notions of the dangers of surprise attack and its prevention, producing the concept of MBFR as the result of an internal NATO debate. This last point needs stressing — the idea of MBFR was a response to political and economic pressures for force reductions in NATO conceived in terms of technical arms control. The Western idea of MBFR did not begin to interact with Soviet ideas in the field of political arms control until Brezhnev's 1971 Tiflis speech inviting the West to "taste the wine" of mutual force reductions. This made it important to trace the evolution of Soviet thinking on arms control in Europe. The political origins and context of this thinking were discussed in Chapter 5, as were Soviet proposals for Atom-Free Zones (AFZ), so it will suffice here to discuss two other manifestations of the Soviet approach to arms control in Europe, the various Rapacki plans for denuclearization and the Soviet proposals for ground observation posts (GOP).

The Political Approach to Arms Control in Europe: 1957-65

There were a total of five Rapacki plans advanced from October 1957[29] to March 1962.[30] They all had three objectives in common: first, securing Western recognition of East Germany; second, the thinning out and eventual withdrawal of FBS; and third, reductions in foreign and indigenous forces in the area of reductions which included the two Germanies, Poland, and Czechoslovakia. Excluding the anti-MLF elements, prominent from 1961 onwards, there was a clear continuity in these Soviet objectives, expressed through Poland, and Soviet aims in the negotiations on the CSCE, FBS, and MBFR. The political success of the Rapacki plans in influencing Western intellectuals and politicians to accept the Soviet concept of the requirements for stabilization in Europe was evident. As early as 1957 George Kennan, in his Reith Lectures, had suggested that all foreign troops should be withdrawn from a denuclearized Central and Eastern Europe within which a neutral Germany could be reunified, and the whole structure guaranteed by a European Security Pact. Similarly, the then leader of the British Labour Party, Hugh Gaitskell, proposed in 1957-58 the disengagement of NATO and WPO forces from a nuclear-free neutral zone including a reunified Germany. His ideas were supported by his Labour Party colleague, Mr. Denis Healey, later Labour Minister of Defence, from 1964 to 1970.[31] Neither these nor other similar proposals for denuclearization were technically adequate from an arms-control viewpoint. Nor were Soviet proposals for ground observation posts (GOP).[32]

Ground Observation Posts

The first Soviet suggestion that GOPs be established at large ports, railway junctions, on main highways, and at airports, to avoid a dangerous concentration of forces, came on May 10, 1955. The very limited number of GOPs, nineteen, was inadequate for effective verification and was linked to proposals for the reduction of armaments that were too far-reaching to be realistic.[33] Mr. Khrushchev's letter of July 2, 1958, accepting the idea of a Surprise Attack Conference[34] suggested that there should be established control posts at railway junctions, big ports, and major highways combined with definite (unspecified) disarmament steps. In the 1958 Surprise Attack Conference the Soviet Union proposed aerial inspection and static ground observation posts. On November 28 they gave the first details of their proposed plans, including a ban on nuclear weapons, at least within the two Germanies; a one-third reduction in conventional forces in the areas covered by NATO and the WPO; an unspecified reduction in foreign bases in the same areas; and a ban on flights of aircraft with nuclear weapons over the high seas and other areas. Apart from aerial inspection, there were to be GOPs at railways, ports, and highways, twenty-eight in the WPO against forty-eight in NATO, plus six each in the Soviet Union and the United States, giving thirty-four in the East as against fifty-four in the West. There were to be no more than six to eight officers at each post, commanded by a national of the observed state, keeping direct visual watch on troop movements.[35]

At first sight, and taken in isolation, these Soviet proposals for inspection appeared similar to those suggested by Western arms controllers to provide mutual reassurance against surprise attack, especially in Europe. However, these inspection proposals were not linked to a balanced scheme of technical arms control in Europe and were technically inadequate to detect preparations for the land-based surprise attack in Europe against which the Soviets were apparently seeking protection. Whereas the Soviet proposal of May 10, 1955, called for an unspecified but "adequate" inspection system, the 1958 proposal amounted to little more than self-inspection. The Aerial Inspection Zones would be covered only by aerial reconnaissance conducted by the state being inspected, albeit with representatives of the other side present. The number of GOPs was also inadequate — the Soviet proposals for 34 posts in the East and 54 in the West were well below an impartial estimate that the minimum requirements for adequate verification would be 60-65 GOPs on either side to cover major river crossings alone plus some 150 GOPs on either side's airfields.[36] Additionally, the Soviet proposals for GOPs were linked to a reduction in the size of foreign armed forces on the territories of European states, that is, disengagement, as well as the removal of nuclear weapons from the two Germanies, that is, denuclearization. No verification for these steps was proposed. So here again, the Soviets were proposing political rather than technical arms control. The four main elements in their measures for stabilizing the NATO–WPO confrontation were: first, the removal of nuclear weapons and their delivery systems from the two Germanies, coupled with their recognition; second, the complete or partial withdrawal of foreign troops from German territory; third, limitations on the conventional and nuclear forces stationed in the adjoining territory, usually Poland and Czechoslovakia; fourth, measures for mutual reassurance against surprise attack with conventional weapons, normally through GOPs and/or aerial inspection.

Basic Positions, 1955-65

The fundamental context of Western and Soviet positions on arms-control issues was thus clearly established by 1965. The Western approach of technical arms control was applied, to a limited degree and with no success, to the NATO–WPO military confrontation. In contrast, the Soviets had used their political-arms-control approach to secure advancement of their political goals, with some success. What was clear in this period, and remained clear in the next decade, was that the two sides' basic approaches remained fundamentally different, technical for the West and political for the East. This was clear from the evolution of their position on MBFR, the CSCE, and FBS.

21 The Moves Towards MBFR and a CSCE: 1965-72

The two major conferences on European security under way in 1975, those on Mutual and Balanced Force Reductions (MBFR) and the Conference on Security and Co-operation in Europe (CSCE), had their origins in, respectively, the intra-NATO debate on political and economic pressures for U.S. Unilateral Force Reductions (UFR) and the Soviet campaign for a general European Security Conference (ESC) to legitimize the status quo of their ideological, political, and military control over Eastern Europe. The two sides maintained the approaches they had established over the previous decade. MBFR emerged as a technical-arms-control measure meeting internal NATO needs, a point that needs stressing — MBFR was a response, conceived in terms of technical arms control, to political and economic pressures from the United States for force reductions in NATO. The Western idea of MBFR did not begin to interact with the Soviet ideas in the field of political arms control until Brezhnev's 1971 Tiflis speech inviting the West to "taste the wine" of mutual force reductions. Even then, the slow progress from 1971 to the preliminary MBFR negotiations of 1973 and the lack of progress in the Mutual Force Reduction (MFR) talks after both sides tabled their initial proposals in October and November 1974 emphasized that the two sides had completely different conceptual approaches to the reduction of forces. The West stuck to the technical-arms-control concept of MBFR, while the Soviet Union stuck to the political-arms-control idea of MFR. The gap between these two proposals might be bridgeable in terms of diplomatic practice, but not in terms of intellectual origins and basic formulation. Provided that this qualification was understood, the evolution of MBFR could then be traced to show how the Western position had evolved. This could then be compared with the evolution of Soviet proposals for an ESC/CSCE.

The U.S. Debate on Forces in Europe and NATO Reactions

The growth of opposition in the U.S. Senate and, to a lesser extent, in Congress to maintaining 310,000 U.S. forces in Western Europe has to be seen partly as a reaction to the global U.S. overcommitment to contain communism everywhere and its resultant direct involvement in the Vietnam War from 1965 to 1973. Additionally, there was a growing argument that domestic priorities were more important than defence spending and that Western Europe was strong enough and wealthy enough to provide for its own defence, or at least a greater share of it. These feelings were typified by Senator Michael Mansfield, the leading critic of U.S. troop involvement in NATO (and globally).

The first evidence that America's European allies were aware of these pressures came with the Harmel report of the North Atlantic Council of December 1967, which for the first time indicated that the Allies were studying the possibility of "balanced force reductions".[1] This showed that NATO supporters would try to head off pressures for U.S. Unilateral Force Reductions (UFR) by putting these in the context of a NATO offer of multilateral East-West talks on mutual force reductions. Before and during these the United States would be unable to reduce its forces unilaterally without prejudicing either the chance of negotiations or their success if they started. This latter eventuality was regarded as unlikely in 1967, certainly by the State Department which, in view of President Johnson's concentration on the Vietnam War, was effectively making U.S. foreign policy towards NATO.

The logical result of these pressures was the Reykjavik Communiqué of the North Atlantic Council meeting of June 24-25, 1968, which spoke of "the study of the possibility of balanced force reductions as between East and West" as the priority arms-control measure being studied by NATO experts and which later referred to the need for intensified work on the possibilities of such reductions

. . . in accordance with the following agreed principles:

a. Mutual force reductions should be reciprocal and balanced in scope and timing.
b. Mutual reductions should represent a substantial and significant step, which will serve to maintain the present degree of security at reduced cost, but should not be such as to risk destabilizing the situation in Europe.
c. Mutual reduction should be consonant with the aim of creating confidence in Europe generally and in the case of each party concerned.
d. To this end, any new arrangement regarding forces should be consistent with the vital security interests of all parties and capable of being carried out effectively.[2]

If this call to the East went unheeded it was scarcely surprising, since the Soviet Union could hope for unilateral Western, particularly U.S., force reductions and remained interested in political rather than technical arms control. The key concept behind MBFR, which was to emerge in the subsequent NATO studies and the NATO negotiating position, was clearly that of an asymmetrical NATO–WPO military balance favouring the WPO, especially in tanks, and creating a balance of deterrence considered as technically unstable in U.S. arms-control thinking. This European assumption clashed with the McNamara view that there was rough parity between NATO and the WPO on the central front.[3] But the *offer* of negotiations on MBFR was acceptable to all members of NATO because it would prevent or delay U.S. UFR. Additionally, if there was a U.S. reduction in forces as part of a negotiated reduction, NATO would be either better off if the Soviet Union accepted the principle of asymmetrical reductions; or not as badly off as if there were no Soviet reductions, if the Soviet Union agreed to cut its forces by an amount equal to the American reduction. Such a U.S. reduction would also put a floor on U.S. forces in NATO, preventing any subsequent UFR.[4]

These studies within NATO and MBFR led to the Rome Communiqué, of May 28, 1970, inviting the East to discuss a proposal for MBFR whose criteria were clearly those of technical arms control:

a. Mutual force reductions should be compatible with the vital security interests of the Alliance and should not operate to the military disadvantage of either side having regard for the differences arising from geographical and other considerations;
b. Reductions should be on a basis of reciprocity, and phased and balanced as to their scope and timing;
c. Reductions should include stationed and indigenous forces and their weapons systems in the area concerned;
d. There must be adequate verification and controls to ensure the observance of agreements on mutual and balanced force reductions.[5]

These concepts had evolved within NATO as a result of studies proceeding from the basis of technical-arms-control premises, to meet the internal needs of the NATO alliance in preventing or limiting U.S. force reductions, so that an intra-alliance policy was being presented as the basis for inter-alliance negotiations.

The U.S. Domestic Debate: 1970-72

That the domestic pressures within the U.S. for force reductions were gathering strength in 1970 was evident from Undersecretary of Defense Elliot Richardson's forthright defence of the maintenance of U.S. forces in NATO at about their current strength of 310,000, down from their 1962 peak of 408,000, despite a balance-of-payments drain estimated at $1.5 billion a year. Additionally, the Mansfield Resolution for UFR was opposed on the grounds that it removed any Warsaw Pact incentive to negotiate on MBFR.[6] Senator Mansfield, who by 1970 was claiming fifty-one Senate backers for his resolution to reduce U.S. forces,[7] replied with an equally trenchant attack on the status quo, arguing that Western Europe was better able to afford to defend itself and that only a token U.S. military presence was necessary to maintain the credibility of the U.S. nuclear guarantee to Western Europe.[8] That the Senator's views on detente grossly exaggerated its nature and extent were evident from this and subsequent statements.

These domestic pressures came to a head in 1971, when Senator Mansfield forced a debate on his proposal to halve the number of U.S. forces in Western Europe. After the Nixon administration exerted the maximum pressure against the resolution and virtually every living major figure in the making of U.S. defence and foreign policy since 1945 had testified against it, the resolution was defeated 61-36, not least because Mr. Brezhnev had accepted the Western offer of MBFR talks the day before the vote. Perhaps more significantly, Mansfield's subsequent November proposal for a 60,000 reduction was defeated by a 54-39 vote. On both occasions, other Senators showed little sign of being under strong pressure from their constituencies to withdraw troops from NATO.[9] Nevertheless, the growing tendency to question the desirability or possibility of maintaining U.S. forces in Europe was evident among the U.S. foreign-policy elite, especially in the Democratic party. The best single study of the issue[10] reflected this uncertainty. The assumptions on which the case for U.S. UFR rested were:

1. a decline in the threat of outright Soviet attack on or intimidation of West Europe;
2. a declining military need for U.S. forces at present levels;
3. a growing European capability to shoulder a substantially larger part of the security burden; and
4. a declining U.S. ability to meet the budgetary and foreign exchange costs of forces in the European theatre while also applying adequate resources to domestic problems.[11]

The conclusions were nevertheless conservative; there was "a continuing need for the present number of U.S. forces in Europe" provided their costs could be shared more evenly.[12] The state of the public and governmental debate in 1970-71 was that "The State Department . . . opposed any reduction because of its demoralising impact on NATO and its undermining effect upon possible force reduction talks with the Warsaw Pact",[13] a view shared by the Joint Chiefs of Staff for fear of the adverse consequences of reduction on the military balance of forces in Europe. The Treasury was concerned over the balance of payments, although this was not a significant factor, and Dr. Kissinger felt that any major cut was unpropitious, politically and strategically, although token reductions might placate congressional opinion.[14] The MBFR options presented at a National Security Council Meeting in November 1970 left open the possibility of modest reductions, as part either of UFR or MBFR.[15] The key conditions to holding off domestic pressures for UFR were the start of MBFR negotiations, acceptable burden-sharing by NATO, and some accommodation on the matter of executive and legislative prerogatives in foreign policy[16] — all conditions which had been met by 1975. The extent to which long-run American interests would be jeopardized by UFR on the Mansfield lines was also emphasized in a major study on U.S. arms-control policy finished in November 1971.[17]

The extent to which these recommendations for maintaining U.S. forces in NATO were to be reflected in official policy became evident during 1973-75, when negotiations on MBFR finally got underway and both the Senate and the administration defined their positions on U.S. forces in Western Europe more clearly. In contrast to these domestic pressures pushing NATO to offer talks on MBFR, Mr. Brezhnev's proposals from 1965 onwards for an ESC/CSCE were primarily instruments of a more assertive Soviet foreign policy, expressed within the framework of political arms control.

An ESC/CSCE: Political Origins, 1965-71

During this period Soviet political-arms-control policy was dominated by two issues. The first, inherited from Mr. Khrushchev, was, as Part IV of this book has shown, the successful campaign to prevent greater West German access to nuclear weapons via the MLF. The second set of issues, introduced by the Soviets from 1966 onwards, resurrected their earlier idea of an ESC that became the CSCE.[18] From the Bucharest meeting of Communist parties in 1966, the ESC became the main vehicle for Soviet expression of interest in arms control in Europe, progressing through the anti-U.S. and -West German 1967 Karlovy Vary declaration of the Political Consultative Committee (PCC) of the WPO to the 1970 Budapest meeting of the PCC, which stressed the need for detente in Europe to be institutionalized in an ESC. Brezhnev's Tiflis speech of May 1971 indicated the Soviet desire to separate the general process of detente from the military aspects of detente in Europe, which were to be dealt with by a conference nominally concerned with MBFR. The Soviet concept of an ESC/CSCE thus evolved from the negative notion of an ESC to contain West Germany to the positive notion of a CSCE and MBFR negotiations to further Soviet political objectives. These included the legitimization of the Soviet sphere of control in Eastern Europe and of the communist governments there, plus U.S.–Western European acceptance of East Germany and the East German and Polish boundaries established in 1945.

Initially, from 1966 to 1969, the ESC was an instrument for containing the threat to the Soviet position in Eastern Europe posed, in their view, by the beginnings of West Germany's *Ostpolitik* and President Johnson's policy of bridge-building from Western to Eastern Europe, both enunciated in 1966. But by 1969, the victory of Chancellor Brandt's Social Democratic Party in West Germany meant a victory for an *Ostpolitik* that represented West Germany's unilateral acceptance of the status quo. This came with the 1970 West German Treaties with the Soviet Union and Poland, the 1971-72 Berlin Accord between the United States, Great Britain, France, and the Soviet Union, and West Germany's 1972 recognition of East Germany. In light of the growing superpower detente, which was to be symbolized by the Moscow Summit meeting of May 1972 between Mr. Brezhnev and President Nixon, the Soviet ESC proposal became, from 1969 onwards, a positive measure to secure multilateral Western European and American endorsement of the existing frontiers and governments in Eastern Europe. This third phase of Soviet policy, starting in 1971 and continuing to the present, stressed the concept of institutionalizing detente through negotiations. By 1973, the CSCE and MBFR negotiations were underway, with the Soviets seeking the political objectives that had characterized their arms-control policy in Europe since 1954.

22 Current Issues in European Arms Control: MBFR, FBS, and CSCE

The initial negotiations on Mutual and Balanced Force Reductions (MBFR) from 1973-78 emphasized how far apart NATO and the Soviet Union remained in their conceptual approaches to the reduction of military forces in Europe. The West stuck to a technical framework within which internal Alliance political pressures could be contained. The Soviets advocated simple force reductions that did not meet the technical-arms-control criteria of MBFR but did meet their requirements for political arms control. Any agreements to reduce forces seemed likely to be nearer to political arms control in their over-all effects, although the actual size of the reductions might not be too far removed from those proposed by NATO. Such a compromise solution would, of course, fit the pattern of East-West arms-control agreements since 1958. In the Conference on Security and Co-operation in Europe (CSCE) the Soviets achieved, in the summer of 1975, their objective of multilateral Western endorsement of their control over Eastern Europe in return for purely nominal concessions to Western demands for greater freedom in the movement of ideas and people and for the advance notification of military manoeuvres. Finally, discussion of Forward-Based Systems (FBS) in the SALT I and II talks and U.S. arms controllers' proposals for reductions in the U.S. stockpile of tactical nuclear weapons in Western Europe had raised political fears among Europeans that the United States might be implicitly or explicitly trying to detach its nuclear deterrent forces in Western Europe from the strategic nuclear deterrent on which Western Europe still depended for its ultimate security. Once again, technical-arms-control proposals were failing to take sufficient account of the political factors involved.

MBFR: Initial Negotiations and Opening Positions

After considerable delay, apparently caused by lack of preparation for negotiations on MBFR,[1] the Soviet Union and its WPO allies finally agreed to preliminary talks lasting from January to May 1973. The

Soviets rejected the technical-arms-control idea that the numerical and geographical advantages enjoyed by the WPO should be off-set by asymmetrical reductions and insisted instead on the political-arms-control idea of equal reductions, leaving the security position of each side nominally unchanged[2] (nominally, because such reductions could, in fact, leave NATO less secure on the Central Front). The WPO delegations to the preliminary talks rejected the term "MBFR" to describe the subject of negotiations and secured a change in title to "negotiations on mutual reduction of forces and armaments and other associated measures".[3] Similarly, at the Washington Summit of June 1973, the final communiqué dropped the word "balanced" from MBFR.[4] In the preliminary MBFR/MFR talks the Soviets succeeded in excluding Hungary as a direct participant, the direct participants being: for the WPO, the Soviet Union, Czechoslovakia, East Germany, and Poland, with Bulgaria, Hungary, and Rumania as observers; for NATO, the United States, Canada, Britain, Belgium, the Netherlands, Luxemburg, and West Germany as direct participants, with the flank countries represented by Denmark and Norway for the northern flank, and Italy, Greece, and Turkey for the southern flank.

The NATO proposal for MBFR presented at the negotiations proper represented the outcome of intra-NATO bargaining on the basis of technical-arms-control considerations that managed to avert British opposition to holding the talks and major intra-alliance disagreements on their desirability, or the desirability of MBFR. Reportedly, the three basic models

. . . for force reductions were, firstly, the symmetrical basic model, with a reduction of 10 per cent of national forces and 30 per cent of foreign forces in West and East Germany, Czechoslovakia, Poland, and the Benelux countries; secondly, the asymmetrical according-to-military-strength model, covering the same area but with reductions of 10 per cent in NATO and 30 per cent in WPO forces; and, thirdly, the asymmetrical according-to-the-area-embraced model, where the area of reduction would be enlarged to include the western part of the Soviet Union, while NATO and WPO forces were reduced by 10 per cent. All three models clearly reflected the belief of NATO's military advisers that there existed a major WPO advantage in conventional forces, necessitating an asymmetrical model of MBFR if NATO's security were not to be brought by reductions in her forces to levels below that required to offer an effective conventional defense all along the Central Front.[5]

The final figures for the military balance on the Central Front used by the United States in its presentation of November 22, 1973,[6] naturally supported the idea of an asymmetrical quantitative balance, and were:

925,000 WPO ground combat forces, as against 777,000 for NATO; and 15,500 main battle tanks for the WPO and 6,000 tanks for NATO. Of these forces, 199,000 were U.S. ground units, out of a total for U.S. forces in Europe, including air and naval units, of 310,000; these compared to Soviet ground forces on the Central Front of 470,000. The U.S. proposal was for a two-phase reduction. In Phase I, the United States would withdraw 29,000 men from unspecified units while the Soviets would withdraw 68,000 men, all from specified tank units; no allied forces on either side would be withdrawn. In Phase II, to be negotiated after Phase I had been agreed, both sides would reduce to a common ceiling of 700,000 ground forces, including allied units. In contrast, the Soviets proposed reductions whose effect would be to symbolize detente and limit West Germany's military strength, that is, political arms control. On October 26, 1973, shortly before the MFR talks opened, Mr. Brezhnev summarized the five principles that should, in the Soviet view, govern these negotiations. These were:

1. That reductions should include both foreign and indigenous forces;
2. That both land and air forces should be included;
3. That force units with nuclear weapons should be reduced;
4. That the reductions should not disturb the existing relationship of forces in Central Europe and the continent as a whole; and
5. That the reductions should be achieved either by equal percentage cuts or by equal numerical cuts.

These principles were restated in the Soviet opening statement of October 30 which was rapidly followed, on November 8, by a WPO package for force reductions, containing four main items. First, both foreign and indigenous forces of all eleven states who were full participants would be included in a three-stage reduction proportionate to the size of their forces. In Stage I (1975) there would be an equal manpower reduction of 20,000 from each of the two sides; in Stage II (1976) the reduction would be 5 per cent on either side; and in Stage III (1977) there would be a further 10 per cent reduction (Brezhnev's Point 5). Second, the Stage I reductions would include nuclear and air units as well as ground forces (Brezhnev's Points 2 and 3). Third, reductions would be achieved by symmetrical trade-offs, with the withdrawals of a WPO unit being matched by the withdrawal of a NATO unit of similar size (Brezhnev's Point 4). Fourth, foreign units withdrawn would take all their equipment with them, while indigenous units would be disbanded. These were clearly proposals for MFR, not for MBFR. The difference between the U.S. proposal for technical arms control and that of the Soviets for political arms control was indicated by the final force levels: 700,000 for NATO and WPO in the U.S. offer; 820,000 for NATO and

1.15 million for the WPO in the U.S.S.R. proposal. Between November 1973 and July 1975 the NATO delegations were able only to clarify the different technical terms in the two proposals. There remained four major differences between the two sides: first, NATO wanted cuts to start with the United States and the Soviet Union, while the Soviet Union wanted these to begin with national and foreign troops; second, NATO wanted these to be limited to ground forces, while the Soviet Union wished to include ground and air forces; third, NATO proposed to include only conventional forces, while the Soviet Union wanted to include nuclear forces (FBS); and, fourth, NATO adhered to the principle of asymmetrical reductions to produce MBFRs while the Soviet Union continued to advocate equal reductions to produce MFR. The most important feature of these U.S.–NATO proposals was that they constituted technical arms control, as defined earlier, and had their intellectual origins in the arms-control thinking of the late 1950s and early 1960s. Whether or not their conclusions about the military balance in Central Europe were correct was less significant than the fact that it would be extremely difficult, if not impossible, to bridge the gap between Western proposals for technical arms control by the normal process of diplomatic negotiations. The diplomatic stalemate in these talks from July 1975 to the present (July 1978), despite new proposals by both sides, which were only minor variations on those described above, emphasized that agreement would take a political decision, probably between the new U.S. President, Jimmy Carter, and Mr. Brezhnev.

The Changing U.S. View of MBFR

There had, however, been significant shifts in the U.S. position on its forces in Europe. The North Vietnamese conquest of South Vietnam and the fall of Cambodia and Laos to the communists in their respective civil wars in 1975 had effectively ended U.S. political and military involvement in South-East Asia, leaving it free to concentrate on Western Europe, which continued to be the area of most vital interest to the United States. Additionally, the financial problem of the balance-of-payments drain posed by U.S. forces in Europe had been dealt with in the Senate. The Jackson–Nunn Amendment, introduced by two pro-NATO Senators, was adopted by Congress on October 23, 1973. It provided for U.S. forces in Western Europe to be reduced by the percentage by which its NATO allies failed to offset their NATO-related balance-of-payments deficits with the United States. America's Western European allies had reluctantly complied with this enforced solution, which would clearly continue, in order to undercut criticism of the balance-of-payments costs of U.S. forces in Western Europe.

In addition, the Nunn Amendment of August 1974 required the U.S. to reduce the non-combat component of total U.S. military strength in Europe by 18,000 men by June 30, 1976, allowing the Secretary of Defense to increase the combat component by the amount of the reductions. While the Soviet Union had appeared displeased in the MBFR negotiations that the United States was converting support forces to combat forces, the net effect was to prevent them from assuming that the United States would continue to run down its forces. These measures also helped to meet the Canby criticism that NATO forces were wrongly postured to fight a long war, with large support facilities, whereas the Soviet Union and her WPO allies were designed to fight a short, blitzkreig war with far fewer support facilities.[7] One interesting implication for MBFR was that the United States could actually improve its combat-to-support ratio if its first-stage reduction of 28,500 was taken primarily from support troops, something the United States offer would allow.

Mini-Nukes, FBS, and the Vladivostok Accord

One of the central underlying issues in the MBFR negotiations, the credibility of the U.S. nuclear guarantee to Western Europe, was affected by technical innovations in the tactical-nuclear-weapons field and changes in U.S. strategic nuclear policy. Both were too complex to be covered in detail, especially as they sparked a continuing debate in strategic circles. But the chief features of both could be noted in so far as they affected the MBFR negotiations.

It became evident in hearings in 1973[8] that the U.S. Army was planning to modernize its tactical-nuclear-weapons systems with a new generation of cleaner, lower-yield nuclear weapons, colloquially known as "mini-nukes". Proponents of this plan argued that these would increase NATO's deterrent capability versus the WPO by making NATO's first use of tactical nuclear weapons more credible because it would involve less collateral damage to civilian lives than existing tactical nuclear weapons, many of which were larger than necessary to destroy their targets. Additionally, mini-nukes would utilize superior U.S. technology to offset the WPO's quantitative advantages.[9] Opponents of mini-nukes argued that they would lessen crisis stability and repeat the errors of the late 1950s in assuming that technology could remedy NATO's conventional inferiority.[10] Similarly revived was the 1950s debate over whether tactical nuclear weapons meant NATO could offer a credible defence with fewer troops, as was first thought, or would require more troops to sustain the larger casualties caused by nuclear weapons, as war games seemed to demonstrate. U.S. policy makers seemed undecided on these issues and confusion was added by the ambiguous U.S. Declaration of May 23, 1974, to the Conference of the Committee on Disarmament (CCD) that the U.S. government had no intention of lowering the firebreak between conventional and tactical nuclear weapons by modernizing its tactical-nuclear-weapons stock-pile, implying that the United States was, in fact, developing mini-nukes.[11] An initial U.S.–U.S.S.R. reduction of 20,000 to 30,000 men in MBFR would be too small to be significantly affected by changes in tactical-nuclear-weapons doctrine. But in so far as mini-nukes made it technically easier for the United States to implement the tactical nuclear phase of NATO's strategy of flexible response, they could be seen as lessening Western European political fears that the United States would not implement its nuclear guarantee and therefore as facilitating a small, negotiated reduction in U.S. forces, one of whose main functions was to guarantee the U.S. nuclear guarantee. Changes in U.S. strategic doctrine were also designed to reinforce the credibility of this guarantee.

Secretary of Defense James Schlesinger's policy statement of January 10, 1974, and his subsequent annual defence statement of March 4 enunciated two new criteria for determining the size and capabilities of U.S. strategic forces: sizing and selective targeting. By sizing, he meant that the adequacy of U.S. strategic forces would now be determined by relative comparisons with those of the Soviet Union, taking into ac-count Soviet capabilities for a counterforce first strike and suggesting that the United States would insist on meaningful symmetry, off-setting any Soviet attempt to acquire significant qualitative or quantita-tive advantages in strategic weapons. The concept of selective targeting was separate from, but related to, the idea that the U.S. President should have selective options for retaliation in the event of a limited Soviet move against the United States and not be confined to making non-credible threats to strike only at Soviet cities. Underlying the ideas of sizing and selective targeting was the belief that criteria for deter-rence had to be reassessed in an era of counterforce capabilities and an apparent Soviet belief that such capabilities would be productive of political gains. This was especially true for the United States, which had to protect both itself and its allies in Western Europe.[12] Here, again, the implications for MBFR seemed to be that the United States was moving to reassure its NATO allies of the credibility of the U.S. nuclear guarantee in an age of Soviet strategic superiority (at least quantita-tively). Secretary Schlesinger certainly stressed this point in his Senate testimony in hearings which also dealt with the issue of Forward-Based Systems (FBS) for delivering tactical nuclear weapons.[13]

These hearings demonstrated that U.S. arms-control thinking had lost none of its technical emphasis. Alain C. Enthoven, former Assistant Secretary of Defense, Systems Analysis, and Paul C. Warnke, former Assistant Secretary of Defense, International Security Affairs, both criticized FBS, especially Quick Reaction Alert (QRA) aircraft as being vulnerable to a surprise attack. They therefore created the classic arms-control problem of creating an incentive for the opponent, in this case the Soviet Union, to strike first. This in turn created an incentive for NATO to strike first, leading to Schelling's position of fear of surprise attack becoming a cause of surprise attack. Although acknowledging the importance attached by Western European governments to FBS as symbols of the U.S. nuclear guarantee, Messrs. Enthoven and Warnke advocated the phasing out of QRA aircraft and their replacement by Poseidon Submarine-Launched Ballistic Missiles (SLBM), together with a reduction in the U.S. stockpile of tactical nuclear weapons in Western Europe from 7,000 to 1,000. This could, they argued, be done in consultation with Western European governments which would alleviate their fears.[14] As has already been noted, the Soviets had never shared, indeed, had probably never understood, the technical-arms-control arguments against FBS, but were aware of the political importance attached to them by Western European governments. The Soviet Union had therefore demanded in SALT I that FBS be counted as strategic weapons because they could, theoretically, strike the Soviet Union on one-way missions, and had raised this issue in the SALT II negotiations from 1973 to 1978. Having exploited the FBS issue for political ends, the Soviets only temporarily dropped their demand that FBS be included in the Vladivostok Accord of November 24, 1974, once it was clear that this was unacceptable to the United States, thanks to Dr. Kissinger's firmness in rejecting these Soviet demands. It was apparent, from the ease with which the Soviets gave in on the FBS issue that they had no real fears here, but had manufactured a non-issue that enabled them to give up nothing (limits on FBS) to achieve something (the Vladivostok Accord). One clear lesson for the MBFR negotiations was that unreasonable Soviet demands derived from political arms control could echo the requirements of technical arms control. But this did not mean that the Soviet Union had accepted technical-arms-control thinking, only that different approaches to arms control could lead to similar demands.

The CSCE

In striking contrast to the lack of progress on MBFR and FBS was the success of the CSCE. The final declaration of the thirty-five nation conference was signed by their heads of state on August 1, 1975. Essentially, it gave Mr. Brezhnev what the Soviet Union had been seeking for thirty years: formal Western recognition of the sphere of ideological and political control it had gained in the Second World

War. In exchange, the West gained theoretical provisions for a freer movement of peoples and ideas between Eastern and Western Europe, provisions likely to be interpreted in a very limited way by the communists. So, in one sense, the conference was a triumph for Mr. Brezhnev. But, in a broader perspective, it could be argued that the underlying realities of political and military power in Europe remained unchanged, so that all the conference did was to provide a multilateral recognition of the status quo. Whether the CSCE document constituted arms control was debatable, since the only confidence-building measure was an agreement, on a voluntary basis, to give twenty-one days' notice of military manoeuvres by more than 25,000 men. For the Soviet Union and Turkey, which had Asian borders, the promise applied only to a 155-mile zone along European borders.[15] But this idea of advance warning of manoeuvres was an arms-control measure which had existed since 1955. In this sense this aspect of the CSCE represented yet another victory for political arms control, since the promise of advance notification of manoeuvres was voluntary. It would not prevent Soviet manoeuvres within their sphere of control, where they had troops stationed in every country except Rumania. In a wider context the CSCE as a whole could be seen as a triumph of political arms control. The original Soviet proposal for an ESC had included discussions on both the political and military aspects of European security. But by accepting the Western idea of separating out the discussions on military security in the MBFR negotiations and rejecting the Western demand that progress in the CSCE should be linked to progress on MBFR, Mr. Brezhnev had dodged the technical-arms-control problems of MBFR that could have delayed indefinitely the conclusion of the CSCE. This in turn increased the likelihood of a political-arms-control solution to the MBFR talks, on the lines I have indicated, to complement the CSCE.

23 Arms Control as a Political Process: 1958-78

It should be clear from the discussions of strategic arms control (the Vladivostok Accord and SALT II) and arms control in Europe (MBFR, FBS, and CSCE) in the preceding chapters that the fundamental dichotomy between technical and political arms control remained. In practice, the United States had come to adopt the political-arms-control procedure of using nominal arms-control agreements to symbolize superpower detente. But in theory, and in diplomatic practice, the United States was still striving for technical-arms-control measures and only accepted political arms control as a second-best solution.

Arms control had always sought to deal with the instability that arose from the technical characteristics of particular weapons systems. The assumption was that since the threat to stability was primarily technical in nature, it could be dealt with through agreements that were isolated or insulated from the general context of superpower relations and, where applicable, from local political problems. In contrast, political arms control stressed the need to regulate the dangers that arose from a military confrontation in politically unstable or unsettled areas. It stressed that primary attention must be given to adjusting the specific political context in which the confrontation occurred, as happened in the Moscow Summit. This was the basic distinction that developed between the Western technically oriented arms-control approach and the Soviet politically oriented approach to the problems of strategic stability. Even though the distinction has proved valid, the former approach sometimes recognized the relevance of the political context while the latter recognized that some form of mutually agreed technical and numerical parity was necessary for agreement on mutual politico-military limitations.

Since the distinction between technical and political arms control became clearer when the two were operationalized within the context of the agreements reached between the superpowers (as has been done in the preceding Chapters 4 to 22) the difference between the two approaches will be analysed in the light of this information.

The Evolution of Arms Control in Theory and Practice

As Chapter 3 showed, arms control originated in the mid-1950s as part of the intellectual development of Western, primarily American, strategic thinking that began with the work of systems analysts in the Second World War. From this experience, it had become evident that independent analysis of military systems or deployments could reveal unsuspected side effects or deficiencies. In 1947, the Charles River Studies that were conducted by the Massachusetts Institute of Technology's (MIT) Lincoln Laboratories, and other similar studies, showed that the most economical allocation of the limited U.S. re-sources for strategic deterrence was a mixture of air defence and offen-sive forces, rather than the USAF's intended concentration on the Strategic Air Command's (SAC) offensive forces. The crucial transition to arms-control theory from technical systems analyses, with quite separate and largely internal political implications, came with Wohlstetter's 1954 study on SAC's plans for overseas bases. Wohlstetter and his colleagues came to both explicit technical conclusions about the high vulnerability of the proposed basing system to surprise attack and the implicit political conclusion that this vulnerability could pro-vide an inherent technological incentive for pre-emption. From the viewpoint of systems analysis, he was undoubtedly correct to explore the implications of such a worst-case assumption. It was incorrect, however, to assume, as most American strategists did, that this techni-cal conclusion supported the political assumption that the Soviet Union would always exploit such probabilistic technical advantages.

Thus, the technical emphasis of arms control became a dominant intellectual feature, but one that was divorced from political reality. The Gaither Committee of 1957 stressed the potential vulnerability of the SAC to Soviet missiles but made this theoretical Soviet advantage the basis for incorrect assumptions about Soviet perceptions that were built into the American approach to the 1958 Surprise Attack Confer-ence and contributed to its failure. Because the arms controllers tended to share the then prevalent perceptions of U.S. strategists, they adopted the view of U.S.–U.S.S.R. relations as a zero-sum two-person game. This trend was reinforced by the games theorists since their analytical tools were largely limited to handling two-person games. Like systems analysts, the games theorists could offer new insights, but from a deceptively apolitical viewpoint. They should have made more ex-plicit the distinction between working hypotheses of worst-case analysis or two-person games and the political assumptions or conclu-sions embodied in a study.

Schelling's dominant intellectual bias towards two-person games theory, which heavily influenced arms-control thinking, was evident from his first major contribution to strategic theory, *The Strategy of Conflict*,[1] a collection of papers on games theory whose relevance to strategy was not always clear. Nevertheless, he was able to say in 1962 that the major intellectual problems of arms control had been solved. However, this was before he wrote *Arms and Influence*, a brilliant exploration of the psychological implications of deterrence within an implicit two-person framework, in which he evolved notions of compellance and deterrence that assumed basically identical perceptions and values by both players.[2] His Harvard colleague, Roger Fisher, was, until the early 1970s, almost alone in emphasizing that other governments had to be considered as composing a complex of bureaucratic and personal actors, each with a set of perceptions unlike those of the United States.[3]

The scientists' refinement of arms-control theory so that it was in accord with their paradigms of scientific methodology completed the development of classical arms-control theory from the 1958 Surprise Attack Conference through to the 1961 break-up of the Geneva test-ban talks. Although 1961-62 was probably the last time for a decade that arms-control theory could be questioned, it had also become, in Kuhn's sense, a paradigm which, since it was untested, could not be prematurely rejected. Paradoxically, arms control was also so closely linked to the political concept of detente that to question it was apparently to question detente.

This paradox remained central to the evolution of arms control in practice, by making the idea of detente through nominal arms control part of a theoretically apolitical theory. Nominal arms control became the chief modality for superpower detente because the technical and non-political qualities claimed for arms control by its advocates made it the ideal means for the Kennedy, Johnson, Nixon, and Ford administrations to move towards a political understanding with the Soviet Union without appearing to do so until the 1972 Moscow Summit. The essentially political nature of arms control also explained the failure to reach any arms-control agreements outside the context of superpower relations, wherein the underlying drive for understanding was always present. But since this drive was for political understanding, it could not extend to securing the technical requirements of arms control through the PTB, NPT, SALT I and II, or the partial measures. Consequently, none of these restrained military competition. Once the idea of political arms control had been elaborated, the technical requirements for restraint were dropped in order to secure superpower understanding. Therefore, unlike political arms control, technical arms control in practice bore little relationship to technical arms control in theory.

Subsequent developments in arms-control thinking did not alter this conclusion.

The Evolution of Arms-Control Thinking: 1962-75

The technical-arms-control thinking described in Chapter 3 remained dominant for at least a decade, and its technical influence continued to shape U.S. approaches to certain aspects of arms control until the present. After 1963-64, the outpouring of books on arms control was reduced to a trickle. Jeremy J. Stone's summary of the prospects for arms control in 1965 reiterated the idea of an Anti-Ballistic Missiles (ABM) moratorium by the United States and the Soviet Union, proposed a mutual "bomber bonfire", and considered the dim prospects for missile disarmament and, more optimistically, the chance of a pause in strategic-weapons procurement.[4] These were all impeccable technical-arms-control proposals, but were unrelated to the political environment between the superpowers. Far more interesting, because it was one of the few arms-control works that was sensitive to the nuances of political dialogue between the governments of the super-powers, was Stone's later work, *Strategic Persuasion*. He rightly concluded that "We have not really taken to heart the possibilities inherent in the notion of 'co-operation between adversaries'. . . because we have not been able to distinguish those shades of relationship that this notion demands."[5] Far more conventional was Dougherty and Lehman's[6] summation of the prospects for arms control in the late 1960s — when technical arms-control concepts dominated and the NPT and an ABM freeze were the chief candidates for effective action, in a technical sense.

Hedley Bull's interim assessment of the arms-control thinking of 1958-62 rightly emphasized how, initially, "There was a sense of being at the threshold of a new era in arms control, reflected in proposals to expand governmental machinery for dealing with arms control, in hopes placed in the goal of what was called 'stable deterrence' and above all in the confidence that was displayed in study and research as a means of improving the prospects of peace and security."[7] He went on to ask what progress had been made since 1960 on the goals that the "new thinking" had mapped out and concluded that the answer was a paradox: "On the one hand the world is a great deal safer than it was at the beginning of the decade, at all events against the danger of nuclear war. But on the other hand the progress of arms control, while it has not been negligible, has been slight and the contributions it has made to the strengthening of international security are problematical."[8]

These improvements in international security included adequate superpower command and control and the emergence of a stable balance of terror the stability of which was unlikely to be threatened in the foreseeable future[9] (an over-optimistic prediction). The effects of the formal arms-control agreements reached were, not negligible, but more in the symbolic than substantive area; but there had been no progress towards stabilizing the balance of deterrence at a minimum level of force.[10] The positive lessons to be drawn were that tacit agreements are more important than formal ones and that "the chief function of formal agreements may sometimes be the symbolic one of demonstrating 'progress' and facilitating the conclusion of further agreements rather than the intrinsic contribution they make to military security."[11] Additionally, it was "time that the study of arms control was redirected towards an examination of fundamentals . . . the research that has been carried out since [the new thinking emerged] now on a massive scale and under the aegis of large institutions, has tended to be encased within these latter assumptions [of the new thinking] which are now aging."[12] This last point, on the institutionalization of the arms-control thinking of 1958-62 needed to be emphasized. The biggest single step in this direction was, of course, the establishment of the Arms Control and Disarmament Agency (ACDA) where the technical-arms-control thinking of 1958-62 was de rigueur.[13] The NPT of 1968 represented the agency's greatest triumph and the dominance of classical arms-control thinking. Similarly, the Harvard–MIT arms-control seminar, the breeding ground for the new ideas of the early 1960s, continued to elaborate on the application of these ideas to particular problems, rather than to question the underlying assumptions of the arms-control theories that its members had played key roles in formulating. The debates on the deployment of ABM and MIRV were conducted within the framework of technical-arms-control thinking, which became accepted by Senators and journalists who were sympathetic to the arms controllers' case for restraining the strategic arms race. The ideas of MAD and of the strategic arms race as an action-reaction phenomenon became the conventional wisdom of Washington.[14]

Scientists who were active in the field continued to reinforce the technical emphasis of classical arms-control thinking and to make political judgments on the basis of technical evidence, judgments which the evidence did not always support.[15]

It was appropriate, therefore, that the study on "New Directions in Arms Control" of 1972-73, comparable in importance to the Daedalus study of 1960, should have been initiated, "because of a widespread feeling within the arms control community that it had been living off the intellectual capital generated in the early 1960's."[16] The conclusion was that:

A brief comparison of the papers prepared for the 1973 study and for the major 1959 and 1960 study efforts is useful for charting the ensuing changes in concerns and efforts of students of arms control. The earlier study stressed strategic and technical issues of deterrence, vulnerability, surprise attack, verification and inspection, adjudication and enforcement, all of which were analyzed from essentially a technocratic and international perspective. Only two papers dealt with the formation of U.S. arms control policy. The 1973 study, in contrast, focused more on how domestic arms decisions are made.

Of the papers from the 1973 study, the largest group reflects a growing feeling that "arms control begins at home" and deals with U.S. military programs and policies: how Defense Department budgets, policies and programs are evolved, and how they might be brought under closer control. Many of these papers manifest the current political and intellectual concern with the problem of bureaucratic decision-making. A smaller group of papers deals with the role of strategy and doctrine in arms decisions, and a third section considers the roles of weapons, doctrine, agreements and negotiations in the international setting.[17]

These trends continued until about 1975-76, with the arms-control community concentrating on bureaucratic politics, weapons-system case studies and arms-race analysis as their principle fronts for advance. In bureaucratic politics the works of Allison and Halperin were notable in suggesting that decisions on weapons development and deployment are often the result of games that bureaucrats (and politicians) play, in which positions are determined by internal bureaucratic forces and domestic political decisions.[18] Although a valuable insight, this school of analysis often seemed to overstress the domestic at the expense of the international political environment. Weapons-system case studies, especially on MIRV and the survivability of the sea-borne deterrent, provided a much fuller technical background to the problems that control weapons development and deployment.[19] But the conclusions, especially on MIRV, seemed technically deterministic in their suggestion that there was perhaps no way in which MIRV deployment and increasing missile accuracy could have been stopped. This certainly highlighted one of the central failures of technical arms control, the failure to impose any significant restraints on the development and deployment of new weapons systems, with the partial exception of ABM where deployment has been halted but development has not. The corollary that if weapons systems could not be contained their political effects could be was not drawn. Analysts of the arms race, notably Gray and Wohlstetter, questioned the action-reaction model of the arms race, arguing that the strategic-weapons acquisition process of the superpowers was much more complex than this simple theory suggested. While no adequate theory of the arms race yet existed, it was clear that it was the Soviet Union that was "racing" to acquire a strategic superiority that it believed would be politically productive. This school of thinking also questioned the adequacy of MAD as a strategic doctrine for the United States in the 1970s.[20]

Two studies of SALT tended to reinforce the technical-arms-control view that these agreements were a substantive restraint on the strategic arms race and represented a major victory for arms-control thinking. Clemens's book[21] repeated every cliché of arms-control and detente thinking, while the contributors to Willrich and Rhinelander,[22] technical arms controllers to a man, welcomed SALT but with an interesting occasional scepticism as to what had really been achieved. The third study of SALT[23] was more interesting because it drew on a conference[24] at which several interesting points of dissent from the arms-control orthodoxy could be detected, although this still dominated the over-all proceedings. It was even suggested that the Soviets sought political advantages from the SALT negotiations and might seek to exploit a quantitative strategic advantage for political ends. A further note of dissent was entered by Elizabeth Young[25] who concluded that, "during the sixties the superpowers have colluded in presenting to the world a series of insignificant treaties"[26] on arms control, the most deficient of which, in terms of achieving its objectives, was the NPT. But despite her astringent scepticism, the political role of arms control eluded her; perhaps her book could better have been titled *A Farewell to Technical Arms Control and a Welcome to Political Arms Control.*

Similarly, despite the resurgence of academic interest in arms control and the new directions that it was taking, the political dimension remained strangely neglected, even though it was central to any understanding of the role of arms control in superpower relations. Dr. Kissinger occasionally alluded to this in his briefings on arms accords, but remained bent on proving that the Emperor really did have clothes on, that is, that his arms-control measures negotiated with the Soviets really did impose restraints on weapons development and deployment. The Soviets, for their part, remained convinced that the Emperor was adequately clothed in political terms, since their policy of political arms control had reaped them such dividends in terms of detente and strategic superiority.

Political Arms Control in Practice: 1958-78

Political arms control has been referred to as if it were an explicit theory. This has been done to simplify comparison with arms control; it is, as was indicated in Chapter 1, a description of the implicit assumptions underlying the Soviets' approach to the problem of strategic stability. Their approach has been essentially political. Both the

Soviets' perceptions and their actions, under both Mr. Khrushchev and Mr. Brezhnev, were as coherent as if they had been acting in accordance with an explicit theory of political arms control. When strategic stability or deterrence vis-à-vis the United States seemed threatening to the Soviets, as in the case of West Berlin from 1959 to 1968, they always sought to remove the political causes of the threat to their political interests or survival, rather than to deal, as arms control sought to, with the symptoms of this instability in isolation from its underlying causes. Indeed, at no time since 1958 have the Soviets shown significant signs of accepting either the arms-control diagnosis or remedies for threats to stability, starting with those related to the vulnerability of land-based ICBMs. Since by 1978 the Soviets were capable of understanding the arms-control viewpoint, the conclusion must be that they have rejected it, except as a self-fulfilling prophecy that has been influencing the United States.

Moreover, the Soviet acceptance of arms control as an incorrect analysis that has influenced the American government explains why nominal arms-control agreements have emerged as the chief modality for, initially, superpower detente in 1963 and then for an increasingly broad understanding of the mutuality of their interests, with the NPT and SALT I and the SALT II/MBFR discussions. Logically, the Soviet Union could deal with what its leadership saw as a political threat, such as West Berlin or the MLF, either by unilateral or bilateral action. Once the unilateral solutions failed, a co-operative solution with the United States left the Soviets facing the same problem as the arms controllers; the other superpower, whose agreement was essential to any solution, perceived the problem differently. Neither the Soviet Union nor America's allies ever found it easy to convince successive U.S. administrations that what Americans saw as strategic problems with political overtones were usually primarily political problems. In dealing with these problems, therefore, the Soviets were forced into a nominal acceptance of the arms-control framework as one within which to discuss political solutions to political threats to stability, as in the 1958 Surprise Attack Conference, or to minimize political threats to their interest, as with West Germany's catalytic potential, the limitation of which was one of the objectives of the 1958-61 discussions on a nuclear test ban and the main aim of initial talks on an NPT from 1961 to 1965. The use of nominal arms-control measures to ensure detente in 1963 was partially the result of a Partial Test Ban's unique suitability for embodying such detente and partially the logical outcome of the Soviet Union's emerging policy of political arms control, which was manifested in the 1963 partial measures. After initial difficulties over the nuclear-sharing issue, the United States came in practice to adopt a policy that was closer to political than technical arms control. It did so in the series of partial measures from 1964 onwards and in the major bilateral measures. The full extent of the change was not apparent until 1972-76, since it was usually argued by technical arms controllers that any particular measure represented the maximum amount of arms control that was feasible under the circumstances. Such reasoning left it unclear where technical arms control in practice became political arms control.

Thus political arms control developed as a reaction to technical arms control. The Soviets recognized that the American perception of strategic problems was primarily technical and that they would have to discuss what they saw as political problems in an arms-control framework, the theoretically apolitical nature of which made it ideal for achieving political agreements without appearing to do so. As the bilateral Soviet-American relationship became more clearly defined through agreements that were couched in terms of the explicit theoretical framework of technical arms control, political arms control became a more coherent theory and one that acquired the reverse image of technical arms control. Whether consciously or not, the Soviet leadership became increasingly explicit about its approach to strategic stability. It stressed political understandings as the best means of controlling those undesirable developments in military technology that threatened Soviet political (not technological) interests.

Arms Control and Arms Limitation in Europe

From the preceding analysis of the respective American and Soviet approaches to strategic stability, it would seem unlikely that technical arms control would be any more successful in the future than in the past, since it attempted to deal with technical symptoms in isolation from their political causes. The only exception would be unilateral Western measures of arms control, such as replacing Minuteman ICBM with mobile ICBM and hardening FBS. Arms control between the West and the Soviet Union remained impossible until the Soviets accepted the validity of arms-control analysis, which seemed unlikely. Ironically, arms control had been, and would continue to be, of immense political value both internally and externally in promoting detente and stabilizing the strategic balance. It was also valuable indirectly in providing a suitable framework for political solutions by the superpowers, rather than directly through securing technical solutions to instability.

Political arms control, on the other hand, was better adapted to dealing with the problems of superpower understanding. It has usually involved a Soviet reaction to a U.S. arms-control initiative, and this cycle could continue if the Soviet leadership remained relatively cautious. There have been indications that they may not do so; for example, they used their relatively unsuccessful 1967 ESC proposals to pressure NATO into the CSCE/MBFR/SALT II set of negotiations, and thereby accentuated Western European sensitivities about the nature and extent of the American nuclear guarantee. But now that they have reached recognized strategic parity with or superiority over the United States, a more positive Soviet use of political arms control may be expected, especially in Europe.

Technical and Political Arms Control: A Synthesis or a Continuing Dichotomy?

Superpower negotiations since President Johnson's explicit acceptance of the NPT as a modality for detente in October 1966 have raised the obvious question of whether the American removal of the technical requirements for arms control in the agreements that have already been reached with the Soviet Union have not brought its government's policy nearer to that of political arms control. The argument for a convergence between the superpowers' views on strategic stability has also been strengthened by the growing Soviet sophistication in discussions of strategic issues at SALT and elsewhere. This suggests that the Soviet political leadership may now be able to understand the political implications of the technical changes that favour a first strike. While both the United States and the Soviet Union have moved closer to understanding each other's approaches and to remedying, respectively, the political defects in arms-control theory and the lack of technical knowledge in political arms control, this process cannot be described as convergence between, or a synthesis of, the two approaches.

Intellectually, the dichotomy between arms-control theory and arms limitation remains as great as it was implicitly when the two approaches emerged in 1958. What has happened is that these American and Soviet theories of strategic stability have had the modifications necessary to superpower understanding superimposed on their basically irreconcilable intellectual assumptions by negotiators and political leaders. This book has tried to underline the different assumptions of technical and political arms control, and to show how these two quite dissimilar approaches enabled nominal arms control to become the chief modality for superpower understanding. Suggestions have been made as to why the theoretical difference between technical and political arms control has remained. In the final analysis, nominal arms control has continued to serve as a modality for the two detentes, first between the superpowers and then within Europe. Arms control remains primarily a matter of politics, not technology. So long as this is recognized, arms control can contribute to improved superpower relations that are based on a true equality of strategic strength and similar political perceptions.

EPILOGUE: An Epitaph for Arms Control

President Carter's attempts, since 1977, to translate technical arms control into U.S. policy on an unprecedented scale have produced an equally unprecedented debate on the adequacy of the principles and policy recommendations of traditional arms control. This questioning of arms control and strategy had started about 1974, but assumed a much greater intellectual and political importance once the Carter administration revealed the depth of its commitment to established theories and policies. The resultant debate had the welcome effect of refocusing attention on the more fundamental questions of arms control that this book has tried to answer. These are, first, whether the underlying assumptions of the mainstream of arms-control theory are correct and, second, whether we have had, or can have, effective technical arms control. My conclusions, that these underlying assumptions were incorrect, that technical arms control has not been, and will not be, possible, and that it has been replaced by political arms control, were justified by the evidence of theory and practice from 1958 to 1976 and by subsequent developments to early 1978. By then, however, it was clear that the Carter administration's arms-control policies were so radical, as were the reactions they provoked, as to require a separate assessment at as late a date as possible. Hence this Epilogue.[1]

This is an interim evaluation of the new debate on arms control and strategy as it bears on my discussion of arms-control theory and of those of the Carter administration's arms-control policies that affect my evaluation of the chances of securing technical arms control. The biggest single objection to my critique of technical arms control would be that the United States had never *really* tried to implement it, settling for the second-best option of political arms control. But President Carter's arms-control policies provided, for the first time, at least a partial answer to the question of what would happen if the United States sought technical, not political, arms control. For my purposes, the details of the Carter administration's policy proposals are less relevant than the broader questions these raise. The debate on these details involved highly complex, technical discussions where different analysts reached diametrically opposed conclusions. So, once again, the fundamental issues of arms control were in danger of being submerged by technical *minutiae* or obscured for political reasons. The current politicization and resultant polarization of the U.S. strategic and arms-control debate have been beneficial insofar as they have brought these fundamental issues into the political arena where they belong, since, to paraphrase Clemenceau, arms control is too important to be left to arms controllers. It also reinforced my argument that the political aspects of arms control have always been the important ones. The undesirable effect of this politicization was that it translated balanced, scholarly analyses and judgments into partisan political positions—my scepticism of the Carter administration's chances of achieving technical arms control is analytical, *not* political. Paradoxically, the present administration's policies are open to criticism from traditional-arms-control thinkers, as well as from the new, revisionist, arms-control theorists. Since these revisionists are re-opening the questions the original theories of arms control posed, these need recapitulating.

The Principles of Arms Control

The central innovation of arms-control thinking was the idea that modern military technology could in itself become a cause of war, creating undesirable instabilities in the strategic balance between the superpowers — and other states — from which no party could benefit. The superpowers' shared interest in avoiding such instabilities, through unilateral or bilateral measures, would therefore override their rivalries, with arms-control considerations supplementing the traditional factors determining the development and deployment of military forces. The arms-control objectives of making war less likely to occur, especially by accident, and less destructive if it did occur, did not necessarily mean that forces or defence budgets could be reduced, or technological innovations halted. On the contrary, more rather than fewer forces, more rather than less defence spending, and an increased, not a decreased, rate of technological innovation could be required where these contributed to stability. Arms control was to be seen as an integral, and crucial, part of a nation's military strategy, contributing in the proper Clausewitzian sense to its political goals: arms control was, ultimately, one means of securing strategic ends, not an end in itself. The best illustration of arms control as part of a national strategy dictating increased forces was the build-up, from 1961, of U.S. strategic forces to the levels required to implement the doctrine of Mutual Assured Destruction (MAD). Although arms controllers criticized the level of these forces as excessive, they were arguing over the means to achieve ends they approved. They did not deny that, in principle, U.S. strategic forces needed to be modernized and increased to ensure stability. The same argument was made in 1978 by revisionist arms controllers. In terms of arms-control theory, the increasing tendency to equate arms control *per se* with decreased forces and defence spending, a tendency encouraged by the Nixon, Ford, and Carter administrations, was thus fallacious. It blurred the crucial distinction between arms control and disarmament, since it was precisely the idea that security would be increased as weapons were reduced — that is, by disarmament — that the traditional arms controllers opposed. They argued that, for example, reducing nuclear weapons to very low levels, or abolishing them (a declared goal of President Carter), would decrease stability. Even a numerically small violation of an agreement to this end would give the violator(s) a major advantage and, since such violations could not be detected, all parties would, if rational, commit them. Moreover, the removal of nuclear weapons would increase the utility of large conventional armies, like those possessed by the Soviet Union and China, creating additional instabilities. Thus, although the objectives of arms control were clear, the modalities of achieving these objectives were not. It was clear that arms control would not always be served by reducing forces; quite the reverse, in fact.

There were, therefore, opportunities for widespread and legitimate disagreements over how to translate the objectives of arms control into specific policies, and over what priorities should be assigned to the five major arms-control problem areas. These were and are: the strategic balance; nuclear testing; nuclear-weapons proliferation; the NATO–Warsaw Pact military balance; and conventional-arms transfers to the Third World. In each area, the aim was, obviously, to prevent inadvertent instability. But, at this level of abstraction, arms-control objectives were motherhood objectives. Since inadvertent instability could serve no rational interests, everybody was for arms control in principle, once this new principle was understood. The real differences arose, then as now, over the modalities of reaching these objectives, their attainability, and their relative importance. The three issues were interrelated. The arms controllers stressed the initial necessity of securing limited measures which could be implemented successfully, unilaterally or bilaterally, rather than more far-reaching measures which could not be agreed on, and/or which might not work. This meant that there would always be disputes over which measures were, in fact, desirable and practicable, desirable but impracticable, or undesirable if practicable. For example, the 1963 three-power Partial Test Ban (PTB) treaty was defended as the most practicable step towards a universal Comprehensive Test Ban (CTB) treaty. However, liberal critics of the PTB saw it as an inadequate measure that would not significantly limit nuclear testing and that would delay progress towards a CTB. Conservative critics saw even a PTB as enabling the Soviets to secure a lead in nuclear weapons technology, a lead a CTB would increase, while a PTB would make such a CTB more likely. The PTB's proponents and opponents thus agreed over their ultimate arms-control objectives, increasing strategic stability and limiting nuclear proliferation, but disagreed on whether these ends were best secured through a PTB, or a CTB, or both, or neither. There was a further difficulty. Even if the 1963 PTB made the strategic balance between the superpowers more stable, it could increase the threat to stability posed by the nuclear powers (France and China) who refused to sign, and it could increase the incentives for potential nuclear proliferators, like India and Israel, to go nuclear. These arguments over the 1963 PTB were repeated over the 1974 Threshold Test Ban Treaty (TTBT) and the accompanying Peaceful Nuclear Explosions Treaty (PNET), both signed in 1976, whose ratification by the U.S. Senate has been effectively suspended while the Carter administration seeks a CTB. Here again, the questions posed are essentially the same as those of 1963. Over the CTB, as over the PTB, TTBT, and PNET, there were important differences within the arms-control community, where the traditionalist majority favoured a CTB, but a revisionist minority opposed a CTB as unverifiable, and therefore destabilizing. In the broader political context, the PTB debate similarly foreshadowed the current debate on President Carter's proposed CTB and, more importantly, his proposed SALT II agreement. In 1963, the decisive political (as distinct from the narrower arms-control) issue was whether President Kennedy should, or should not, seek such a politically significant agreement, symbolizing detente with Mr. Khrushchev, so soon after the 1963 Cuban missile crisis. The PTB, like SALT II, was thus a symbolic, as well as a substantive, issue.

Arms Control: The New Debate

The difficulty of using even the original theories of arms control to produce specific arms-control policy proposals, and of evaluating their merits and demerits, is thus clear. The problem has been compounded by the emergence of three distinct schools of arms-control analysts, with opposing policy prescriptions. In the absence of any generally accepted, non-pejorative names, I have called these the revisionist, the traditionalist, and the realist schools. Because the revisionists are a major new group, they require the most consideration here. They question both established arms-control thinking and policy prescriptions (which were the prescriptions of technical, or traditional, arms control) and the realist approach of adopting political arms control as the actual policy of the United States while clothing it in the rhetoric of technical arms control. The distinction between traditional arms-control thinking and traditionalist policies has become increasingly important, because the traditionalists have devoted most of their attention, since 1963, to elaborating policy proposals based on a generally accepted set of theoretical assumptions. Inevitably, these proposals have tended to become accepted, both by the arms-control community and by the broader public of politicians and voters, as ends in themselves (as has happened with the 1972 SALT I agreements). These were criticized by traditional arms controllers for their technical deficiencies, but on the premise that the chief means of achieving strategic stability was through SALT. This would be true only if the theoretical underpinnings of SALT were correct, which was very doubtful. The realists claimed to share the theoretical assumptions and ultimate goals of the traditionalists, and to be implementing their policy proposals, sacrificing only the minimum of technical content needed to secure negotiable agreements. Since this minimum was almost all of the technical content necessary for effective technical restraints, the realists' claim was disingenuous. It also made it intellectually difficult and politically unwise for the realists to elaborate either the theory behind, or the practice of, political arms control. Presumably this was so that political arms control could make an immediate contribution to traditional arms-control goals, while facilitating a later, and larger, contribution through technical-arms-control agreements. Although this later contribution seemed increasingly unlikely to be achieved by political arms control, the immediate gains could still be defended as providing some increase in stability, albeit a modest one, if coupled with the appropriate unilateral policies.

The revisionists argued that the traditional arms controllers had originally identified the correct objectives of arms control, which should form an integral part of strategic objectives. What was needed was a return to these basic principles, as well as a re-evaluation of traditionalist theories and policies in the light of these principles. Essentially, traditionalist policies could not work, and could, indeed, be counter-productive, because they were based on theories that did not correspond to realities, being incorrect in their analyses of the causes of strategic (and other) arms races, nuclear proliferation, technological innovation, and the role of domestic (including bureaucratic) factors in arms races. The underlying problem was a Western, largely American, cultural myopia that incorporated highly ethnocentric, mechanistic assumptions into theories of arms control and strategy, and for these a universal validity was claimed. Whatever most of the U.S. arms-control community believed at any time was treated as the ultimate and final truth, providing a necessary and sufficient set of theoretical explanations and policy prescriptions which should be accepted by Washington and Moscow, as well as by lesser powers. Such reasoning naturally produced the fallacy of mirror-imaging, the assumption that the Soviet leadership should view arms races, and measures for their control, in the same way the mainstream of American arms controllers did. If they did not, this was attributed to Soviet backwardness, to be remedied by an education that would raise their "learning curve" on arms control. By definition, neither America's adversaries (especially the Soviet Union) nor her allies could have any valid alternative to traditional-arms-control theories or policies, so that any failure on their part to follow American policy prescriptions was seen as irrational. The United States was therefore cast in an evangelical role, converting the rest of the world to the true faith of arms control, by persuasion where possible, and by force — in the sense of economic and technical sanctions — where not. To the revisionists, the cumulative errors of this approach to arms control meant that it was necessary to return to first principles. A prerequisite of understanding how these principles worked in the real world, and how these could be translated into effective arms-control policies, was the replacement of the assumption of knowledge with that of ignorance. Since arms-control theories provided an incorrect description of arms races, their prescriptions for controlling such races were necessarily wrong, often dangerously so, as with SALT I. So, paradoxically, a failure to reach a SALT II, or even a cessation of SALT, would actually contribute to the objectives of arms control by forcing the United States to face up to realities. These included the bankruptcy of arms-control theory and of the policy of seeking strategic stability almost exclusively through SALT. Instead, stability should be sought by increases in U.S. strategic and tactical nuclear forces and, perhaps, in those of her British and French allies.

Intellectually, the revisionist arms controllers reinforced my criticisms of arms control's theoretical assumptions and my argument that those arms-control agreements reached, or reachable, have not met the traditional arms controllers' technical criteria for effectiveness. The revisionist assessment of political-arms-control agreements as potentially destabilizing in the current context of U.S. internal and external politics echoes my stress on the importance of the political content and context of arms-control agreements. Between 1963 and 1972 these agreements codified and advanced a superpower detente, thereby contributing to strategic stability and making technical arms control possible, and so the agreements were of value, albeit decreasing value. The failure of SALT I meant that subsequent political-arms-control measures were trying to shore up a collapsing detente, and indeed, by their conspicuous failure, politically and technically, were contributing to its collapse. Any SALT II agreement can now make only a marginal contribution to strategic stability, and could inhibit the unilateral U.S. and allied measures needed to stabilize a potentially unstable strategic balance. The failure of the SALT process could stimulate a balanced reassessment of the defects of traditionalist and realist thinking in arms control, as well as of the revisionist critique of these.

The political element in the arms-control debate itself has both helped and hindered this necessary reconsideration of basics. The majority of revisionists are, in political shorthand, conservative hawks (Republican and Democratic), either overtly, like Paul Nitze and Senator Henry M. Jackson (D–Wash.), or in terms of their policy recommendations, like Donald G. Brennan, Colin S. Gray, Albert Wohlstetter, and William R. van Cleave. This is because the majority of traditionalist arms controllers have been, again in over-simplified terms, either liberal doves (mostly Democratic), such as Paul Warnke, Marshall D. Shulman, and Senator Edward Kennedy (D–Mass.), or supporters of similar policies, like Jerome H. Kahan, Dr. Herbert Scoville, Jr., and Messrs. Alain C. Enthoven and Wayne K. Smith. These political factors have produced the proposition that all revisionist criticisms of traditionalist thinking were wrong, because revisionists were hawks, which was as intellectually indefensible as the converse, that all traditionalist propositions were wrong, because all traditionalists were doves. For political purposes, of course, such propositions were used. The hearings on Paul Warnke's nomination as both chief SALT negotiator and Director of the Arms Control and Disarmament Agency (ACDA) showed that shades of analytical meaning were irrelevant to the political question of whether individuals or groups were for or against these nominations, especially as President Carter made this a test-case of support for his arms-control policies. Opponents of these policies, led by Paul Nitze, mounted a major attack, so Paul Warnke was confirmed as chief SALT negotiator by only fifty-eight to forty Senate votes (less than the two-thirds majority required to approve SALT II), and as Director of ACDA by seventy to twenty-nine votes — again a narrow enough majority to indicate to the new President that SALT would encounter major domestic political, as well as analytical, criticism. Mr. Warnke's resignation in late 1978, whatever the causes, was symptomatic of the difficulties facing traditional arms controllers.

Nor was it inappropriate for SALT, and arms control, to become a political issue. The issues involved were central to the survival of the United States and its allies and, ultimately, to the survival of the world.

The American public and America's allies were therefore entitled to influence the President's arms-control policies. Arms-control analysts could rightly object if their views were distorted for political or personal reasons — and personalities play a much larger role in strategic debates than strategists usually suggest. But analysts involved in political debates were subject to the same political rules as the other participants. The polarization of revisionists and traditionalists left the realists in an excluded middle position, which was largely untenable because it was under attack from revisionists and traditionalists. Both agreed that the realists had failed to produce technical arms control, the revisionists arguing that they had produced undesirable strategic policies (unilateral U.S. restraint) and had induced false political hopes (for detente). Traditionalists sought to maintain strategic restraint and detente through technical arms control. Again, this evolution of the arms-control debate reflected the erosion of the basic political and analytical consensus behind SALT I and detente. Advocates of the realist position implicitly argued that, after trying for technical arms control, President Carter would have to settle for political arms control, but with less effect because of problems his search for the former had caused within the United States and among the Soviet leaders. By late 1978 this was happening.

President Carter's Arms-Control Policies

The three major traditional-arms-control objectives stressed by the new President were: the stability of the strategic balance, to be secured by a SALT II; a halt to all nuclear testing, via a universal CTB, primarily to complement SALT II; and a halt to nuclear proliferation. He also sought a major reduction in conventional arms transfers to the Third World and a more stable NATO–Warsaw Pact balance, through unilateral measures and through the continuing negotiations on Mutual and Balanced Force Reductions (MBFR). President Carter's SALT and strategic policies most clearly demonstrated his commitment to technical arms control, but they must be considered in the context of his other arms-control policies. The questions raised by the CTB have been summarized. Neither France nor China will become a party to a CTB, as they reject the traditional-arms-control arguments involved. Although the Soviet Union agreed to forego the rights to conduct Peaceful Nuclear Explosions that they secured under the PNET, it too has shown no interest in the technical-arms-control arguments for a CTB. It is also questionable whether the Soviets would accept such a major restraint on their nuclear weapons technology for long. A Soviet Union that continues to reject the technical-arms-control case for a CTB cannot reasonably be expected to observe its provisions, at least for long.

A similar rejection of the Carter administration's attempts to secure technical arms control was the Soviets' refusal to limit their conventional arms transfers to the Third World. Such transfers, which include Cuban and Warsaw Pact (possibly Soviet) combat personnel, have undergone a major quantitative and qualitative increase. Restraints were also opposed by Third World acquirers of arms and by suppliers outside the United States, notably in Western Europe. The Soviets have also continued to reject the basic arms-control concept that force reductions in Europe should be mutual and balanced, making it questionable how much longer the five-year-old MBFR talks can continue without results. The Warsaw Pact acceptance, in 1978, of the NATO principle of reductions to a common personnel ceiling of 700,000 was qualified both by their insistence that the Warsaw Pact forces currently totalled only 805,000 compared to Western estimates of 950,000 and by the continuing increase of Soviet and Warsaw Pact forces to unparalleled levels. These bear no relation to any Soviet requirements for defence against NATO or for the control of her Eastern European empire, and include major new nuclear forces designed for use against Western Europe — Eurostrategic forces — notably the SS-20 Intermediate Range Ballistic Missile (IRBM) and the Backfire-B bomber. This build-up explains the growing NATO, especially West German, view that, if superpower arms-control measures affect their security interests, as with restraints on the Long Range Cruise Missile (LRCM) or on the transfer of LRCM technology to NATO members, these are no longer matters for the United States and/or the Soviet Union to decide alone. In the view of Western Europeans and America's other major allies, the same holds true of any other arms-control measures sought by the United States, from the deployment (or non-deployment) of enhanced radiation weapons (the neutron bomb) in Western Europe, to the type and level of conventional arms to be supplied either to U.S. allies in Asia or to China. They will not accept U.S. arms-control policies that conflict with their interests, especially since most allied analysts and policy makers are so sceptical of traditional-arms-control thinking as to be, in effect, revisionist arms controllers.

President Carter's non-proliferation policies have been rejected, in whole or in part, by all his major allies, for the same basic reason: the allies accepted neither these policies nor the arms-control analyses underlying them. As with the 1968 NPT, their view is that the Soviet Union's interest in stopping nuclear proliferation has virtually nothing to do with the traditional-arms-control arguments against it, being based, instead, on the likelihood of potential proliferators, being anti-Soviet, if not pro-American or pro-Chinese. They also oppose the traditionalist view that the spread of the technical capability to manufacture nuclear weapons via nuclear power plants must be equated with the spread of usable nuclear-weapons options. For strategic and economic reasons, none of America's allies can see any realistic alternative, for the next decade or more, to nuclear power as a substitute for oil. They also know that, even among the traditional arms controllers, there are major differences over which mix of non-proliferation policies is best, given that proliferation cannot now be halted, only limited. With the differing objectives and policies of the realist and revisionist arms controllers competing with those of the traditionalists it has become impossible to talk of a single clearly identified and accepted arms-control analysis of nuclear proliferation. There are, rather, competing groups with conflicting analyses and policies, such as the Ford/Mitre group, whose approach President Carter has adopted,[2] and others. The American and traditional-arms-control penchant for exclusively technical solutions to problems which are only partly technical, and whose technical content is in itself hotly disputed, helped undermine Carter's non-proliferation policies. Since the realist arms controllers have no coherent alternatives, the revisionists are more realistic in saying that the problems of nuclear proliferation must be rethought. There will be no simple answers, and non-proliferation measures can do no more than try to inhibit proliferation. Traditionalists and realists alike are moving, reluctantly, to the same conclusion.

The failure of Carter's traditional-arms-control policies in every major area besides SALT means that his failure there is symptomatic of the inadequacies of these policies and their theoretical assumptions. As Annex I shows, the March 1977 U.S. Comprehensive Proposals were for a SALT II incorporating almost every measure suggested by traditional arms controllers. These proposals represented a genuine attempt to persuade the Soviets to discuss a SALT II stabilizing a strategic balance through traditional, technical-arms-control measures. The extent to which the Soviets rejected every important technical restraint is evident from a comparison of the 1977 U.S. Comprehensive Proposals with the SALT II provisions agreed to by the end of 1978. As the Soviets clearly understood the reasoning behind these restraints, it is now clear that they have decided that traditional-arms-control objectives and policies are inappropriate for the Soviet Union, both now and for some years ahead. This was consistent with my earlier conclusions, and confirms the similar revisionist arguments. Further confirmation is to be found in the Soviet failure to reciprocate unilateral U.S. initiatives towards strategic restraint, notably President Carter's June 1977 cancellation of the B-1 strategic bomber, his closedown of the Minuteman III ICBM production lines, and his deferment of LRCM deployment and of the development and deployment of the M-X, particularly in its mobile basing modes. The Soviets ignored these actions, increasing their strategic forces and budgets at the same rates as previously. Consequently, no foreseeable SALT II agreement could contribute, in a technical sense, to strategic stability. Nor would it contribute to political stability. The realist arms controllers were essentially correct in arguing that it was the best agreement that could be reached, given the Carter administration's strategic policies, but whether, under these circumstances, an agreement was worth having was doubtful.

Over all, then, President Carter's attempts to secure technical arms control were as clear as their failure. This was primarily caused by the inadequacies of traditional-arms-control thinking, but its rejection by the Soviet Union was particularly significant and disturbing. The Soviets were rejecting the central arms-control notion that the technical or political problems created by inadvertent instabilities in the strategic, or local, military balances should be managed cooperatively, not competitively. Thus their actions further undercut both traditional (technical) and realist (political) approaches to arms control which were already undermined by technological and political changes. This left the revisionist approach as the one most likely to produce effective arms-control analyses and policies for the United States and her allies. What these new arms-control policies should be is far too large a question to answer here, but I must repeat my conclusions that the old arms-control theories and policies are now no longer adequate. We are moving into a much less stable, much more dangerous world, in which the objectives of arms control are going to be more important but less easy to reach. Arms controllers and strategists must therefore respond to these new challenges with new ideas and new policies, recognizing that both the problems and the solutions to them must correspond to the real world, where political considerations and differences are paramount.

December, 1978

Annex I President Carter's SALT II Proposals, 1977–78

	1977 March (Moscow) Proposals Comprehensive Plan[1]	1978 Draft Agreement as of December 1978[2]
SALT II Treaty, Running until 1985		
Strategic Delivery Vehicles (SDV), Total	1,800–2,000	2,250
Sublimits		
MIRVed SDV (including bombers)[3]	1,100–1,200	1,320
MIRVed ICBM and SLBM	–	1,200
MIRVed ICBM[4]	550	820
Heavy ICBM	150	313
Long-Range Cruise Missiles (LRCM)	Range limited to: ALCM 2,500 km (1,553 mi.) GLCM 600 km (350 mi.)	2,500 km[5] (1,553 mi.) 600 km (350 mi.)
U.S.S.R. Backfire Bomber	Not to be deployed strategically, operationally, against the U.S.[6]	
Treaty Protocol Restraints on Strategic Force Modernization and Mobile ICBM Deployment	U.S. would not develop: (a) MK12A MIRV (for MMIII ICBM); (b) MX large, mobile ICBM. U.S.S.R. would not deploy: (a) SS-16 Mobile ICBM.	U.S. could deploy: (a) a new ICBM MIRVed or single warhead: type unknown); (b) Trident I and II SLBM. U.S.S.R. could deploy: (a) a new ICBM (single warhead: type unknown); (b) SS–NX–17 and 18 SLBM plus a new SLBM.

Annex I (Cont'd.)

1977 March (Moscow) Proposals Comprehensive Plan[1]	1978 Draft Agreement as of December 1978[2]
U.S. and U.S.S.R. *would agree to:*	*U.S. and U.S.S.R.* ~~*would agree not to:*~~
(a) limit ICBM and SCBM flight tests to six per year for each class of system, ICBM and SLBM;[7]	(a) significantly improve existing strategic systems, except for improvements in existing guidance systems, which could not be verified;
(b) ban the development of all follow-on ICBM and SLBM systems.	(b) test or deploy mobile ICBM's in a mobile mode during the Protocol's life, possibly including the Soviet SS–16 ICBM. Missiles intended for deployment on the Protocol's expiry could be tested from fixed launchers (e.g., MX and SS–16);
	(c) test or deploy LRCM with ranges exceeding 2,500 km;[8]
	(d) deploy LRCM with ranges of over 600 km on platforms other than strategic bombers, but such systems (land-, air-, or sea-launched) could be developed and tested up to the 2,500 km range.[8]

SOURCES: Richard Burt, "The Scope and Limits of SALT", *Foreign Affairs*, Vol. 56, no. 4 (July 1978), pp. 751–70; *The New York Times*; *The Washington Post*; *Arms Control Today*, 1977 and 1978; *Strategic Survey* (London: IISS, 1977).

Annex I (Cont'd.)

NOTES:

1. The fall-back "Deferral Plan" followed the 1974 Vladivostock Accord. Limits on U.S. LRCM and U.S.S.R. Backfire bombers would be discussed later.

2. The three-tier SALT II structure comprises: a Treaty lasting until 1985; a three-year Protocol (starting date uncertain); and a Statement of Principles for a SALT III.

3. U.S. bombers carrying LRCM count as MIRVed SDV. Whether other LRCM-carrying aircraft, notably proposed U.S. conversions of wide-bodied commercial jets, would be included is unclear. The U.S.S.R. has argued that they would be, either under these limits or within a separate subceiling.

4. The Comprehensive Proposals constituted the first attempt to limit MIRVed ICBM, reflecting U.S. concern with the first-strike potential represented by these, especially Soviet heavy ICBM. The 1978 sublimit was too high to reduce this potential and allowed the U.S.S.R. to MIRV *all* their heavy ICBM (SS-9 and -18).

5. Testing and deployment of long-range ALCM are restricted to strategic bombers, U.S. B-52s, and Soviet *Bear* and *Bison*. It is unclear whether this limit applies only to nuclear-armed ALCM or includes also those with conventional warheads, or whether the range limits are based on a straight-line course from launch to target, or include an additional range (up to one quarter of the total) to allow the ALCM to evade Soviet defences.

6. Soviet undertakings to limit Backfires' refuelling capabilities and not to base Backfires operationally where they could reach the U.S. would be difficult to verify and unenforceable in a crisis.

7. Such tests are essential to develop the high confidence needed for a counter-force first strike, so these limitations would have lessened the Soviet threat to the U.S. land-based forces and communications.

8. Verification of deployed LRCM ranges is impossible, all LRCM components can be tested clandestinely, and technological developments will extend the range and/or throweight capabilities of deployed LRCM.

Annex II The U.S.–Soviet Strategic Balance under the Interim Agreement (SALT I) 1972–77: Static Measurements

	Deliverable Warheads			Equivalent Megatonnage EMT (expressed as two-thirds power of the explosive yield)			Missile Throweight (million lbs.)			Strategic Bombers (SB)/Bomber Payload (million lbs.)		
	1972	1977	1978	1972	1977	1978	1972	1977	1978	1972	1977	1978
U.S.A.												
ICBM	1,304	2,154			1,460		2.1	2.2		445 SB/ 29.6	373 SB/ 22.8	
SLBM	2,832	5,120			830		0.76	1.1				
Long-Range Bombers	4,867	4,056		7,900	4,400		—	—				
Totals	9,003	11,330	c.11,000	7,900	6,690		2.86	3.3				
U.S.S.R.												
ICBM	1,600	2,647		n.a.	2,950		6.0	7.8		135 SB/ 4.7	135 SB/ 4.7	
SLBM	845	909		n.a.	860		1.0	1.3				
Long-Range Bombers	270	270		780	780		—	—				135 SB/ 4.7
Totals	2,715	3,826	c.4,500	780	4,590		7.0	9.1				

	1972	1977	1978
United States			
B–52D/F (First deployed, 1956)	172	147	75
B–52G/H (First deployed, 1959)	283	226	241
Total	455	373	316
Soviet Union			
Tu95–Bear (First deployed, 1956)	100	100	100
Mya–4 Bison (First deployed, 1956)	35	35	35
Total	135	135	135

SOURCE: IISS, *The Military Balance 1972–73, 1977–78* (London: 1972, 1977). Figures are for July of each year.

NOTE: U.S.–U.S.S.R. strategic bomber forces comprised the following aircraft; both forces suffer severely from aging, especially the U.S. B-52s, which face very heavy Soviet air defences.

Notes

Chapter 1

1. The MAD doctrine, as enunciated by Secretary of Defense Robert S. McNamara, held that the United States (and the Soviet Union) required only those nuclear forces sufficient to inflict unacceptable damage on an aggressor, even after absorbing the maximum possible counterforce first strike from the aggressor. "Unacceptable damage" was defined as "one-fifth to one-fourth of her [Soviet] population and one-half of her industrial capability". Robert S. McNamara, *Statement Before the Senate Armed Services Committee on the* FY *1969-73 Defense Program and 1969 Defense Budget* (Washington, D.C.: Department of Defense, 1968), p. 50.

2. At its simplest, the theory held that any strategic force deployments by one superpower produced an overreaction from the other. Thus Soviet deployment of a thin Anti-Ballistic Missile (ABM) system would lead to U.S. deployment of a thicker ABM system and Multiple Independently Targetable Re-entry Vehicles (MIRV) which in turn would lead to Soviet deployment of still thicker ABM and MIRV systems. The classic statement on this theory was George W. Rathjens's monograph, *The Future of the Strategic Arms Race* (New York: Carnegie Endowment for International Peace, 1969). This summarized the findings of a study group including Robert S. McNamara.

3. See the Introduction to John Garnett, ed., *Theories of Peace and Security: A Reader in Contemporary Strategic Thought* (London: Macmillan, 1970), p.24. For an attack on the orthodoxy of MAD, see Fred C. Iklé (Director of the U.S. Arms Control and Disarmament Agency — ACDA, 1973-76), "Can Nuclear Deterrence Last Out the Century?", *Foreign Affairs*, Vol. 51, no. 2 (January 1973), pp. 267-85; and the reply in defence of MAD by Wolfgang H. Panofsky, "The Mutual-Hostage Relationship Between America and Russia", *Foreign Affairs*, Vol. 52, no. 1 (October 1973), pp. 109–18.

4. See "Texts of Major Arms Control Agreements", Appendix C, in John H. Barton and Lawrence D. Weiler, eds., *International Arms Control: Issues and Agreements*, by the Stanford Arms Control Group (Stanford: Stanford University Press, 1976). The group's interpretations of these agreements were those of technical arms controllers.

5. The different U.N. bodies for disarmament and arms-control negotiations are easily confused. In chronological order, these have been: (1) The U.N. Disarmament Commission (1952 to present) — established in 1952 with twenty-six members, expanded in 1959 to include all members of the General Assembly. It has not met since 1965; (2) The Ten Nation Disarmament Conference (TNDC), 1959–60 — established in 1959. This body was formally called the Ten Nation Disarmament Committee. Legally, however, it was not a committee, but only a group of states called together to discuss disarmament and arms control. The less confusing, informal usage of Ten Nation Disarmament *Conference* (TNDC) was therefore widely adopted and has been used here; (3) The Eighteen Nation Disarmament Conference (ENDC), 1961–69 — an enlarged TNDC. Like the TNDC, the ENDC was formally a *committee*; (4) The Conference of the Committee on Disarmament (CCD), 1969–78 — an ENDC increased to twenty-six members in 1969 and thirty-one in 1975. The CCD incorporated the term "Conference" into its formal title, whilst retaining the confusing name of "Committee"; (5) The Committee on Disarmament,

1978 — effectively a CCD with thirty-five members. This body also retained the misleading title of "Committee".

6. For these reasons, most official statements up to and including 1971 have been taken from *United States Documents on Disarmament, 1945-71* (hereafter referred to as *U.S. Doc. D.*). Since then, Dr. Kissinger's downgrading of the Arms Control and Disarmament Agency (ACDA), plus his intensely secretive and personalized diplomacy, have made these documents an inadequate source of this book, although still of great value as a reference source. For consistency, the military background has been based on the International Institute for Strategic Studies (hereafter referred to as IISS) publications *The Military Balance* (from 1959 onwards) and *Strategic Survey* (from 1966 onwards).

7. For example, Philip Green's work, especially *Deadly Logic: The Theory of Nuclear Deterrence* (Columbus: Ohio State University Press, 1966), provided a useful critical starting point, but was unbalanced in its attacks on Herman Kahn.

Chapter 2

1. See Thomas S. Kuhn, *The Structure of Scientific Revolutions,* 2nd enlarged ed. (Chicago: University of Chicago Press, 1970). In Kuhn's terms, the arms controllers' technical approach was a paradigm that accorded with, and was therefore acceptable to, the underlying paradigms of science. See Kuhn's postscript, "Paradigms and Community Structure", ibid., pp. 176-81. Interviews confirmed the scientists' difficulties in discussing political propositions conflicting with their paradigms of science and politics.

2. On the role of PSAC and scientists involved in strategic-arms-control policy formulation, see George B. Kistiakowsky, *A Scientist at the White House: The Private Diary of President Eisenhower's Special Assistant for Science and Technology* (Cambridge, Mass., and London: Harvard University Press, 1976), especially the introduction by Charles S. Maier. Kistiakowsky was a member of PSAC from November 1957, after the post-Sputnik expansion into a major advisory body, and he became Special Assistant for Science and Technology to the President in July 1959, holding this post until January 20, 1961. He had already emerged as an influential proponent of technical arms control, especially at the 1958 Surprise Attack Conference (see Chapter 4), a position he maintained on his return to private life. See, for example, George W. Rathjens and George B. Kistiakowsky, "The Limitation of Strategic Arms", *Scientific American,* Vol. 222, no. 1 (January 1970), pp. 19–25.

3. Robert Gilpin, *American Scientists and Nuclear Weapons Policy* (Princeton: Princeton University Press, 1962).

4. I. F. Stone, "The Test Ban Comedy", *New York Review of Books,* Vol. 14, no. 9 (May 7, 1970), pp. 14–22.

5. Harold K. Jacobsen and E. Stein, *Diplomats, Scientists and Politicians: The United States and the Nuclear Test Ban Negotiations* (Ann Arbor: University of Michigan Press, 1966).

6. Lincoln Bloomfield, Walter C. Clemens, and Franklyn Griffiths, *Khrushchev and the Arms Race: Soviet Interests in Arms Control and Disarmament, 1954-1964* (Cambridge, Mass.: MIT Press, 1966).

7. John W. Spanier and Joseph L. Nogee, *The Politics of Disarmament: A Study in Soviet-American Gamesmanship* (New York: Praeger, 1962).

8. Arthur H. Dean, *Test Ban and Disarmament: The Path of Negotiation* (New York: Harper and Row, for the Council on Foreign Relations, 1966).

9. Sir Michael Wright, *Disarm and Verify: An Expanation of the Central Difficulties of National Policies* (London: Chatto and Windus; Toronto: Clarke, Irwin, 1964).

10. Lt.-Gen. E. L. M. Burns, *A Seat at the Table: The Struggle for Disarmament* (Toronto: Clarke, Irwin, 1972).

11. See Marshall D. Shulman, *Stalin's Foreign Policy Reappraised* (Cambridge,

Mass.: Harvard University Press, 1963), Chaps. 5, 8; ibid. (New York: Atheneum, 1965), pp. 104-38, 176-98.

12. Gilpin, *American Scientists and Nuclear Weapons Policy*, p. 138.

13. Ibid., pp. 142-43.

14. The Baruch plan of 1946 proposed that all atomic energy projects should be placed under the guardianship of an international agency, following which the United States would place its nuclear plants and atomic weapons under the custody of this agency. The result would have been to institutionalize the U.S. nuclear monopoly and was therefore unacceptable to the Soviet Union, but the plan was a superb piece of "gamesmanship", putting the Soviets at a great propaganda disadvantage. This was partly because the Baruch plan was, strictly speaking, the Acheson–Baruch plan, as U.S. Secretary of State Dean Acheson heavily modified Baruch's original proposal, via the Acheson–Lilienthal Report, to secure this political effect. See Bernard G. Bechhoefer, *Postwar Negotiations for Arms Control* (Washington, D.C.: Brookings Institution, 1961), pp. 27-28. For the 1955 Russian proposals, see ibid., pp. 270–325.

15. *U.S. Doc. D., 1959*, Vol. I, p. 462.

16. Gilpin, *American Scientists and Nuclear Weapons Policy*, p. 160.

17. *U.S. Doc. D., 1945–1959*, Vol. II, pp. 778–87, especially p. 783.

18. Ibid., pp. 868–74, especially p. 871.

19. Gilpin, *American Scientists and Nuclear Weapons Policy*, pp. 179–81.

20. Of the civilians, four (Dr. Hans Bethe, Chairman; Dr. Harold Brown; Dr. Herbert Scoville, Jr.; and Dr. Herbert York) were to become notable advocates of technical arms control, Dr. Brown becoming U.S. Secretary of Defense in 1977. The other three (Dr. Carson Mark, Mr. Doyle Northrup, and Dr. Roderick Spence) appeared slightly more favourable to U.S. testing but were prepared to concede the disadvantages of not negotiating. The four military members would accept a properly safeguarded Comprehensive Test Ban (CTB) as institutionalizing Soviet inferiority in nuclear testing and safeguarding U.S. security. That the Bethe panel saw its role as reassessing the technical possibilities for negotiations on a test ban, a significant political step, was recognized in retrospect by those of its members interviewed. See also Jacobsen and Stein, *Diplomats, Scientists and Politicians*, pp. 46–50.

21. See Jacobsen and Stein, ibid., pp. 50–53, and Kistiakowsky, *A Scientist at the White House*, Introduction, pp. xliii–xliv, especially the revealing comment by Maier that "Eisenhower wanted rigidly to separate technical discussions from political negotiations", although these negotiations showed it was difficult, if not impossible, "to keep the two components apart", p. xliv.

22. See Gilpin, *American Scientists and Nuclear Weapons Policy*, especially pp. 186–222. In Kistiakowsky, ibid., Maier argues in footnote 33 that Gilpin's discussion of the Geneva inspection system was "perhaps overly critical", p. xlv.

23. See, for example, Thomas C. Schelling and Morton H. Halperin, with the assistance of Donald G. Brennan, *Strategy and Arms Control* (New York: The Twentieth Century Fund, 1961), Chaps. 7–10. This book summarized the very influential 1960 Summer Study on Arms Control, conducted under the auspices of the American Academy of Arts and Sciences, the participants and visitors being listed in ibid., pp. 147–48.

24. Gilpin, *American Scientists and Nuclear Weapons Policy*, pp. 251–52.

25. Dean, *Test Ban and Disarmament*, pp. 88–90.

26. *U.S. Doc. D., 1962*, Vol. II, pp. 792–807.

Chapter 3

1. The Eisenhower administration's doctrine of "sufficiency" (re-adopted by President-elect Richard M. Nixon in 1968 and later) was elaborated by Secretary of the Air Force Quarles from August 1956 onwards. See Samuel P. Huntingdon, *The Common Defense: Strategic Programs in National Politics* (New York: Columbia University Press, 1961), pp. 99–106. In footnote 118 he emphasizes that

"throughout the airpower debate, Administration supporters stressed the 'absolute' character of nuclear airpower and Administration critics its 'relative' character", pp. 455–56. See also Seyom Brown, *The Faces of Power: Constancy and Change in United States Foreign Policy from Truman to Johnson* (New York: Columbia University Press, 1968), Parts II and III, pp. 31–124. The Eisenhower policy of "sufficiency" was vulnerable to intellectual and practical criticism, but worked, because it was based on a combination of the Administration's willingness to treat nuclear weapons as equivalent to conventional weapons, to be used as local military situations required, as set out in NSC-168 (recently declassified); with the overwhelming U.S. superiority in strategic airpower, documented in Edgar M. Bottome, *The Missile Gap: A Study of the Formulation of Military and Public Policy* (Cranbury, N.J.: Fairleigh Dickinson University Press, 1971) and Colin S. Gray, "Gap Prediction and America's Defense: Arms Race Behaviour in the Eisenhower Years", *Orbis*, Vol. 16, no. 1 (Spring 1972), pp. 257–74.

2. See Albert Wohlstetter's "Delicate Balance of Terror", *Foreign Affairs*, Vol. 37, no. 2 (January 1959), pp. 211–34, a theoretical elaboration of the consequences of the Strategic Air Command's (SAC) vulnerability to a first strike that he had analysed in Albert Wohlstetter *et al.*, "Selection and Use of Strategic Air Bases", RAND Report R-266 (April 1954), and "Protecting U.S. Power to Strike Back in the 1950s and 1960s", RAND Report R-290 (April 1956).

3. For McNamara's definition of "unacceptable damage", see Chap. 1 of this book (footnote 1).

4. See the discussion of incentives for pre-emption in Schelling and Halperin, *Strategy and Arms Control*, pp. 9–31.

5. Ibid., p. 31.

6. The most influential summary of this view was Henry A. Kissinger, "Limited War: Nuclear or Conventional? A Reappraisal", *Daedalus*, Special Issue on Arms Control, Vol. 89, no. 4 (Fall 1960), pp. 800–17. Kissinger elaborated these arguments in his *The Necessity for Choice: Prospects of American Foreign Policy* (New York: Harper and Brothers, 1961), which reversed his earlier advocacy of the widespread deployment and early use of tactical nuclear weapons. See his *Nuclear Weapons and Foreign Policy* (New York: Harper and Brothers, for the council on Foreign Relations, 1957).

7. Thomas C. Schelling, "Arms Control: Proposal for a Special Surveillance Force", *World Politics*, Vol. 13, no. 1 (October 1960), pp. 1–18.

8. Schelling and Halperin, *Strategy and Arms Control*, pp. 3, 4.

9. Ibid., p. 143.

10. See Bernard Brodie and Arnold Wolfers, eds., *The Absolute Weapon: Atomic Power and World Order* (New York: Harcourt Brace, 1946); and William L. Borden, *There Will Be No Time: The Revolution in Strategy* (New York: Macmillan, 1946); in 1946, Borden said much that Albert Wohlstetter was not to say until 1958-59.

11. John Foster Dulles, "The Evolution of Foreign Policy", *U.S. Department of State Bulletin*, Vol. 30, no. 761 (January 25, 1954), pp. 107–10. This anticipated his more widely publicized, although slightly different, statement of this doctrine in his "Policy for Security and Peace", *Foreign Affairs*, Vol. 32, no. 3 (April 1954), pp. 353-64.

12. Bernard Brodie, "Unlimited Weapons and Limited War", *The Reporter*, Vol. 11 (November 18, 1954), pp. 16–21; Henry A. Kissinger, "Military Policy and Defense of the 'Grey' Areas", *Foreign Affairs*, Vol. 33, no. 3 (April 1955), pp. 416-28.

13. William W. Kaufmann, *The Requirements of Deterrence*, Memorandum No. 7, Center of International Studies (Princeton: Princeton University Press, 1954).

14. Kissinger, *Nuclear Weapons and Foreign Policy*. For the composition of the central study group, see Kissinger's Preface, ibid., p. xiii. It included his later antagonist on SALT, Paul Nitze, who argued then that Kissinger distorted the group's findings, whilst Kissinger "never really forgave Nitze", see Bruce Mazlish, *Kissinger: The European Mind in American Policy* (New York: Basic Books, 1976), pp. 109–10.

15. Robert E. Osgood, *Limited War: The Challenge to American Strategy* (Chicago: University of Chicago Press, 1957).
16. John Foster Dulles, "Challenge and Response in United States' Policy", *Foreign Affairs*, Vol. 36, no. 1 (October 1957), pp. 25–43.
17. Morton H. Halperin, *Limited War in the Nuclear Age* (New York: Wiley, 1963).
18. Herman Kahn, *On Thermonuclear War*, 1st ed. (Princeton: Princeton University Press, 1960).
19. Klaus Knorr and Thornton Read, eds., *Limited Strategic War: Essays on Nuclear Strategy* (New York: Praeger, 1962).
20. For an elaboration of these concepts of rationality derived from game theory, see James N. Rosenau, "Paradigm Lost: Five Actors in Search of the Interactive Effects of Domestic and Foreign Affairs", paper prepared for Symposium on National Strategy in a Decade of Change, sponsored by the Stanford Research and Foreign Policy Research Institutes, Arlie House (February 18, 1972); and Anatol Rapoport, "A Critique of Strategic Thinking", in Roger Fisher, ed., *International Conflict and Behavioral Science* (New York: Basic Books, 1964), pp. 211–37.
21. See the recently declassified Gaither Committee report, U.S. Congress, Joint Commission on Defense Production, *Deterrence and Survival in the Nuclear Age (Gaither Report of 1957)*, Report to the President by the Security Resources Panel of the Science Advisory Committee, November 1957 (Washington, D.C.: U.S. Government Printing Office, 1976). Although highly classified when completed in 1957, the report's essentials were quickly leaked to the press; see Morton H. Halperin, "The Gaither Committee and the Policy Process", *World Politics*, Vol. 13, no. 3 (April 1961), pp. 360–91. The Committee's findings were paralleled by the Rockefeller Study, Rockefeller Brothers Fund, *International Security: The Military Aspect* (Garden City, N.J.: Doubleday, 1958).

Chapter 4

1. Johan J. Holst, "Strategic Arms Control and Stability: A Retrospective Look", in Johan J. Holst and William Schneider, Jr., eds., *Why ABM?: Policy Issues in the Missile Defense Controversy* (New York: Pergamon, 1969), pp. 245–84. Dr. Holst (now Undersecretary of State in the Norwegian Ministry of Defence) gave an extremely accurate account of the conference. Both his account and interviews emphasized the totally opposed approaches of the Western, especially American, delegations and governments and those of the Soviets. The United States saw it as a gathering of arms-control experts — although the only existing ones were on the Western side — convened to discuss extremely elaborate technical-arms-control schemes for avoiding surprise attack, as they defined it. This was evident from the six Western proposals, tabled on November 18, 19, and 24, and December 3, 5, and 17. See *U.S. Doc. D.*, *1945-1959*, Vol. II, pp. 1230–64, 1275–97, and 1306–16. The Soviets, in contrast, were preoccupied with the political potential for a military clash in a divided Europe, particularly one brought about by West German revanchists as shown by their proposals of November 17 and 28, and December 12. See *U.S. Doc. D.*, *1945-1959*, Vol. II, pp. 1227, 1264–75, 1298–1302.
2. By this, Schelling meant that it sometimes made strategic sense to suggest that one might behave irrationally; see Thomas C. Schelling, *Arms and Influence* (New Haven: Yale University Press, 1966).
3. Robin Ranger, "Arms Control Within A Changing Political Context", *International Journal*, Vol. 26, no. 4 (Autumn 1971), pp. 735–52.
4. *U.S. Doc. D.*, *1945-1959*, Vol. II, pp. 932-41.
5. The 1955 U.S. open-skies proposal would have allowed completely free aerial reconnaissance by each superpower over the other's home territory and in Europe. This would have removed the advantage the Soviets enjoyed of secrecy in their strategic deployments, an advantage that dwindled with the American U-2 photographic reconnaissance planes over the Soviet Union, beginning in 1956 and only ceasing in 1960, when a U-2 was brought down by the Soviets and President

Eisenhower promised to cease such flights. Effectively, the open-skies proposal has been implemented by the introduction, from 1961 onwards, of the reconnaissance satellite.

6. *U.S. Doc. D.*, *1945-1959*, Vol. II, pp. 1084–87.

7. Ibid., pp. 1087–90.

8. See Saville R. Davis, "Recent Policy Making in the United States Government", *Daedalus*, Special Issue on Arms Control, Vol. 89, no. 4 (Fall 1960), pp. 951–66; Davis emphasized Dulles's personal dominance over the modalities of policy and his ability to change these as he thought fit.

9. *U.S. Doc. D.*, *1945-1959*, Vol. II, pp. 1129–31.

10. Holst and Schneider, eds., *Why ABM?*, p. 254.

11. Ibid., pp. 254–55.

Chapter 5

1. *U.S. Doc. D.*, *1945–1959*, Vol. II, pp. 1217–19.

2. See Alastair Buchan and Philip Windsor, *Arms and Stability in Europe: A British–French–German Enquiry* (London: Chatto and Windus for the ISS, 1963), especially pp. 6–8, 28–31, 49–50, and 110, for a discussion, from a European view, of these ultimatums and their effects.

3. Quoted by Donald G. Brennan, Review of Carl von Clausewitz's *On War* (Princeton: Princeton University Press, 1976), edited and translated by Michael Howard and Peter Paret, in *Survival*, Vol. 20, no. 1 (London: IISS, January–February 1978), p. 38.

4. These figures are based on Bruce M. Russet and Carolyn C. Cooper, *Arms Control in Europe*, Monograph Series in *World Affairs*, Vol. 4, no. 2 (Denver, Colo.: University of Denver Press, 1966–67), pp. 49–57, and Appendix, "Major Proposals for Arms Control in Europe, 1947–64", pp. 79–85.

5. Although known as the Herter plan, its official title was the "Western Peace Plan". The text is in *U.S. Doc. D.*, *1945–1959*, Vol. II, pp. 1413–19.

6. Text in *The New York Times*, September 20, 1959. For the full effects of this statement, see Philip Windsor, *Berlin, City on Leave: A History of Berlin 1945–1962* (London: Chatto and Windus, 1963), pp. 209–12; and, for an Atlanticist-oriented account of the interaction between the relevant strategic and political issues, especially in West German politics, see James L. Richardson, *Germany and the Atlantic Alliance: The Interaction of Strategy and Politics* (Cambridge, Mass.: Harvard University Press, 1966). On the Camp David Summit and its aftermath, the United States return to support for the status quo in Berlin, and Soviet acceptance of this, see ibid., pp. 271–78.

7. Richardson, *Germany and the Atlantic Alliance*, pp. 293–96, 321–23.

8. *U.S. Doc. D.*, *1945–1959*, Vol. II, pp. 1452–74.

9. *U.S. Doc. D.*, *1960*, pp. 4–16.

10. *U.S. Doc. D.*, *1945–1959*, Vol. II, p. 1459.

11. Bechhoefer, *Postwar Negotiations for Arms Control*, p. 524.

12. U.N. General Assembly Resolution 1378 (XIV), *U.S. Doc. D.*, *1945–1959*, Vol. II, p. 1545.

13. *U.S. Doc. D.*, *1960*, pp. 68–71.

14. *U.S. Doc. D.*, *1961*, pp. 374–84.

15. Ibid., pp. 439–42, including the U.S. reservation that in practice it would insist on verification of arms retained as well as destroyed.

16. *U.S. Doc. D.*, *1965*, pp. 260–62.

17. The details are taken from Bechhoefer, *Postwar Negotiations for Arms Control*; and United Nations, *The United Nations and Disarmament, 1945–1970* (New York: 1971).

18. The changing membership of the successive negotiating bodies reflected the success of the Soviet Union's policy. The U.N. Disarmament Commission Subcommittee (1954–1957) comprised the Soviet Union, the United States, Great Britain, Canada, and France. At the 1958 Conference of Experts, the Soviet Union,

Poland, Czechoslovakia, and Rumania claimed to represent the Eastern bloc, the West sending experts from the United States, Great Britain, Canada, and France. The Surprise Attack Conference saw each side adding what was in practice an additional state to their bloc delegation, Albania for the East and Italy for the West. The same countries supplied the Eastern and Western delegations to the TNDC and ENDC, except for the Soviet Union's replacement of Albania by Bulgaria. The ENDC's eight Third World members were: two Latin American states that the United States could influence — Brazil and Mexico; one traditional neutral — Sweden — respectful of its Soviet neighbour; an African supporter of the United States — Ethiopia; an independent — Nigeria; an Arab client of the Soviet Union — Egypt; and two Asian neutrals favourably disposed to the Soviet Union — Burma and India.

19. Although the CCD, like the TNDC and ENDC, was not a U.N. body, it reported to the U.N. General Assembly First (political) Committee at the annual fall U.N. General Assembly meetings. In 1978 the CCD comprised thirty-one members with the addition, on January 1, 1975, of West and East Germany, Iran, Peru, and Zaire, but still reflected the old troika principle of the ENDC. The West was represented by the United States, with seven allies, Canada, France (still refusing to take its seat though suggesting it might), Great Britain, Italy, Japan, the Netherlands, and West Germany. The East had the Soviet Union and its seven allies, Bulgaria, Czechoslovakia, East Germany, Hungary, Mongolia, Poland, and Rumania. The neutral "bloc", although far from being a bloc, consisted of the fifteen states of Argentina, Brazil, Burma, Egypt, Ethiopia, India, Iran, Mexico, Morocco, Nigeria, Pakistan, Peru, Sweden, Yugoslavia, and Zaire. The political allegiances of these neutrals have, of course, shifted since the days of the ENDC (1961–69) and will continue to do so. The 1978 U.N. Special Session on Disarmament (U.N. SSOD) agreed to enlarge the CCD to thirty-five members and abolish the superpower co-chairmanship. France agreed to participate.

Chapter 6

1. Thomas W. Wolfe, *Soviet Power and Europe 1945–1970* (Baltimore: Johns Hopkins Press, 1970), Chap. VI, pp. 100–17.

2. See Robert F. Kennedy, *Thirteen Days: A Memoir of the Cuban Missile Crisis*, Afterword by Richard E. Neustadt and Graham T. Allison (New York: W. W. Norton, 1969) for a description of the crisis and its effects on the main protagonists. The Afterword (pp. 109–50) emphasizes the lessons the *United States* analysts drew from the crisis. They ignored the key issue of the effect on the *Soviet* leadership of their humiliation by the United States' overwhelming strategic nuclear and local conventional superiority, a superiority *Thirteen Days* glosses over.

3. See *U.S. Doc. D., 1962*, Vol. I, p. 625 (the crucial extract from McNamara's speech was reprinted in ibid., pp. 622–28); and see William W. Kaufmann, *The McNamara Strategy* (New York, Evanston, and London: Harper and Row, 1964), pp. 114–20. Additionally, the shift away from the Ann Arbor strategy was influenced by RAND studies conducted in 1962–63, which demonstrated that damage limitation would decline over the next few years. See James Schlesinger (U.S. Secretary of Defense, 1973–75), "The Changing Environment for Systems Analysis", in S. Enke, ed., *Defense Management* (Englewood Cliffs, N.J.: Prentice-Hall, 1967), pp. 89–112.

4. See *U.S. Doc. D., 1962*, Vol. II, pp. 966–72 for the text of the "Radio–Television Address by President Kennedy on the Cuban Crisis, October 22, 1962"; especially ibid., p. 970. The President also stressed the United States' determination to defend West Berlin "by whatever action is needed", ibid., p. 971.

5. "Towards a Strategy of Peace", (ACDA publication no. 17, 1963), reprinted in *U.S. Doc. D., 1963*, pp. 215–22, excerpt from p. 218.

6. Theodore Sorensen, *Kennedy* (New York: Harper and Row, 1965), pp. 727–40.

7. Philip C. Jessup and Howard J. Taubenfeld, *Controls for Outer Space and the Antarctic Analogy* (New York: Columbia University Press, 1959), p. 153, and map opposite p. 144 showing National Claims and IGY bases.

8. *U.S. Doc. D.*, 1945–1959, Vol. II, pp. 1006–07, and the "U.S. Circular Note Regarding Antarctica", May 3, 1958, pp. 1020–27.

9. Jessup and Taubenfeld, *Controls for Outer Space and the Antarctic Analogy*, p. 182.

10. Evan Luard, "The Background of the Negotiations to Date", in Evan Luard, ed., *First Steps to Disarmament: A New Approach to the Problems of Arms Reductions* (London: Thames and Hudson, 1965), pp. 36–37.

11. *U.S. Doc. D.*, 1945–1959, Vol. II, p. 1552. The Treaty text is in ibid., pp. 1550–59.

12. See *U.S. Doc. D.*, 1964, pp. 195–203; *U.S. Doc. D.*, 1967, pp. 283–90; *U.S. Doc. D.*, 1971, pp. 934–35; *Arms Control Report* (Washington, D.C.: ACDA Publication No. 89, July 1976), p. 15.

13. *U.S. Doc. D.*, 1945–1959, Vol. II, maps on pp. 1596–99.

14. Alexander Rich and Aleksandr P. Vinogradov, "Arctic Disarmament", *The Bulletin of the Atomic Scientists*, Vol. 20, no. 9 (November 1964), pp. 22-23.

15. President Eisenhower on December 29 stated that while the voluntary moratorium expired on December 31: "Although we shall consider ourselves free to resume nuclear weapons testing, we shall not resume nuclear weapons tests without announcing our intention in advance of any resumption." On December 30, Mr. Khrushchev stated he would not resume testing unless the Western powers did. See *U.S. Doc. D.*, 1945–1959, Vol. II, pp. 1590–91.

16. See Schelling, "Arms Control: Proposal for a Special Surveillance Force"; and Schelling and Halperin, *Strategy and Arms Control*; although neither mentions a "hotline" arrangement *per se.*

17. The most comprehensive summation of these was in the significantly titled U.S. Working Paper, "Reduction of the Risk of War Through Accident, Miscalculation or Failure of Communication", submitted to the ENDC on December 12, 1962, *U.S. Doc. D.*, 1962, Vol. II, pp. 1214–25.

18. Hedley Bull, *The Control of the Arms Race: Disarmament and Arms Control in the Missile Age*, 1st ed. (London: Weidenfeld and Nicolson, for the ISS, 1961); 2nd rev. ed. (New York: Praeger, 1965), p. 174 in 1st ed., at the end of his Chap. 10, "Arms Control and Surprise Attack", pp. 158–74.

19. U.S. Working Paper, "Reduction of the Risk of War Through Accident, Miscalculation or Failure of Communication", pp. 1214–25.

20. See *U.S. Doc. D.*, 1963, pp. 156–60, for the April 5 agreement; the Memorandum of Understanding establishing a "Direct Communications Link" is on pp. 236–38.

21. See Philip Windsor, "Observation Posts", in Luard, ed., *First Steps to Disarmament*, Chap. 4, pp. 85–99.

22. See Chap. 4.

Chapter 7

1. See Chap. 23 and Epilogue.

2. Donald G. Brennan and Morton H. Halperin stressed this link in "Policy Considerations of a Nuclear Test Ban", in Donald G. Brennan, ed., *Arms Control, Disarmament and National Security* (New York: Braziller, 1961), drawn from the special issue on arms control of *Daedalus*, Vol. 89, no. 4 (Fall 1960), pp. 234–60.

3. Jacobsen and Stein, *Diplomats, Scientists and Politicians*, pp. 425–26; and Dean, *Test Ban and Disarmament*, pp. 41–42.

4. Whether the U.S. offer was politically realistic was doubtful. Jerome B. Wiesner wrote that "we had reason [during the Senate debate on the PTB] to wonder whether a comprehensive treaty would . . . have been acceptable given any number of inspections", *Where Science and Politics Meet* (New York: McGraw-Hill, 1965), p. 167. Wiesner felt five inspections a year would suffice, ibid., p. 167. The U.S. Senate gave its advice and consent to ratification of the PTB by 80–19 votes only after a major campaign for ratification by President Kennedy, including the commitment to conduct a vigorous underground testing program demanded by the Joint Chiefs of Staff. Jacobsen and Stein, *Diplomats, Scientists, and Politicians*, pp. 458–64.

5. *U.S. Doc. D.*, *1962*, Vol. II, p. 1241; the Soviet December 10 offer is on p. 1184.

6. Jacobsen and Stein, *Diplomats, Scientists and Politicians*, pp. 432–35.

7. *U.S. Doc. D.*, *1963*, pp. 244–46.

8. "Treaty Banning Nuclear Weapon Tests in the Atmosphere, in Outer Space and Under Water, August 5, 1963", *U.S. Doc. D.*, *1963*, pp. 291–93.

9. "Communiqué and Report of the Conference of Experts to Study the Possibility of Detecting Violations of a Possible Agreement on the Suspension of Nuclear Tests, August 21, 1958", *U.S. Doc. D.*, *1945–1959*, Vol. II, pp. 1090–1111, especially pp. 1094–95.

10. The first were launched in October 1963, the second pair in July 1964, and the third pair in July 1965. All functioned correctly. See Dean, *Test Ban and Disarmament*, pp. 21–22.

11. Wright, *Disarm and Verify*, p. 113.

12. See *U.S. Doc. D.*, *1965*, pp. 4–5, 9–10.

13. Ibid., pp. 9–10.

14. SIPRI *Yearbook 1969–1970* (Stockholm: Almquist and Wicksell, 1970), pp. 384–87, Table 26.2.

15. SIPRI *Yearbook 1968–1969* (Stockholm: Almquist and Wicksell, 1969), pp. 241–58.

16. See Chap. 23 and Epilogue.

17. Philip Windsor, "Current Tensions in NATO", *The World Today*, Vol. 26, no. 7 (July 1970), pp. 289–95.

18. Ibid., p. 290.

19. Robert E. Hunter, "The Future of Soviet-American Détente", *The World Today*, Vol. 24, no. 7 (July 1968), pp. 281–90.

Chapter 8

1. U.N. General Assembly Resolution 1962 (XVIII), *U.S. Doc. D.*, *1963*, p. 644–45.

2. Khrushchev's address in Moscow is in ibid., pp. 640–43.

3. Ibid., p. 664.

4. *U.S. Doc. D.*, *1964*, pp. 165–71.

5. "Treaty on Principles Governing the Activities of States in the Exploration and Use of Outer Space, Including the Moon and Other Celestial Bodies, January 27, 1967", reprinted in *U.S. Doc. D.*, *1967*, pp. 38–43.

6. See, for example, *U.S. Doc. D.*, *1945–1959*, Vol. II, pp. 733, 871, 914–15.

7. Ibid., pp. 1275–84.

8. Ibid., p. 1279.

9. Donald G. Brennan, "Arms and Arms Control in Outer Space", in Lincoln P. Bloomfield, ed., *Outer Space: Prospects for Man and Society*, 1st ed. (Englewood Cliffs, N.J.: Prentice-Hall, 1962); 2nd rev. ed. (New York: Praeger, 1968), pp. 145–77.

10. Bull, *The Control of the Arms Race*, Chap. 11, pp. 175-92.

11. See Brennan, "Arms and Arms Control in Outer Space".

12. Soviet Foreign Minister Andrei Gromyko accepted this "demilitarization" of outer space in his September 19 address to the United Nations. See *U.S. Doc. D.*, *1963*, p. 523.

13. *The United Nations and Disarmament 1945–1970* (New York: United Nations, 1971), p. 177.

14. *U.S. Doc. D.*, *1966*, pp. 809–81, and *U.S. Doc. D.*, *1967*, pp. 38–43.

15. *U.S. Doc. D.*, *1966*, p. 655.

16. See McNamara's statement of November 3, reprinted in *U.S. Doc. D.*, *1967*, pp. 559–60.

17. SIPRI *Yearbook 1969–1970* (Stockholm: Almquist and Wicksell, 1970), Chap. 3, pp. 92–184.

18. See *U.S. Doc. D.*, *1969*, pp. 112–13 and 747–49.

19. Ibid., pp. 373–80.

20. Ibid., p. 486.

21. *U.S. Doc. D., 1970*, pp. 475–79.

22. For full details of the treaty's negotiations and implications, see Garcia Robles, *The Denuclearization of Latin America* (New York: Carnegie Endowment for International Peace, 1967); and "The Treaty for the Prohibition of Nuclear Weapons in Latin America" (Treaty of Tlatelolco), sipri *Yearbook 1969–1970*, Part ii, pp. 218–56; and *United Nations and Disarmament*, Chap. 15, pp. 327–48.

23. Article 16(b) (i); italics mine. The treaty is reprinted in *U.S. Doc. D., 1967*, pp. 69–83; sipri *Yearbook 1969–1970*, pp. 237–53.

24. George H. Quester, "Missiles in Cuba, 1970", *Foreign Affairs*, Vol. 49, no. 3 (April 1971), pp. 493–506, especially p. 503.

25. Ibid.

26. There were also strong bureaucratic and political constraints against a ban only on flight testing. See John Newhouse, *Cold Dawn: The Story of* salt (Toronto: Holt, Rinehart and Winston, 1973), pp. 178–83.

27. For the origins and implications of this Convention, see Robin Ranger, "The Canadian Contribution to the Control of Chemical and Biological Warfare", Wellesley Paper No. 5 (Toronto: Canadian Institute of International Affairs, 1976), pp. 38–44. The Convention is reprinted in Appendix E, pp. 57–61.

28. Ranger, ibid., pp. 51–52.

Chapter 9

1. See Marshall D. Shulman, *Beyond the Cold War* (New Haven and London: Yale University Press, 1966), p. 88.

2. These ideas were expounded by President Johnson's chief advisor on European affairs, Zbigniew Brzezinski, subsequently President Jimmy Carter's Special Assistant for National Security Affairs (January 1977–present), in Zbigniew Brzezinski, *Alternative to Partition: For a Broader Conception of America's Role in Europe* (New York: McGraw-Hill, for the Council on Foreign Relations, 1965).

3. *U.S. Doc. D., 1964*, pp. 7–9.

4. Ibid., pp. 12–17.

5. Ibid., pp. 101–05.

6. See John L. Sutton and G. Kemp, *Arms to Developing Countries, 1945–1965*, Adelphi Paper No. 28 (London: iss, October 1966); G. Kemp, "Dilemmas of the Arms Traffic", *Foreign Affairs*, Vol. 48, no. 2 (January 1970), pp. 274–84.

7. See iss, *The Military Balance, 1964–65* (London: 1964), pp. 3–4, 22, and 37.

8. See *U.S. Doc. D., 1964*, pp. 137–39, 284–93, 509–17.

9. Ibid., p. 8.

10. *U.S. Doc. D., 1962*, Vol. i, p. 359.

11. *U.S. Doc. D., 1964*, pp. 15–16.

12. Proliferation had been second only in importance to strategic stability for the United States and other Western arms controllers from the time arms control emerged. See, for example, National Planning Association, *The nth Country Problem and Arms Control* (Washington, D.C.: 1960) Leonard Beaton and John Maddox, *The Spread of Nuclear Weapons* (London: Chatto and Windus, for the iss, 1962). This view became official United States policy with the Director of the Arms Control and Disarmament Agency, William C. Foster's "New Directions in Arms Control and Disarmament", *Foreign Affairs*, Vol. 43, no. 4 (July 1965), pp. 587–601.

Chapter 10

1. Under this agreement the United States was willing to provide the Polaris missile and technological information which would enable Great Britain to construct nuclear-powered submarines carrying Polaris Submarine-Launched Ballistic Missiles (slbm) with U.K.-built thermonuclear warheads. This force would be under the ultimate independent control of the British Prime Minister. See "Nassau Communiqué by President Kennedy and Prime Minister Macmillan, December 21, 1962", in *U.S. Doc. D., July–December 1962*, Vol. #ii, pp. 1274–76. The

agreement has to be placed in its post-Cuban-missile-crisis context of the uncertainty of whether the Cold War would get worse, or be replaced by detente. But Macmillan also negotiated brilliantly, securing an extraordinary extension of nuclear aid from Kennedy, an extension that obviously alarmed the Soviets by its future implications: after Nassau, was it really unreasonable to fear that the same logic *could* lead to a similar offer to West Germany?

2. See Karl Kaiser, *German Foreign Policy in Transition: Bonn Between East and West* (London, Oxford, and New York: Oxford University Press, for the Harvard Center for International Affairs, the Twentieth Century Fund, and the Royal Institute of International Affairs, 1968), Chap. 6, in particular pp. 74–100.

3. See Philip Windsor, *Germany and the Management of Detente* (London: Chatto and Windus, for the ISS, 1971).

4. Adam B. Ulam's masterly *Expansion and Coexistence: The History of Soviet Foreign Policy 1917–1967* (New York: Praeger, 1968) can be criticized for its overemphasis on the importance of China in Soviet foreign policy.

5. Chiefly through provision of the Lanchow gaseous-diffusion plant, which provided the highly enriched uranium (U–235) essential for the atomic (fission) trigger for hydrogen (fusion) explosions. Why the Soviets provided *this* aid remains a puzzle, whilst suggesting that they, too, can make major mistakes. See Walter C. Clemens, Jr., *The Arms Race and Sino-Soviet Relations* (Stanford: The Hoover Institution on War, Revolution and Peace, Stanford University, 1968), in particular pp. 15–24.

Chapter 11

1. See R. Ranger, "Death of a Treaty: A Diplomatic Obituary?", *International Relations*, Vol. 3, no. 7 (April 1969), pp. 482–97. Whilst retrospective evaluations of one's own predictions are notoriously favourable, the title of my article makes clear my doubts that the 1968 NPT could fulfil its *technical*-arms-control tasks and would, in practice, only marginally inhibit proliferation. This proved to be the case: by 1977–78 it was clear that proliferation had re-emerged (more accurately, finally emerged) as a major arms-control problem, that the NPT was largely irrelevant to limiting proliferation, and that, in the world of real politics, strategy, and economics, the classical technical-arms-control theories (c. 1958–66) of the causes of proliferation, and therefore of its control, were largely irrelevant. See Chaps. 17, 18, and Epilogue.

2. William B. Bader, *The United States and the Spread of Nuclear Weapons* (New York: Pegasus, for the Center of International Studies, Princeton University, 1968). Bader emphasized the inherent tensions between the American desire, first, to inhibit the proliferation of nuclear weapons to undesirable (by United States criteria) states; second, to facilitate the use of "peaceful" nuclear power where possible; and third, to utilize "controlled dissemination" within NATO.

3. This view, for example, is reflected in Elizabeth Young, *The Control of Proliferation: The 1968 Treaty in Hindsight and Forecast*, Adelphi Paper No. 56 (London: ISS, April 1969), and even more so in the official U.S. account, United States Arms Control and Disarmament Agency, Publication 48, *International Negotiations on the Treaty on the Non-proliferation of Nuclear Weapons* (Washington, D.C.: U.S. Government Printing Office, January 1969).

4. For the relationship between the introduction of the two-key system and the MLF, see Irving Heymont, "The NATO Nuclear Bilateral Forces", *Orbis*, Vol. 9, no. 4 (Winter 1966), pp. 1025–41; Thomas C. Wiegle, "The Origins of the MLF Concept, 1957–1960", *Orbis*, Vol. 12, no. 2 (Summer 1968), pp. 465–89; and Wilfred L. Kohl, "Nuclear Sharing in NATO and the Multilateral Force", *Political Science Quarterly*, Vol. 80, no. 1 (March 1965), pp. 88–109. Kohl stressed that the MLF originated in 1960 in a secret State Department document, written primarily by Robert R. Bowie, and presented to the December 1960 North Atlantic Council "by the United States Secretary of State Christian A. Herter as a 'concept' for discussion", ibid., p. 91. The most complete account of the MLF's political development and defects remains

Henry A. Kissinger's *The Troubled Partnership* (New York: McGraw-Hill, for the Council on Foreign Relations, 1965), Chap. 5, pp. 127–59; and the MLF's conceptual framework, elaborated by Morton A. Kaplan in "Problems of Coalition and Deterrence", in Klaus Knorr, ed., NATO and American Security (Princeton: Princeton University Press, 1959), pp. 127–50.

5. Bader, *The United States and the Spread of Nuclear Weapons*, pp. 28–29.

6. Ibid.

7. Typical statements of the Soviet position on dissemination, which changed little in style or substance from 1957 onwards, may be found in *U.S. Doc. D., 1945–1959*, Vol. II, pp. 849–68, 878, and 1473–74.

8. For a detailed analysis of the difference between Soviet declaratory policy and action, see Benjamin S. Lambeth, "Nuclear Proliferation and Soviet Arms Control Policy", *Orbis*, Vol. 14, no. 2 (Summer 1970), pp. 298–325.

9. General Assembly Resolution 1665 (XVI), December 4, *U.S. Doc. D., 1961*, p. 694.

10. General Assembly Resolution 1664 (XVI), December 4, ibid., p. 693.

11. *U.S. Doc. D., 1962*, Vol. I, p. 88.

12. See ibid., pp. 83–86, especially p. 84.

13. Alastair Buchan, *The Multilateral Force: An Historical Perspective*, Adelphi Paper No. 13 (London: ISS, October 1964), p. 4, quoting the President's December 18, 1962, question, "How does that produce security when you have 10, 20, 30 nuclear powers . . .?"

14. This debate was summarized by Lt.-Gen. E. L. M. Burns in "Can the Spread of Nuclear Weapons Be Stopped?", *International Organization*, Vol. 19, no. 4 (Autumn 1965), pp. 851–69.

15. Ibid., p. 860.

16. These ideas of eventual lessening of U.S. control were elaborated by one of the MLF's chief supporters, Robert R. Bowie, in "Strategy and the Atlantic Alliance", *International Organization*, Vol. 17, no. 3 (Summer 1963), pp. 709–32, especially pp. 722–26. The ultimate release formula for the MLF was that its use would require two affirmative votes, one by the United States and one by the majority decision of the European members; see Thomas C. Wiegle, "Nuclear Consultation Processes in NATO", *Orbis*, Vol. 16, no. 2 (Summer 1972), p. 469.

17. Kissinger, *The Troubled Partnership*, pp. 134–35.

18. See, for example, the *Washington Star*, January 15, 1965; and the *Washington Post*, January 22, 1965. According to both, the Committee included Arthur Dean, former Chairman of the U.S. delegation to the Eighteen Nation Disarmament Conference (ENDC); Allen Dulles, former head of the CIA; Gen. Alfred Gruenther, former commander of SACEUR; Dr. George Kistiakowsky, former science advisor to President Eisenhower; John McCloy, former High Commissioner in Germany; James A. Perkins, President of Cornell University; and Herbert F. York, former Director, Defense Research and Engineering (DDRE), all of whom would have been influential in its discussions. Also included were the Chairman of the Board of International Trade Corporation, and the President of English Electric.

19. For a detailed account of the relationship between the MLF and NPG, see Harlan Cleveland, *The Transatlantic Bargain: NATO Past and Future* (New York: Harper and Row, for the Council on Foreign Relations, 1970), in particular, pp. 50–51.

20. Later published as Karl W. Deutsch, *Arms Control and the Atlantic Alliance: Europe Faces Coming Policy Decisions* (New York: Wiley, 1967).

Chapter 12

1. *U.S. Doc. D., 1965*, pp. 347–49.

2. *U.S. Doc. D., 1966*, pp. 159–60.

3. See, for example, ACDA Deputy Director Adrian S. Fisher's March 22 statement, ibid., pp. 160–68.

4. *U.S. Doc. D., 1967*, pp. 338–41.

5. *U.S. Doc. D., 1965*, p. 347.

6. See, for example, the statements made by President Johnson and Acting Secretary of State George Ball, on July 5 and 6 (1966), respectively, in *U.S. Doc. D., 1966*, pp. 405–07.
7. Ibid., pp. 640–44.
8. *U.S. Doc. D., 1966*, pp. 649–55.
9. Report by Secretary of State Rusk to President Johnson on the NPT on July 2, 1968, *U.S. Doc. D., 1968*, pp. 470–78, especially p. 478.

Chapter 13

1. This distinction was stressed by Alastair Buchan, and the importance of *contrôle* to the West Europeans is summarized in Kohl, "Nuclear Sharing in NATO and the Multilateral Force", especially pp. 102–07. The attitudes of the major West European powers involved in the MLF/NPT debate, towards both this debate and the broader issues raised by control and *contrôle* over nuclear weapons within NATO, showed the relative commonality of British, French, and West German interests and the inability of United States policy makers to understand the validity of these interests, especially if these conflicted with whatever the then current United States policy was. See Catherine McArdle Kelleher, *Germany and the Politics of Nuclear Weapons* (New York: Columbia University Press, 1975); Wilfred L. Kohl, *French Nuclear Diplomacy* (Princeton: Princeton University Press, 1971); and Andrew J. Pierre, *Nuclear Politics: The British Experience With An Independent Strategic Force 1939–1970* (London: Oxford University Press, 1972).
2. See, for example, Soviet Representative Tsarpkin's statement of June 2, printed in *U.S. Doc. D., 1965*, pp. 219–25.
3. Ibid., pp. 102–11.
4. William C. Foster, "New Directions in Arms Control and Disarmament", pp. 587–601.
5. *U.S. Doc. D., 1965*, pp. 347–49.
6. Ibid., pp. 443–46.
7. The U.S. and U.S.S.R. Draft Resolutions tabled (in 1965) before the U.N. General Assembly on October 26 and 27, respectively, reflected their differing approaches. See ibid., pp. 498–500.
8. *U.S. Doc. D., 1966*, pp. 159–60.
9. See ibid., pp. 253–55, 302–03, 306–07.

Chapter 14

1. *U.S. Doc. D., 1967*, pp. 338–41.
2. Ibid., pp. 613–16.
3. Statement by Secretary of State Rusk to the Senate Foreign Relations Committee on the NPT on July 10, 1968; *U.S. Doc. D., 1968*, pp. 493–96.
4. The text of the Treaty on the Non-proliferation of Nuclear Weapons, July 1, 1968, is reprinted in ibid., pp. 461–65.
5. See, for example, U.S. statements in ibid., pp. 13, 505, and 520.
6. *The New York Times*, November 13, 1969.
7. See R. Ranger, "The NPT Two Years on: Lessons for SALT", *The World Today*, Vol. 26, no. 11 (November 1970), pp. 453–57; and Ryukichi Imai, *Nuclear Safeguards*, Adelphi Paper No. 86 (London: IISS, March 1972).
8. *The New York Times*, March 6, 1972.
9. See Thomas W. Wolfe, *The SALT Experience: Its Impact on U.S. and Soviet Strategic Policy and Decisionmaking*. RAND Report R–1686–PR, September 1975.
10. S. Ex. Report No. 9, 90th Congress, 2nd Session, printed in *U.S. Doc. D., 1968*, pp. 642–67.
11. Ibid., pp. 656–57.
12. Ibid., pp. 657–67, see especially p. 657.
13. Ibid., p. 659.

14. See my "NATO's Reaction to Czechoslovakia", *The World Today*, Vol. 25, no. 1 (January 1969), pp. 19–25, especially p. 25.

15. I attempted to reflect this in ibid.

16. Quoted in ibid., p. 19.

17. *International Herald Tribune*, November 29, 1968.

18. Ibid., October 26, 1968.

19. See John Newhouse, *Cold Dawn*, pp. 135–36; Moscow responded on November 12 by indicating its willingness to start SALT.

20. Secretary McNamara's views were similar to those in George W. Rathjens's *The Future of the Strategic Arms Race*. Those who reviewed the original paper included such well-known technical arms controllers as Paul M. Doty, Bernard T. Feld, Richard L. Garwin, Carl Kaysen, George B. Kistiakowsky, Franklin A. Long, Robert S. McNamara, Marshall D. Shulman, Jeremy J. Stone, and Richard H. Ullman. See pp. iii–iv, introduction by Joseph E. Johnson, President, Carnegie Endowment for International Peace, who wrote that "the paper represents a substantial consensus", p. iv.

21. See the Russian statements in *U.S. Doc. D.*, 1968, pp. 703–13, 739–47.

22. U.S. Government, *U.S. Foreign Policy for the 1970s: A New Strategy for Peace* (Washington, D.C.: U.S. Government Printing Office, February 18, 1970). For the Nixon–Kissinger view of their success in implementing their objectives, see *U.S. Foreign Policy for the 1970s: Shaping a Durable Peace*, A Report to the Congress by Richard Nixon, President of the United States, May 3, 1973 (Washington, D.C.: U.S. Government Printing Office, 1973).

23. For this and other signs of President Nixon's more political approach to the NPT, see, for example, his News Conference of March 4, in *U.S. Doc. D.*, 1969, pp. 66–67.

24. See Ninth Annual ACDA Report, reprinted in *U.S. Doc. D.*, 1969, pp. 733–65.

25. *U.S. Doc. D.*, 1969, p. 315.

26. My discussions in Washington in the summer of 1969 confirmed that this was the administration's preferred timetable and that the Soviet failure to react was viewed as inimical to arms control, while the Soviet approach was still seen in terms of American arms-control thinking.

27. See *The New York Times*, November 13, 1969. For a masterly survey of the over-all *political* issues involved in the German question and detente, see Philip Windsor, *Germany and the Management of Detente*.

28. *U.S. Doc. D.*, 1969, p. 499.

29. Ibid., pp. 576–77 and 609–15.

30. S. Encel and Allan McKnight, "Bombs, Power Stations and Proliferation", *Australian Quarterly*, Vol. 42 (March 1970), pp. 15–26.

31. *U.S. Doc. D.*, 1970, pp. 78–81.

Chapter 15

1. On the nuclear proliferation position of India and of the potential Nth powers before India's 1974 nuclear test, see Ashok Kapur, *India's Nuclear Option: Atomic Diplomacy and Decision Making* (New York: Praeger, 1976), especially pp. 1–25, 93–144, and 220. On India and other Nth powers, see George H. Quester, *The Politics of Nuclear Proliferation* (Baltimore: Johns Hopkins Press, 1973), and SIPRI, *The Near-Nuclear Countries and the NPT* (Stockholm: Almquist and Wicksell, 1972), and Shelton L. Williams, *The U.S., India, and the Bomb* (Baltimore: Johns Hopkins Press, 1969).

2. The difference between the technical capability to manufacture nuclear weapons and the strategic motivations for doing so had been spelt out in Alastair Buchan, ed., *A World of Nuclear Powers?* (Englewood Cliffs, N.J.: Prentice-Hall, for The American Assembly, Columbia University, 1966).

3. Statement of French Ambassador Armand Berard on June 12, 1968, *U.S. Doc. D.*, 1968, pp. 429–31. France had also ceased assistance to Israel's nuclear program.

4. See Andrew J. Pierre, *Nuclear Politics: The British Experience*, pp. 325–42.

5. See *U.S. Doc. D., 1968*, pp. 620–23, for details of the U.S. position on safeguards at signature.

6. Leonard Beaton, "Nuclear Fuel-for-All", *Foreign Affairs*, Vol. 45, no. 4 (July 1967), pp. 662–69.

7. Security Council Resolution 225 (June 19, 1968), *U.S. Doc. D., 1968*, p. 444.

8. See *The Times*, August 29, 1968, and *Hansard*, Vol. IV (July 19, 1968), respectively. China's admission to the Security Council in 1971, with a veto, made these guarantees worthless.

9. See, for example, Secretary McNamara's justification for deploying a "relatively light and reliable Chinese-orientated ABM system" for the defence of cities against a possible *irrational* Chinese nuclear attack. See "Address by Secretary of Defense McNamara to United Press International Editors and Publishers, September 18, 1967", reprinted in *U.S. Doc. D., 1967*, pp. 382–94, especially pp. 392–93.

10. R. Ranger, "Death of a Treaty", p. 488.

11. Ibid., p. 488.

Chapter 16

1. On India, see Ashok Kapur, *India's Nuclear Option*; on Israel, Fuad Jabber's dated, but comprehensive, *Israel and Nuclear Weapons: Present Options and Future Strategies* (London: Chatto and Windus, for the ISS, 1971); on Japan, John E. Endicott, *Japan's Nuclear Option: Political, Technical, and Strategic Factors* (New York: Praeger, 1975). The best recent summaries are G. S. Bhargava, *India's Security in the 1980s*, Adelphi Paper No. 125 (London: IISS, Summer 1976); William Epstein, *The Last Chance: Nuclear Proliferation and Arms Control* (New York: The Free Press, 1976); Ted Greenwood, George W. Rathjens, and Jack Ruina, *Nuclear Power and Weapons Proliferation*, Adelphi Paper No. 130 (London: IISS, Winter 1976); Lloyd Jensen, *Return from the Nuclear Brink: National Interest and the Nuclear Nonproliferation Treaty* (Lexington, Mass.: D. C. Heath, 1974); Geoffrey Kemp, Robert L. Pflatzgraff, Jr., Uri Ra'anan, eds., *The Superpowers in a Multinuclear World* (Lexington, Mass.: D. C. Heath, 1974); Robert M. Lawrence and Joel Larus, eds., *Nuclear Proliferation Phase II* (Lawrence: University of Kansas, for the National Security Education Program of New York University, 1974); John Maddox, *Prospects for Nuclear Proliferation*, Adelphi Paper No. 113 (London: IISS, Spring 1975); Onkar Marwah and Ann Schulz, *Nuclear Proliferation and the Near-Nuclear Countries* (Cambridge, Mass.: Ballinger, 1975); Peter G. Mueller, *On Things Nuclear: The Canadian Debate* (Toronto: Canadian Institute of International Affairs, 1977); and SIPRI, *Nuclear Proliferation Problems* (Stockholm: Almquist and Wicksell, 1974).

2. See R. Ranger, "The Canadian Perspective", in Frederick S. Northedge, ed., *The Foreign Policies of the Powers*, 2nd rev. ed. (London: Faber and Faber, 1974), pp. 269–95.

3. Quester, *The Politics of Nuclear Proliferation*, p. 154. For a typical Canadian reaction to India's nuclear test, see Barrie Morrison and Donald M. Page, "India's Option: The Nuclear Route to Achieve Goal as World Power", *International Perspectives* (Ottawa: Department of External Affairs, July–August 1974), pp. 23–28; for a reasoned defence of the Indian position see Dr. Ashok Kapur's letter in ibid. (November–December 1974), pp. 55–56. For the U.S. reaction see George H. Quester, "Can Proliferation Now Be Stopped?", *Foreign Affairs*, Vol. 53, no. 1 (October 1974), pp. 77–97, and Lincoln P. Bloomfield, "Nuclear Spread and World Order", *Foreign Affairs*, Vol. 53, no. 4 (July 1975), pp. 743–55.

4. Maddox, *Prospects for Nuclear Proliferation*, p. 17.

5. See K. Subrahmanyam, Director of the [Indian] Institute of Defence Studies and Analyses, "Indian Attitudes Towards the NPT", in SIPRI, *Nuclear Proliferation Problems*, pp. 259–76; K. Subrahmanyam, "An Indian Nuclear Force in the Eighties", in *The Institute of Defence Studies and Analyses Journal* (New Delhi: April 6, 1973); and G. S. Bhargava, *India's Security in the 1980s*.

6. Beaton and Maddox, *The Spread of Nuclear Weapons*, p. 136.

7. Ibid., p. 141.

8. The best generally accepted (except by the Indian government) account of what he called the Chinese "punitive expedition" was Neville Maxwell's *India's China War* (London: Jonathan Cape, 1970), summarized in Neville Maxwell, "China and India: The Un-Negotiated Dispute", *China Quarterly*, Vol. 43 (July–September 1970), pp. 47–80.

9. Major-General D. Som Dutt, *India and the Bomb*, Adelphi Paper No. 30 (London: ISS, November 1966), p. 1.

10. Ibid., p. 6.

11. See, for example, Indian statements, *U.S. Doc. D.*, *1967*, pp. 692–98; and *U.S. Doc. D.*, *1968*, pp. 325–36.

12. The details are in *Strategic Survey* (London: ISS, 1969), pp. 66–72, "The Sino-Soviet Dispute".

Chapter 17

1. Japanese *White Paper on Defense*, translated in *Survival*, Vol. 13, no. 1 (London: ISS, January 1971), p. 3.

2. For Japanese reservations on the treaty itself, see *U.S. Doc. D.*, *1968*, pp. 309–14.

3. Yair Evron, Review of Fuad Jabber's *Israel and the Bomb*, in *Survival*, Vol. 14, no. 5 (September–October 1972), pp. 253–54. I am indebted to Dr. Evron for his insights into Israel's position.

4. The key article was "U.S. believes Israel has more than 10 nuclear weapons", *Boston Globe*, July 31, 1975, by William Beecher, the Globe's diplomatic correspondent and, in 1973–75, Principal Deputy Assistant Secretary of Defense for Public Affairs. This estimate was confirmed in a rare "semi-public" briefing by Central Intelligence Agency (CIA) officials in March 1976; see *The Guardian Weekly*, March 21, 1976. For the suggestion of Israel's readiness to use nuclear weapons in the 1973 War, see *Time*, "How Israel Got the Bomb", April 12, 1976, pp. 21–22; see also Lawrence Freedman, "Israel's Nuclear Policy", *Survival*, Vol. 17, no. 3 (London: IISS, May–June 1975), pp. 114–19.

5. Yair Evron, "Israel and the Atom: The Uses and Misuses of Ambiguity, 1957–1967", *Orbis*, Vol. 17, no. 4 (Winter 1974), pp. 1326–43.

6. *U.S. Doc. D.*, *1968*, pp. 402–04, especially p. 403.

Chapter 18

1. For simplicity's sake the common acronym of SALT I has been used to cover the May 1972 package of agreements limiting strategic arms. These are reprinted in *Survival*, Vol. 14, no. 4 (July–August 1972), pp. 128–99. See Appendix — Table.

2. See *Excerpts of Dr. Henry Kissinger's Briefing on SALT for Members of Congress*, Official Text from USIS, American Embassy, London, June 16, 1972; and *Excerpts of Dr. Henry Kissinger's Briefing Question and Answer Session*, Official Text from USIS, American Embassy, London, June 19, 1972.

3. This interdependence was summarized in the "Basic Principles of Relations" of May 29, 1972, *Survival*, Vol. 14, no. 4 (July–August 1972), pp. 191–92. The central principles (first to fourth) are reprinted at Appendix. These principles of relations were violated the next year by the Soviet encouragement of the Arab attack on Israel in October 1973, and by their arms shipments to the Arabs during the war.

4. For an excellent critique of this over-simplified theory of the arms race, a theory which, arguably, reflected the influence of two-person game theory and McNamara's excessively apolitical approach to strategic problems, see Colin S. Gray, "The Arms Race Phenomenon", *World Politics*, Vol. 24, no. 1 (October 1971), pp. 39–79; and, Colin S. Gray, "The Urge to Compete: Rationales for Arms Racing", *World Politics*, Vol. 26, no. 2 (January 1974), pp. 207–33.

5. Emerging evidence now suggests that the United States would have deployed MIRV for technical and bureaucratic reasons and pressures independently of Soviet

ABM deployment or non-deployment. See Ted Greenwood, *Making the* MIRV: *A Study of Defense Decision Making* (Cambridge, Mass.: Ballinger, 1975); and Ronald L. Tammen, MIRV *and the Arms Race: An Interpretation of Defense Strategy* (New York: Praeger, 1973). The best over-all account of the U.S. missile defence policy from its origins to 1970 is in Benson D. Adams, *Ballistic Missile Defense* (New York: American Elsevier, 1971).

6. These views are summarized in the writings of Dr. Herbert Scoville, Jr., to whom I am indebted for his great assistance in my research and his illuminating discussion of the differences between effective arms control and the policies practised by Presidents Kennedy, Johnson, Nixon, and Ford. See, for example, Dr. Herbert Scoville, Jr., *Towards a Strategic Arms Limitation Agreement* (New York: Carnegie Endowment for International Peace, 1970). Like George Rathjens's *The Future of the Strategic Arms Race,* Dr. Scoville's monograph resulted from a 1969 Carnegie Endowment strategic arms policy study group, chaired by Dr. Harold Brown, U.S. Secretary of Defense, 1977 to date (Introduction, p. iii). See also, Scoville, "Beyond SALT I", *Foreign Affairs,* Vol. 50, no. 3 (April 1972), pp. 488-500; with Betty G. Lall and Robert E. Hunter, "The Arms Race: Steps Towards Constraint", *International Conciliation,* no. 587 (March 1972); "Strategic Forum: The SALT Agreements", *Survival,* Vol. 14, no. 5 (September–October 1972), pp. 210-12.

7. These arms-control arguments were advanced from the early 1960s on; the pro-arms-control view of ABM systems, condemning them, was summarized in Abram Chayes and Jerome B. Wiesner, eds., ABM: *An Evaluation of the Decision to Deploy an Antiballistic Missile System* (New York: Signet, 1969). The pro-ABM-systems reply was Holst and Schneider, eds., *Why* ABM? In Holst and Schneider, Donald G. Brennan pointed out that the Soviet Major-General Nikolai A. Talenski's pro-ABM article, "Anti-Missile Systems and Disarmament", *International Affairs* (Moscow), Vol. 7, no. 10 (November 1964), pp. 15–17, was a response to an anti-ABM paper by Jeremy J. Stone addressed to Talenski and other Russians in 1964. Such exchanges also took place at the international Pugwash conferences of scientists.

8. Talenski, "Anti-Missile Systems and Disarmament".

9. *U.S. Doc. D., 1967,* pp. 60–61.

10. Ibid., p. 270.

11. Ibid., pp. 108–10.

12. See Robert S. McNamara, *The Essence of Security: Reflections in Office* (New York: Harper and Row, 1968). Curiously, these reflections are merely a collection of speeches and statements made in office. McNamara has never provided a proper memoir, a strange and serious omission.

13. *U.S. Doc. D., 1964,* pp. 7–9.

14. *U.S. Doc. D., 1966,* pp. 730–31.

15. *U.S. Doc. D., 1967,* pp. 382–94. See also Morton H. Halperin, "The Decision to Deploy the ABM: Bureaucratic and Domestic Politics in the Johnson Administration", *World Politics,* Vol. 25, no. 1 (October 1972), pp. 62–95.

16. See, for example, ABM, MIRV, SALT, *and the Nuclear Arms Race,* Hearings before the Sub-committee on Arms Control, International Law and Organization, of the Committee on Foreign Relations, United States Senate, Ninety-First Congress, Second Session, March–June 1970 (Washington, D.C.: U. S. Government Printing Office). When the Operations Research Society of America (ORSA) conducted an entirely legitimate investigation into the quality of the operations research in the ABM debate, it underlined the deep divisions in the strategic community; see ORSA, "The Nature of Operations Research and the Treatment of Operations Research Questions in the 1969 Safeguard Debate", *Operations Research,* Vol. 19, no. 5 (September 1971), pp. 1123–1258; this investigation was attacked as political and unprofessional, see *Operations Research,* Vol. 20, no. 1 (January–February 1972), pp. 205–46, and Federation of American Scientists (FAS) Newsletter, Special Issue on ORSA ABM Report, Vol. 24, no. 9 (December 1971).

17. For a partially inside account of American policy making for SALT and the SALT negotiations, see John Newhouse, *Cold Dawn*; and for a devastating review (also

partially inside), William R. Van Cleave, "The SALT Papers: A Torrent of Verbiage or a Spring of Capital Truths?", *Orbis*, Vol. 17, no. 4 (Winter 1974), pp. 1396–1401.

18. For details of the U.S. 1971 package, see *The New York Times*, July 24, 1971, and September 24, 1971; details of the negotiations are taken from Dr. Kissinger's briefing, reprinted in NATO *Review* (July–August 1972), and confidential sources.

19. For the texts of the SALT I agreements, and related treaties, see Barton and Weiler, *International Arms Control*, Appendix C, pp. 368–82.

20. These views were expressed in the testimony of Richard L. Garwin, Stanley Hoffman, Jerome H. Kahan, Hon. Edward Kennedy, Roman Kolkowitz, Wolfgang Panofsky, George Rathjens, Dr. Marshall D. Shulman, and Paul C. Warnke, all long-time technical arms controllers, in *Hearings before the Committee on Foreign Relations, Ninety-Second Congress, Second Session on the ABM Treaty and the Interim Agreement*, June 19, 20, 21, 26, 28, and 29, and July 20, 1972.

21. Barry M. Blechman and Alton Quanbeck, "The Arms Accord: Everyone Gains", *Washington Post*, June 4, 1972, reprinted in ibid. (*Hearings*), p. 32.

22. Ibid. (*Hearings*), pp. 394 and 400.

23. See Scoville, *Towards a Strategic Arms Limitation Agreement*; Scoville, Lall, and Hunter, "The Arms Race: Steps Towards Constraint"; and Mason Willrich and John B. Rhinelander, SALT: *The Moscow Agreements and Beyond* (New York: Free Press, for the American Society of International Law, 1974), pp. 225–76.

24. See Scoville, "Strategic Forum: The SALT Agreements". Scoville stressed the need to plug qualitative loopholes in SALT I, notably MIRV testing, and secure reductions in force levels; Yu. Kulish of Moscow claimed that the strategic arms race had been limited; Pierre Gallois of Paris and Donald G. Brennan of New York pointed out that limiting ABM meant accepting the doctrine of MAD, while the freeze on offensive missiles left the Soviet Union with a quantitative advantage.

Chapter 19

1. Joseph Kruzel, "SALT II: The Search for a Follow-On Agreement", *Orbis*, Vol. 17, no. 2 (Summer 1973), pp. 340–41.

2. Newhouse, *Cold Dawn*, p. 181.

3. Ibid., pp. 174–75.

4. See Willrich and Rhinelander, SALT: *The Moscow Agreements and Beyond*, pp. 339–42.

5. Ibid., pp. 343-45.

6. See L. Gelb, "Kissinger Said to Offer Halt on New Missiles", *The New York Times*, March 31, 1974.

7. See Henry R. Myers, "Extending the Nuclear Test Ban"; and Herbert F. York, "The Great Test Ban Debate". These two articles originally appeared in *Scientific American* (January and November 1972); reprinted in Herbert F. York, *Arms Control: Readings from Scientific American* (San Francisco: W. H. Freeman, 1973), pp. 283–93 and pp. 294–302, respectively.

8. See *Aviation Week and Space Technology* SALT 1–2. Articles reprinted from the regular issues to provide a background . . . of SALT. The two-year period covered in this publication begins in March 1974.

9. *The New York Times*, November 25, 1974, and December 3, 1974. See also Vladivostok Accord, *Joint Soviet-American Statement on Strategic Arms Limitation, 24 November 1974*, reprinted in *Survival*, Vol. 17, no. 1 (January–February 1975), p. 32.

10. For a critical assessment, see my "The Politics of Arms Control After Vladivostok", *Millenium*, Vol. 4, no. 1 (Spring 1975), pp. 52–66.

11. Paul H. Nitze, "Vladivostok and SALT II", *The Review of Politics*, Vol. 37, no. 2 (April 1975), pp. 147–60, and Paul H. Nitze, "Assuring Strategic Stability in an Era of Detente", *Foreign Affairs*, Vol. 54, no. 2 (January 1976), pp. 207–32.

12. Paul H. Nitze, "SALT, The Strategic Balance Between Hope and Scepticism", *Foreign Policy*, no. 17 (Winter 1974–75), pp. 136–56, especially p. 154.

13. David Aaron, "A New Concept", *Foreign Policy*, no. 17 (Winter 1974–75).

14. Nitze, "SALT, The Strategic Balance Between Hope and Scepticism", p. 154.

15. Ibid.
16. See Lynn E. Davis and Warner R. Schilling, "All You Ever Wanted to Know about MIRV and ICBM Calculations But Were Not Cleared to Ask", *Journal of Conflict Resolution*, Vol. 17, no. 2 (June 1973), pp. 207–42, especially pp. 237–40.
17. *The New York Times*, November 25, 1974.
18. The most accurate summaries of Soviet "violations" of SALT I which have provided the source material, are: Colin S. Gray, "SALT I Aftermath: Have the Soviets Been Cheating?", *Air Force*, Vol. 58, no. 11 (November 1975), pp. 28–33; and Tad Szulc, "Have We Been Had?", *The New Republic*, June 7, 1975, pp. 11–15. On Dr. Kissinger's increasingly desperate attempts to suppress evidence of these "violations" and secure a SALT II, see Adm. Elmo Zumwalt, USN (Ret.), *On Watch: A Memoir* (New York: Quadrangle, 1976), pp. xi–xv, pp. 308–461, especially Chap. 17, "Kissingerology", and pp. 395–423.
19. See Fred C. Iklé, "After Detection—What?", *Foreign Affairs*, Vol. 39, no. 2 (January 1961), pp. 208–20, referring to detection of violations of arms-control agreements.
20. See Aaron Latham, "Kissinger's Bluff Is Called", *New York*, April 12, 1976, pp. 30–35.

Chapter 20

1. *U.S. Doc. D., 1945–1959*, Vol. II, pp. 1230–64.
2. Ibid., p. 1243.
3. Ibid., pp. 1251–52.
4. Ibid., pp. 1284–97.
5. Ibid., p. 1290.
6. Ibid., p. 1306.
7. Ibid., p. 1317.
8. Brennan, *Arms Control, Disarmament and National Security*; Hedley Bull, *The Control of the Arms Race*; Ernest W. Lefever, ed., *Arms and Arms Control* (New York: Praeger, 1962); Schelling and Halperin, *Strategy and Arms Control*.
9. Bull, *The Control of the Arms Race*, p. 169.
10. *U.S. Doc. D., 1960*, pp. 68–71.
11. Buchan and Windsor, *Arms and Stability in Europe*, pp. vi–ix.
12. Ibid., pp. 16–17.
13. Ibid., p. 112.
14. Ibid., p. 115.
15. Ibid., pp. 120–23.
16. Ibid., pp. 126–36.
17. Ibid., p. 127.
18. U.S. Working Paper, "Reduction of the Risks of War Through Accident, Miscalculation, or Failure of Communication", *U.S. Doc. D., 1962*, pp. 1214–25, see Chap. 6, note 17.
19. Buchan and Windsor, *Arms and Stability in Europe*, pp. 136–37.
20. See Philip Windsor, "Observation Posts", and Michael Howard, "Inspected Zones", in Luard, ed., *First Steps to Disarmament*, pp. 85–99 and 121–31.
21. See, for example, James E. Dougherty and J. F. Lehman, Jr., eds., *Arms Control for the Late Sixties* (Toronto: Van Nostrand, 1967), proceedings of the Third International Arms Control Symposium, in Philadelphia, April 1966.
22. Bechhoefer, *Postwar Negotiations for Arms Control*, pp. 531–35.
23. *U.S. Doc. D., 1962*, pp. 1214–25.
24. Ibid., p. 1218.
25. Ibid., pp. 1219–24.
26. *U.S. Doc. D., 1965*, pp. 110–11.
27. *U.S. Doc. D., 1964*, pp. 112–18.
28. The report of the National Citizens Commission on International Co-operation prepared for the White House Conference on International Co-operation (November 28–December 1, 1965), *U.S. Doc. D., 1965*, pp. 555–81, especially p. 570.

29. See Chap. 4.

30. For details, see Chap. 5, p. 40. The plans were introduced on October 2, 1957, February 14 and November 4, 1958, October 9, 1961, and March 28, 1962. See *U.S. Doc. D., 1945–1959*, Vol. II, pp. 889–92, 944–48, 1217–19; *U.S. Doc. D., 1962*, pp. 201–05.

31. See, for example, Hugh Gaitskell, "Disengagement: Why? How?", *Foreign affairs*, Vol. 36, no. 4 (January 1958), pp. 539–56; Denis Healey, *A Neutral Belt in Europe* (London: Fabian Society, Fabian Tract 311, 1958); their ideas and those of a significant section of elite Western opinion in favour of disengagement were summarized in: Michael Howard, *Disengagement in Europe* (Harmondsworth, Middlesex: Penguin Books, 1958).

32. Not to be confused with the Grand Old Party, the Republicans in the United States.

33. *U.S. Doc. D., 1945–1959*, Vol. I, pp. 456–72.

34. Ibid., Vol. II, pp. 1084–87.

35. See also Chap. 4 of this book.

36. Among the few published assessments of the capabilities of GOP is Windsor, "Observation Posts".

Chapter 21

1. See "The Harmel Report", *Survival*, Vol. 10, no. 2 (February 1968), pp. 62–64.

2. Reprinted in *Survival*, Vol. 10, no. 9 (September 1968), pp. 297–99.

3. See Alain C. Enthoven and K. Wayne Smith, *How Much is Enough? Shaping the Defense Program 1961–1969* (New York: Harper and Row, 1971).

4. See Roger J. Hill, "MBFR", *International Journal*, Vol. 29, no. 2 (Spring 1974), pp. 243–55.

5. *Survival*, Vol. 12, no. 8 (August 1970), p. 286.

6. Elliot Richardson, "The U.S. and Western Europe", Speech to the Chicago Council on Foreign Relations, January 20, 1970, printed in *Survival*, Vol. 12, no. 3 (March 1970), pp. 86–90.

7. Annette Baker Fox, "Domestic Pressures in North America to Withdraw Forces from Europe", in William T. R. Fox and Warner R. Schilling, eds., *European Security and the Atlantic System* (New York: Columbia University Press, 1973), p. 221.

8. *Survival*, Vol. 12, no. 8 (August 1970), pp. 270–75.

9. See Fox, "Domestic Pressures in North America to Withdraw Forces from Europe".

10. John Newhouse, with M. Croan, E. R. Fried, and T. W. Stanley, *U.S. Troops in Europe: Issues, Costs, and Choices* (Washington, D.C.: Brookings Institution, 1971).

11. Ibid., pp. 147–48.

12. Ibid., p. 161.

13. John Yochelson, "The American Military Presence in Europe: Current Debate in the United States", *Orbis*, Vol. 15, no. 3 (Fall 1971), pp. 784–807, especially p. 794.

14. Ibid., pp. 794–95.

15. Ibid., p. 793.

16. Ibid., p. 806; see also John Yochelson, "MBFR: The Search for an American Approach", *Orbis*, Vol. 17, no. 1 (Spring 1973), pp. 155–75.

17. The latter published in a revised version as: Warner R. Schilling, W. T. R. Fox, C. M. Kelleher, and D. J. Puchala, *American Arms and a Changing Europe: Dilemmas of Deterrence and Disarmament* (New York: Columbia University Press, 1973); see especially pp. 192–93.

18. For details, see Timothy W. Stanley and Darnell M. Whitt, *Detente Diplomacy: United States and European Security in the 1970s* (New York: Dunellen, 1970), p. 14; Michael Palmer, *The Prospects for a European Security Conference* (London: Chatham House, Political and Economic Planning, 1971).

Chapter 22

1. See Lawrence T. Caldwell, *Soviet Security Interests in Europe and* MFR, California Seminar on Arms Control and Foreign Policy, Research Paper No. 72, April 1976.
2. The first coherent statement of the Soviet position was Yu. Kostko, "Mutual Force Reductions in Europe", *Survival*, Vol. 14, no. 5 (September–October 1972), pp. 236–38.
3. "Mutual Force Reductions in Europe — Communiqué of the Exploratory Talks, June 28, 1973", reprinted in *Survival*, Vol. 15, no. 5 (September–October 1973), pp. 240–41.
4. "Joint Soviet–U.S. Communiqué, June 24, 1973", reprinted in ibid., pp. 244–48.
5. K. A. Tortenson, "MBFR: An Introduction", *Internasjonal Politik*, nos. 2–3 (1971), pp. 206–37.
6. This account of the initial positions is taken from my *Mutual and Balanced Force Reductions: Underlying Issues and Potential Developments*, ORAE Memorandum No. M74 (Ottawa: Department of National Defence, January 1976).
7. See, for example, Steven L. Canby, "NATO Muscle More Shadow Than Substance", *Foreign Policy*, no. 8 (Fall 1972), pp. 38–49.
8. *Military Applications of Nuclear Technology*, Hearings before the Sub-committee on Military Applications of the Joint Committee on Atomic Energy, Ninety-Third Congress, Part I, April 16, Part II, May 12 and June 29, 1973 (Washington, D.C.: U.S. Government Printing Office).
9. For an excellent summary of the arguments for mini-nukes, see Colin S. Gray, "Mini-Nukes and Strategy", *International Journal*, Vol. 14, no. 2 (Spring 1974), pp. 216–41; W. S. Bennett, R. R. Sandoval, and R. G. Schreffler, "A Credible Nuclear-Emphasis Defense for NATO"; James H. Polk, "The Realities of Tactical Nuclear Warfare"; and R. C. Richardson, "Can NATO Fashion a New Strategy?", all three in *Orbis*, Vol. 17, no. 2 (Summer 1973), pp. 463–79, pp. 439–47, and pp. 415–38, respectively.
10. See, for example, W. Heisenberg, *The Alliance and Europe: Part I: Crisis Stability in Europe and Tactical Nuclear Weapons*, Adelphi Paper No. 96 (London: IISS, Summer 1973). The classic 1950s case for tactical nuclear weapons was Kissinger, *Nuclear Weapons and Foreign Policy*.
11. "Statement by Ambassador Martin to the CCD", printed in *Survival*, Vol. 16, no. 5 (September–October 1975), pp. 248–49.
12. See Lynn Etheridge Davis, *Limited Nuclear Options: Deterrence and the New American Doctrine*, Adelphi Paper No. 121 (London: IISS, Winter 1975–76).
13. *Nuclear Weapons and Foreign Policy*, Hearings before the Sub-committee on U.S. Security Agreements and Commitments Abroad and the Sub-committee on International Law and Organization of the Committee on Foreign Relations, U.S. Senate, 93rd Congress, Second Session, March 7, 14, and April 4, 1974, pp. 151–211.
14. See ibid., Warnke testimony, pp. 51–65; Enthoven testimony, pp. 65–85; joint testimony, pp. 115–41.
15. For a realistically sceptical analysis of the minimal value of these CBMs in practice, see Johan J. Holst and Karen A. Melander, "European Security and Confidence Building Measures", *Survival*, Vol. 19, no. 4 (July–August 1977), pp. 146–54.

Chapter 23

1. Thomas C. Schelling, *The Strategy of Conflict* (Cambridge, Mass.: Harvard University Press, 1960).
2. See Schelling, *Arms and Influence*; for evidence that his views remained unchanged in the role of arms control, see his "Communications, Bargaining and Negotiations", in *Arms Control and National Security*, Vol. I (New York: Pergamon, 1969), pp. 63–72; R. Ranger and Richard Stubbs, "Mechanistic Assumptions and

United States Strategy", *International Journal*, Vol. 33, no. 3 (Summer 1978), pp. 557–87.

3. See Roger Fisher, *International Conflict for Beginners* (New York: Harper and Row, 1969).

4. Jeremy J. Stone, *Containing the Arms Race* (Cambridge, Mass., and London: MIT Press, 1966).

5. Jeremy J. Stone, *Strategic Persuasion: Arms Limitation Through Dialogue* (New York and London: Columbia University Press, 1967), p. 175.

6. Dougherty and Lehman, eds., *Arms Control for the Late Sixties.*

7. Hedley Bull, "Arms Control: A Stocktaking and Prospectus", in Alastair Buchan, ed., *Problems of Modern Strategy* (London: Chatto and Windus, for the ISS, 1970), pp. 139–58, especially p. 143.

8. Ibid. This conclusion ignores the key role of arms control in acting as the chief modality for superpower detente argued for in this book.

9. Ibid., p. 145.

10. Ibid., pp. 147–52.

11. Ibid., p. 155. This recognized the political role of arms-control agreements.

12. Ibid., p. 158.

13. This was clear from extensive interviews with ACDA personnel in the summer of 1969. See also Harland B. Moulton (formerly of ACDA and then of the National War College), *From Superiority to Parity: The United States and the Strategic Arms Race, 1961–1971* (Westport, Conn.: Greenwood Press, 1973), reviewed by Colin S. Gray, "From Superiority to Sub-Parity", *Orbis*, Vol. 18, no. 1 (Spring 1974), pp. 292–97.

14. For a typical journalist's viewpoint see Chalmers M. Roberts, *The Nuclear Years: The Arms Race and Arms Control 1945–70* (New York: Praeger, 1970).

15. See, for example, *Arms Control: Readings from Scientific American.*

16. "The Search for a New Handle on Arms Control", *Science and Public Affairs*, formerly and subsequently *The Bulletin of the Atomic Scientists* (April 1974), p. 7. The papers from this summer study were published in Special Issue, *Arms, Defense Policy, and Arms Control*, in *Daedalus*, Vol. 104, no. 3 (Summer 1975).

17. Ibid. Participants in the summer study were Graham Allison, Harvard University; Robert Art, Brandeis University; Congressman Les Aspin; Harvey Brooks, Harvard University; Anne Cahn, MIT; Barry Carter, Wilmer, Cutler and Pickering; Abram Chayes, Harvard Law School; Paul Doty, Harvard University; Richard Falk, Princeton University; Charles Ferris, Democratic Policy Committee, U.S. Senate; Edward Fried, Brookings Institution; Richard Garwin, IBM; Thomas Halsted, Carnegie Endowment; Morton H. Halperin, Brookings Institution; Jerry Kahan, Brookings Institution; Milton Katz, Harvard Law School; John Lee, former assistant director, Arms Control and Disarmament Agency; Franklin A. Long, Cornell University; William Niskanen, University of California, Berkeley; George Quester, Cornell University; George Rathjens, MIT; Leonard Rodberg, Institute for Policy Studies; Jack Ruina, MIT; Thomas Schelling, Harvard University; Herbert Scoville, former assistant director, Arms Control and Disarmament Agency; Marshall D. Shulman, Columbia University; John Steinbruner, Harvard University; James Woolsey, staff, U.S. Senate Armed Services Committee.

18. Morton H. Halperin, *Bureaucratic Politics and Foreign Policy* (Washington, D.C.: Brookings Institution, 1974).

19. See, for example, Tammen, *MIRV and the Arms Race*; Ted Greenwood, *Making the MIRV.*

20. For the flavour of the debate on MAD sparked by Secretary of Defense James R. Schlesinger, see, for example, "Focus on the Military Balance, U.S. Strategic Forces and the New Targetting Doctrine", *Orbis*, Vol. 18, no. 3 (Fall 1974), pp. 655–770. The parallel debate on the nature of the strategic arms race was sparked by Dr. Colin S. Gray's articles from 1971, summarized in his *The Soviet-American Arms Race* (Lexington, Mass.: D. C. Heath, 1976) and Albert Wohlstetter's *Legends of the*

Strategic Arms Race (Washington, D.C.: U.S. Strategic Institute, 1975). A shorter version of Wohlstetter's analysis was published in *Foreign Policy*, nos. 15 and 16 (Summer and Fall 1974), with comments by Paul H. Nitze, Joseph Alsop, Morton H. Halperin, and Jeremy J. Stone, pp. 82–92. Articles by Johan J. Holst and Michael Nacht questioning Wohlstetter's arguments appeared in *Foreign Policy*, no. 19 (Summer 1975), with a rebuttal of those and other criticisms by Wohlstetter in *Foreign Policy*, no. 20 (Fall 1975). Full citations are in the Bibliography.

21. Walter C. Clemens, Jr., *The Superpowers and Arms Control: From Cold War to Interdependence* (Lexington, Mass.: D. C. Heath, 1973); for a perceptive review of Clemens's arms-control orthodoxy, see Joseph Kruzel (a former member of the U.S. SALT delegation and an advocate of the bureaucratic politics approach to the subject), "Arms Control at the Crossroads", *The Bulletin of the Atomic Scientists*, Vol. 30, no. 6 (June 1974), pp. 58–60.

22. Willrich and Rhinelander, SALT: *The Moscow Agreements and Beyond.*

23. William R. Kintner and Robert L. Pflatzgraff, Jr., eds., SALT: *Implications for Arms Control in the 1970s* (Pittsburgh: University of Pittsburgh Press, 1973).

24. The Fifth International Arms Control Conference, held in Philadelphia in October 1971, which I attended; the prevalence of technical arms control was still evident, as was the realization of its inadequacies.

25. Elizabeth Young, *A Farewell to Arms Control* (Harmondsworth, Middlesex: Pelican Books, 1972).

26. Ibid., p. 135.

Epilogue

1. My major source has been confidential interviews with the major participants in the new arms-control debate in Canada, the United States, and Western Europe, making footnotes impossible.

2. The Nuclear Energy Policy Study Group, *Nuclear Power Issues and Choices* (Cambridge, Mass.: Ballinger, for the Ford Foundation/MITRE Corp., 1977).

Bibliography

Books

Adams, Benson D. *Ballistic Missile Defense*. New York: American Elsevier, 1971.

Allison, Graham T. *Essence of Decision: Explaining the Cuban Missile Crisis*. Boston: Little, Brown, 1971.

Bader, William B. *The United States and the Spread of Nuclear Weapons*. New York: Pegasus Books, for the Center of International Studies, Princeton University, 1968.

Barnaby, C. F., ed. *Preventing the Spread of Nuclear Weapons*. London: Souvenir Press, 1969.

Barton, John H., and Lawrence D. Weiler, eds. *International Arms Control: Issues and Agreements*. Stanford Arms Control Group. Stanford: Stanford University Press, 1976.

Baylis, John, Ken Booth, John Garnett, and Phil Williams. *Contemporary Strategy: Theories and Policies*. London: Croom Helm, 1975.

Beard, Edmund. *Developing the* ICBM: *A Study in Bureaucratic Politics*. New York: Columbia University Press, 1976.

Beaton, Leonard. *Must the Bomb Spread?* Harmondsworth, Middlesex: Penguin Books, 1966.

_____. *The Reform of Power: A Proposal for an International Security System*. New York: Viking Press, 1972.

_____, and John Maddox. *The Spread of Nuclear Weapons*. London: Chatto and Windus, for the ISS, 1962.

Bechhoefer, Bernard G. *Postwar Negotiations for Arms Control*. Washington, D.C.: Brookings Institution, 1961.

Biddle W. F. *Weapons Technology and Arms Control*. New York: Praeger, 1972.

Blackett, P. M. S. *Studies of War: Nuclear and Conventional*. Edinburgh and London: Oliver and Boyd, 1962.

Blechman, Barry M., Edward M. Gramlich, and Robert W. Hartman. *Setting National Priorities: The 1975 Budget*. Washington, D.C.: Brookings Institution, 1974.

Bloomfield, Lincoln P., ed. *Outer Space: Prospects for Man and Society*. 1st ed. Englewood Cliffs, N.J.: Prentice-Hall, 1962. 2nd rev. ed. New York: Praeger, 1968.

_____, Walter C. Clemens, and F. Griffiths. *Khrushchev and the Arms Race: Soviet Interests in Arms Control and Disarmament 1954–1964*. Cambridge, Mass.: MIT Press, 1966.

Borden, William L. *There Will Be No Time: The Revolution in Strategy*. New York: Macmillan, 1946.

Boskey, Bennett, and Mason Willrich, eds. *Nuclear Proliferation: Prospects for Control*. New York: Dunellen, 1970.

Bottome, Edgar, M. *The Missile Gap: A Study of the Formulation of Military and Public Policy*. Cranbury, N.J.: Fairleigh Dickinson University Press, 1971.

Brennan, Donald G., ed. *Arms Control, Disarmament and National Security*. New York: Braziller, 1961.

Brodie, Bernard. *Strategy in the Missile Age.* 1st ed. Princeton: Princeton University Press, 1959; 2nd ed. 1965.

——. *Escalation and the Nuclear Option.* Princeton: Princeton University Press, 1966.

——. *War and Politics.* New York: Macmillan, 1973.

——, and Arnold Wolfers, eds. *The Absolute Weapon: Atomic Power and World Order.* New York: Harcourt, Brace, 1946.

Brown, Seyom. *The Faces of Power: Constancy and Change in United States Foreign Policy From Truman to Johnson.* New York: Columbia University Press, 1968.

Brzezinski, Zbigniew. *Alternative to Partition: For a Broader Conception of America's Role in Europe.* New York: McGraw-Hill, for the Council on Foreign Relations, 1965.

Buchan, Alastair, ed. *A World of Nuclear Powers?* Englewood Cliffs, N.J.: Prentice-Hall, for The American Assembly, Columbia University, 1966.

——, intro. *Problems of Modern Strategy.* London: Chatto and Windus, for the ISS, 1970.

——, and Philip Windsor. *Arms and Stability in Europe: A British–French–German Enquiry.* London: Chatto and Windus, for the ISS, 1963.

Bull, Hedley. *The Control of the Arms Race: Disarmament and Arms Control in the Missile Age.* London: Weidenfeld and Nicolson, for the ISS, 1961. 2nd rev. ed. New York: Praeger, 1965.

Burns, Lt.-Gen. E. L. M. *A Seat at the Table: The Struggle for Disarmament.* Toronto: Clarke, Irwin, 1972.

Canby, S. L. NATO *Military Policy: Obtaining Conventional Comparability with the Warsaw Pact,* RAND Report R-1088. Santa Monica, Calif.: 1972.

Carnegie Endowment for International Peace. *The Control of Chemical and Biological Weapons.* New York: 1971.

Chayes, Abram, and Jerome B. Wiesner, eds. ABM: *An Evaluation of the Decision to Deploy an Antiballistic Missile System.* New York: Signet Books, 1969.

Clausewitz, Carl von. *On War.* Edited and translated by Michael Howard and Peter Paret. Princeton: Princeton University Press, 1976.

Clemens, Walter C., Jr. *The Arms Race and Sino-Soviet Relations.* Stanford: Stanford University, The Hoover Institution on War, Revolution and Peace, 1968.

——. *The Superpowers and Arms Control: From Cold War to Interdependence.* Lexington, Mass.: D. C. Heath, 1973.

Cleveland, Harlan. *The Transatlantic Bargain:* NATO *Past and Future.* New York: Harper and Row, for the Council on Foreign Relations, 1970.

Coffey, Joseph I. *Strategic Power and National Security.* Pittsburgh, Penn.: University of Pittsburgh Press, 1971.

——, ed. *Nuclear Proliferation: Prospects, Problems, and Proposals.* Philadelphia: The Annals of the American Academy of Political and Social Science, Vol. 430, March 1977.

——. *Arms Control and European Security: A Guide to East–West Negotiations.* London: Chatto and Windus, for the IISS, 1977.

Cox, Arthur M. *The Dynamics of Détente: How to End the Arms Race.* New York: W. W. Norton, 1976.

Daedalus. Journal of the American Academy of Arts and Sciences, Special Issue: *Arms Control.* Holton, Gerald, ed. Fall 1960, Issued as Vol. 89, no. 4, of the Proceedings of the American Academy of Arts and Sciences. (Partially reprinted and rev. as Brennan, Donald G., ed. *Arms Control* — cited above.)

——. Journal of the American Academy of Arts and Sciences, Special Issue: *Arms, Defense Policy, and Arms Control.* Long, Franklin, and G. W. Rathjens, eds. Summer 1975, Issued as Vol. 104, no. 3, of the Proceedings of the American Academy of Arts and Sciences.

Dean, Arthur H. *Test Ban and Disarmament: The Path of Negotiation.* New York: Harper and Row, for the Council on Foreign Relations, 1966.

Deutsch, Karl W. *Arms Control and the Atlantic Alliance: Europe Faces Coming Policy Decisions.* New York: Wiley, 1967.

Dougherty, James E., and J. F. Lehman, Jr., eds. *Arms Control for the Late Sixties.* Toronto: Van Nostrand, 1967.

Endicott, John E. *Japan's Nuclear Option: Political, Technical, and Strategic Factors.* New York: Praeger, 1975.

Enke, Stephen, ed. *Defense Management.* Englewood Cliffs, N.J.: Prentice-Hall, 1967.

Enthoven, Alain C., and K. Wayne Smith. *How Much is Enough? Shaping the Defense Program 1961–1969.* New York: Harper and Row, 1971.

Epstein, William. *The Last Chance: Nuclear Proliferation and Arms Control.* New York: The Free Press, 1976.

Feld, B. T., Ted Greenwood, G. W. Rathjens, and S. Weinberg, eds. *Impact of New Technologies on the Arms Race.* Cambridge, Mass.: MIT Press, 1971.

Fisher, Roger. *International Conflict for Beginners.* New York: Harper and Row, 1969.

——, ed. *International Conflict and Behavioral Science.* New York: Basic Books, 1964.

Foster, R. B., A. Beaufre, and W. Joshua. *Strategy for the West.* New York: Crane, Russak, 1974.

Fox, William T. R., and Warner R. Schilling. *European Security and the Atlantic System.* New York: Columbia University Press, 1973.

Fried, E. R., Alice M. Ravlin, Charles L. Schultze, and Nancy H. Tetters. *Setting National Priorities: The 1974 Budget.* Washington, D.C.: Brookings Institution, 1973.

Frye, Alton. *A Responsible Congress: The Politics of National Security.* New York: McGraw-Hill, for the Council on Foreign Relations, 1975.

Gallagher, P., and Karl F. Speilmann, Jr. *Soviet Decision-Making for Defense: A Critique of U.S. Perspectives on the Arms Race.* New York: Praeger, 1972.

——. *Soviet Military Policy: A Historical Analysis.* London: Praeger, 1966.

Garnett, John, ed. *Theories of Peace and Security: A Reader in Contemporary Strategic Thought.* London: Macmillan, 1970.

Garthoff, Raymond L. *Soviet Strategy in the Nuclear Age.* New York: Praeger, 1958.

——. *The Soviet Image of a Future War.* Washington, D.C.: Public Affairs Press, 1959.

——. *Soviet Military Policy: A Historical Analysis.* London: Faber and Faber, 1966.

Gilpin, Robert. *American Scientists and Nuclear Weapons Policy.* Princeton: Princeton University Press, 1962.

——, and Christopher Wright, eds. *Scientists and National Policy-Making.* New York and London: Columbia University Press, 1964.

Gompert, David C., Michael Mandelbaum, Richard L. Garwin, and John H. Barton. *Nuclear Weapons and World Politics: Alternatives for the Future.* 1980s Project/Council on Foreign Relations. New York: McGraw-Hill, 1977.

Gray, Colin S. *The Soviet-American Arms Race.* Lexington, Mass.: D. C. Heath, 1976.

——. *Strategic Studies and Public Policy: The American Experience* (forthcoming).

Green, Philip. *Deadly Logic: The Theory of Nuclear Deterrence.* Columbus, Ohio: Ohio State University Press, 1966.

Greenwood, Ted. *Making the MIRV: A Study of Defense Decision Making.* Cambridge, Mass.: Ballinger, 1975.

——, Harold A. Feiveson, and Theodore B. Taylor. *Nuclear Proliferation: Motivations, Capabilities, and Strategies for Control.* 1980s Project/Council on Foreign Relations. New York: McGraw-Hill, 1977.

Halperin, Morton H. *Limited War in the Nuclear Age.* New York: Wiley, 1963.

——, ed. *Sino-Soviet Relations and Arms Control.* Cambridge, Mass.: MIT Press, 1967.

——. *Defense Strategies for the Seventies.* Boston: Little, Brown, 1971.

_____. *Bureaucratic Politics and Foreign Policy.* Washington, D.C.: Brookings Institution, 1974.

Healey, Denis. *A Neutral Belt in Europe.* Fabian Tract No. 311. London: Fabian Society, 1958.

Henkin, Louis, ed. *Arms Control: Issues for the Public.* Englewood Cliffs, N.J.: Prentice-Hall, for the American Assembly, Columbia University, 1961.

Hinterhoff, Eugene. *Disengagement.* London: Stevens, 1959.

Hoeber, Francis P., and William Schneider, Jr., eds. *Arms, Men, and Military Budgets: Issues for the Fiscal Year 1977–1978* (with David B. Kassing). New York Crane, Russak, 1976, 1977 and 1978.

Hoerlick, Arnold L., and Myron Rush. *Strategic Power and Soviet Foreign Policy.* Chicago: University of Chicago Press, 1965.

Holst, Johan J., and William Schneider, Jr., eds. *Why ABM?: Policy Issues in the Missile Defense Controversy.* New York: Pergamon, 1969.

_____, and Uwe Nehrlich. *Beyond Nuclear Deterrence: New Aims, New Arms.* New York: Crane, Russak, 1977.

Howard, Michael. *Disengagement in Europe.* Harmondsworth, Middlesex: Penguin Books, 1958.

Hunter, Robert E. *Security in Europe.* 2nd rev. ed. Bloomington, Ind.: Indiana University Press, 1972.

Huntingdon, Samuel P. *The Common Defense: Strategic Programs in National Politics.* New York: Columbia University Press, 1961.

Iklé, Fred C. *How Nations Negotiate.* New York: Harper and Row, 1964.

_____. *Every War Must End.* New York and London: Columbia University Press, 1971.

Jabber, Fuad. *Israel and Nuclear Weapons: Present Options and Future Strategies.* London: Chatto and Windus, for the ISS, 1971.

Jacobsen, Carl G. *Soviet Strategy — Soviet Foreign Policy.* 2nd rev. ed. Glasgow: The University Press, 1974.

Jacobsen, Harold K., and Eric Stein. *Diplomats, Scientists and Politicians: The United States and the Nuclear Test Ban Negotiations.* Ann Arbor: University of Michigan Press, 1966.

Jensen, Lloyd. *Return from the Nuclear Brink: National Interest and the Nuclear Nonproliferation Treaty.* Lexington, Mass.: D. C. Heath, 1974.

Jessup, Phillip C., and Howard J. Taubenfeld. *Controls for Outer Space and the Antarctic Analogy.* New York: Columbia University Press, 1959.

Kahan, Jerome H. *Security in the Nuclear Age: Developing U.S. Strategic Arms Policy.* Washington, D.C.: Brookings Institution, 1975.

Kahn, Herman. *On Thermonuclear War.* 1st ed. Princeton, N.J.: Princeton University Press, 1960. 2nd rev. ed. New York: The Free Press, 1969.

_____. *Thinking About the Unthinkable.* New York: Horizon Press, 1962.

_____. *On Escalation: Metaphors and Scenarios.* New York: Praeger, 1965.

Kaiser, Karl. *German Foreign Policy in Transition: Bonn Between East and West.* New York: Oxford University Press, 1968.

Kalb, Marvin, and Bernard Kalb. *Kissinger.* New York: Dell, 1974, 1975.

Kaplan, Morton A., ed. *SALT: Problems and Prospects.* Morristown, N.J.: General Learning Press, 1973.

Kapur, Ashok. *India's Nuclear Option: Atomic Diplomacy and Decision Making.* New York: Praeger, 1976.

Kaufmann, William W. *The McNamara Strategy.* New York: Harper and Row, 1964.

Kavic, Lorne K. *India's Quest for Security: Defense Policies 1947-1965.* Berkeley, Calif.: University of California Press, 1967.

Kelleher, Catherine McArdle. *Germany and the Politics of Nuclear Weapons.* New York: Columbia University Press, 1975.

Kemp, Geoffrey, Robert L. Pflatzgraff, Jr., and Uri Ra'anan, eds. *The Superpowers in a Multinuclear World.* Lexington, Mass.: D. C. Heath, 1974.

_____, eds. *The Other Arms Race: New Technologies and Non-Nuclear Conflict.* Lexington, Mass.: D. C. Heath, 1975.

Kennedy, Robert F. *Thirteen Days: A Memoir of the Cuban Missile Crisis.* Afterword by Richard E. Neustadt and Graham T. Allison. New York: W. W. Norton, 1969.

Kintner, William R., and Richard B. Foster. *National Strategy in a Decade of Change.* Lexington, Mass.: D. C. Heath, 1973.

_____, and Robert L. Pflatzgraff, Jr., eds. SALT: *Implications for Arms Control in the 1970s.* Pittsburgh, Penn.: University of Pittsburgh Press, 1973.

Kissinger, Henry A. *Nuclear Weapons and Foreign Policy.* New York: Harper and Brothers, for the Council on Foreign Relations, 1957.

_____. *The Necessity for Choice: Prospects of American Foreign Policy.* New York: Harper and Brothers, 1961.

_____. *A World Restored: Metternich, Castlereagh and the Problems of Peace, 1812–1822.* Boston: Houghton Mifflin, 1957. Reprinted in Universal Library, New York: Grosset and Dunlap, 1964.

_____. *The Troubled Partnership: A Re-appraisal of the Atlantic Alliance.* New York: McGraw-Hill, for the Council on Foreign Relations, 1965.

_____. *American Foreign Policy.* 3rd rev. ed. New York: W. W. Norton, 1977.

Kistiakowsky, George B. *A Scientist at the White House: The Private Diary of President Eisenhower's Special Assistant for Science and Technology.* Cambridge, Mass., and London: Harvard University Press, 1976.

Klaiber, W., L. Hadik, J. Harned, J. Sattler, and S. Wasowski. *Era of Negotiations: European Security and Force Reductions.* Lexington, Mass.: D. C. Heath, for the Atlantic Council of the U.S., 1973.

Knorr, Klaus, ed. NATO *and American Security.* Princeton: Princeton University Press, 1959.

_____, and Thornton Read, eds. *Limited Strategic War: Essays on Nuclear Strategy.* New York: Praeger, 1962.

Kohl, Wilfrid L. *French Nuclear Diplomacy.* Princeton: Princeton University Press, 1971.

Kolkowitz, Roman et al., eds. *The Soviet Union and Arms Control: A Super-Power Dilemma.* Baltimore: Johns Hopkins Press, 1970.

Kuhn, Thomas S. *The Structure of Scientific Revolutions.* 2nd enlarged ed. Chicago: University of Chicago Press, 1970.

Lapp, Ralph. *The Weapons Culture.* Baltimore: Penguin Books, 1969.

Larson, Thomas B. *Disarmament and Soviet Policy 1964–1968.* Englewood Cliffs, N.J.: Prentice-Hall, 1969.

Lawrence, Robert M., and Joel Larus, eds. *Nuclear Proliferation Phase II.* Lawrence, Kan.: University of Kansas, for the National Security Education Program of New York University, 1974.

Lefever, Ernest W., ed. *Arms and Arms Control.* New York: Praeger, for the Washington Center of Foreign Policy Research, 1962.

Legault, Albert. *Deterrence and the Atlantic Alliance.* Translated by Archibald Day. Lindsay, Ont.: John Deyell Ltd., for the CIIA, 1966.

_____, and George Lindsey. *The Dynamics of the Nuclear Balance.* 2nd rev. ed. London and New York: Cornell University Press, 1976.

Levine, Robert A. *The Arms Debate.* Cambridge, Mass.: Harvard University Press, 1963.

Licklider, Roy E. *The Private Nuclear Strategists.* Columbus, Ohio: Ohio State University Press, 1971.

Luard, Evan, ed. *First Steps to Disarmament: A New Approach to the Problems of Arms Reductions.* London: Thames and Hudson, 1965.

McNamara, Robert S. *The Essence of Security: Reflections in Office.* New York: Harper and Row, 1968.

Marwah, Onkar, and Ann Schulz. *Nuclear Proliferation and the Near-Nuclear Countries.* Cambridge, Mass.: Ballinger, 1975.

Maxwell, Neville. *India's China War.* London: Jonathan Cape, 1970.

Mazlish, Bruce. *Kissinger: The European Mind in American Policy.* New York: Basic Books, 1976.

Moss, Norman. *Men Who Play God: The Story of the Hydrogen Bomb.* Harmondsworth, Middlesex: Penguin Books, 1970.

Moulton, Harland B. *From Superiority to Parity: The United States and the Strategic Arms Race, 1961–1971.* Westport, Conn.: Greenwood Press, 1973.

Myrdal, Alva. *The Game of Disarmament: How the United States and Russia Run the Arms Race.* New York: Pantheon, 1977.

Newhouse, John. *Cold Dawn: The Story of* SALT. New York: Holt, Rinehart and Winston, 1973.

——, M. Croan, E. R. Fried, and T. W. Stanley. *U.S. Troops in Europe: Issues, Costs, and Choices.* Washington, D.C.: Brookings Institution, 1971.

Noel-Baker, Philip. *The Arms Race: A Program for World Disarmament.* London: John Calder, 1958.

The Nuclear Energy Policy Study Group. *Nuclear Power: Issues and Choices.* Cambridge, Mass.: Ballinger, for the Ford Foundation/MITRE Corp., 1977.

O'Neill, Robert, ed. *The Strategic Nuclear Balance: An Australian Perspective.* Canberra: Australian National University, 1975.

Osgood, Robert E. *Limited War: The Challenge to American Strategy.* Chicago: University of Chicago Press, 1957.

——. NATO: *The Entangling Alliance.* Chicago: University of Chicago Press, 1962.

——, and Robert W. Tucker. *Force, Order, and Justice.* Baltimore: Johns Hopkins Press, 1967.

Palmer, Michael. *The Prospects for a European Security Conference.* London: Chatham House, Political and Economic Planning, 1971.

Pierre, Andrew J. *Nuclear Politics: The British Experience with an Independent Strategic Force 1939–1970.* London: Oxford University Press, 1972.

Planck, Charles R. *The Changing Status of German Reunification in Western Diplomacy, 1955–1966.* Baltimore: Johns Hopkins Press, 1967.

Polmar, Norman. *Strategic Weapons: An Introduction.* New York: Crane, Russak, 1975.

Pranger, Robert J., ed. *Détente and Defense: A Reader.* Washington, D.C.: American Enterprise Institute for Public Policy Research, 1976.

——, and Roger P. Labrie. *Nuclear Strategy and National Security: Points of View.* Washington, D.C.: American Enterprise Institute for Public Policy Research, 1977.

Quester, George H. *The Politics of Nuclear Proliferation.* Baltimore: Johns Hopkins Press, 1973.

——. *Nuclear Diplomacy: The First Twenty-Five Years.* New York: Dunellen, 1970.

Rapoport, Anatol. *Fights, Games and Debates.* Ann Arbor: University of Michigan Press, 1961.

——. *Strategy and Conscience.* New York: Harper and Row, 1964.

——, ed. and intro. *Clausewitz on War,* Introduction. Harmondsworth, Middlesex: Penguin Books, 1968; first published in 1832.

Remington, Robin Alison. *The Warsaw Pact: Case Studies in Communist Conflict Resolution.* Cambridge, Mass.: MIT Press, 1971.

Richardson, James L. *Germany and the Atlantic Alliance: The Interaction of Strategy and Politics.* Cambridge, Mass.: Harvard University Press, 1966.

Roberts, Chalmers M. *The Nuclear Years: The Arms Race and Arms Control 1945–70.* New York: Praeger, 1971.

Robles, Garcia. *The Denuclearization of Latin America.* New York: Carnegie Endowment for International Peace, 1967.

Rosecrance, R. N., ed. *The Dispersion of Nuclear Weapons: Strategy and Politics.* New York and London: Columbia University Press, 1964.

Rotblat, J. *Scientists in the Quest for Peace: A History of the Pugwash Conferences.* Cambridge, Mass.: MIT Press, 1972.

Sapolsky, H. M. *The Polaris System Development: Bureaucratic and Programmatic Success in Government.* Cambridge, Mass.: Harvard University Press, 1972.

Schelling, Thomas C. *The Strategy of Conflict.* Cambridge, Mass.: Harvard University Press, 1960.
———. *Arms and Influence.* New Haven: Yale University Press, 1966.
———, and Morton H. Halperin, with the assistance of Donald G. Brennan. *Strategy and Arms Control.* New York: Twentieth Century Fund, 1961.
Schilling, Warner R., William T. R. Fox, C. M. Kelleher, and D. J. Puchala. *American Arms and a Changing Europe: Dilemmas of Deterrence and Disarmament.* New York: Columbia University Press, 1973.
Shulman, Marshall D. *Stalin's Foreign Policy Reappraised.* Cambridge, Mass.: Harvard University Press, 1963.
———. *Beyond The Cold War.* New Haven and London: Yale University Press, 1966.
Smith, Bruce. *The RAND Corporation: Case Study of a Non-Profit Advisory Corporation.* Cambridge, Mass.: Harvard University Press, 1966.
Sokolovskii, Marshall V. D. *Military Strategy: Soviet Doctrine and Concepts.* Edited with an introduction by R. Garthoff. New York: Praeger, 1963.
———. *Soviet Military Strategy.* Edited with an introduction by T. Wolfe *et al.* Englewood Cliffs, N. J.: RAND – Prentice-Hall, 1963. 3rd ed. (ed. by Dr. Harriet Fast Scott) New York: Crane, Russak, 1975.
Sorensen, Theodore C. *Kennedy.* New York: Harper and Row, 1965.
Spanier, John W., and Joseph L. Nogee. *The Politics of Disarmament: A Study in Soviet-American Gamesmanship.* New York: Praeger, 1962.
Stanley, Timothy W., and D. M. Whitt. *Détente Diplomacy: United States and European Security in the 1970s.* New York: Dunellen, for the Atlantic Council of the U.S., 1970.
Stockholm International Peace Research Institute (SIPRI). *Yearbook of World Armaments and Disarmaments: 1968/69; 1969/70; 1972; 1973; 1974; 1975; 1976; 1977; 1978.* Stockholm: Almquist and Wicksell, 1969, 1970, 1972, 1973, 1974, 1975, 1976, 1977, 1978.
———. *The Near-Nuclear Countries and the NPT.* Stockholm: Almquist and Wicksell, 1972.
———. *Nuclear Proliferation Problems.* Stockholm: Almquist and Wicksell, 1974.
———. *The Arms Trade With the Third World.* Harmondsworth, Middlesex: Penguin Books, 1975.
Stone, Jeremy J. *Containing the Arms Race.* Cambridge, Mass.: MIT Press, 1966.
———. *Strategic Persuasion: Arms Limitation Through Dialogue.* New York and London: Columbia University Press, 1967.
Strachey, John. *On the Prevention of War.* London: Macmillan, 1962.
Tammen, Ronald L. *MIRV and the Arms Race: An Interpretation of Defense Strategy.* New York: Praeger, 1973.
Tsipis, Kosta, A. H. Kahn, and B. T. Feld, eds. *The Future of the Sea-Based Deterrent.* Cambridge, Mass.: MIT Press, 1973.
Ulam, Adam B. *Expansion and Coexistence: The History of Soviet Foreign Policy 1917–67.* New York: Praeger, 1968.
United Nations. *The United Nations and Disarmament 1945–1970.* New York: 1971.
von Riekhoff, Harald. *NATO: Issues and Prospects.* Lindsay, Ont.: John Deyell, for the CIIA, 1967.
Whetten, Lawrence L., ed. *The Future of Soviet Military Power.* New York: Crane, Russak, 1976.
Wiesner, Jerome B. *Where Science and Politics Meet.* New York: McGraw-Hill, 1965.
Williams, Shelton. *The U.S., India and the Bomb.* Baltimore: Johns Hopkins Press, 1969.
Willrich, Mason, and John B. Rhinelander. *SALT: The Moscow Agreements and Beyond.* New York: Free Press, under the auspices of the American Society of International Law, 1974.

Windsor, Philip. *Berlin, City on Leave: A History of Berlin 1945–1962*. London: Chatto and Windus, 1963.
——. *German Reunification*. London: Elek, 1969.
——. *Germany and the Management of Détente*. London: Chatto and Windus, for the ISS, 1971.
Wohlstetter, Roberta. *Pearl Harbor: Warning and Decision*. Stanford: Stanford University Press, 1962.
Wolfe, Thomas W. *Soviet Power and Europe 1945–1970*. Baltimore: Johns Hopkins Press, 1970.
Wright, Sir Michael. *Disarm and Verify: An Explanation of the Central Difficulties and of National Policies*. London: Chatto and Windus, 1964.
York, Herbert. *Race to Oblivion: A Participant's View of the Arms Race*. New York: Simon and Schuster, 1970.
——, comp. and intro. *Arms Control: Readings from Scientific American*. San Francisco: W. H. Freeman, 1973.
——. *The Advisors: Oppenheimer, Teller, and the Superbomb*. San Francisco: W. H. Freeman, 1976.
Young, Elizabeth. *A Farewell to Arms Control?* Harmondsworth, Middlesex: Penguin Books, 1972.
Zumwalt, Elmo R., Jr., Admiral USN (Ret.). *On Watch: A Memoir*. New York: Quadrangle, 1976.

Articles

Aaron, David. "A New Concept". *Foreign Policy*, no. 17, Winter 1974–75, pp. 157–65.
Arms Control Association. *Arms Control Today* (formerly ACA *Newsletter*). Washington, D.C.: April 1972 onward.
Aron, Raymond. "The Evolution of Modern Strategic Thought". In *Problems of Modern Strategy*, edited by Alastair Buchan. London: Chatto and Windus, for the ISS, 1970, pp. 13–45.
Aviation Week and Space Technology SALT I–2. Special issue with articles reprinted from the regular issue of *Aviation Week and Space Technology* to provide a background for a more complete understanding of the Strategic Arms Limitation Talks (SALT) under way between the U.S. and the Soviet Union. The two-year period covered in this publication begins in March 1974. New York: Reginald A. Hubley, for McGraw–Hill.
Beaton, Leonard. *The Western Alliance and the McNamara Doctrine*. Adelphi Paper No. 11. London: ISS, August 1964.
——. "Nuclear Fuel-for-All". *Foreign Affairs*, Vol. 45, no. 4, July 1967, pp. 662–69.
Beecher, William. "U.S. believes Israel has more than 10 nuclear weapons". *Boston Globe*, July 31, 1975.
Bennett, W. S., R. R. Sandoval, and R. G. Schreffler. "A Credible Nuclear-Emphasis Defense for NATO". *Orbis*, Vol. 17, no. 2, Summer 1973, pp. 463-79.
Bertram, Christoph. *Mutual Force Reductions in Europe: The Political Aspects*. Adelphi Paper No. 84. London: IISS, January 1972.
——, ed. *The Future of Arms Control: Part I: Beyond SALT II*. Adelphi Paper No. 141. London: IISS, Spring 1978.
——, ed. *The Future of Arms Control: Part II: Arms Control and Technological Change: Elements of a New Approach*. Adelphi Paper No. 146. London: IISS, Summer 1978.
Bhargava, G. S. *India's Security in the 1980s*. Adelphi Paper No. 125. London: IISS, Summer 1976.
Blackett, P. M. S. "Critique of Some Contemporary Defence Thinking". *Encounter*, Vol. 16, no. 4, April 1961, pp. 9–17.
Bowie, Robert R. "Strategy and the Atlantic Alliance". *International Organization*, Vol. 17, no. 3, Summer 1963, pp. 722–26.

Brennan, Donald G. "Arms and Arms Control in Outer Space". In *Outer Space: Prospects for Man and Society*, edited by Lincoln Bloomfield. 1st ed. New York: The American Assembly of Columbia University, 1962. 2nd rev. ed. New York: Praeger, 1968, pp. 145–77.

———, and Morton H. Halperin. "Policy Considerations of a Nuclear Test Ban". In *Arms Control, Disarmament and National Security*, edited by Donald G. Brennan. New York: Braziller, 1961, pp. 234–60.

Brenner, Michael J. "Tactical Nuclear Strategy and European Defense". *International Affairs*, Vol. 51, no. 1, January 1975, pp. 23–42.

Brodie, B. "Unlimited Weapons and Limited War". *The Reporter*, Vol. 11, November 18, 1954, pp. 16–21.

———. "Were We So (Strategically) Wrong?" *Foreign Policy*, no. 5, Winter 1971–72, pp. 151–61.

Bromke, Adam. "The CSCE and Eastern Europe". *The World Today*, Vol. 29, no. 5, May 1973, pp. 196–206.

Brown, Seyom. "A Cooling-Off Period for U.S.–Soviet Relations". *Foreign Policy*, no. 28, Fall 1977, pp. 3–21.

Brown, Thomas A. *Models of Strategic Stability*. The Southern California Arms Control and Foreign Policy Seminar, August 1971.

Buchan, Alastair. *The Multilateral Force: A Historical Perspective*. Adelphi Paper No. 13. London: ISS, October 1964.

———. "P. M. S. Blackett and War". *Encounter*, Vol. 17, no. 2, August 1961, pp. 56–59.

Bull, Hedley. "Strategic Studies and Its Critics". *World Politics*, Vol. 20, no. 4, July 1968, pp. 593–605.

———. "Arms Control: A Stocktaking and Prospectus". Reprinted in *Problems of Modern Strategy*, edited by Alastair Buchan. London: Chatto and Windus, for the ISS, 1970, pp. 139–58.

Bundy, McGeorge. "To Cap the Volcano". *Foreign Affairs*, Vol. 49, no. 1, October 1969, pp. 1–20.

Burns, Arthur Lee. "Must Strategy and Conscience Be Disjointed?" *World Politics*, Vol. 17, no. 4, July 1965, pp. 687–702.

———. *Ethics and Deterrence: A Nuclear Balance Without Hostage Cities?* Adelphi Paper No. 69. London: ISS, July 1970.

Burns, Lt.-Gen. E. L. M. "Can the Spread of Nuclear Weapons Be Stopped?" *International Organization*, Vol. 19, no. 4, Autumn 1965, pp. 851–69.

———. "The Non-Proliferation Treaty: Its Negotiations and Prospects". *International Organization*, Vol. 23, no. 4, Autumn 1969, pp. 788–807.

Burt, Richard. *New Weapons Technologies: Debate and Directions*. Adelphi Paper No. 126. London: IISS, Summer 1976.

———. "Arms Control and Soviet Strategic Forces: The Risks of Asking SALT to Do Too Much". *The Washington Review of Strategic and International Studies*, Vol. 1, no. 1, January 1978, pp. 19–33.

Cahn, Anne, H., F. A. Long, and G. W. Rathjens. "The Search for a New Handle on Arms Control". *The Bulletin of the Atomic Scientists*, Vol. 30, no. 4, April 1974, p. 7.

Caldwell, Lawrence T. *Soviet Attitudes to SALT*. Adelphi Paper No. 75. London: ISS, February 1971.

———. *Soviet Security Interests in Europe and MFR*. California Seminar on Arms Control and Foreign Policy, April 1976.

Canby, Steven L. "NATO Muscle More Shadow Than Substance". *Foreign Policy*, no. 8, Fall 1972, pp. 38–49.

———. *The Alliance and Europe: Part IV: Military Doctrine and Technology*. Adelphi Paper No. 109. London: IISS, Winter 1974–75.

———. "Dampening Nuclear Counterforce Incentives: Correcting NATO's Inferiority in Conventional Military Strength". *Orbis*, Vol. 19, no. 1, Spring 1975, pp. 47–71.

Chayes, A., F. A. Long, and G. W. Rathjens. "Threshold Treaty: A Step Backwards". *The Bulletin of the Atomic Scientists*, Vol. 31, no. 1, January 1975, p. 16.

Coffey, Joseph I. "The Savor of SALT". *The Bulletin of the Atomic Scientists*, Vol. 29, no. 5, May 1973, pp. 9–15.

——. *New Approaches to Arms Reductions in Europe*. Adelphi Paper No. 105. London: IISS, Autumn 1974.

——. "Détente, Arms Control and European Security". *International Affairs*, Vol. 52, no. 1, January 1976, pp. 39–52.

Cohen, Samuel T., and W. C. Lyons. "A Comparison of U.S. –Allied and Soviet Tactical Nuclear Force Capabilities and Policies". *Orbis*, Vol. 19, no. 1, Spring 1975, pp. 72–92.

Davis, Lynn Etheridge. *Limited Nuclear Options: Deterrence and the New American Doctrine*. Adelphi Paper No. 121. London: IISS, Winter 1975–76.

——, and Warner R. Schilling. "All You Ever Wanted to Know About MIRV and ICBM Calculations But Were Not Cleared to Ask". *Journal of Conflict Resolution*, Vol. 17, no. 2, June 1973, pp. 207–42.

Davis, Saville R. "Recent Policy Making in the United States Government". *Daedalus*, Special Issue on Arms Control, Vol. 89, no. 4, Fall 1960, pp. 951–66.

Doty, Paul, Albert Carnesale, and Michael Nacht. "The Race to Control Nuclear Arms", *Foreign Affairs*, Vol. 55, no. 1, October 1976, pp. 119–32.

Dougherty, James E. "The Soviet Union and Arms Control". *Orbis*, Vol. 17, no. 3, Fall 1973, pp. 737–77.

Dulles, John Foster. "The Evolution of Foreign Policy". *U.S. Department of State Bulletin*, Vol. 30, no. 761, January 25, 1954, pp. 107–10.

——. "Policy for Security and Peace". *Foreign Affairs*, Vol. 32, no. 3, April 1954, pp. 353–64.

——. "Challenge and Response in United States Policy". *Foreign Affairs*, Vol. 36, no. 1, October 1957, pp. 25–43.

Dutt, Major-General D. Som. *India and the Bomb*. Adelphi Paper No. 30. London: ISS, November 1966.

Eayrs, James. "Arms Control on the Great Lakes". *Disarmament and Arms Control*. New York: Pergamon, Vol. 2, Autumn 1962.

Encel, S., and Allan McKnight. "Bombs, Power Stations and Proliferation". *Australian Quarterly*, Vol. 42, March 1970, pp. 15–26.

Enthoven, Alain C. "U.S. Forces in Europe: How Many? Doing What?" *Foreign Affairs*, Vol. 53, no. 3, April 1975, pp. 513–32.

Evron, Yair. Review of Fuad Jabber's *Israel and the Bomb*. In *Survival*, Vol. 14, no. 5, September–October 1972, pp. 253–54.

——. "Israel and the Atom: The Uses and Misuses of Ambiguity, 1957–1967". *Orbis*, Vol. 17, no. 4, Winter 1974, pp. 1326–43.

——. *The Role of Arms Control in the Middle East*. Adelphi Paper No. 138. London: IISS, Autumn 1977.

Facer, Roger. *The Alliance and Europe: Part III: Weapons Procurement in Europe — Capabilities and Choices*. Adelphi Paper No. 108. London: IISS, Winter 1974/75.

Federation of American Scientists (FAS) Newsletter, Special Issue on ORSA ABM Report, Vol. 24, no. 9, December 1971.

Feld, Bernard T. "The Charade of Piecemeal Arms Limitation". *The Bulletin of the Atomic Scientists*, Vol. 31, no. 1, January 1975, pp. 8–16.

Fischer, Robert Lucas. *Defending the Central Front: The Balance of Forces*. Adelphi Paper No. 127. London: IISS, Autumn 1976.

Foster, William C. "New Directions in Arms Control and Disarmament". *Foreign Affairs*, Vol. 43, no. 4, July 1965, pp. 587–601.

——. "Strategic Weapons: Prospects for Arms Control". *Foreign Affairs*, Vol. 47, no. 3, April 1969, pp. 413–21.

Freedman, Lawrence. "Israel's Nuclear Policy". *Survival*, Vol. 17, no. 3, May–June 1975, pp. 114–20.

Frye, Alton. "Strategic Restraint, Mutual and Assured". *Foreign Policy*, no. 27, Summer 1977, pp. 3–26.

Gaitskell, H. "Disengagement: Why? How?" *Foreign Affairs*, Vol. 36, no. 2, January 1958, pp. 539-56.

Gelber, Harry G. "Technical Innovation and Arms Control". *World Politics*, Vol. 26, no. 4, July 1974, pp. 509–41.

Gray, Colin S. "The Arms Race Phenomenon". *World Politics*, Vol. 24, no. 1, October 1971, pp. 39–79.

_____. "What RAND Hath Wrought". *Foreign Policy*, no. 4, 1971, pp. 111–29.

_____. "Strategists: Some Views Critical of the Profession". *International Journal*, Vol. 26, no. 4, Autumn 1971, pp. 771–90.

_____. " 'Gap' Prediction and America's Defense: Arms Race Behaviour in the Eisenhower Years". *Orbis*, Vol. 16, no. 1, Spring 1972, pp. 257–74.

_____. "The Arms Race is About Politics". *Foreign Policy*, no. 9, Winter 1972–73, pp. 117–29.

_____. "The Urge to Compete: Rationales for Arms Racing". *World Politics*, Vol. 26, no. 2, January 1974, pp. 207–33.

_____. "Mini-Nukes and Strategy". *International Journal*, Vol. 14, no. 2, Spring 1974, pp. 216–41.

_____. "SALT II and the Strategic Balance". *British Journal of International Studies*, Vol. 1, no. 3, October 1975, pp. 183–208.

_____. "SALT I Aftermath: Have the Soviets Been Cheating?" *Air Force*, Vol. 58, no. 11, November 1975, pp. 28–33.

_____. "Theater Nuclear Weapons: Doctrines and Postures". *World Politics*, Vol. 28, no. 2, January 1976, pp. 300–14.

_____. "SALT: Time to Quit". *Strategic Review*, Vol. 4, no. 4, Fall 1976, pp. 14–22.

_____. "Détente, Arms Control and Strategy: Perspectives on SALT". *The American Political Science Review*, Vol. 70, no. 4, December 1976, pp. 1242–56.

_____. "Across the Nuclear Divide — Strategic Studies, Past and Present". *International Security*, Vol. 2, no. 1, Summer 1977, pp. 24–46.

_____. "Who's Afraid of the Cruise Missile?" *Orbis*, Vol. 21, no. 3, Fall 1977, pp. 517–31.

_____. *The Future of Land-Based Missile Forces*. Adelphi Paper No. 140. London: IISS, Winter 1977.

Green, Philip. "Method and Substance in the Arms Debate". *World Politics*, Vol. 16, no. 4, July 1964, pp. 642–67.

_____. "Science, Government and the Case of RAND: A Singular Pluralism". *World Politics*, Vol. 20, no. 2, January 1968, pp. 301 –26.

Greenwood, Ted. *Reconnaissance, Surveillance and Arms Control*. Adelphi Paper No. 88. London: IISS, June 1972.

_____, and Michael L. Nacht. "The New Nuclear Debate: Sense or Nonsense?" *Foreign Affairs*, Vol. 52, no. 4, July 1974, pp. 761–80.

_____. George W. Rathjens, and Jack Ruina. *Nuclear Power and Weapons Proliferation*. Adelphi Paper No. 130. London: IISS, Winter 1976.

Griffiths, Franklyn. "Inner Tensions in the Soviet Approach to Disarmament". *International Journal*, Vol. 22, no. 4, Autumn 1967, pp. 593–6.16.

_____. *Genoa Plus 51: Changing Soviet Objectives in Europe*. Wellesley Paper No. 4. Toronto: Canadian Institute of International Affairs (CIIA), June 1973.

Halperin, Morton H. "The Gaither Committee and the Policy Process". *World Politics*, Vol. 13, no. 3, April 1961, pp. 360–91.

_____. "The Decision to Deploy the ABM: Bureaucratic and Domestic Politics in the Johnson Administration". *World Politics*, Vol. 25, no. 1, October 1972, pp. 62–95.

Harmel Report (The). Reprinted in *Survival*, Vol. 10, no. 2, February 1968, pp. 62–64.

Heisenberg, Wolfgang. *The Alliance and Europe: Part I: Crisis Stability in Europe and Tactical Nuclear Weapons.* Adelphi Paper No. 96. London: IISS, Summer 1973.

Heymont, Irving. "The NATO Nuclear Bilateral Forces". *Orbis,* Vol. 9, no. 4, Winter 1966, pp. 1025–41.

Hill, Roger J. "MBFR". *International Journal,* Vol. 29, no. 2, Spring 1974, CIIA, pp. 242–55.

Hoeber, Francis P. *Slow to Take Offense: Bombers, Cruise Missiles, and Prudent Deterrence.* Monograph. Washington, D. C.: Center for Strategic and International Studies, Georgetown University, 1977.

Holst, Johan J. "Strategic Arms Control and Stability: A Retrospective Look". In *Why ABM?: Policy Issues in the Missile Defense Controversy,* edited by Johan J. Holst and William Schneider, Jr. New York: Pergamon, 1969, pp. 245–47.

_____. "A Strategic Arms Race? What is Really Going On?" *Foreign Policy,* no. 19, Summer 1975, pp. 155–62.

Howard, Michael. "The Relevance of Traditional Strategy". *Foreign Affairs,* Vol. 51, no. 2, January 1973, pp. 253–66.

Hunt, Kenneth. *The Alliance and Europe: Part II: Defence with Fewer Men.* Adelphi Paper No. 98. London: IISS, Summer 1973.

Hunter, Robert E. "The Future of Soviet-American Détente". *The World Today,* Vol. 24, no. 7, July 1968, pp. 281–90.

Iklé, Fred C. "After Detection — What?" *Foreign Affairs,* Vol. 39, no. 2, January 1961, pp. 208–20.

_____. "Arms Control and Disarmament". *World Politics,* Vol. 14, no. 4, July 1962, pp. 713–22.

_____. "Can Nuclear Deterrence Last Out the Century?" *Foreign Affairs,* Vol. 51, no. 2, January 1973, pp. 267–85.

Imai, Ryukichi. *Nuclear Safeguards.* Adelphi Paper No. 86. London: IISS, March 1972.

International Affairs: A Monthly Journal of Political Analysis. Chekhov, Moscow Region, U.S.S.R.: All-Union Znaniye Society, 1955 onwards.

Jacobsen, Carl G. SALT: MBFR: *Soviet Perspectives on Security and Arms Negotiations.* ORAE Memorandum No. M53. Ottawa: Defence Research Analysis Establishment, April 1974.

Kahan, Jerome H. "Where to for SALT II?" *Washington Post,* November 19, 1972.

Kaiser, Karl. "The Great Nuclear Debate". *Foreign Policy,* no. 30, Spring 1978, pp. 83–110.

Kaplan, Morton A. "Problems of Coalition and Deterrence". In *NATO and American Security,* edited by Klaus Knorr. Princeton, N.J.: Princeton University Press, 1959, pp. 127–50.

Kaufmann, William W. *The Requirements of Deterrence.* Memorandum No. 7. Princeton, N.J.: Center of International Studies, Princeton University, 1954.

Kemp, Geoffrey. *Arms and Security: The Egypt–Israel Case.* Adelphi Paper No. 52. London: ISS, October 1968.

_____. "Dilemmas of the Arms Traffic". *Foreign Affairs,* Vol. 48, no. 2, January 1970, pp. 274–84.

_____. *Nuclear Forces for Medium Powers: Part I: Targets and Weapons Systems.* Adelphi Paper No. 106. London: IISS, Autumn 1974.

_____. *Nuclear Forces for Medium Powers: Parts II and III: Strategic Requirements and Options.* Adelphi Paper No. 107. London: IISS, Autumn 1974.

Kissinger, Henry A. "Military Policy and Defense of the 'Grey' Areas". *Foreign Affairs,* Vol. 33, no. 3, April 1955, pp. 416–28.

_____. "Arms Control, Inspection and Surprise Attack". *Foreign Affairs,* Vol. 38, no. 4, July 1960, pp. 557–75.

_____. "Limited War: Conventional or Nuclear? A Reappraisal". *Daedalus,* Special Issue on Arms Control, Vol. 89, no. 4, Fall 1960, pp. 800–17.

_____. In Excerpts of Dr. Henry Kissinger's Briefing on S.A.L.T. for Members of Congress. Official Text from USIS, American Embassy, London, June 16, 1972.
_____. In Excerpts of Dr. Henry Kissinger's Briefing on SALT for Members of Congress. Official Text from USIS, American Embassy, London, June 16, 1972.
_____. "Briefings on SALT". NATO Review, Vol. 20, nos. 7–8, July–August 1972, pp. 6–12.
_____. "Press Statement by U.S. Secretary of State Dr. Kissinger 24 November 1974". Survival, Vol. 17, no. 1, January–February 1975, pp. 33-34.
_____. "The Vladivostok Accord". Background briefing by Henry Kissinger, December 3, 1974. Survival, Vol. 17, no. 4, July–August 1975, pp. 191–98.
Klein, J. "Les aspects militaires de la détente en Europe et les perspectives d'une réduction mutuelle des forces dans un cadre regional". Études Internationales, mars–juin 1973, pp. 121–58.
Kohl, W. L. "Nuclear Sharing and the Multilateral Force". Political Science Quarterly, Vol. 80, no. 1, March 1965, pp. 88–109.
Kostko, Yu. "Mutual Force Reductions in Europe". Survival, Vol. 14, no. 5, September–October 1972, pp. 236-88.
Kramish, A. The Watched and the Unwatched: Inspection in the Non-Proliferation Treaty. Adelphi Paper No. 36. London: ISS, June 1967.
Kruzel, Joseph. "SALT II: The Search for a Follow-On Agreement". Orbis, Vol. 17, no. 2, Summer 1973, pp. 334–63.
_____. "Arms Control at the Crossroads". The Bulletin of the Atomic Scientists, Vol. 30, no. 6, June 1974, pp. 58–60.
Lambeth, Benjamin S. "Nuclear Proliferation and Soviet Arms Control Policy". Orbis, Vol. 14, no. 2, Summer 1970, pp. 298–325.
Latham, Aaron. "Kissinger's Bluff Is Called". New York, April 12, 1976, pp. 30–35.
Leitenberg, Milton. "Soviet Secrecy and Negotiations on Strategic Weapon Arms Control and Disarmament". Bulletin of Peace Proposals, no. 4, 1974, pp. 427–40.
_____. "The SALT Ceilings and Why They Are So High". British Journal of International Studies, Vol. 2, no. 2, July 1976, pp. 149–63.
Lethes, Nathan. "Weakening the Belief in General War: Schelling on Strikes". World Politics, Vol. 19, no. 4, July 1967, pp. 709–19.
Levine, Robert A. "Facts and Morals in the Arms Debate". World Politics, Vol. 14, no. 2, January 1962, pp. 239–58.
Lodal, Jan M. "Assuring Strategic Stability: An Alternate View". Foreign Affairs, Vol. 54, no. 3, April 1976, pp. 462–81.
_____. "Verifying SALT". Foreign Policy, no. 24, Fall 1976, pp. 40–64.
Long, Franklin A. "Should We Buy the Vladivostok Agreement?" The Bulletin of the Atomic Scientists, Vol. 31, no. 2, February 1975, pp. 5–6.
Lowrance, William W. "Nuclear Futures for Sale: To Brazil from West Germany, 1975". International Security, Vol. 1, no. 2, Fall 1976, pp. 147–66.
Luttwak, Edward. "The Strategic Balance 1972". The Washington Papers. No. 3. The Center for Strategic and International Studies, Georgetown University, Washington, D.C. New York: The Library Press, 1972.
_____. "The U.S.–U.S.S.R. Nuclear Weapons Balance". The Washington Papers. No. 13. The Center for Strategic and International Studies, Georgetown University, Washington, D.C. Beverly Hills, London: Sage Publications, 1974.
_____. "Strategic Power: Military Capabilities and Political Utility". The Washington Papers. No. 38. The Center for Strategic and International Studies, Georgetown University, Washington, D.C. Beverly Hills, London: Sage Publications, 1976.
_____. "SALT and the Meaning of Strategy". The Washington Review of Strategic and International Studies, Vol. 1, no. 2, April 1978, pp. 16–28.
Mackintosh, Malcolm. The Evolution of the Warsaw Pact. Adelphi Paper No. 58. London: ISS, June 1969.
Maddox, John. Prospects for Nuclear Proliferation. Adelphi Paper No. 113. London: IISS, Spring 1975.

Marks, Anne W., ed. NPT: *Paradoxes and Problems*. Carnegie Endowment for International Peace. Washington, D.C.: Arms Control Association, 1975.

Maxwell, Neville. "China and India: The Un-Negotiated Dispute". *China Quarterly*, Vol. 43, July–September 1970, pp. 47–80.

Maxwell, Stephen. *Rationality in Deterrence*. Adelphi Paper No. 50. London: ISS, August 1968.

Mueller, Peter G. *On Things Nuclear; The Canadian Debate*. Toronto: Canadian Institute of International Affairs, 1977.

Multan, W., and A. Towpik. "Western Arms Control Policies in Europe Seen from the East". *Survival*, Vol. 16, no. 3, May–June 1974, pp. 127–32.

Myrdal, Alva, L. B. Pearson, and S. Zuckerman. *The Control of Proliferation: Three Views*. Adelphi Paper No. 29. London: ISS, October 1966.

Nacht, Michael L. "The Vladivostok Accord and American Technological Options". *Survival*, Vol. 17, no. 3, May–June 1975, pp. 106–13.

_____. "A Strategic Arms Race: The Delicate Balance of Error". *Foreign Policy*, no. 19, Summer 1975, pp. 163–77.

National Planning Association. *Strengthening the Government for Arms Control*. Washington, D.C.: 1960.

_____. Special Project Committee on Security through Arms Control. *1970 Without Arms Control*. Planning Pamphlet No. 104. Washington. D.C.: 1958.

_____, and William C. Davidon, Christoph Hohenemser, and Marvin I. Kalkstein. *The Nth Country Problem and Arms Control*. Planning Pamphlet No. 108. Washington, D.C.: 1960.

Nerlich, Uwe. *The Alliance and Europe: Part V: Nuclear Weapons and East-West Negotiation*. Adelphi Paper No. 120. London: IISS, Winter 1975–76.

Nitze, Paul H. "SALT, The Strategic Balance Between Hope and Scepticism". *Foreign Policy*, no. 17, Winter 1974–75, pp. 136-56.

_____. "Soviets' Negotiating Style Assayed". *Aviation Week and Space Technology*, February 17, 1975. Reprinted in special issue from the regular issues, covering the two-year period beginning in March 1974, pp. 49–56.

_____. "Vladivostok and SALT II". *The Review of Politics*, Vol. 37, no. 2, April 1975, pp. 147–60.

_____. "Assuring Strategic Stability in an Era of Détente". *Foreign Affairs*, Vol. 54, no. 2, January 1976, pp. 207–32.

_____. "Deterring our Deterrent", *Foreign Policy*, no. 25, Winter 1976–77, pp. 195–210.

Nye, Joseph S. "Nonproliferation: A Long-Term Strategy". *Foreign Affairs*, Vol. 56, no. 3, April 1978, pp. 601–23.

Operations Research Society of America (ORSA). "The Nature of Operations Research and the Treatment of Operations Research Questions in the 1969 Safeguard Debate". *Operations Research*, Vol. 19, no. 5, September 1971, pp. 1123–1258.

_____. *Operations Research*, Vol. 20, no. 1, January–February 1972, pp. 205–45.

Panofsky, Wolfgang K. H. "The Mutual-Hostage Relationship Between America and Russia". *Foreign Affairs*, Vol. 52, no. 1, October 1973, pp. 109–18.

Pflatzgraff, Robert L., Jr., and Jacquelyn K. Davis. *The Cruise Missile: Bargaining Chip or Defense Bargain?* Special Report. Cambridge, Mass.: Institute for Foreign Policy Analysis, January 1977.

Pierre, Andrew J. "Nuclear Diplomacy: Britain, France and America". *Foreign Affairs*, Vol. 49, no. 2, January 1971, pp. 283–301.

_____. "The SALT Agreement and Europe". *The World Today*, Vol. 28, no. 7, July 1972, pp. 281–88.

Pranger, Robert J., and Dale R. Tahtinen. *Nuclear Threat in the Middle East*. Foreign Affairs Study No. 23. Washington, D.C.: American Enterprise Institute for Public Policy Research, July 1975.

Quanbeck, Alton H., and Barry M. Blechman. *Strategic Forces: Issues for the Mid-Seventies.* Washington, D.C.: Brookings Institution, 1973.
———, and Archie L. Wood, with the assistance of Louisa Thoron. *Modernizing the Strategic Bomber Force: Why and How.* Washington, D.C.: Brookings Institution, 1976.
Quester, George H. "Missiles in Cuba, 1970". *Foreign Affairs,* Vol. 49, no. 3, April 1971, pp. 493–506.
———. "Can Proliferation Now Be Stopped?" *Foreign Affairs,* Vol. 53, no. 1, October 1974, pp. 77–97.
Ranger, Robin. "NATO's Reaction to Czechoslovakia". *The World Today,* Vol. 25, no. 1, January 1969, pp. 19–26.
———. "Death of a Treaty: A Diplomatic Obituary?" *International Relations,* Vol. 3, no. 7, April 1969, pp. 482–97.
———. "The NPT Two Years On: Lessons for SALT". *The World Today,* Vol. 26, no. 11, November 1970, pp. 453–57.
———. "The Political Involvement of the Soviet Union". In Robert S. Jordan, ed. *Europe and the Super Powers.* Boston: Allyn and Bacon, 1971, pp. 47–70.
———. "Arms Control Within a Changing Political Context". *International Journal,* Vol. 26, no. 4, Autumn 1971, pp. 735–52.
———. "MBFR: Political or Technical Arms Control?" *The World Today,* Vol. 30, no. 10, October 1974, pp. 411–18.
———. "The Canadian Perspective". In *The Foreign Policies of the Powers,* edited by Frederick S. Northedge. 2nd rev. ed. London: Faber and Faber, 1974, pp. 269–95.
———. "The Politics of Arms Control After Vladivostok". *Millenium,* Vol. 4, no. 1, Spring 1975, pp. 52–66.
———. *Mutual and Balanced Force Reductions: Underlying Issues and Potential Developments.* ORAE Memorandum No. M74. Ottawa: Operational Research and Analysis Establishment, Department of National Defence, January 1976.
———. *The Canadian Contribution to the Control of Chemical and Biological Warfare.* Wellesley Paper No. 5. Toronto: Canadian Institute of International Affairs, 1976.
———. "Arms Control in Theory and Practice". *The Year Book of World Affairs 1977.* Vol. 31, pp. 122–137. London: Stephens and Sons, for the London Institute of World Affairs, 1977.
———, and Richard Stubbs. "Mechanistic assumptions and United States Strategy". *International Journal,* Vol. 33, no. 3 (Summer 1978), pp. 557–72.
Rapoport, Anatol. "A Critique of Strategic Thinking". In *International Conflict and Behavioral Science,* edited by Roger Fisher. New York: Basic Books, 1964, pp. 211–37.
Rathjens, George W. *The Future of the Strategic Arms Race: Options for the 1970s.* New York: Carnegie Endowment for International Peace, 1969.
———, Abram Chayes, and J. P. Ruina. *Nuclear Arms Control Agreements: Process and Impact.* Washington, D.C.: Carnegie Endowment for International Peace, 1974.
Record, Jeffrey, with Thomas I. Anderson. *U.S. Nuclear Weapons in Europe: Issues and Alternatives.* Washington, D.C.: Brookings Institution, March 1974.
Rich, Alexander, and Aleksandr P. Vinogradov. "Arctic Disarmament". *The Bulletin of the Atomic Scientists,* Vol. 20, no. 9, November 1964, pp. 22–23.
Rockefeller Report on the Problems of U.S. Defense. Special Studies Report II. *International Security: The Military Aspect.* America at Mid-Century Series. Garden City, N.Y.: Doubleday, 1958.
Rosecrance, Richard. *Strategic Deterrence Reconsidered.* Adelphi Paper No. 116. London: IISS, Spring 1975.
Rosenau, James N. "Paradigm Lost: Five Actors in Search of the Interactive Effects of Domestic and Foreign Affairs". Paper prepared for a symposium on National

Strategy in a Decade of Change, sponsored by the Stanford Research Institute and Foreign Policy Research Institute, Arlie House, February 18, 1972.

Rowen, Henry S. "The Need for a New Analytical Framework". A review of *Security in the Nuclear Age*, by Jerome Kahan. In *International Security*, Vol. 1, no. 2, Fall 1976, pp. 130–46.

Russet, Bruce M., and Carolyn C. Cooper. *Arms Control in Europe: Proposals and Political Constraints*. Monograph series in *World Affairs*, Vol. 4, no. 2. Denver, Colo.: University of Denver, 1966–67.

Schelling, Thomas C. "Arms Control: Proposal for a Special Surveillance Force". *World Politics*, Vol. 13, no. 1, October 1960, pp. 1–18.

———. "Communications, Bargaining and Negotiations". *Arms Control and National Security*, Vol. I, pp. 63-72. New York: Pergamon, 1969.

Scoville, Herbert, Jr. *Toward a Strategic Arms Limitation Agreement*. New York: Carnegie Endowment for International Peace, 1970.

———. "Beyond SALT One". *Foreign Affairs*, Vol. 50, no. 3, April 1972, pp. 488–500.

———. "Strategic Forum: The SALT Agreements". *Survival*, Vol. 14, no. 5, September–October 1972, pp. 210–12.

———. "The SALT Negotiations". *Scientific American*, Vol. 237, no. 2, August 1977, pp. 24–31.

———, Betty G. Lall, and Robert E. Hunter. "The Arms Race: Steps Towards Restraint". *International Conciliation*, no. 587. New York: Carnegie Endowment for International Peace, March 1972.

Shulman, Marshall D. "Toward a Western Philosophy of Coexistence". *Foreign Affairs*, Vol. 52, no. 1, October 1973, pp. 35–58.

———. "On Learning to Live with Authoritarian Regimes". *Foreign Affairs*, Vol. 55, no. 2, January 1977, pp. 325–38.

Slocombe, W. *The Political Implications of Strategic Parity*. Adelphi Paper No. 77. London: ISS, May 1971.

Smart, Ian. "Reviewing Non-Proliferation". *The World Today*, Vol. 31, no. 6, June 1975, pp. 223–25.

Stockholm International Peace Research Institute. *Force Reductions in Europe*. Stockholm: Almquist and Wicksell, 1974.

Stone, I. F. "The Test Ban Comedy". *New York Review of Books*, Vol. 14, no. 9, May 7, 1970, pp. 14–22.

Stone, Jeremy J. "When and How to Use SALT". *Foreign Affairs*, Vol. 48, no. 2, January 1970, pp. 262–73.

Sutton, John L., and Geoffrey Kemp. *Arms to Developing Countries, 1945–1965*. Adelphi Paper No. 28. London: ISS, October 1966.

Survival. "Japanese White Paper on Defense" (translated). Vol. 13, no. 1, January 1971, pp. 3–4.

———. "Statement by Ambassador Martin to the CCD". Vol. 16. no. 5, September–October 1973, pp. 248–49.

Szulc, Tad. "Have We Been Had?" *The New Republic*, June 7, 1975, pp. 11–15.

Talenski, Major-Gen. Nikolai A. "Anti-Missile Systems and Disarmament". *International Affairs* (Moscow), Vol. 7, no. 10, November 1964, pp. 15–17.

Time. "How Israel Got the Bomb". April 12, 1976, pp. 21–22.

Tortenson, K. A. "MBFR: An Introduction". *Internasjonal Politik*, nos. 2–3, 1971, pp. 206–37.

Tsipis, Kosta. "Cruise Missiles". *Scientific American*, Vol. 236, no. 2, February 1977, pp. 20–29.

United Nations. *Effects of the Possible Use of Nuclear Weapons and the Security and Economic Implications for States of the Acquisition and Further Development of these Weapons*. Report of the Secretary General transmitting the study of his consultative group. New York: U.N. Department of Political and Security Council Affairs, 1968.

United States Government. "U.S. Foreign Policy for the 1970s — A New Strategy for Peace". Washington, D.C.: U.S. Government Printing Office, February 18, 1970.

Van Cleave, William R. Testimony: International Negotiation, Hearings Before the Sub-committee on National Security and International Operations of the Committee on Government Operations, U.S. Senate, Ninety-Second Congress, Second Session, Part 7, July 25, 1972.
———. "Political Negotiating Asymmetries: Insult in SALT I". Paper prepared for Sixth International Arms Control Symposium, Philadelphia, November 2, 1973.
———. "The SALT Papers: A Torrent of Verbiage or a Spring of Capital Truths?" Orbis, Vol. 17, no. 4, Winter 1974, pp. 1396–1400.
———. "SALT on the Eagle's Tail". Strategic Review, Vol. 4, no. 2, Spring 1976, pp. 44–55.
Vershbow, Alexander R. "The Cruise Missile: The End of Arms Control?" Foreign Affairs, Vol. 55, no. 1, October 1976, pp. 133–46.
Vincent, R. J. Military Power and Political Influence: The Soviet Union and Western Europe. Adelphi Paper No. 119. London: Autumn 1975.
Vladivostok Accord. Joint Soviet-American Statement on Strategic Arms Limitation, 24 November 1974. Reprinted in Survival, Vol. 17, no. 1, January–February 1975, p. 32.
Warnke, Paul C. "Apes on a Treadmill". Foreign Policy, no. 18, Spring 1975, pp. 12–29.
———. "We Don't Need A Devil (To Make or Keep Our Friends)". Foreign Policy, no. 25, Winter 1976–77, pp. 78–87.
Wettig, Gerhard. "Soviet Policy on the Non-Proliferation of Nuclear Weapons 1966–68". Orbis, Vol. 13, no. 3, Winter 1969, pp. 1058–84.
Wiegle, Thomas C. "The Origins of the MLF Concept, 1957–1960". Orbis, Vol. 12, no. 2, Summer 1968, pp. 465–89.
———. "Nuclear Consultation Processes in NATO". Orbis, Vol. 16, no. 2, Summer 1972, pp. 462–87.
Windsor, Philip. Western Europe in Soviet Strategy. Adelphi Paper No. 8. London: ISS, January 1964.
———. "The Boundaries of Détente". The World Today, Vol. 25, no. 6, June 1969, pp. 255–63.
———. "Current Tensions in NATO". The World Today, Vol. 26, no. 7, July 1970, pp. 289–95.
———. ". . . But Europe Shouldn't". Foreign Policy, no. 8, Fall 1972, pp. 92–99.
———. "NATO's Twenty-Five Years". The World Today, Vol. 30, no. 5, May 1974, pp. 181–87.
———. "The State of NATO". The World Today, Vol. 31, no. 8, August 1975, pp. 318–25.
———. "A Watershed for NATO". The World Today, The Royal Institute of International Affairs, Vol. 33, no. 11, November 1977, pp. 409–16.
Wohlstetter, Albert et al. Selection and Use of Strategic Air Bases. RAND Report R-266, April 1954.
———. Protecting U.S. Power to Strike Back. RAND Report R-290, April 1956.
———. "The Delicate Balance of Terror". Foreign Affairs, Vol. 37, no. 2, January 1959, pp. 211–34.
———. "Is There a Strategic Arms Race?" Foreign Policy, Pt. 1, no. 15, Summer 1974, pp. 3–20.
———. "Rivals, But No 'Race' ". Foreign Policy, Pt. 2, no. 16, Fall 1974, pp. 48–81.
———. "How to Confuse Ourselves". Foreign Policy, no. 20, Fall 1975, pp. 170–98.
———. Legends of the Strategic Arms Race. Washington, D.C.: United States Strategic Institute, 1975.
———. "Spreading the Bomb Without Quite Breaking the Rules". Foreign Policy, no. 25, Winter 1976–77, pp. 88–96, 145–79.
Wolfe, Thomas W. The SALT Experience: Its Impact on U.S. and Soviet Strategic Policy and Decisionmaking. RAND Report R-1686-PR, September 1975.
Wyle, Frederick W. "European Security: Beating the Numbers Game". Foreign Policy, no. 10, Spring 1973, pp. 41–54.

Yochelson, John. "The American Military Presence in Europe: Current Debate in the United States". *Orbis*, Vol. 15, no. 3, Fall 1971, pp. 784–807.
____. "MBFR: The Search for an American Approach". *Orbis*, Vol. 17, no. 1, Spring 1973, pp. 155–75.
Young, Elizabeth. *The Control of Proliferation: The 1968 Treaty in Hindsight and Forecast*. Adelphi Paper No. 56. London: ISS, April 1969.
____. "To Guard the Sea". *Foreign Affairs*, Vol. 50, no. 1, October 1971, pp. 136–47.
"Z". "The Year of Europe?" *Foreign Affairs*, Vol. 52, no. 2, January 1974, pp. 237–48.
Zumwalt, Adm. Elmo R. USN (Ret.). "An Assessment of the Bomber-Cruise Missile Controversy". *International Security*, Vol. 2, no. 1, Summer 1977, pp. 47–58.

U.S. Senate and Congressional Hearings

Strategic and Foreign Policy Implications of ABM *Systems*. Hearings before the Sub-committee on International Organization and Disarmament Affairs of the Committee on Foreign Relations, U.S. Senate, Ninety-First Congress, First Session, Part I, March 1969, Part II and III, May and July 1969. Washington, D.C.: U.S. Government Printing Office.
Diplomatic and Strategic Impact of Multiple Warhead Missiles. Hearings before the Sub-committee on National Security Policy and Scientific Developments of the Committee on Foreign Affairs, House of Representatives, Ninety-First Congress, First Session, July and August 1969. Washington, D.C.: U.S. Government Printing Office.
ABM, MIRV, SALT *and the Nuclear Arms Race*. Hearings before the Sub-committee on Arms Control, International Law and Organization of the Committee on Foreign Relations, U.S. Senate, Ninety-First Congress, Second Session, March-June 1970. Washington, D.C.: U.S. Government Printing Office.
Prospects for a Comprehensive Nuclear Test Ban Treaty. Hearings before the Sub-committee on Arms Control, International Law and Organization of the Committee on Foreign Relations, U.S. Senate, Ninety-Second Congress, Second Session, July 1971. Washington, D.C.: U.S. Government Printing Office.
Prospects for a Comprehensive Nuclear Test Ban Treaty. Committee Print, a staff report prepared for the use of the Sub-committee on Arms Control, International Law and Organization of the Committee on Foreign Relations, U.S. Senate, Ninety-Second Congress, First Session, November 1971. Washington, D.C.: U.S. Government Printing Office.
The Geneva Protocol of 1925. Hearings before the Committee on Foreign Relations, U.S. Senate, Ninety-Second Congress, Second Session, March 1971. Washington, D.C.: U.S. Government Printing Office.
Strategic Arms Limitation Agreements. Hearings before the Committee on Foreign Relations, U.S. Senate, Ninety-Second Congress, Second Session, June/July 1972. Washington, D.C.: U.S. Government Printing Office.
Military Applications of Nuclear Technology. Hearing before the Sub-committee on Military Applications of the Joint Committee on Atomic Energy, Congress of the United States, Ninety-Third Congress, First Session, April/June 1973. Washington, D.C.: U.S. Government Printing Office.
U.S. Security Issues in Europe: Burden Sharing and Offset, MBFR *and Nuclear Weapons*. Committee Print, a staff report prepared for the use of the Sub-committee on U.S. Security Agreements and Commitments Abroad of the Committee on Foreign Relations, U.S. Senate, Ninety-Third Congress, First Session, December 2, 1973. Washington, D.C.: U.S. Government Printing Office.
U.S. Chemical Warfare Policy. Hearings before the Sub-committee on National Security Policy and Scientific Developments of the Committee on Foreign Affairs, House of Representatives, Ninety-Third Congress, Second Session, May 1974. Washington, D.C.: U.S. Government Printing Office.
Nuclear Weapons and Foreign Policy. Hearings before the Sub-committee on U.S. Security Agreements and Commitments Abroad and the Sub-committee on

International Law and Organization of the Committee on Foreign Relations, U.S. Senate, Ninety-Third Congress, Second Session, March–April 1974, Washington, D.C.: U.S. Government Printing Office.

U.S.–U.S.S.R. Strategic Policies. Hearing before the Sub-committee on Arms Control, International Law and Organization of the Committee on Foreign Relations, U.S. Senate, Ninety-Third Congress, Second Session, March 1974. Washington, D.C.: U.S. Government Printing Office.

Briefing on Counterforce Attacks. By Secretary of Defense, James R. Schlesinger. Hearing before the Sub-committee on Arms Control, International Law and Organization of the Committee on Foreign Relations, U.S. Senate, Ninety-Third Congress, Second Session, September 1974. Washington, D.C.: U.S. Government Printing Office.

Prohibition of Chemical and Biological Weapons. Hearing before the Committee on Foreign Relations, U.S. Senate, Ninety-Third Congress, Second Session, December 1974. Washington, D.C.: U.S. Government Printing Office.

Soviet Compliance with Certain Provisions of the 1972 SALT I Agreements. Hearing before the Sub-committee on Arms Control of the Committee on Armed Services, U.S. Senate, Ninety-Fourth Congress, First Session, March 1975. Washington, D.C.: U.S. Government Printing Office.

Conference on Security and Co-operation in Europe. Hearing before the Sub-committee on International Political and Military Affairs of the Committee on International Relations, House of Representatives, Ninety-Fourth Congress, First Session, May 1975. Washington, D.C.: U.S. Government Printing Office.

The Vladivostok Accord: Implications to U.S. Security, Arms Control, and World Peace. Hearings before the Sub-committee on International Security and Scientific Affairs of the Committee on International Relations, House of Representatives, Ninety-Fourth Congress, First Session, June and July 1975. Washington, D.C.: U.S. Government Printing Office.

Analyses of Effects of Limited Nuclear Warfare. Committee Print prepared for Sub-committee on Arms Control, International Organizations and Security Agreements of the Committee on Foreign Relations, U.S. Senate, Ninety-Fourth Congress, First Session, September 1975. Washington, D.C.: U.S. Government Printing Office.

Nuclear Proliferation: Future U.S. Foreign Policy Implications. Hearings before the Sub-committee on International Security and Scientific Affairs of the Committee on International Relations, House of Representatives, Ninety-Fourth Congress, First Session, October and November 1975. Washington, D.C.: U.S. Government Printing Office.

Warnke Nomination. Hearings before the Committee on Foreign Relations, U.S. Senate, Ninety-Fifth Congress, First Session, on Nomination of Paul C. Warnke to be Director of the United States Arms Control and Disarmament Agency, with the Rank of Ambassador During His Tenure of Service as Director, February 1977. Washington, D.C.: U.S. Government Printing Office.

Consideration of Mr. Paul C. Warnke to Be Director of the U.S. Arms Control and Disarmament Agency and Ambassador. Hearings together with Individual Views, Committee on Armed Services, U.S. Senate, Ninety-Fifth Congress, First Session, February 1977. Washington, D.C.: U.S. Government Printing Office.

Annual Defense Department Report. FY 1975, James R. Schlesinger, March 4, 1974; FY 1976 and 1971, February 5, 1975; FY 1977, Donald H. Rumsfeld, January 27, 1976, FY 1978, January 17, 1977; FY 1979, Harold Brown, February 2, 1978. Washington, D.C.: U.S. Government Printing Office.

Documents

The International Institute for Strategic Studies (IISS), London (until 1972, the Institute for Strategic Studies—ISS). The Military Balance. 1959, 1960, 1961,

1962–63, 1963–64, 1964–65, 1966–67, 1967–68, 1968–69, 1969–70, 1970–71, 1971–72, 1972–73, 1973–74, 1974–75, 1975–76, 1976–77, 1977–78, 1978–79.
————. *Strategic Survey*. 1966, 1967, 1968, 1969, 1970, 1971, 1972, 1973, 1974, 1975, 1976, 1977.
United States Arms Control and Disarmament Agency. *International Negotiations on the Treaty on the Non-Proliferation of Nuclear Weapons*. Publication No. 48. Washington, D.C.: U.S. Government Printing Office, January 1968.
United States Documents on Disarmament 1945–1971. 1945–1959—Vol.ɪ: 1945–1956; Vol. ɪɪ: 1957–1959; 1960; 1961; 1962—Vol. ɪ: January–June 1962; Vol.ɪɪ: July–December 1963; 1964; 1965; 1966; 1967; 1968; 1969; 1970; 1971; 1972; 1973; 1974; 1975; 1976; 1977. Washington D.C.: U.S. Government Printing Office.

Index